The Jacqueline Rose Reader

The Jacqueline Rose Reader

JACQUELINE ROSE

Edited and with an introduction by
JUSTIN CLEMENS *and* BEN NAPARSTEK

DUKE UNIVERSITY PRESS
Durham & London
2011

Designed by Amy Ruth Buchanan
Typeset in Arno Pro by Keystone
Typesetting, Inc.
Library of Congress Cataloging-in-
Publication Data and republication
acknowledgments appear on the last
printed page of this book.

*This publication is supported by a grant from
the Research and Research Training Committee,
Faculty of Arts, The University of Melbourne.*

Acknowledgments for previously printed
material appear at the end of this book.

CONTENTS

Reading Jacqueline Rose: An Introduction

JUSTIN CLEMENS AND BEN NAPARSTEK

To encounter Jacqueline Rose's work is an extraordinary intellectual experience. From her early writings on feminism and psychoanalysis, through her readings of Marcel Proust, Virginia Woolf, and J. M. Coetzee, to her ongoing analyses of the Israel–Palestine conflict, she has pursued a project without precedent in contemporary thought. At the heart of this project is a set of brilliant theoretical innovations centered on the concept of fantasy—a concept which Rose reconfigures and deploys in such a way as to illuminate hitherto unexamined connections between the most intimate personal experiences and the most public actions of nation-states. In this introduction, we signpost the key way stations of her trajectory, and outline how and why her contribution has proved so influential for understanding some of the most pressing political issues of the present.

In some ways, Rose's work is exemplary of a certain kind of literary intellectual formation. She has published scholarly monographs on authors such as J. M. Barrie and Sylvia Plath; she has written technical articles on key theoretical concepts and canonical literary texts, as well as elegant essays on a variety of topics in a less academic frame; she has reviewed for high-end magazines and daily newspapers; she has translated important psychoanalytic documents from French, including works by Jacques Lacan and Moustapha Safouan. Rose's erudition, commitment, and incisiveness are patent in all her work, from her specialist studies to her ambitious examinations of deep historical messianic tendencies working in and through the self-destructive militarism of the contemporary Israeli state. Today, her impact is legible in academic fields such as comparative literature and cinema studies, postcolonial and cultural studies, as well as in applied psychoanalysis. Reviews of her work—whether in daily newspapers or in specialist academic journals—

consistently resort to such locutions as "wonderful clarity and originality," "verve, imagination and ingenuity," and "formidably intelligent, eloquent and knowledgeable" in an attempt to convey something of its powers.

On the other hand, Rose's work has at once extended and perturbed the traditional literary critical mode in which she was trained and of which she remains an outstanding exponent. Rose completed her doctorate at the University of London, where she was supervised by Frank Kermode, himself one of the first major British humanities scholars to show an interest in contemporary French thought. Yet, as her ongoing analyses of Jewish nationalism shows, Rose is also deeply politically engaged. Her role in broaching and sustaining an open debate about Israel through her various published interventions and public discussions, and as the co-founder of Independent Jewish Voices (signatories include Harold Pinter, Eric Hobsbawm, and Mike Leigh), is testament to her political dedication and effectiveness. Major thinkers as diverse as Edward Said, Slavoj Žižek, and Avi Shlaim have all acclaimed the importance of her political interventions; her writings have been the subject of public debate from Melbourne to Montreal.

Certainly, there's nothing especially novel about linking literature to politics under one heading or another—what else did the great Marxist critics such as George Lukacs, Walter Benjamin, and Theodor Adorno do, not to mention feminist critics such as Virginia Woolf? What is striking, however, about Rose's project is *how* she does it, her motivations and aims, and the particular forms of attentiveness she brings to her materials. Rose's willingness to engage with difficult issues is noteworthy, whether that difficulty stems from their intellectual complexity, or from their political volatility, or both. One might think here of *The Last Resistance*, which includes "Deadly Embrace," an essay that calls for a less pathologizing understanding of suicide bombers, and "The Hidden Life of Vladimir Jabotinsky," in which she reads the literary texts of Jabotinsky, father of right-wing Revisionist Zionism, as casting doubt on the militancy of his political convictions. It is at such points of tension within discourse that Rose seeks for real political lessons.

Above all, what at once drives and binds the agile diversity of Rose's work is a commitment to a radical, singular kind of feminism, which enables her to move from the smallest, most intimate, and literally often unspeakable elements of individuality to the greatest geopolitical formations and deformations—and then back again. It is Rose's feminism that further enables her to collect articles about shame, contemporary celebrity culture, and South Africa's Truth and Reconciliation Commission in a single book (as she does in

On Not Being Able to Sleep), without thereby losing focus or persuasiveness. On the contrary, part of Rose's achievement has been to show how *not* making such apparent leaps is itself a failure of traditional forms of criticism and theory; or, from the other side, that making such links *without* being guided by the problematic of sexual difference is also going to miss something essential about political community.

In other words, the ceaseless movements of topic and genre in Rose's writing are themselves a kind of political act, one that is undoubtedly founded on the fundamental feminist principle that "the personal is political." This means that even the most apparently idiosyncratic elements of an individual life are themselves the expression and outcome of larger social processes, that politics is deeply inscribed within the very places that are supposedly apolitical—and that such self-dissimulation is a key feature of politics itself. The feminist principle declares that social processes are in some way iniquitous, divisive, and exploitative; that at their center is a problematic of sexual difference; that this problematic can and must be used as leverage for political claims that are at once blatantly material (e.g., contesting sexual violence and ensuring economic equality) and apparently abstract (e.g., interrogating representations of femininity); and that, quite literally, these struggles have to begin at home. Part of the point of declaring "the personal is political" is to expose the public-private distinction as itself politically motivated and, to that extent, a condition of injustice.

But the converse also holds true for Rose, for the political is also personal. This is one reason why psychoanalysis is so crucial: psychoanalysis places sexual difference at the heart of all of its developmental stories of the human, and maintains that primordial sexual fantasies continue to govern very different phenomena of the social body. Political life in general remains a form of sexual experience, and cannot properly be understood—or transformed—without an attention to this sexual character. Hence Sigmund Freud himself kept returning to the problem of the foundations of politics in primal fantasies, often in terms that can seem outrageously mythopoeic, such as in *Totem and Taboo* (1913) or in *Group Psychology and the Analysis of the Ego* (1921). In this context, such psychoanalytic concepts as the unconscious, identification, and fantasy come to be deployed at a distance from their origins in clinical practice, in the attempt to understand the relationships between guilt and law or the tendencies to regression of individuals in "passionately excited mobs" (as Freud put it).

Yet, in its insistence on the abiding unconscious character of politics, psychoanalysis also exposes something of the radical instability of sexual difference itself, something that renders sexuality recalcitrant to the very cultures that it founds, and which, furthermore, constantly presses against the public bulwarks that are erected to contain it. Even more profoundly, sexuality comes to appear as something like the point at which all representations of identity founder, a fundamental difference that is neither exactly natural nor cultural, and which always evades any reconciliation worthy of the name. As Freud's *Civilization and Its Discontents* (1930) suggests, civilization itself breeds divisiveness and dissent as part of its essential processes. Without some kind of "repression," that is, without stringent controls exerted over sexuality, no society whatsoever is possible; however, such controls themselves necessarily create their own discontents, as repressed sexual drives reemerge in transubstantiated, near-unrecognizable, and often virulent forms.

Finally, psychoanalysis matters for Rose because it is—as Anna O., one of Josef Breuer's patients proclaimed—a "talking cure." This means that, in addition to its insistence on the roguishness of sexuality for human beings, psychoanalysis not only listens to their representations of sexuality with an unprecedented sensitivity, but wagers that such a listening can have a therapeutic benefit. As is evident in every great psychoanalytic orientation, from classical Freudianism itself, through Melanie Klein and Jacques Lacan and beyond, psychoanalysis attends not only to the explicit statements of its patients, but to what they cannot say or, indeed, to what they say without saying about knowing what they don't know. Psychoanalysis thinks of the rifts, opacities, equivocations, inconsistencies, and so on, that traverse and punctuate all self-representations, as having unspeakable meaning for the patient—meanings that literally render the patient sick through his or her own desire.

Representations, censorship, and primal affects are thereby bound together in such complex knots that they preclude any easy analysis and prevent any easy untangling. To underestimate the complexity of the mind, or to think that one can intervene there with the tools of pure reason alone, has lobotomy as its end and emblem. Against the surgical or biochemical strike, then, psychoanalysis affirms a lingering, finely-tuned attention to the impasses and curlicues of the subject's incessant self-elaborations. That this attention may fail as a matter of course is also part of the risk of psychoanalysis.

It is here that psychoanalysis—at least at its nondogmatic best—necessarily has recourse to art and literature. Jacques Lacan, for example, liked to remind his auditors of the indispensability of a literary formation: "How could we forget that Freud constantly, and right until the end, maintained that such a background was the prime requisite in the training of analysts, and that he designated the age-old *universitas litterarum* as the ideal place for its institution?"[1] Lacan's point is that psychoanalysis is, above all, a symbolic practice, one which takes place on the field and attends to the function of signification. In such a context, literature comes to provide materials, illustrations, inspiration, and models for psychoanalysis. Certainly, psychoanalysis is not simply a literary pursuit, for a number of reasons (we will return to some of these below, as they are of import for Rose's own work); yet it simply cannot do without some relation to the literary (think of the origins of the "Oedipus complex" itself in Sophoclean drama).

Lacan is, of course, one of the great thinkers of the twentieth century whom Rose herself—along with the feminist theorist Juliet Mitchell—helped to introduce to the Anglophone world in the important co-edited volume *Feminine Sexuality: Jacques Lacan and the école freudienne* (1982). This was a collaborative work in a variety of ways. *Feminine Sexuality* not only includes major essays by Lacan, but by other members of his school. It has not one editor, but two—both women. Rose and Mitchell not only selected but also contributed notable introductory essays (we include an extract from Rose's in this collection). Rose herself did the translations. The selected material—of all the diverse work of Lacan and his school—focuses on the issue of "feminine sexuality."

The topic had a directly political valency in the historical and national context of the publication. It added to a crucial intra-psychoanalytic debate dating back at least to the 1920s, as it intervened into an Anglophone feminist and left-wing situation in which Freud and psychoanalysis were once again falling foul of certain politically committed critics. As Rose notes in the essay "Femininity and Its Discontents," psychoanalysis in Britain was "accused of inherent conservatism which rationalises and perpetuates the subordination of women under capitalism, or else fails to engage with that subordination at the level of material life."[2] In other words, the very decision of Mitchell and Rose to translate such work was a means of shifting, broadening, and elevating the debate.

Feminine Sexuality was not a standard single-authored academic monograph translated by a single translator for a clearly delimited audience, but a collaborative project that, in its very principles of selection and in its decisions about translation, diverged both from the theoretical prejudices then dominating its own situation *and* the very materials that it was making available to an English-speaking public. At the moment that it sought to affect the situation into which it was intervening, this act of translation also questioned the possibilities of refashioning community, its structures of address and reception. The brilliant introductions by Mitchell and by Rose—well informed, lucid, and theoretically sophisticated—proved influential in the subsequent uptake of Lacanian psychoanalysis in the English-speaking world. Not only did Mitchell and Rose make available and justify the usefulness of Lacanian psychoanalysis for English-language feminism, but thereby gave both a decisive impetus and critical import whose theoretical consequences are still felt today.

Rose reflects on this situation in her introduction to that volume. As she writes, moreover, in her "Translator's Note": "I have chosen for the most part to follow the predominant English usage of the masculine pronoun in cases where gender was grammatically determined in the original. My early attempt to correct this throughout by the consistent use of 'he/she,' 'his/her,' or of 'she/her' alone, produced either an equality or a 'supremacy' of the feminine term, the absence of which this book attempts to analyse and expose."[3] One could hope for no better example of the formula *traduttore, traditore* ("translator, traitor"), but in a sense that is not merely negative: Rose here stages her critique both of Lacan and of English grammar by means of hesitant fidelity, and not through polemical confrontation. Even more subtly, she thereby enacts what Lacan proposes about femininity, its quiet divagations from the impositions of masculinity by inhabiting its routines and vitiating them from within.

Translation is clearly an integral part of what Rose does, and its demands cannot be separated from her own political commitments. Lacan rigorously insisted that sexual difference was essentially a *symbolic* difference, a difference that is, strictly speaking, neither quite natural nor cultural. This insight has clearly been of central importance to Rose. Human sexuality is at once unnaturally plastic—there are no correlates with human sexuality, its "polymorphous perversity," elsewhere in the animal world—yet it resists any will that attempts to shape it to its own ends. The very definition of the repressed is that it returns, and it returns in often very nasty forms. As Rose puts it, "For Lacan, the unconscious undermines the subject from any position of certainty, from any relation of knowledge to his or her psychic processes and history, and simultaneously reveals the fictional nature of the sexual category to which every human subject is none the less assigned. In Lacan's account, sexual identity operates as a law—it is something enjoined on the subject."[4] That identity is constituted neither by biological programs nor simply by positive social laws, but by the operations of language itself, and that this identity must be at once sexual and unconscious is given a feminist twist by Rose. If Lacan's own political convictions were enigmatic at best, Rose puts his theoretical innovations to work in a more clearly political frame.

Sexual identity is a fictional category—although no less real for that—and is in each individual's case built up out of identifications and fantasies about what it means to be a sexual creature. The definition of the "feminine" is not inscribed in the genes or on the body, but produced out of the relationship to linguistically established social phantasms. "Psychoanalysis," as Rose says, "does not produce that definition. It gives an account of how that definition is produced" (ooo herein). The psychoanalytic account, moreover, is quite clear that such a definition is never fully established in and by the bodies it marks. Femininity, Rose writes, "is neither simply achieved nor ever complete."[5]

Precisely because sexual identity is a forever-incomplete-becoming and not a given, Rose turns her attention to the means and modes of its assumption. As ever with political writers since Plato, the education of the young must be a central concern; what psychoanalysis adds to the august history of educational innovations is an account of their impossibility. With characteristic irony, Freud wrote in "Analysis Terminable and Interminable" (1937), "It almost looks like analysis were the third of those 'impossible' professions in which one can be quite sure of unsatisfying results. The other two, much older-established, are the bringing-up of children and the government of nations."[6] Note how the institutions of raising children and political governance come in Freud's remarks to be joined by the practice that sees all human experience as grounded in unconscious sexuality. And note how Freud insinuates that such institutions betray their own ideals in their very pursuit, and how, above all, training and education become centrally implicated in self-betrayal in the act of transmission itself.

This psychoanalytic insight is deployed in Rose's groundbreaking scholarly monograph, *The Case of Peter Pan, or, The Impossibility of Children's Fiction* (1984), which began as her doctoral dissertation. One of the indispensable tools in the education of children is so-called children's literature: it is one of the chief means by which children are taught to read, to identify, and to act correctly; it aims at inculcating literacy, identity, and morality at once. Of course, such literature is not really *children's* literature at all, but a self-denying depository of adult fantasies *about* what children are or should be, what they want and what they should not. If certain classic texts of children's fiction succeed extraordinarily well at such tasks, they can, paradoxically, do so insofar as they also fail to do so, or, at least, in doing so expose their own machinations in unexpected ways.

The case of J. M. Barrie's *Peter Pan*, a very peculiar transgeneric text, is exemplary in this regard. The character Peter Pan began life as part of a novel not intended for children at all, entered a stage play, was re-edited and republished with illustrations, and became a prose piece in its own right, as well giving rise to an enormous number of other adaptations, including stage musicals and Disney animations. How and why could Peter Pan—a flying boy who has decided never to grow up—become such an abidingly popular figure?

As Rose writes in "The Return of Peter Pan," the introduction to the republished version of her book (1992), "What seemed to me to make *Peter Pan* so significant was the way that, as a cultural myth, it undoes itself, or offers the tools for its own undoing, as it goes."[7] She continues: "*Peter Pan* is a front—a cover not as concealer but as vehicle—for what is most unsettling and uncertain about the relationship between adult and child. It shows innocence not as a property of childhood, but as a portion of adult desire" (xii). Whatever a "child" is, it is to be at the mercy of adult anxieties about what a child is; but, since an "adult" is only constituted as adult in relation to children, it is in the torsions of children's fictions that adulthood reveals itself, its unconfessed desires and projections, "more truly and more strange" (to invoke Wallace Stevens's poem "Tea at the Palaz of Hoon").

It is precisely at this point that we are returned to the origins of psychoanalysis itself: in the disturbing crises occasioned by the terrors of child abuse. In her influential collection of articles *Sexuality in the Field of Vision* (first published by Verso in 1986, and republished in their prestigious "Radical Thinkers" series in 2005), Rose revisits the recurrent birth pangs of the psychoanalytic project. The problems hinge on the constitutionally unstable status of fantasy. Notoriously, Freud discovers or invents psychoanalysis at the very moment that he ceases to believe that his patients' stories of child abuse are *simply* matters of fact.

According to the "seduction theory," which Freud is usually held to have abandoned in 1897–98, the origins of neuroses derive from the sexual abuse of children by a parental figure, emblematically the *father*. The trauma suffered by this external sexual assault on the infantile mind is unable to be properly integrated, and becomes the primary cause of neuroses in later life. Freud, however, modified this theory under pressure of certain anxieties about the facts, or rather about their status: for example, that the overwhelming prevalence of such accusations was itself suspicious; that the line between fact and fiction in the unconscious was extremely difficult to establish, if not entirely impossible; and that the reality of the alleged cause was in any case subordinate to its effects.

Yet that first seduction theory that Freud is seen by some as having subsequently betrayed was already more sophisticated than this sketch—not to mention many of its critics—admit. As Jean Laplanche and J. B. Pontalis write in a classic account of Freud's constant revisions of the structure and situation of fantasy, "The very words, *theory of sexual seduction*, should arrest our attention: the elaboration of a schema to explain the aetiology of neuroses, and not the purely clinical observation of the frequency of the seduction of children by adults, nor even a simple hypotheses that such occurrences would preponderate among the different kinds of traumas."[8] In other words, even the seduction theory at its most apparently empirical implied that fantasy occupied a structural position in the psyche, and such a position further entailed that there be a dialectical relationship between "fantasy" and "reality." No reality was free of fantasy; without fantasy, no reality.

The extraordinarily unsettled—and unsettling nature—of fantasy has led to all sorts of abiding problems for psychoanalysis itself. How, indeed, can the experience of a "real" trauma be gauged against the experience of a "fantasied" trauma? Where, exactly, does fantasy sit? Is it exogenous or endogamous? Innate or experiential? Is it simply defensive, or does it have other functions as well? The concept of fantasy, in a word, at once seems to make possible new accounts of psychic reality, at the very moment that it pulls the rug out from under their effectiveness.

Rose's own contribution to this debate is at once modest and genuinely inventive. It is modest insofar as it doesn't purport to unlock its diverse materials with any single "master key." The concept that may seem closest to performing this function in her work—"fantasy"—is precisely one whose essence is to evade any such mastery. In other words, the import of Rose's work cannot be separated from its theoretical restraint. Picking up on the difficulties that seem invariably to plague the critical accounts of fantasy, Rose demonstrates, with noteworthy generosity, that critics such as Kate Millett and Jeffrey Masson (the author of a controversial book titled *The Assault on Truth: Freud's Suppression of the Seduction Theory*) go seriously astray. In their allegations that Freud falsified evidence of child sexual abuse, they have to falsify the evidence against Freud in turn. Worse still, their falsifications have the unfortunate unexpected consequence of condemning the very persons whose experiences they are supposedly defending. As Rose writes of Masson's claims,

The psychoanalytic attention to fantasy does not, however, discredit the utterance of the patient. To argue that Freud dismissed the traumas of his patients as "the fantasies of hysterical women who invented stories and told lies" is a total misconstrual of the status psychoanalysis accords to fantasy, which was never assigned by Freud to the category of willful untruth. In fact Freud's move was the reverse—towards a dimension of reality all the more important for the subject because it goes way beyond anything that can, or needs to be, attested as fact. By seeing fantasy as a degradation of speech, by turning reality into nothing more than what can be empirically established as the case, it is Masson himself who places human subjects in the dock.[9]

Rose's task in this book is to interpret the unknowing, fantastic self-excesses of discourse in a feminist frame. *Sexuality in the Field of Vision* contains coruscating readings of diverse representations of femininity—of works by Freud, George Eliot, Leonardo da Vinci, and Shakespeare, among others—as well as a series of superb critiques of technical psychoanalytic concepts and their relationship to issues bearing on vision, spectacle, and imagination.

In three pieces that have changed the face of film studies, "The Imaginary," "The Cinematic Apparatus," and "Woman as Symptom," Rose clarifies both key psychoanalytic concepts and their application in cinema studies. As she notes, the "proliferation of references to psychoanalysis in literature on the cinema is probably exceeded only by the number of references to the camera and geometrical optics in the literature of psychoanalysis itself."[10] This close but asymmetrical bond between psychoanalysis and cinema studies implicates the technologies of cinema and the screen of the mind. Rose returns to some of the central psychoanalytic texts from which film studies was then drawing, in order to bring out the difficulties of such a reliance—pointing out how often sexual difference came to be elided in various theorizations of the "cinematic apparatus." Bristling with detailed, informed, and innovative argumentation, these essays remain classics, cited again and again for their arguments and their insights by scholars of visual culture.

From children's fictions to the fractured imbrication of feminist desires with their Others, the importance of fantasy is the constant. Rose's next book turned to one of the most controversial English-language poets, Sylvia Plath. As it happens, Rose's own book quickly became enmired in a controversy of its own—a dispute with the estate of the poet, then controlled by Ted Hughes, Plath's husband at the time of her suicide, and by Hughes's sister Olwyn.

Plath, as Rose points out, poses a set of painful difficulties for any feminist reader, not least because the power of Plath's poetry may seem to be complicated both internally and externally by politically fraught identifications. A battery of questions arises. Plath, not a Jew, nonetheless draws on Holocaust imagery in the service of her poetry: how can she compare her own psychological turbulence to the extermination of six million persons? Plath, a major female poet, committed suicide in tormented circumstances: how is it possible for a feminist to affirm her poetry and her actions, without simply resorting to guilt and blame, whether of "men" or of Plath herself? Plath, though a confessional poet, nonetheless fabricates events as if they were actualities in order to squeeze more power from her words: how to resist the temptation to impute a real-world correlate to each and every poetic image without explaining away their fictional power—and thereby Plath's own creative genius?

This is where the problem of fantasy once again cannot be evaded. As Rose wrote in the *London Review of Books* (22 August 2002) of her dispute with "the Estate," "Grant a fantasy a reality of its own and it crosses the barrier into the real world."[11] The protest pivoted on Rose's interpretation of "The Rabbit Catcher," a poem which seethes with an ambiguous sadomasochistic violence, mixing and inverting person and place, corroding experience and landscape with its intensities. Rose quotes Plath:

It was a place of force—
The wind gagging my mouth with my own blown hair,
Tearing off my voice, and the sea
Blinding me with its lights, the lives of the dead
Unreeling in it, spreading like oil.

Did the "events" there presented "really" ever happen? Is "Rabbit Catcher" a poem of rage or of desire? Or both? Or of something else? Is the eponymous "rabbit catcher" a figure for the male hunter or for the female body? Is this a war of sexes or of species or of the self-against-itself? On Rose's own account, Hughes accused Rose of "stealing" his life with her interpretations, replacing it with salacious, gossipy fantasies of what transpired and, in doing so, threatening to "humiliate" Plath's children with deleteriously sexualized images of their mother.[12] When it comes to a figure like Plath, Rose notes, it is just as impossible to write a biography of her as *not* to write a biography of her. What this means, among other things, is that Plath's "confessional" poetry puts reality into question as an integral part of its elaboration. Writing poetry about her own life was an essential part of Plath's life, but to read this poetry is to realize that her crucial life events involved the immixture of fantasies which often have no clear or consistent empirical referent. To make "reality" the tribunal of the verse is therefore to seriously mistake what Plath's poetry is up to; it is, peculiarly, to ignore its properly *poetic* activity. As Rose's work everywhere demonstrates, "fantasy" and "reality" cannot simply be opposed, for "there is no history outside its subjective realisation."[13]

Slowly but surely Rose's focus on fantasy can be seen to be moving into a more explicitly geopolitical frame, as the chapter on "Daddy" included here makes clear. *Why War? Psychoanalysis, Politics, and the Return to Melanie Klein* collects papers first presented in a variety of contexts, then as Bucknell Lectures in 1992. These papers engage themes as diverse as the inner relationship between truth and war, Margaret Thatcher and Ruth Ellis (the last woman to be hanged in England, in 1955), and Shakespeare and the death drive. Moreover, as the book's subtitle suggests, it shows Rose engaged in a strenuous re-reading of the work of Melanie Klein, one of the greatest of all psychoanalysts, focusing particularly on the radical negativity that Klein posits at the origins of subjectivity. In doing so, Rose draws a connection with politics, not only in the possible application of Kleinian concepts, but in their very emergence: the famous disputes between Anna Freudians and Kleinians, "as is well known, were staged at the height of the Second World War."[14] To take this negativity and this historical conflict seriously is to be forced to recognize the limits of all struggles for liberation, their ineradicable tendency to turn on themselves, to fuse and confuse demands for justice with the operations of tyranny.

States of Fantasy—first given as the Clarendon Lectures in English Literature 1994 and since the inspiration for a concerto by Mohammed Fairouz, which, performed by the Borromeo Quartet, premiered at the Lincoln Center in New York in September 2010—reads problems of racism and nationalism through a sequence of literary and autobiographical texts and their ways of representing the politics of the places in which they are set: Amos Oz and Raja Shehadeh in Israel, Rian Malan in South Africa, Bessie Head in Botswana/South Africa, Kazuo Ishiguro in England. Since none of the bases of political life—the divisions between self and other, man and woman, child and adult, *ethnos* and *xenos*, and so on—can have any purchase outside of the fantasies which support them, Rose targets not only the points at which these fantasies come into conflict with so-called realities, but how they are at variance with themselves. For Rose, no fantasy is innocent in its own terms; no fantasy emerges without harboring unintended guests or without engendering undesirable consequences; no fantasy can function without implicating others. As Rose writes in the introduction to *States of Fantasy*, included in this reader, "To place 'state' and 'fantasy' together is not only to propose a new theoretical turn but is also . . . to uncover the history of their intimate relation" (136 herein). The history thereby uncovered will necessarily be a *traumatic* one, cobbled together with ellipses, and pulsing with inadmissible affects. The work of the critic is in part to reconstruct and re-inflect what has been censored, and to do so in such a way as to decline its more murderous impulses.

In its attention to Israel, *States of Fantasy* sees Rose steadily moving toward the center of her most recent politically engaged writing on the Middle East (indeed, she says that it was feeling a need to explore further its historical preconditions that led her to the question of Zionism). The other major focus of the book is on South Africa. That these two countries are linked somehow for Rose is troubling but unavoidable: but although the specter of apartheid, as reality and as fantasmatic reality, can never be far away, she refuses any easy analogy between the two. The differences can never be elided, either, a point Rose stresses was made by Edward Said, who insisted on the distinction between white settlers in Africa and Jews fleeing European anti-Semitism, at the same time as he made the link between the victims of apartheid and the state of Israel today.[15] Great Britain and its multifarious, malignant residues of empire are implicated in both histories. The South African writers about whom Rose has now written extensively include Wulf Sachs, Nadine Gordimer, Bessie Head, and J. M. Coetzee, and in every case she is concerned to explore their particular ambivalences, and even their complicities with the states—in all senses of that word—they are contesting. In such studies, the difficulties of self-localization and address become paramount. How, for instance, can one write out of an identification with the oppressed, when understanding or even empathy is simultaneously sustained by that oppression? How can such identifications be more than recuperative fantasy projections? Such questions are, as always, linked by Rose to the question of feminism.

As Rose writes in "Dorothy Richardson and the Jew," "A fair amount has been written about the presence of anti-Semitism in modernist writing, especially with reference to T. S. Eliot and Ezra Pound; much less about the anti-Semitism of women modernist writers. This may be another version of a problem that has recently become familiar to feminism—the limits to its earlier celebration of women writers, the point where feminism has had to acknowledge the other agendas and blindspots of oppression which that celebration apparently had to ignore."[16] If Rose puts psychoanalysis to work in the service of feminism, then she also uses psychoanalysis to curb the excesses of dogmatic feminism, as she uses it to construct surprising and powerful accounts of certain kinds of political formation. She is certainly against victimhood as an identity, to the point where she argues that it can become a source of new atrocities in its turn, as when horrific events—such as the Holocaust—are turned into alibis for brutal state suppression of other minorities. Nonetheless, she also tries to avoid laying the blame for certain injustices on any one agency, given the overdeterminations of the unconscious, the constitutive forgetting that troubles all memory, the contradictions in every act.

Yet the sophistications of Rose's position hardly lead her to a cynicism or quietism; on the contrary, what they do is impel her, again and again, to reflect on the problems of re-education, of social change, of the attempted reform of institutions in order to transmit corrected doctrine. As she points out, even the enthusiasm within some academic departments of literature for psychoanalysis as "negative capability"—the affirmation of doubts, hesitancies, contradictions, and so on—purged psychoanalysis both of its extremities of affect and its attention to effective politics. Rose discusses some of the political consequences of such institutional failures in her 2000 translation of, and introduction to, the 1983 text of Moustapha Safouan, in *Jacques Lacan and the Question of Psychoanalytic Training* (a slightly different version of this essay also appears in *On Not Being Able to Sleep*). There she writes,

> There is a feminist point, or rather a point about feminism, to be made here. From a position outside or against institutions, many feminists of the 1970s (myself included) have risen up the institutional hierarchy in such a way that it is no longer viable to base any claim for political radicalism on the status of the outsider to the institution, on an uneasy belonging inside its walls. It seems appropriate, then, to start asking what is wrong with institutions from the inside. There might be much for feminism in an examination of the precise ways in which power entrenches itself in institutions, beyond the more easy disclaimer that makes all institutions necessarily authoritarian, patriarchal, non-viable. As Safouan puts the question in relation to psychoanalysis: In what ways might an institution constitute a piece of acting out against its own main discovery?[17]

"Men make their own history," Marx famously writes in *The Eighteenth Brumaire of Louis Bonaparte*, "but they do not make it just as they please."

Psychoanalysis adds: humans make their own histories through the fantasies that traverse them. We have already noted the importance of translating and translations for Rose; we can now add that translation is one way in which she pursues her own essays in self-criticism. Academic or technical translations, which are now so often done by graduate students or underpaid professionals, are often treated as elementary rungs up a symbolic scholarly ladder (when they are not simply done for peanuts). It is clear that, in translating Safouan, neither of these can truly be motivations for Rose. Safouan himself is a magnificent translator—notably of *The Interpretation of Dreams* into Arabic, and *Othello* into demotic Egyptian—in whose hands translations themselves become political acts, and are theorized as such. Likewise, in translating, Rose clearly places her own ideals on the line, in order that she might be forced to take new directions: ideals of scholarship, ideals of praxis, ideals of friendship.

Friendship networks, state institutions, teaching, and scholarship are all intimately related—as Rose's work itself constantly emphasizes—and it would be instructive to trace Rose's own career through the optic of her elective and institutional affinities, not least because of her own theorization of the vagaries of institutional processes. She herself trained at such august academic institutions as Oxford University, the Sorbonne, and the University of London; she has for a long time held a professorial position at Queen Mary's College, University of London, with visiting lectureships at U.S. universities and elsewhere. She has had intellectual exchanges with such scholars, writers, psychoanalysts, and editors as Jenny Uglow, Marina Warner, Edward Said, Avi Shlaim, Judith Butler, Julia Kristeva, Sally Alexander, Christopher Bollas, and Mary-Kay Wilmers, among many others (in this regard, it is illuminating to examine not only the topics and references, but also the dedications and acknowledgments in her books).

Despite the wider sociological import that such an investigation of a successful feminist scholar's career might have—in its charting of shifts in intellectual capital from the 1970s to the present day, from the emergence of gender studies as a viable academic program through postcolonialism and queer theory and beyond—we wish only to pick up a single strand here. This strand is, in accordance with the most basic psychoanalytic doctrine, familial. Rose's sister Gillian was herself a well-known academic, a philosopher whose work on Hegel, law, and the Holocaust has proven very influential worldwide. Her death, in 1995, played a key role in Rose's shift into writing fiction. It is "To my sister Gillian Rose" that Rose dedicates her novel *Albertine* (2001), named after a female character central to Marcel Proust's *A la recherche du temps perdu* (*In Search of Lost Time*). The link between Rose's growing interest in Israel and Gillian's work on Jewish philosophy is the subject of the memorial address "On Gillian Rose," which concludes *The Last Resistance*.

Here we are confronted by a generic shift on Rose's part: from essays and extended studies to a novel, from criticism to fiction. We are confronted by a different kind of translation work: a novel that rewrites another novel, at once homage and critique. And not just any novel, but one of the monuments of European modernism. To Proust's *roman d'Albertine*, identified with the volumes *The Prisoner* and *The Fugitive* (although the orphan Albertine is of course introduced much earlier in the sequence), Rose has responded with a rendering from the perspectives of Albertine and her friend Andrée, thereby emphasizing the singularities of voice and position in the elaboration of narrative. We are confronted by the problem of sexuality, in which an apparently heterosexual relationship ciphers and betrays homosexual, "perverse," elements. We are confronted by familial, social, and political intensities: Proust's masterpiece famously traverses the intricate milieux of Paris society, in which the glamorous whirl of aristocracy and the *haute bourgeoisie* intersect with the noxious labyrinths of anti-Semitic prejudice surrounding the Dreyfus Affair. So the motifs of capture and incarceration, fleeing and hiding, transformation and transience, loss and commemoration are put to work at every level in *Albertine* by Rose, interweaving the themes of family, sex, sexuality, race, class, nation, and religion—right up to the point where it becomes impossible to separate art from autobiography.

Rose's following book, *On Not Being Able to Sleep* (2003)—the dense literary allusions compressed into the title also denoting the insomniac restlessness of thought—collects a decade's work of essays and reviews with a new form of accessibility and a shift from theory to journalism, part of her increasing commitment to writing for the *London Review of Books*. The essays range over a variety of topics, from the poet Anne Sexton to the contemporary psychoanalyst Christopher Bollas, from "the cult of celebrity" to South Africa's Truth and Reconciliation Commission. Here "shame," one of the primal, most distressing affects of humankind, steps in as the new focus for the vagaries of the psyche. Linked as it is to appearance and exposure, the public and publicity, shame proves to be a red thread linking the innocent cruelty of the uninhibited infant to the murderousness of states. Yet shame can also "be a blessing, the heart's desire, something coveted and pursued."[18] The intensities of shame can be the result of acts done or undone; one can, paradoxically, be ashamed for one's shamelessness, feel shame for not being ashamed, or feel ashamed for the other who should be shamed but does not feel it. Rose's discussion of shame draws for its examples on literature, psycho-analysis, and philosophical works, as well as on major political events, extend-ing her work on the links between fantasy and affect into the realms of celebrity and mass-media gossip.

How is it that shame and shamelessness enter a dialectical relationship in which the most intimate, visceral humiliations find themselves played out in the grand violence of states? Rose's controversial *The Question of Zion* (2005) consolidates her engagement with one of the most enduring and distressing conflicts of our time, a conflict in which, as a Jewish writer, she feels herself deeply implicated. *The Question of Zion* is an intervention into the fraught discourses that swarm about the constitution and actions of the Israeli state, as she ventures an understanding of the inner dimensions of Zionism. Rose traces a fierce messianic streak running through secular Jewish national-ism, which silences the self-critical spirit of political Zionism's very progeni-tors, including Ahad Ha'am, Theodor Herzl, and Martin Buber, and renders present-day Israel tragically impervious to critique. As in her work on Plath and feminism, Rose here demonstrates how victimhood can deleteriously fossilize into an identity, arguing that the nation has become entrapped by a relentless psychic logic in which their own traumatic histories now serve as both the raison d'être for the Israeli state and a limitless rationale for sub-jugating the Palestinians—a process that Rose describes as "the militarisation of suffering."

The Question of Zion is a particularly bold intervention, in part because it raises the question of how, in such a case, to intervene at all? Is it possible to condemn the actions of Israel and not be compromised by anti-Semitism? What are the risks of even entering into this debate, such as it is? The fact is that any non-Jewish critic of Israel runs the risk of being challenged to defend their antiracist credentials, while a Jewish critic of Israel may be in turn always be charged with being a "self-hating-Jew"—a phenomenon about which Rose has written a short piece, "On the Myth of Self-Hatred," her contribution to the set of essays published by Independent Jewish Voices in 2008.[19]

The impact of *The Question of Zion* has been extraordinary. It was trans-lated into Hebrew and Arabic and drew highly positive notices in publications such as *Ha'aretz*, the *London Review of Books*, and the *Observer*. Other re-sponses to the book have sometimes been vitriolic, as might be expected given the intensity of feeling that drives the issue. Amnon Rubinstein, in a hallucinatory review in the *Jerusalem Post*, fulminated: "Iran's president is not alone in wanting to wipe Israel off the map."[20] (In fact, Rose describes the Zionist desire for a homeland for a persecuted people as legitimate on the second page of her book.) The Israeli psychoanalyst Avner Falk posed the question "How did Jacqueline Rose acquire her anti-Semitic anti-Zionism?"[21] When Rose participated in a public debate in support of the motion that "Zionism Today is the Real Enemy of the Jews" (her speech appears in this collection), one of the members of the losing side, the conservative columnist Melanie Phillips, described her as one of "three Jewish persecutors of Israel who strutted their repellent stuff," the others being the distinguished "new" Israeli historian Avi Shlaim and the award-winning campaigning journalist Amira Hass.[22] (The outcome was surprising, given that an online poll before the debate registered more than 3,000 against and a few hundred in favor of the motion.) Rose has even been accused by the novelist Howard Jacobson of being the playwright Caryl Churchill's "Jewish midwife" in the delivery of the latter's play *Seven Jewish Children* (Rose's defense of which is included in this reader).

Such vituperative criticisms are, notably, enunciated in tones distinctly different from Rose's own. Her own voice is often highly self-questioning, and her conclusions qualified, self-confessedly provisional; she also welcomes public responses to her essays, replying in an open and accessible way to strenuous questioning, whether on the letters pages of daily newspapers, or in academic lecture halls or online forums. Rose's riposte to the attacks of Churchill's play, for example, was originally published on the *Guardian's* "Comment Is Free" opinion site.

It is therefore also worth underlining here her role as a *teacher*, as someone professionally engaged not only in the often solitary realm of closeted reading and writing, but in the transmission of knowledge between persons and across generations. Yet teaching concerns more than simply transmitting information. As we have seen, this relationship is a persistent theme in Rose's writings—its necessary difficulties and failures, as much as its glories—and it is therefore significant that her writing often develops out of ongoing discussions with her students in courses. For many years, Rose regularly taught an undergraduate seminar, "Literature, History, Politics: South African Writing in the Era of Apartheid and After," and since 2005 has been teaching "Palestine-Israel, Israel-Palestine: Politics and the Literary Imagination." Three other courses have defined Rose's tenure at Queen Mary—"Reading Psychoanalysis Reading Literature," "Freud and Proust," and "Psychoanalysis and Modern Culture"—and her enduring commitment to teaching psychoanalysis is further reflected in the intercollegiate forum she co-teaches with Daniel Pick, "Psychoanalytic Thought, History and Political Life."

Queen Mary's location in London's East End means that Rose's students tend to come from extraordinarily diverse national, ethnic, and religious backgrounds—British, Egyptian, Palestinian, Israeli, Somalian, Pakistani—and this plurality offers a unique opportunity for dialogue. As Rose herself notes, any pedagogy worthy of the name cannot be a unilateral imposition of knowledge; rather, it is the teacher who has to listen and learn from her interlocutors if she is indeed to teach.

If Rose had laid some of the groundwork for *The Question of Zion* in her academic studies, she consolidated her understanding of Israeli politics in 2002, when she made a documentary *Dangerous Liaisons: Israel and America* for Channel Four in the United Kingdom. The film shows Rose again moving into a new medium and a new kind of genre—television journalism—and, in doing so, becoming an interviewer of key voices in the Israeli-Palestinian conflict, including Benjamin Netanyahu and Noam Chomsky. It bears noting that *The Question of Zion* itself draws extensively on a range of materials, political and theological tracts, literary texts, historical and statistical studies, as well as interviews with a range of people, including Jewish settlers in the Occupied Territories. This process—of continuing to listen intently to others despite their often wildly different beliefs, actions, and demands—is, at the very least, an ethical one. It suggests that the labels "pro-Palestinian" and "anti-Israeli" are not only not simple designators of clearly demarcated positions, but that they silence attempts at a proper discussion by buoying a spurious logic of blame. As Rose writes in her book on Plath, "One does not become pure as the other falls into the dirt."[23]

Israel-Palestine is also the dominant subject of her most recent collection, *The Last Resistance* (2007), in which the power of unconscious fantasies in the establishment and perpetuation of modern states is again key. All these essays were written post–September 11, with the worsening of the Israel-Palestine conflict and the ongoing war in Iraq. The volume shows Rose at her angriest and most elegiac, but without ever losing her theoretical edge—witness the essay "Freud and the People, or Freud Goes to Abu Ghraib," in which she investigates how Freud's own ambivalence about the alleged shamelessness of the "common people" can help us to understand some of the humiliating actions of the American torturers in Iraq. But the theoretical linchpin of the collection is "Mass Psychology" (first published, in 2004, as the preface to the New Penguin Classics translation of Freud's text of the same name, and reproduced in this reader). Rose discusses the ways in which Freud came to reconceive the relations between individual psychopathology and varieties of group action, ranging from the sustained hyper-organization of nations and armies to the punctual hysterias of fandom and frenzied teenage enthusiasms.

In tracking Rose's development in this preface, we have had to present her arguments more simply and bluntly than she does herself. This point is worth reflecting on. If, for purposes of clarity and following the generic constraints of such "introductions" to such "readers" as the present one, we try to situate, in however minimal a manner, Rose's contribution to important debates as plainly as possible, this very clarity necessarily has something reductive, misleading, even brutal about it. Moreover, it treats Rose's writing as if her style— or, more accurately, *styles*—were simply a rhetorical ornament, something that could be shorn from the prose without loss of meaning or impact. This is to miss something essential. After all, Lacan opened his own famous collection of essays, the *Ecrits*, with a short commentary on Buffon's maxim: "Style is the man himself." Surely style can also be the woman herself? Rose is an extraordinarily readable writer, and even virulent critics of her politics can admit (if grudgingly) the power and seductiveness of her style. Indeed, her style undoubtedly contributes to what these critics find threatening about Rose's work. Her prose is never harsh or violent, even when directly confronting political opponents: complex, meditative, supple, Rose's sinuous lines tend to generate a kind of "pleasure of the text" (to advert to the title of Roland Barthes's well-known book), gently concatenating syncopations as they incline from one topic to the next. These rhythms have a poetic aspect, as if Rose's own criticism was engaged in a mimetic admiration of its objects, of Plath and Proust and Woolf. She moves easily from colloquialisms to complex concepts, and back again. Rose often begins and ends a piece of writing with a question or a quotation, rather than with a summary assertion; her aphorisms tend to be exploratory, rather than apodictic. In the case of "Daddy," the chapter, which concludes her monograph on Plath, ends with Plath's own voice—a paragraph-long passage from Plath's journals with which she rounds off. It is inquiry and otherness that guides her, not doctrine or command. Moreover, as we have been implying, Rose can modulate her style for different audiences and different contexts, from technical psychoanalytic studies to prose fiction to newspaper opinion columns.

Yet, precisely because of this stylistic mastery, it could—wrongly—appear that Rose's work is not always logically argued or structured, being perhaps more akin to a sequence of stunning *aperçus* strung together in an associative way. Rather than "if x, then y follows," we often find ourselves following diverging augmentations: "x and y and z and. . . ." Moreover, the twists and drifts of her writing can seem to make her overall argument elusive at the moment she is in fact writing most clearly. And if her occasionally eccentric punctuation (a medley of semicolons and dashes) exacerbates this sense of elusiveness, Rose's interest in the profuse operations of language is surely related to the linguistic milieu of her childhood. In *Love's Work*, Gillian Rose recalled their grandparents' "macaronic medley of tongues," their father's "strict, clipped conformity to the Queen's English," and their stepfather's "love of the underside of the language, pronounced with a Dublin lilt."[24]

It is instructive that Jacqueline Rose's prose is suffused with metaphors of tracking and path-following. "A line which runs"; "came at least halfway to meet"; "not a million miles from"; "runs back and forth across the space of"; "runs into and up against": such phrases evoke a graphic picture of intellectual inquiry as a process of ceaseless movement, energy, and slippage. However, Rose's logic is always more than just associative, if "associative" means an arbitrary, idiosyncratic meandering without universal traction or consequence. On the contrary, an essential conviction of psychoanalysis is that the truth insists in the apparent disconnectedness of such associations; that such associations are both "free" and "constrained" in a way that exceeds the usual meaning of these terms; that such indirection is in fact the only way to evade the deadlocks of prohibition; and that the defiles of desire are not altered by, and certainly not captured by, "telling it straight."

Rose herself likes to reexamine ready-to-wear figures of speech, which have become so commonsensical that they are no longer even thought about (at the very moment that they pass for truth). She will often entreat readers to ' return to look more closely at an earlier and apparently banal remark. Unexpected utterances are interrogated for their illuminating force. Take, for instance, her focus on the plea of "apathy" that an unnamed South African Indian woman submitted to the Truth and Reconciliation Commission. The application—rejected by the commissioners because, although it was agreed apathy did fall within the ambit of the inquiry, it did not constitute quite enough of a sin of omission, was not *quite enough* of an offense—nonetheless touches directly on key political problems. As Rose asks, "How can you fully disclose something whose chief property is deficiency, to be in some sense absent from history and missing to yourself?"[25] In part, Rose's style is an attempt to answer such impossible questions, only insofar as, in its ceaseless turns and returns, it offers possible answers that it then immediately complicates.

If the singularity of Rose's style finds its authorization in its conceptual principles and the demands of its objects, the pleasures of texts are at once personal and political, as she also so persuasively demonstrates. At its limits, such singularity becomes exemplary. It is perhaps, finally, in her style that Rose is at once most herself—and most other to herself, as well.

Rose's style is not confined simply to her writing; her personality as an intellectual bears noting, too, not least because she is a writer who foregrounds the personal and reminds us, most obviously through her use of the first-person pronoun, that the voice of her essays is always that of an embodied agent. (The personal, after all, is the political, and vice versa.) For Rose is not just a striking belletrist, but also a compelling presenter of her ideas. In Janet Malcolm's book *The Silent Woman: Sylvia Plath and Ted Hughes* (1994) —a study of Plath's afterlife as the subject of biography—Rose disarms the *New Yorker* journalist celebrated for her caustic tone. From her experience meeting Rose to discuss her conflicts with the Plath estate, Malcolm builds the following picture of her immaculate poise.

> I was greeted by a small, attractive woman in her early forties, wearing a short and close-fitting skirt and a sweater, whose face was framed by a great deal of artfully unruly blond hair, and whose whole person was surrounded by a kind of *nimbus of self-possession*.[26] During our meeting her manner was engaging—neither too friendly nor too distant—and on a scale of how people should conduct themselves with journalists I would give her a score of 99. That she was an adept of a theory of criticism whose highest values are uncertainty, anxiety, and ambiguity was a curious but somewhat unameliorating facet of her formidable clarity, confidence, and certainty.[27]

What Malcolm observes as a paradox between Rose's assured persona and frequently hesitant prose may not, in fact, be paradoxical at all, since outward confidence is often the psyche's answer to anxiety. Our interview with Rose, which concludes this volume, however, puts paid to one journalist's description of her as "fervently private."[28] In other ways, her self-presentation squares more easily with her thought. Rose, no less than in Malcolm's account, remains an avowed fashionista who has never seen the accoutrements of "femininity" as incompatible with her political principles. For Rose, a woman's intellectual authority need in no way derive from aping the dominant characteristics of men. In a piece written for a birthday *Festschrift* for the *London Review of Books* editor Mary-Kay Wilmers, Rose wrote, "I love the fact that Mary-Kay is a small person (in height) like me, and like to see this, oddly, as a political statement."[29] Rose went on to recall her first job interview at the University of East Anglia, when she prompted one panel member to remark, "But she is so young and thin, she will crack under the administrative strain!" Just as Rose's writing critiques dominant images of mastery, so her charisma cuts against one feminist view of power as the preserve of the towering patriarch.

Like Plath, whose engagements with the popular she compellingly defends, Rose takes mass culture seriously, seeing it as a repository for group psychic unrest. In "The Cult of Celebrity," for example, she confesses to being an unabashed reader of *Hello!* magazine. And if there is risk for an intellectual in embracing popular culture, it is the no-less-hazardous wager of her work to read politics through the visor of fantasy, which we've posited as the closest thing to a unifying trope in her work. As she writes in *States of Fantasy*, "There is a common assumption that fantasy has tended to be excluded from the political rhetoric of the Left because it is not serious, not material, too flighty and hence not worth bothering about" (126 herein). In fact, Rose shows, what escapes inquiry as "trivial" or "obvious" is often precisely what's most worth bothering about, because it exposes the psyche's defensive blockage of thought. Perhaps the closest that Rose ever comes to proffering a manifesto is in that same introduction to *States of Fantasy*, included in this reader, where she suggests that the terms "state and fantasy" should replace "culture and identity" in modern theory: " 'Identity' seems too 'hard,' 'culture' too 'soft.' . . . [But] however far it travels, the term 'state' always holds its reference to the founding political condition of the modern world. And 'fantasy,' however much it threatens subjects with the prospect of its own and their dissolution, keeps sight of the peculiarities with which identities, not only consciously but also unconsciously, make and unmake themselves" (136 herein).

In *The Haunting of Sylvia Plath*, Rose explored the fantasmatic agenda behind Ted Hughes's editing of Plath's posthumously published writings in her chapter "The Archive," which she describes as "a reading—of necessity speculative—of the editing of Plath's work."[30] So it is fitting to conclude this introduction with a short note about the principles of selection for this reader. As we have tried to show, the "Rose Archive" is not simply a coherent whole; nor, by the same token, is it simply incoherent. Rather, it is a ceaseless knotting and re-knotting of disparate threads. This knotting, moreover, is not merely a consequence of external, empirical happenstances, but has an immanent theoretical and political justification. So if there are certainly unifying tendencies to be discerned in the Rose archive, these tendencies are ramifying rather than reductive: the movement of her work constantly presses toward a unity that it also denies. This movement has itself a crucial import for understanding something about the times in which we live.

Given the variety and extent of Rose's publications, we needed to give a sense of this range.[31] We have reproduced extracts from her monographs, as well as self-contained essays, reviews, and, finally, the combative tactical interventions that conclude this volume, in which intellectual life moves decisively into the public sphere. We wanted, moreover—again given the pedagogical aspects of such readers—to give a sense both of the unity and diversity of her work under guiding subdivisions. We have thus presented the selections under the following headings: Analysis, Nation, Representations, Interventions. These headings, whose justification should by now be evident, hopefully enable a useful summation of Rose's animating preoccupations, just as the selected pieces are intended to give the uninitiated reader of Rose a sense of her protean intellectual engagements. At best, we hope that readers hitherto unfamiliar with her work will be induced to seek out her published materials to date, and to continue to follow the writings of one of the most important contemporary psychoanalytic, feminist, and political thinkers.

As the extracts in this reader attest, Jacqueline Rose is a major public intellectual of and for our times.

PART I   Analysis

Analysis

We open this reader with a sample of Rose's writings on psychoanalysis. Rose launched her publishing career with translations and studies of Lacanian analysis, which were decisive in introducing Jacques Lacan's work to an English-speaking audience and promoting the radical political possibilities of this theory for British feminism. Along with other feminist translator-critics of a similar generation, such as Gayatri Spivak, Toril Moi, Peggy Kamuf, and the late Barbara Johnson, Rose played a central role in introducing post–Second World War French thought to an Anglophone readership. Yet Rose didn't simply emerge as an exegete or adherent of Lacan, applying or extending Lacanian concepts to new fields. On the contrary, her technical psychoanalytic work has moved increasingly away from the arcana of high Lacanian doctrine toward detailed studies of other psychoanalytic orientations. Rose's work on Melanie Klein, or on such contemporary analysts as Christopher Bollas, shows her willingness to engage with the entire tradition of psychoanalysis in an open and nondoctrinaire manner. Moreover, her subjects—among them, sexual hierarchies, murderous political fantasies, and general group psychology—typically have serious implications for other disciplines. The essays selected here move chronologically forward, from Rose's early essays on "Femininity and Its Discontents" and "Feminine Sexuality," through the work on the death drive in Melanie Klein, to a more recent introduction to a new translation of Freud's *Mass Psychology and Other Writings*.

These essays show that psychoanalysis, when properly understood, is the opposite of the dogmatic discourse it is often caricatured as being. Psychoanalysis is an investigation into the endlessly inventive powers of the psyche, as Freud's development showed—from his foundational writings, such as *Studies on Hysteria* and the *Interpretation of Dreams*, all the way to *Moses and Monotheism* and beyond. Freud constantly changed his positions under the pressure of new evidence—whether gleaned from listening to his own patients, the discovery of immanent theoretical difficulties, research in related scientific fields, or political events of such magnitude as the First World War. For psychoanalysis was never only an enterprise founded on what Lacan later referred to as "the golden tonsils" of the hysterical women Freud and Josef Breuer treated in their private practice, but a discourse which took the problems of sex—its formation, operations, and consequences—to be central to all human life. In doing so, psychoanalysis became one of the very few modern professions in which women, almost immediately, began to play at least as significant a role as men.

This is not to say that feminism and psychoanalysis are the same kind of practice, but psychoanalysis certainly offers useful concepts for feminism and, at the same time, can challenge political feminism in difficult but productive ways. So runs Rose's argument in her essay "Femininity and Its Discontents" (1983). Against the dominant strain in left-wing English-language feminism— particularly in *English* feminism—that insisted on the primacy of "material" and "materialist" analyses in feminist theory, Rose countered that psycho-analysis reveals something in femininity itself that cannot be reduced to class or economic positions. She shows how psychoanalysis is often characterized in such a way (as simply a "theory," for example) so as to have lost the battle in advance. Rose reveals how many feminist criticisms of psychoanalysis repeat the very blind spots that inspired the development of psychoanalysis in the first place. For Rose, what makes psychoanalysis scandalous and corrosive to some is precisely its emphasis on the unconscious: that is, the revelation of the inexorable failures of identity. In a striking defense of Freud's assault on naïve empiricism, Rose demonstrates how the resistance to the unconscious is often driven by an unjustifiable belief in the absoluteness of "psychic cohe-sion" and can lead to positions with unfortunate political consequences.

In "Feminine Sexuality" (1982), originally published as an introduction to Rose's and Juliet Mitchell's translation of Lacanian texts on *Feminine Sexuality*, Rose provides what remains a classic account of Lacan's work. She emphasizes the close relationship between sexuality and the unconscious in Lacan's writ-ing, and also the fictional and fantasmatic status of subjectivity (which is all the more compelling, however, for not being simply reducible to any empiri-cal reality). "Reality" and "fiction" are not opposed in the realms of subjec-tivity, since reality itself is always in part the outcome of psychic processes of fiction-making. The putative identity and unity of the psyche are themselves fictions and, as such, are menaced and destabilized by the very operations and materials required for their elaboration. Above all, language itself (what Lacan denominated "the symbolic") is key: Lacan's work shows how allegedly bio-logical instincts are actually the by-products of systems of representation. "Woman" is therefore an effect of the laws of language, and any positing of an "essence" to "woman" can be seen as an imposture—one which feminist theorists can draw on psychoanalysis to unmask and transform.

In line with one crucial aspect of psychoanalysis, Rose consistently probes those elements in thought that are extreme and insistent but often seen as unapproachable and therefore overlooked. As she remarks in her discussion of "Negativity in the Work of Melanie Klein," Klein herself "saw her task as one of excavation, as the retrieval of something which even Freud . . . had barely been able to approach" (61 herein). Noting that "a post-Lacanian orthodoxy" in the humanities "has blocked access to Klein," Rose attempts a rereading of the notorious "Controversial Discussions," a series of debates between Kleinians and Anna-Freudians at the British Psycho-Analytic Society in En-gland in 1943–1944, at the height of the Second World War. Rose discusses the contributions of Paula Heimann, Susan Isaacs, and Joan Rivière to the debate, taking the problem of negativity qua the destructive instincts as her red thread through the thickets of the controversy. The key authorizing text for the discussants is Freud's classic paper "Negation" (1925), and from it Rose de-velops a sequence of issues that continue to plague psychoanalysis today: the origins, status, and powers of the ego; the role of anxiety in both fixing and precipitating psychic development; the power of negativity to subvert both biology and chronology; and the unsettling relationships between institu-tions, politics, and psychoanalytic concepts.

Rose returns to Freud's own essays on the links between the individual psyche and mass action in the introductory essay she contributed to the new Penguin Modern Classics translation of *Mass Psychology and Other Writings* (2004), which includes *The Future of an Illusion* and *Moses the Man and Monotheistic Religion*. Here Rose sketches a certain line of Freud's own per-sonal and theoretical trajectory, drawing out the crucial fact that "from the very earliest moments of our lives . . . we are 'peopled' by others. Our 'psyche' is a social space" (86 herein). From the mid-1910s, Freud's recognition that the problem of narcissism necessarily blurs any clear distinction between "self" and "others" induces him to develop his "second topography," in which the poor ego attempts to fend off the irreducible, competing demands of reality, the id, and the superego. In doing so, Freud is constrained to acknowledge that among the primary needs of the self is the passion to be acknowledged by others. Moreover, as Rose argues, it "is central to Freud's thinking on this topic that what binds people together, for better and worse, is their commitment to an internal ideal" (90 herein). The concept of "identification" is therefore recalibrated to explain, on the one hand, how people can at once identify with a group (e.g., ethnicity, class, or nation) and, on the other hand, simultaneously act as if such an identification—in such a way as might be seen to threaten the unity of any group—makes each of them special. Love of a "leader" (whether a person or an ideal) is the key. For Freud, one loves to be loved, and the leader must always also be a lover. Yet love, as psychoanalysis shows, is always also ambivalent, and the leader is finally a mask for the loathed primal father. This ambivalence is, for Freud, a literally murderous ambivalence, as he places "a primary parricide at the origins of all culture" (97 herein). This conviction plays throughout Freud's later work, and the themes Rose discerns in her rereading of these major Freudian texts on group dynamics are the very themes of sexuality, identification, fantasy, and the political that have concerned her throughout her career.

—*Justin Clemens and Ben Naparstek*

1

Femininity and Its Discontents

Is psychoanalysis a "new orthodoxy" for feminism? Or does it rather represent the surfacing of something difficult and exceptional but important for feminism, which is on the verge (once again) of being lost? I will argue that the second is the case, and that the present discarding of psychoanalysis in favour of forms of analysis felt as more material in their substance and immediately political in their effects is a *return* to positions whose sensed inadequacy for feminism produced a gap in which psychoanalysis could—fleetingly—find a place.[1] What psychoanalysis offered up in that moment was by no means wholly satisfactory and it left many problems unanswered or inadequately addressed, but the questions which it raised for feminism are crucial and cannot, I believe, be approached in the same way, or even posed, from anywhere else. To ask what are the political implications of psychoanalysis for feminism seems to me, therefore, to pose the problem the wrong way round. Psychoanalysis is already political for feminism—political in the more obvious sense that it came into the arena of discussion in response to the internal needs of feminist debate, and political again in the wider sense that the repudiation of psychoanalysis by feminism can be seen as linking up with the repeated marginalisation of psychoanalysis within our general culture, a culture whose oppressiveness for women is recognised by us all.

Before going into this in more detail, a separate but related point needs to be made, and that is the peculiarity of the psychoanalytic object with which feminism engages. Thus to ask for effects from psychoanalysis in the arena of political practice is already to assume that psychoanalytic practice is apolitical.[2] Recent feminist debate has tended to concentrate on theory (Freud's theory of femininity, whether or not psychoanalysis can provide an account of women's subordination). This was as true of Juliet Mitchell's defense of Freud as it has been of many of the more recent replies.[3] The result has been that psychoanalysis has been pulled away from its own practice. Here the challenge to psychoanalysis by feminists has come from alternative forms of therapy (feminist therapy and co-counseling). But it is worth noting that the way psychoanalysis is engaged with in much recent criticism already divests it of its practical effects at this level, or rather takes this question as settled in advance (the passing reference to the chauvinism of the psychoanalytic institution, the assumption that psychoanalysis depoliticises the woman analysand). In this context, therefore, the common theory/practice dichotomy has a very specific meaning in that psychoanalysis can only be held accountable to "practice" if it is assumed not to be one, or if the form of its practice is taken to have no purchase on political life. This assumes, for example, that there is no politics of the psychoanalytic institution itself, something to which I will return.

Both these points—the wider history of how psychoanalysis has been placed or discarded by our dominant culture, and the detaching of psychoanalysis from its practical and institutional base—are related, in as much as they bring into focus the decisions and selections which have already been made about psychoanalysis before the debate even begins. Some of these decisions, I would want to argue, are simply wrong—such as the broad accusation of chauvinism levelled against the psychoanalytic institution as a whole. In this country at least, the significant impetus after Freud passed to two women—Anna Freud and Melanie Klein. Psychoanalysis in fact continues to be one of the few of our cultural institutions which does not professionally discriminate against women, and in which they could even be said to predominate. This is not of course to imply that the presence of women inside an institution is necessarily feminist, but women have historically held positions of influence inside psychoanalysis which they have been mostly denied in other institutions where their perceived role as "carers" has relegated them to a subordinate position (e.g., nursing); and it is the case that the first criticisms of Freud made by Melanie Klein can be seen to have strong affinities with later feminist repudiation of his theories.

For those who are hesitating over what appears as the present "impasse" between feminism and psychoanalysis, the more important point, however, is to stress the way that psychoanalysis is being presented for debate—that is, the decisions which have already been made before we are asked to decide. Much will depend, I suspect, on whether one sees psychoanalysis as a new form of hegemony on the part of the feminist intelligentsia, or whether it is seen as a theory and practice which has constantly been relegated to the outside of dominant institutions and mainstream radical debate alike—

an "outside" with which feminism, in its challenge to both these traditions, has its own important forms of allegiance.

Components of the Culture

In England, the relationship between the institution of psychoanalysis and its more general reception has always been complex, if not fraught. Thus in 1968, Perry Anderson could argue that major therapeutic and theoretical advances inside the psychoanalytic institution (chiefly in the work of Melanie Klein) had gone hand in hand with, and possibly even been the cause of, the isolation of psychoanalysis from the general culture, the slowness of its dissemination (until the Pelican Freud started to appear in 1974, you effectively had to join a club to read the *Standard Edition* of Freud's work), and the failure of psychoanalysis to effect a decisive break with traditions of empiricist philosophy, reactionary ethics, and an elevation of literary "values," which he saw as the predominant features of our cultural life.[4] Whether or not one accepts the general "sweep" of his argument, two points from that earlier polemic seem relevant here.

Firstly, the link between empiricist traditions of thought and the resistance to the psychoanalytic concept of the unconscious. Thus psychoanalysis, through its attention to symptoms, slips of the tongue, and dreams (that is, to what *insists* on being spoken against what is *allowed* to be said), appears above all as a challenge to the self-evidence and banality of everyday life and language; which have also, importantly, constituted the specific targets of feminism. If we use the (fairly loose) definition which Anderson provided for empiricism as the unsystematic registration of things as they are and the refusal of forms of analysis which penetrate beneath the surface of observable social phenomena, the link to feminism can be made. For feminism has always challenged the observable "givens" of women's presumed natural qualities and their present social position alike (especially when the second is justified in terms of the first). How often has the "cult of common sense," the notion of what is obviously the case or in the nature of things, been used in reactionary arguments against feminist attempts to demand social change? For Anderson in his article of 1968, this espousal of empiricist thinking provided one of the chief forms of resistance to Freud, so deeply committed is psychoanalysis to penetrating behind the surface and conscious manifestations of everyday experience.

Secondly, the relationship between this rejection of psychoanalysis and a *dearth* within British intellectual culture of a Marxism which could both theorise and criticise capitalism as a social totality. This second point received the strongest criticism from within British Marxism itself, but what matters here is the fact that both Marxism *and* psychoanalysis were identified as forms of radical enquiry which were unassimilable to bourgeois norms. In the recent feminist discussion, however—notably in the pages of *Feminist Review*—Marxism and psychoanalysis tend to be posited as antagonistic; Marxism arrogating to itself the concept of political practice and social change, psychoanalysis being accused of inherent conservatism which rationalises and perpetuates the subordination of women under capitalism, or else fails to engage with that subordination at the level of material life.

In order to understand this, I think we have to go back to the earlier moment. For while the argument that Marxism was marginal or even alien to British thought was strongly repudiated, the equivalent observation about psychoanalysis seems to have been accepted and was more or less allowed to stand. This was perhaps largely because no one on the Left rushed forward to claim a radicalism committed to psychoanalytic thought. *New Left Review* had itself been involved in psychoanalysis in the early 1960s, publishing a number of articles by Cooper and Laing, and there is also a strong tradition, which goes back through Christopher Caudwell in the 1930s, of Marxist discussion of Freud.[5] But the main controversy unleashed by Anderson's remarks centered around Marxism; in an earlier article Anderson himself had restricted his critique to the lack of Marxism and classical sociology in British culture, making no reference to psychoanalysis at all.[6] After 1968, *New Left Review* published Althusser's famous article on Lacan and one article by Lacan, but for the most part the commitment to psychoanalysis was not sustained even by that section of the British Left which had originally argued for its importance.[7]

Paradoxically, therefore, the idea that psychoanalysis was isolated or cut off from the general culture could be accepted to the extent that this very marginalisation was being *reproduced* in the response to the diagnosis itself. Thus the link between Marxism and Freudian psychoanalysis, as the twin poles of a failed radicalism at the heart of British culture, was broken. Freud was cast aside at the very moment when resistance to his thought had been identified as symptomatic of the restrictiveness of bourgeois culture. Juliet Mitchell was the exception. Her defence of Freud needs to be seen as a redress of this omission, but also as a critique of the loss of the concept of the unconscious in the very forms of psychoanalysis (for example, Laing) sponsored by the British Left (the second problem as the cause of the first).[8] In this context the case for psychoanalysis was part of a claim for the fundamentally anti-empiricist and radical nature of Freudian thought. That this claim was made via feminism (could perhaps *only* be made via feminism) says something about the ability of feminism to challenge the orthodoxies of both Left and Right.

Thus the now familiar duo of "psychoanalysis and feminism" has an additional and crucial political meaning. Not just psychoanalysis *for* feminism or feminism *against* psychoanalysis, but Freudian psychoanalysis and feminism *together* as two forms of thought which relentlessly undermine the turgid resistance of common-sense language to all forms of conflict and political change. For me this specific sequence has been ironically or negatively confirmed (that is, it has been gone over again backward) by the recent attempt by Michael Rustin to relate psychoanalysis to socialism through a combination of F. R. Leavis and Melanie Klein—the very figures whose standing had been taken as symptomatic of that earlier resistance to the most radical aspects of Freudian thought (Klein because of the confinement of her often challenging ideas to the psychoanalytic institution itself; Leavis because of the inappropriate centrality which he claimed for the ethics of literary form and taste).[9] I cannot go into the details of Rustin's argument here, but its ultimate conservatism for feminism is at least clear; the advancement of "mothering," and by implication of the role of women as mothers, as the psychic basis on which socialism can be built (the idea that psychoanalysis can *engender* socialism seems to be merely the flip side of the argument which accuses psychoanalysis of producing social conformity).

This history may appear obscure to many feminists who have not necessarily followed the different stages of these debates. But the diversion through this cultural map is, I think, important insofar as it can illustrate the ramifications of feminist discussion over a wider political spectrum, and also show how this discussion—the terms of the argument, the specific oppositions proposed—have in turn been determined by that wider spectrum itself.

Thus it will have crucial effects, for instance, whether psychoanalysis is discussed as an addition or supplement to Marxism (in relation to which it is then found *wanting*), or whether emphasis is laid on the concept of the unconscious. For while it is indeed correct that psychoanalysis was introduced into feminism as a theory which could rectify the inability of Marxism to address questions of sexuality, and that this move was complementary to the demand within certain areas of Marxism for increasing attention to the ideological determinants of our social being, it is also true that undue concentration on this aspect of the theory has served to cut off the concept of the unconscious, or at least to displace it from the centre of the debate. (This is graphically illustrated in Michèle Barrett's book, *Women's Oppression Today*, in which the main discussion of psychoanalysis revolves around the concept of ideology, and that of the unconscious is left to a note appended at the end of the chapter.)[10]

Femininity and Its Discontents

One result of this emphasis is that psychoanalysis is accused of "functionalism," that is, it is accepted as a theory of how women are psychically "induced" into femininity by a patriarchal culture, and is then accused of perpetuating that process, either through a practice assumed to be *prescriptive* about women's role (this is what women *should* do), or because the very effectiveness of the account as a *description* (this is what is demanded of women, what they are *expected* to do) leaves no possibility of change.

It is this aspect of Juliet Mitchell's book which seems to have been taken up most strongly by feminists who have attempted to follow through the political implications of psychoanalysis as a critique of patriarchy.

Thus Gayle Rubin, following Mitchell, uses psychoanalysis for a general critique of a patriarchal culture which is predicated on the exchange of women by men.[11] Nancy Chodorow shifts from Freud to later object relations theory to explain how women's child-caring role is perpetuated through the earliest relationship between a mother and her child, which leads in her case to a demand for a fundamental change in how childcare is organised between women and men in our culture.[12] Although there are obvious differences between these two readings of psychoanalysis, they nonetheless share an emphasis on the social exchange of women, or the distribution of roles for women, across cultures: "Women's mothering is one of the few universal and enduring elements of the sexual division of labour."[13]

The force of psychoanalysis is therefore (as Janet Sayers points out) precisely that it gives an account of patriarchal culture as a transhistorical and cross-cultural force.[14] It therefore conforms to the feminist demand for a theory which can explain women's subordination across specific cultures and different historical moments. Summing this up crudely, we could say that psychoanalysis adds sexuality to Marxism, where sexuality is felt to be lacking, and extends beyond Marxism where the attention to specific historical instances, changes in modes of production etc., is felt to leave something unexplained.

But all this happens at a cost, and that cost is the concept of the unconscious. What distinguishes psychoanalysis from sociological accounts of gender (hence for me the fundamental impasse of Nancy Chodorow's work) is that whereas for the latter, the internalisation of norms is assumed roughly to work, the basic premise and indeed starting point of psychoanalysis is that it does not. The unconscious constantly reveals the "failure" of identity. Because there is no continuity of psychic life, so there is no stability of sexual identity, no position for women (or for men) which is ever simply achieved. Nor does psychoanalysis see such "failure" as a special-case inability or an individual deviancy from the norm. "Failure" is not a moment to be regretted in a process of adaptation, or development into normality, which ideally takes its course (some of the earliest critics of Freud, such as Ernest Jones, did, however, give an account of development in just these terms). Instead "failure" is something endlessly repeated and relived moment by moment throughout our individual histories. It appears not only in the symptom, but also in dreams, in slips of the tongue, and in forms of sexual pleasure which are pushed to the sidelines of the norm. Feminism's affinity with psychoanalysis rests above all, I would argue, with this recognition that there is a resistance to identity at the very heart of psychic life. Viewed in this way, psychoanalysis is no longer best understood as an account of how women are fitted into place (even this, note, is the charitable reading of Freud). Instead psychoanalysis becomes one of the few places in our culture where it is recognised as more than a fact of individual pathology that most women do not painlessly slip into their roles as women, if indeed they do at all. Freud himself recognised this increasingly in his work. In the articles which run from 1924 to 1931, he moves from that famous, or rather infamous, description of the little girl struck with her "inferiority" or "injury" in the face of the anatomy of the little boy and wisely accepting her fate ("injury" as the *fact* of being feminine), to an account which quite explicitly describes the process of becoming "feminine" as an "injury" or "catastrophe" for the complexity of her earlier psychic and sexual life ("injury" as its *price*).[15]

Elizabeth Wilson and Janet Sayers are, therefore, in a sense correct to criticise psychoanalysis when it is taken as a general theory of patriarchy or of gender identity, that is, as a theory which explains how women wholly internalise the very mode of being which is feminism's specific target of attack; but they have left out half the (psychoanalytic) story. In fact the argument seems to be circular. Psychoanalysis is drawn in the direction of a general theory of culture or a sociological account of gender because these seem to lay greater emphasis on the pressures of the "outside" world, but it is this very pulling away from the psychoanalytic stress on the "internal" complexity and difficulty of psychic life which produces the functionalism which is then criticised.

The argument about whether Freud is being "prescriptive" or "descriptive" about women (with its associated stress on the motives and morals of Freud himself) is fated to the extent that it is locked into this model. Many of us will be familiar with Freud's famous pronouncement that a woman who does not succeed in transforming activity to passivity, clitoris to vagina, mother for father, will fall ill. Yet psychoanalysis testifies to the fact that psychic illness or distress is in no sense the prerogative of women who "fail" in this task. One of my students recently made the obvious but important point that we would be foolish to deduce from the external trappings of normality or conformity in a woman that all is in fact well. And Freud himself always stressed the psychic cost of the civilising process for all (we can presumably include women in that "all" even if at times he did not seem to do so).

All these aspects of Freud's work are subject to varying interpretation by analysts themselves. The first criticism of Freud's "phallocentrism" came from inside psychoanalysis, from analysts such as Melanie Klein, Ernest Jones, and Karen Horney who felt, contrary to Freud, that "femininity" was a quality with its own impetus, subject to checks and internal conflict, but tending ultimately to fulfillment. For Jones, the little girl was "typically receptive and acquisitive" from the outset; for Horney, there was from the beginning a "wholly womanly" attachment to the father.[16] For these analysts, this development might come to grief, but for the most part a gradual strengthening of the child's ego and her increasing adaptation to reality should guarantee its course. Aspects of the little girl's psychic life which were resistant to this process (the famous "active" or "masculine" drives) were defensive. The importance of concepts such as the "phallic phase" in Freud's description of infantile sexuality is not, therefore, that such concepts can be taken as the point of insertion of patriarchy (assimilation to the norm). Rather their importance lies in the way that they indicate, through their very artificiality, that something was being *forced*, and in the concept of psychic life with which they were accompanied. In Freud's work they went hand in hand with an increasing awareness of the difficulty, not to say impossibility, of the path to normality for the girl, and an increasing stress on the fundamental divisions, or splitting, of psychic life. It was those who challenged these concepts in the 1920s and 30s who introduced the more normative stress on a sequence of development, and coherent ego, back into the account.

I think we go wrong again, therefore, if we conduct the debate about whether Freud's account was developmental or not entirely in terms of his own writing. Certainly the idea of development is present at moments in his work. But it was not present *enough* for many of his contemporaries, who took up the issue and reinstated the idea of development precisely in relation to the sexual progress of the girl (her passage into womanhood).

"Psychoanalysis" is not, therefore, a single entity. Institutional divisions within psychoanalysis have turned on the very questions about the phallocentrism of analysts, the meaning of femininity, the sequence of psychic development and its norms, which have been the concern of feminists. The accusations came from analysts themselves. In the earlier debates, however, the reproach against Freud produced an account of femininity which was more, rather than less, normative than his own.

The politics of Lacanian psychoanalysis begin here. From the 1930s, Lacan saw his intervention as a return to the concepts of psychic division, splitting of the ego, and an endless (he called it "insistent") pressure of the unconscious against any individual's pretension to a smooth and coherent psychic and sexual identity. Lacan's specific target was "ego-psychology" in America, and what he saw as the dilution of psychoanalysis into a tool of social adaptation and control (hence the central emphasis on the concepts of the ego and identification which are often overlooked in discussions of his ideas). For Lacan, psychoanalysis does not offer an account of a developing ego which is "not *necessarily* coherent," but of an ego which is "necessarily *not* coherent," that is, which is always and persistently divided against itself.[17]

Lacan could therefore be picked up by a Marxist like Althusser not because he offered a theory of adaptation to reality or of the individual's insertion into culture (Althusser added a note to the English translation of his paper on Lacan criticising it for having implied such a reading), but because the force of the unconscious in Lacan's interpretation of Freud was felt to undermine the mystifications of a bourgeois culture proclaiming its identity, and that of its subjects, to the world.[18] The political use of Lacan's theory therefore stemmed from its assault on what English Marxists would call bourgeois "individualism." What the theory offered was a divided subject out of "synch" with bourgeois myth. Feminists could legitimately object that the notion of psychic fragmentation was of little immediate political advantage to women struggling for the first time to find a voice, and trying to bring together the dissociated components of their life into a political programme. But this is a very different criticism of the political implications of psychoanalysis than the one which accuses it of forcing women into bland conformity with their expected role.

Psychoanalysis and History: The History of Psychoanalysis

What, therefore, is the political purchase of the concept of the unconscious on women's lived experience? And what can it say to the specific histories of which we form a part?

One of the objections which is often made against psychoanalysis is that it has no sense of history, and an inadequate grasp of its relationship to the concrete institutions which frame and determine our lives. For even if we allow for a moment the radical force of the psychoanalytic insight, the exclusiveness or limited availability of that insight tends to be turned, not against the culture or state which mostly resists its general (and publicly funded) dissemination, but against psychoanalysis itself.[19] The "privatisation" of psychoanalysis comes to mean that it only refers to the individual as private, and the concentration on the individual as private is then seen as reinforcing a theory which places itself above history and change.

Again I think that this question is posed back to front, and that we need to ask, not what psychoanalysis has to say about history, but rather what is the history of psychoanalysis, that is, what was the intervention of psychoanalysis into the institutions which, at the time of its emergence, were controlling women's lives? And what was the place of the unconscious, historically, in that? Paradoxically, the claim that psychoanalysis is ahistorical dehistoricises it. If we go back to the beginnings of psychoanalysis, it is clear that the concept of the unconscious was radical at exactly that level of social "reality" with which it is so often assumed to have nothing whatsoever to do.

Recent work by feminist historians is of particular importance in this context. Judith Walkowitz, in her study of the Contagious Diseases Acts of the 1860s, shows how state policy on public hygiene and the state's increasing control over casual labour relied on a category of women as diseased (the suspected prostitute subjected to forcible examination and internment in response to the spread of venereal disease in the port towns).[20] Carol Dyhouse has described how debates about educational opportunity for women constantly returned to the evidence of the female body (either the energy expended in their development towards sexual reproduction meant that women could not be educated, or education and the overtaxing of the brain would damage their reproductive capacity).[21] In the birth control controversy, the Malthusian idea of controlling the reproduction, and by implication the sexuality, of the working class served to counter the idea that poverty could be reduced by the redistribution of wealth.[22] Recurrently in the second half of the nineteenth century, in the period immediately prior to Freud, female sexuality became the focus of a panic about the effects of industrialisation on the cohesion of the social body and its ability to reproduce itself comfortably. The importance of all this work (Judith Walkowitz makes this quite explicit) is that "attitudes" towards women cannot be consigned to the sphere of ideology, assumed to have no purchase on material life, so deeply implicated was the concept of female sexuality in the legislative advancement of the state.[23]

Central to all of this was the idea that the woman was wholly responsible for the social well-being of the nation (questions of social division transmuted directly into the moral and sexual responsibility of subjects), or where she failed in this task, that she was disordered or diseased. The hysteric was either the overeducated woman, or else the woman indulging in nonprocreative or uncontrolled sexuality (conjugal onanism), or again the woman in the lock hospitals which, since the eighteenth century, had been receiving categories refused by the general hospitals ("infectious diseases, 'fever,' children, maternity cases, mental disorders, as well as venereal diseases").[24] It was these hospitals which, at the time of the Contagious Diseases Acts, became the place of confinement for the diseased prostitute in a new form of collaborative relationship with the state.

This is where psychoanalysis begins. Although the situation was not identical in France, there are important links. Freud's earliest work was under Charcot at the Salpêtrière Clinic in Paris, a hospital for women: "Five thousand neurotic indigents, epileptics, and insane patients, many of whom were deemed incurable."[25] The "dregs" of society comprised the inmates of the Salpêtrière (psychoanalysis does not start in the Viennese parlour). Freud was working under Charcot, whose first contribution to the study of hysteria was to move it out of the category of sexual malingering and into that of a specific and accredited neurological disease. The problem with Charcot's work is that while he was constructing the symptomatology of the disease (turning it into a respected object of the medical institution), he was reinforcing it as a special category of behavior, visible to the eye, and the result of a degenerate hereditary disposition.

Freud's intervention here was two-fold. Firstly, he questioned the visible evidence of the disease—the idea that you could know a hysteric by looking at her body, that is, by reading off the symptoms of nervous disability or suscep- tibility to trauma. Secondly (and this second move depended on the first), he rejected the idea that hysteria was an "independent" clinical entity, by using what he uncovered in the treatment of the hysterical patient as the basis of his account of the unconscious and its universal presence in adult life.

The "universalism" of Freud was not, therefore, an attempt to remove the subject from history; it stemmed from his challenge to the category of hys- teria as a principle of classification for certain socially isolated and confined individuals, and his shifting of this category into the centre of everybody's psychic experience: "Her hysteria can therefore be described as an acquired one, and it presupposed nothing more than the possession of what is probably a very wide-spread proclivity—the proclivity to acquire hysteria."[26] The rea- son why the two moves are interdependent is because it was only by penetrat- ing behind the visible symptoms of disorder and asking what it was that the symptom was trying to *say*, that Freud could uncover those unconscious desires and motives which he went on to expose in the slips, dreams, and jokes of individuals paraded as normal. Thus the challenge to the entity "hysteria," that is, to hysteria *as* an entity available for quite specific forms of social control, relied on the concept of the unconscious. "I have attempted," wrote Freud, "to meet the problem of hysterical attacks along a line other than *descriptive*."[27] Hence Freud's challenge to the visible, to the empirically self- evident, to the "blindness of the seeing eye."[28] (Compare this with Charcot's photographs offered as the evidence of the disease.) It is perhaps this early and now mostly forgotten moment which can give us the strongest sense of the force of the unconscious as a concept against a fully social classification relying on empirical evidence as its rationale.

The challenge of psychoanalysis to empiricist forms of reasoning was therefore the very axis on which the fully historical intervention of psycho- analysis into late nineteenth-century medicine turned. The theories of sex- uality came after this first intervention (in *Studies on Hysteria*, Freud's remarks on sexuality are mostly given in awkward footnotes suggesting the importance of sexual abstinence for women as a causal factor in the etiology of hysteria). But when Freud did start to investigate the complexity of sexual life in re- sponse to what he uncovered in hysterical patients, his first step was a similar questioning of social definitions, this time of sexual perversion as "innate" or "degenerate," that is, as the special property of a malfunctioning type.[29] In fact, if we take dreams and slips of the tongue (both considered before Freud to result from lowered mental capacity), sexuality and hysteria, the same movement operates each time. A discredited, pathological, or irrational form of behaviour is given its psychic value by psychoanalysis. What this meant for the hysterical woman is that instead of just being looked at or examined, she was allowed to *speak*.

Some of the criticisms which are made by feminists of Freudian psychoanalysis, especially when it is filtered through the work of Lacan, can perhaps be answered with reference to this moment. Most often the emphasis is laid either on Lacan's statement that "the unconscious is structured like a language," or on his concentration on mental representation and the ideational contents of the mind. The feeling seems to be that the stress on ideas and language cuts psychoanalysis off from the materiality of being, whether that materiality is defined as the biological aspects of our subjectivity, or as the economic factors determining our lives (one or the other and at times both).

Once it is put like this, the argument becomes a version of the debate within Marxism over the different instances of social determination and their hierarchy ("ideology" versus the "economic") or else it becomes an accusation of idealism (Lacan) against materialism (Marx). I think this argument completely misses the importance of the emphasis on language in Lacan and of mental representation in Freud. The statement that "the unconscious is structured like a language" was above all part of Lacan's attempt to establish a continuity between the seeming disorder of the symptom or dream and the normal language through which we recognise each other and speak. And the importance of the linguistic sign (Saussure's distinction between the signifier and the signified) was that it provided a model internal to language itself of that form of indirect representation (the body speaking because there is something which cannot be said) which psychoanalysis uncovered in the symptomatology of its patients.[30] Only if one thing can stand for another is the hysterical symptom something more than the logical and direct manifestation of physical or psychic (and social) degeneracy.

This is why the concept of the unconscious—as indicating an irreducible discontinuity of psychic life—is so important. Recognition of that discontinuity in us all is in a sense the price we have to pay for that earlier historical displacement.

Feminism and the Unconscious

It is, however, this concept which seems to be lost whenever Freud has been challenged on those ideas which have been most problematic for feminism, insofar as the critique of Freudian phallocentrism so often relies on a return to empiricism, on an appeal to "what actually happens" or what can be *seen* to be the case. Much of Ernest Jones's criticism of Freud, for example, stemmed from his conviction that girls and boys could not conceivably be ignorant of so elementary a fact as that of sexual difference and procreation.[31] And Karen Horney, in her similar but distinct critique, referred to "the manifestations of so elementary a principle of nature as that of the mutual attraction of the sexes."[32] We can compare this with Freud: "From the point of view of psychoanalysis the exclusive sexual interest felt by men for women is also a problem that needs elucidating and is not a self-evident fact based upon an attraction that is ultimately of a chemical nature."[33] The point is not that one side is appealing to "biology" (or "nature") and the other to "ideas," but that Freud's opening premise is to challenge the self-evidence of both.

The feminist criticism of Freud has of course been very different since it has specifically involved a rejection of the evidence of this particular norm: the normal femininity which, in the earlier quarrel, Freud himself was considered to have questioned. But at this one crucial level—the idea of an unconscious which points to a fundamental division of psychic life and which therefore challenges any form of empiricism based on what is there to be observed (even when scientifically tested and tried)—the very different critiques are related. In *Psychoanalysis and Feminism*, Juliet Mitchell based at least half her argument on this point, but it has been lost. Thus Shulamith Firestone, arguing in *The Dialectic of Sex* that the girl's alleged sense of inferiority in relation to the boy was the logical outcome of the observable facts of the child's experience, had to assume an unproblematic and one-to-one causality between psychic life and social reality with no possibility of dislocation or error.[34] The result is that the concept of the unconscious is lost (the little girl rationally recognises and decides her fate) and mothering is deprived of its active components (the mother is seen to be only subordinate and in no sense powerful for the child).[35] For all its more obvious political appeal, the idea that psychic life is the unmediated reflection of social relations locks the mother and child into a closed subordination which can then only be broken by the advances of empiricism itself.

Full mastery of the reproductive process is in sight, and there has been significant advance in understanding the basic life and death process. The nature of ageing and growth, sleep and hibernation, the chemical functioning of the brain and the development of consciousness and memory are all beginning to be understood in their entirety. This acceleration promises to continue for another century, or however long it takes to achieve the goal of Empiricism: total understanding of the laws of nature.[36]

Shulamith Firestone's argument has been criticised by feminists who would not wish to question, any more than I would, the importance of her intervention for feminism.[37] But I think it is important that the part of her programme which is now criticised (the idea that women must rely on scientific progress to achieve any change) is so directly related to the empiricist concept of social reality (what can be *seen* to happen) which she offers. The empiricism of the goal is the outcome of the empiricism at the level of social reality and psychic life. I have gone back to this moment because, even though it is posed in different terms, something similar seems to be going on in the recent Marxist repudiation of Freud. Janet Sayers's critique of Juliet Mitchell, for example, is quite explicitly based on the concept of "what actually and specifically happens" ("in the child's environment" and "in the child's physical and biological development").[38]

Utopianism of the Psyche

Something else happens in all of this which is probably the most central issue for me: the discarding of the concept of the unconscious seems to leave us with a type of utopianism of psychic life. In this context it is interesting to note just how close the appeal to biology and the appeal to culture as the determinants of psychic experience can be. Karen Horney switched from one to the other, moving from the idea that femininity was a natural quality, subject to checks, but tending on its course, to the idea that these same checks, and indeed most forms of psychic conflict, were the outcome of an oppressive social world. The second position is closer to that of feminism, but something is nonetheless missing from both sides of the divide. For what has happened to the unconscious, to that divided and disordered subjectivity which, I have argued, had to be recognised in us all if the category of hysteria as a peculiar property of one class of women was to be disbanded? Do not both of these movements make psychic conflict either an accident or an obstacle on the path to psychic and sexual continuity—a continuity which, as feminists, we recognise as a myth of our culture only to reinscribe it in a different form on the agenda for a future (postrevolutionary) date?

Every time Freud is challenged, this concept of psychic cohesion as the ultimate object of our political desires seems to return. Thus the French feminist and analyst Luce Irigaray challenges Lacan not just for the phallocentrism of his argument; but because the Freudian account is seen to cut women off from an early and untroubled psychic unity (the primordial state of fusion with the mother) which feminists should seek to restore. Irigaray calls this the "imaginary" of women (a reference to Lacan's idea of a primitive narcissism which was for him only ever a fantasy). In a world felt to be especially alienating for women, this idea of psychic oneness or primary narcissism has its own peculiar force. It appears in a different form in Michèle Barrett's and Mary McIntosh's excellent reply to Christopher Lasch's thesis that we are witnessing a regrettable decline in the patriarchal family.[39] Responding to his accusation that culture is losing its superego edge and descending into narcissism, they offer the particularly female qualities of mothering (Chodorow) and a defense of this very "primary narcissism" in the name of women against Lasch's undoubtedly reactionary lament. The problem remains, however, that whenever the "feminine" comes into the argument as a quality in this way we seem to lose the basic insight of psychoanalysis—the failure or difficulty of femininity for women, *and* that fundamental psychic division which in Freud's work was its accompanying and increasingly insistent discovery. If I question the idea that psychoanalysis is the "new orthodoxy" for feminists, it is at least partly because of the strong political counterweight of this idea of femininity which appears to repudiate both these Freudian insights together.

To return to the relationship between Marxism and psychoanalysis with which I started, I think it is relevant that the most systematic attack we have had on the hierarchies and organisation of the male Left gives to women the privilege of the personal in a way which divests it (*has* to divest it) of complexity at exactly this level of the conflicts and discontinuities of psychic life.[40] Like many feminists, the slogan "the personal is political" has been central to my own political development; just as I see the question of sexuality, as a political issue which *exceeds* the province of Marxism ("economic," "ideological," or whatever), as one of the most important defining characteristics of feminism itself. But the dialogue between feminism and psychoanalysis, which is for me the arena in which the full complexity of that "personal" and that "sexuality" can be grasped, constantly seems to fail.

In this article, I have not answered all the criticisms of psychoanalysis. It is certainly the case that psychoanalysis does not give us a blueprint for political action, or allow us to deduce political conservatism or radicalism directly from the vicissitudes of psychic experience. Nor does the concept of the unconscious sit comfortably with the necessary attempt by feminism to claim a new sureness of identity for women, or with the idea of always conscious and deliberate political decision-making and control (psychoanalysis is *not* a voluntarism).[41] But its challenge to the concept of psychic identity is important for feminism in that it allows into the political arena problems of subjectivity (subjectivity *as* a problem) which tend to be suppressed from other forms of political debate. It may also help us to open up the space between different notions of political identity—between the idea of a political identity for feminism (what women require) and that of a feminine identity for women (what women are or should be), especially given the problems constantly encountered by the latter and by the sometimes too easy celebration of an identity amongst women which glosses over the differences between us.

Psychoanalysis finally remains one of the few places in our culture where our experience of femininity can be spoken as a problem that is something other than the problem which the protests of women are posing for an increasingly conservative political world. I would argue that this is one of the reasons why it has not been released into the public domain. The fact that psychoanalysis cannot be assimilated directly into a political programme as such does not mean, therefore, that it should be discarded, and thrown back into the outer reaches of a culture which has never yet been fully able to heed its voice.

Feminine Sexuality: Jacques Lacan and the *école freudienne*

The link between sexuality and the unconscious is one that was constantly stressed by Lacan: "We should not overlook the fact that sexuality is crucially underlined by Freud as being strictly consubstantial to the dimension of the unconscious."[1] Other accounts, such as that of Ernest Jones, described the acquisition of sexual identity in terms of ego development and/or the maturation of the drives. Lacan considered that each of these concepts rests on the myth of a subjective cohesion which the concept of the unconscious properly subverts. For Lacan, the description of sexuality in developmental terms invariably loses sight of Freud's most fundamental discovery—that the unconscious never ceases to challenge our apparent identity as subjects.

Lacan's account of subjectivity was always developed with reference to the idea of a fiction. Thus, in the 1930s he introduced the concept of the "mirror stage," which took the child's mirror image as the model and basis for its future identifications.[2] This image is a fiction because it conceals, or freezes, the infant's lack of motor coordination and the fragmentation of its drives. But it is salutary for the child, since it gives it the first sense of a coherent identity in which it can recognise itself. For Lacan, however, this is already a fantasy— the very image which places the child divides its identity into two. Furthermore, that moment only has meaning in relation to the presence and the look of the mother who guarantees its reality for the child. The mother does not (as in D. W. Winnicott's account) mirror the child to itself; she grants an image *to* the child, which her presence instantly deflects.[3] Holding the child is, therefore, to be understood not only as a containing, but as a process of referring, which fractures the unity it seems to offer. The mirror image is central to Lacan's account of subjectivity, because its apparent smoothness and totality is a myth. The image in which we first recognise ourselves is a *misrecognition*. Lacan is careful to stress, however, that his point is not restricted to the field of the visible alone: "The idea of the mirror should be understood as an object which reflects—not just the visible, but also what is heard, touched and willed by the child."[4]

Lacan then takes the mirror image as the model of the ego function itself, the category which enables the subject to operate as "I." He supports his argument from linguistics, which designates the pronoun as a "shifter."[5] The "I" with which we speak stands for our identity as subjects in language, but it is the least stable entity in language, since its meaning is purely a function of the moment of utterance. The "I" can shift, and change places, because it only ever refers to whoever happens to be using it at the time.

For Lacan the subject is constituted through language—the mirror image represents the moment when the subject is located in an order outside itself to which it will henceforth refer. The subject is the subject *of* speech (Lacan's "*parle-être*"), and subject *to* that order. But if there is division in the image, and instability in the pronoun, there is equally loss, and difficulty, in the word. Language can only operate by designating an object in its absence. Lacan takes this further, and states that symbolisation turns on the object *as* absence. He gives as his reference Freud's early account of the child's hallucinatory cathexis of the object for which it cries, and his later description in *Beyond the Pleasure Principle* of the child's symbolisation of the absent mother in play.[6] In the first example, the child hallucinates the object it desires; in the second, it throws a cotton reel out of its cot in order to symbolise the absence and the presence of the mother. Symbolisation starts, therefore, when the child gets its first sense that something could be missing; words stand for objects, because they only have to be spoken at the moment when the first object is lost. For Lacan, the subject can only operate within language by constantly repeating that moment of fundamental and irreducible division. The subject is therefore constituted in language *as* this division or splitting (Freud's *Ichspaltung*, or splitting of the ego).

Lacan termed the order of language the symbolic, that of the ego and its identifications the imaginary (the stress, therefore, is quite deliberately on symbol and image, the idea of something which "stands in"). The real was then his term for the moment of impossibility onto which both are grafted, the point of that moment's endless return.[7]

Lacan's account of childhood then follows his basic premise that identity is constructed in language, but only at a cost. Identity shifts, and language speaks the loss which lay behind that first moment of symbolisation. When the child asks something of its mother, that loss will persist over and above anything which she can possibly give, or say, in reply. Demand always "bears on something other than the satisfaction which it calls for," and each time the demand of the child is answered by the satisfaction of its needs, so this "something other" is relegated to the place of its original impossibility.[8] Lacan terms this "desire." It can be defined as the "remainder" of the subject, something which is always left over, but which has no content as such. Desire functions much as the zero unit in the numerical chain—its place is both constitutive *and* empty.

The concept of desire is crucial to Lacan's account of sexuality. He considered that the failure to grasp its implications leads inevitably to a reduction of sexuality back into the order of a need (something, therefore, which could be satisfied). Against this, he quoted Freud's statement: "We must reckon with the possibility that something in the nature of the sexual instinct itself is unfavourable to the realisation of complete satisfaction."[9]

At the same time "identity" and "wholeness" remain precisely at the level of fantasy. Subjects in language persist in their belief that somewhere there is a point of certainty, of knowledge, and of truth. When the subject addresses its demand outside itself to another, this other becomes the fantasied place of just such a knowledge or certainty. Lacan calls this the Other—the site of language to which the speaking subject necessarily refers. The Other appears to hold the "truth" of the subject and the power to make good its loss. But this is the ultimate fantasy. Language is the place where meaning circulates—the meaning of each linguistic unit can only be established by reference to another, and it is arbitrarily fixed. Lacan, therefore, draws from Saussure's concept of the arbitrary nature of the linguistic sign—introduced in his *Course on General Linguistics*—the implication that there can be no final guarantee or securing of language. There is, Lacan writes, "no Other of the Other," and anyone who claims to take up this place is an imposter (the Master and/or psychotic).

Sexuality belongs in this area of instability played out in the register of demand and desire, each sex coming to stand, mythically and exclusively, for that which could satisfy and complete the other. It is when the categories "male" and "female" are seen to represent an absolute and complementary division that they fall prey to a mystification in which the difficulty of sexuality instantly disappears: "To disguise this gap by relying on the virtue of the 'genital' to resolve it through the maturation of tenderness . . . , however piously intended, is nonetheless a fraud."[10] Lacan therefore argued that psychoanalysis should not try to produce "male" and "female" as complementary entities, sure of each other and of their own identity, but should expose the fantasy on which this notion rests.

As Juliet Mitchell has pointed out in her account of early psychoanalytic debates on femininity,[11] there is a tendency, when arguing for the pre-given nature of sexual difference, for the specificity of male and female drives, to lose sight of the more radical aspects of Freud's work on sexuality—his insistence on the disjunction between the sexual object and the sexual aim, his difficult challenge to the concept of perversion, and his demand that heterosexual object-choice be explained and not assumed.[12] For Lacan, the "vicissitudes" of the instinct ("instinct" was the original English translation for the German word "*trieb*") cannot be understood as a deviation, accident or defence on the path to a normal heterosexuality which would ideally be secured. Rather the term "vicissitude" indicates a fundamental difficulty inherent in human sexuality, which can be seen in the very concept of the drive.

The concept of the drive is crucial to the discussion of sexuality because of the relative ease with which it can be used to collapse psychoanalysis into biology, the dimension from which, for Lacan, it most urgently needed to be retrieved. He rejected the idea of a gradual "maturation" of the drive, with its associated emphasis on genital identity (the "virtue" of the genital) because of the way it implies a quasi-biological sequence of sexual life. Instead he stressed the resistance of the drive to any biological definition.

The drive is not the instinct precisely because it cannot be reduced to the order of need (Freud defined it as an internal stimulus only to distinguish it immediately from hunger and thirst). The drive is divisible into pressure, source, object, and aim; and it challenges any straightforward concept of satisfaction—the drive can be sublimated and Freud described its object as "indifferent." What matters, therefore, is not what the drive *achieves*, but its *process*. For Lacan, that process reveals all the difficulty which characterises the subject's relationship to the Other. In his account, the drive is something in the nature of an appeal, or searching out, which always goes beyond the actual relationships on which it turns. Although Freud did at times describe the drive in terms of an economy of pleasure (the idea that tension is resolved when the drive achieves its aim), Lacan points to an opposite stress in Freud's work. In *Beyond the Pleasure Principle*, when Freud described the child's game with the cotton reel, what he identified in that game was a process of pure repetition which revolved around the object as lost. Freud termed this the death drive. Analysts since Freud (specifically Melanie Klein) have taken this to refer to a primordial instinct of aggression. For Freud there could be no such instinct, in that all instincts are characterised by their aggression, their tenacity or insistence (exactly their *drive*). It is this very insistence which places the drive outside any register of need, and beyond an economy of pleasure. The drive touches on an area of excess (it is "too much"). Lacan calls this *jouissance* (literally "orgasm," but used by Lacan to refer to something more than pleasure, which can easily tip into its opposite).

In Lacan's description of the transformation of the drive (its stages), the emphasis is always on the loss of the object around which it revolves, and hence on the drive itself as a representation. Lacan therefore took one step further Freud's own assertion that the drive can only be understood in terms of the representation to which it is attached, by arguing that the structure of representation is present in the very process of the drive. For Lacan, there is always distance in the drive and always a reference to the Other (he added to the oral and anal drives the scopic and invocatory drives whose objects are the look and the voice). But because of its relation to the question of sexual difference, he made a special case for the genital drive in order to retrieve it from the residual biologism to which it is so easily assimilated: "There is no genital drive. It can go and get f . . . [. . .] on the side of the Other."[13] In one of his final statements, Lacan again insisted that Freud had seen this, despite his equation of the genital and the reproductive at certain moments of his work.[14]

When Lacan himself did refer to biology, it was in order to remind us of the paradox inherent in reproduction itself, which, as Freud pointed out, represents a victory of the species over the individual. The "fact" of sexed reproduction marks the subject as "*subject to*" death.[15] There is a parallel here with the subject's submission to language, just as there is an analogy between the endless circulation of the drive and the structure of meaning itself ("a topological unity of the gaps in play").[16] At moments, therefore, it looks as if Lacan too is grounding his theory of representation in the biological facts of life. But the significant stress was away from this, to an understanding of how representation determines the limits within which we experience our sexual life. If there is no straightforward biological sequence, and no satisfaction of the drive, then the idea of a complete and assured sexual identity belongs in the realm of fantasy.

The structure of the drive and what Lacan calls the "nodal point" of desire are the two concepts in his work as a whole which undermine a normative account of human sexuality, and they have repercussions right across the analytic setting. Lacan considered that an emphasis on genital maturation

tends to produce a dualism of the analytic relationship which can only reinforce the imaginary identifications of the subject. The case of Dora illustrates
only too well that the question of feminine sexuality brings with it that of
psychoanalytic technique. Thus by insisting to Dora that she was in love with
Herr K., Freud was not only defining her in terms of a normative concept of
genital heterosexuality, he also failed to see his own place within the analytic
relationship, and reduced it to a dual dimension operating on the axes of
identification and demand. By asking Dora to realise her "identity" through
Herr K., Freud was simultaneously asking her to meet, or reflect, his own
demand. On both counts, he was binding her to a dual relationship in which
the problem of desire has no place. For Lacan, there was always this risk that
psychoanalysis will strengthen for the patient the idea of self-completion
through another, which was the fantasy behind the earliest mother-child
relationship. If the analyst indicates to the patient that he or she "desires this
or that object," this can only block the emergence of desire itself.[17]

Lacan, therefore, defined the objective of analysis as the breaking of any
imaginary relationship between patient and analyst through the intervention
of a third term which throws them both onto the axis of the symbolic. The
intervention of a third term is the precondition of language (the use of the
three basic pronouns "I"/"you"/"he-she-it"), and it can be seen in the structure of the Oedipus complex itself. What matters here, however, is that the
symbolic sets a limit to the "imaginary" of the analytic situation. Both analyst
and patient must come to see how they are constituted by an order which
goes beyond their interaction as such: "The imaginary economy only has a
meaning and we only have a relation to it in so far as it is inscribed in a
symbolic order which imposes a ternary relation."[18]

By focusing on what he calls the symbolic order, Lacan was doing no more
than taking to its logical conclusion Freud's preoccupation with an "historic
event" in the determination of human subjectivity. But for Lacan this is not
some mythical moment of our past, it is the present order in which every
individual subject must take up his or her place. His concern to break the
duality of the analytic situation was part of his desire to bring this dimension
back into the centre of our understanding of psychic life. The subject and the
analytic process must break out of the imaginary dyad which blinds them to
what is happening outside. As was the case with Freud, the concept of castration came into Lacan's account of sexuality as the direct effect of this emphasis. For Lacan, the increasing stress on the mother-child relationship in
analytic theory, and the rejection of the concept of castration had to be seen

as related developments, because the latter only makes sense with reference to the wider symbolic order in which that relationship is played out.

> Taking the experience of psychoanalysis in its development over sixty years, it comes as no surprise to note that whereas the first outcome of its origins was a conception of the castration complex based on paternal repression, it has progressively directed its interests towards the frustrations coming from the mother, not that such a distortion has shed any light on the complex.[19]

This was at the heart of Lacan's polemic. He considered that it was the failure to grasp the concept of the symbolic which has led psychoanalysis to concentrate increasingly on the adequacies and inadequacies of the mother-child relationship, an emphasis which tends to be complicit with the idea of a maternal role (the concept of mothering).[20] The concept of castration was central to Lacan because of the reference which it always contains to paternal law.

Addressing Melanie Klein, Lacan makes it clear that the argument for a reintroduction of the concept of desire into the definition of human sexuality is a return to, and a reformulation of, the law and the place of the father as it was originally defined by Freud ("a dimension . . . increasingly evaded since Freud").[21]

> Melanie Klein describes the relationship to the mother as a mirrored relationship: the maternal body becomes the receptacle of the drives which the child projects onto it, drives motivated by aggression born of a fundamental disappointment. This is to neglect the fact that the outside is given for the subject as the place where the desire of the Other is situated, and where he or she will encounter the third term, the father.[22]

Lacan argued, therefore, for a return to the concept of the father, but this concept is now defined in relation to that of desire. What matters is that the relationship of the child to the mother is not simply based on "frustration and satisfaction" ("the notion of frustration [which was never employed by Freud]"), but on the recognition of her desire.[23] The mother is refused to the child insofar as a prohibition falls on the child's desire to be what the mother desires (not the same, note, as a desire to possess or enjoy the mother in the sense normally understood).

> What we meet as an accident in the child's development is linked to the fact that the child does not find himself or herself alone in front of the

mother, and that the phallus forbids the child the satisfaction of his or her own desire, which is the desire to be the exclusive desire of the mother.[24]

The duality of the relation between mother and child must be broken, just as the analytic relation must be thrown onto the axis of desire. In Lacan's account, the phallus stands for that moment of rupture. It refers mother and child to the dimension of the symbolic which is figured by the father's place. The mother is taken to desire the phallus not because she contains it (Klein), but precisely because she does not. The phallus therefore belongs somewhere else; it breaks the two-term relation and initiates the order of exchange. For Lacan, it takes on this value as a function of the androcentric nature of the symbolic order itself. But its status is in itself false, and must be recognised by the child as such. Castration means first of all this—that the child's desire for the mother does not refer *to* her but *beyond* her, to an object, the phallus, whose status is first imaginary (the object presumed to satisfy her desire) and then symbolic (recognition that desire cannot be satisfied).

The place of the phallus in the account, therefore, follows from Lacan's return to the position and law of the father, but this concept has been reformulated in relation to that of desire. Lacan uses the term "paternal metaphor," metaphor having a very specific meaning here. First, as a reference to the act of substitution (substitution is the very law of metaphoric operation), whereby the prohibition of the father takes up the place originally figured by the absence of the mother. Secondly, as a reference to the status of paternity itself which can only ever logically be *inferred*. And thirdly, as part of an insistence that the father stands for a place and a function which is not reducible to the presence or absence of the real father as such.

> To speak of the Name of the Father is by no means the same thing as invoking paternal deficiency (which is often done). We know today that an Oedipus complex can be constituted perfectly well even if the father is not there, while originally it was the excessive presence of the father which was held responsible for all dramas. But it is not in an environmental perspective that the answer to these questions can be found. So as to make the link between the Name of the Father, in so far as he can at times be missing, and the father whose effective presence is not always necessary for him not to be missing, I will introduce the expression *paternal metaphor*.[25]

Finally, the concept is used to separate the father's function from the idealised or imaginary father with which it is so easily confused and which is exactly the figure to be got round, or past: "Any discourse on the Oedipus complex which fails to bring out this figure will be inscribed within the very effects of the complex."[26]

Thus when Lacan calls for a return to the place of the father he is crucially distinguishing himself from any sociological conception of role. The father is a function and refers to a law, the place outside the imaginary dyad and against which it breaks. To make of him a referent is to fall into an ideological trap: the "prejudice which falsifies the conception of the Oedipus complex from the start, by making it define as natural, rather than normative, the predominance of the paternal figure."[27]

There is, therefore, no assumption about the ways in which the places come to be fulfilled (it is this very assumption which is questioned). This is why, in talking of the genetic link between the mother and child, Lacan could refer to the "vast social connivance" which *makes* of her the "privileged site of prohibitions."[28] And why Safouan, in an article on the function of the real father, recognises that it is the intervention of the third term which counts, and that nothing of itself requires that this should be embodied by the father as such.[29] Lacan's position should be read against two alternative emphases—on the actual behavior of the mother alone (adequacy and inadequacy), and on a literally present or absent father (his idealisation and/or deficiency).

The concept of the phallus and the castration complex can only be understood in terms of this reference to prohibition and the law, just as rejection of these concepts tends to lose sight of this reference. The phallus needs to be placed on the axis of desire before it can be understood, or questioned, as the differential mark of sexual identification (boy or girl, having or not having the phallus). By breaking the imaginary dyad, the phallus represents a moment of division (Lacan calls this the subject's "lack-in-being") which reenacts the fundamental splitting of subjectivity itself. And by jarring against any naturalist account of sexuality ("phallocentrism . . . strictly impossible to deduce from any pre-established harmony of the said psyche to the nature it expresses") the phallus relegates sexuality to a strictly other dimension—the order of the symbolic outside of which, for Lacan, sexuality cannot be understood.[30] The importance of the phallus is that its status in the development of human sexuality is something which nature *cannot* account for.

When Lacan is reproached with phallocentrism at the level of his theory, what is most often missed is that the subject's entry into the symbolic order is equally an exposure of the value of the phallus itself. The subject has to recognise that there is desire, or lack in the place of the Other, that there is no ultimate certainty or truth, and that the status of the phallus is a fraud (this is, for Lacan, the meaning of castration). The phallus can only take up its place by indicating the precariousness of any identity assumed by the subject on the basis of its token. Thus the phallus stands for that moment when prohibition must function, in the sense of whom may be assigned to whom in the triangle made up of mother, father, and child, but at that same moment it signals to the subject that "having" only functions at the price of a loss and "being" as an effect of division. Only if this is dropped from the account can the phallus be taken to represent an unproblematic assertion of male privilege, or else lead to reformulations intended to guarantee the continuity of sexual development for both sexes (Jones).

It is that very continuity which is challenged in the account given here. The concept of the phallus and the castration complex testify above all to the problematic nature of the subject's insertion into his or her sexual identity, to an impossibility writ large over that insertion at the point where it might be taken to coincide with the genital drive. Looking back at Jones's answer to Freud, it is clear that his opposition to Freud's concept of the phallic phase involves a rejection of the dimension of desire, of the loss of the object, of the difficulty inherent in subjectivity itself. Just as it was Freud's failure to apply the concept of castration literally to the girl child which brought him up against the concept of desire.[31]

The subject then takes up his or her identity with reference to the phallus, but that identity is thereby designated symbolic (it is something enjoined on the subject). Lacan inverts Saussure's formula for the linguistic sign (the opposition between signifier and signified), giving primacy to the signifier over that which it signifies (or rather creates in that act of signification). For it is essential to his argument that sexual difference is a legislative divide which creates and reproduces its categories. Thus Lacan replaces Saussure's model for the arbitrary nature of the linguistic sign:

(which is indeed open to the objection that it seems to reflect a theory of language based on a correspondence between words and things), with this model:[32]

TREE

"Any speaking being whatever" must line up on one or other side of the divide.[33]

Sexual difference is then assigned according to whether individual subjects do or do not possess the phallus, which means not that anatomical difference *is* sexual difference (the one as strictly deducible from the other), but that anatomical difference comes to *figure* sexual difference, that is, it becomes the sole representative of what that difference is allowed to be. It thus covers over the complexity of the child's early sexual life with a crude opposition in which that very complexity is refused or repressed. The phallus thus indicates the reduction of difference to an instance of visible perception, a *seeming* value.

Freud gave the moment when boy and girl child saw that they were different the status of a trauma in which the girl is seen to be lacking (the objections often start here). But something can only be *seen* to be missing according to a preexisting hierarchy of values ("there is nothing missing in the real").[34] What counts is not the perception but its already assigned meaning— the moment therefore belongs in the symbolic. And if Lacan states that the symbolic usage of the phallus stems from its visibility (something for which he was often criticised), it is only insofar as the order of the visible, the apparent, the seeming is the object of his attack. In fact he constantly refused any crude identification of the phallus with the order of the visible or real ("one might say that this signifier is chosen as what stands out as most easily seized upon in the realm of sexual copulation"), and he referred it instead to that function of "veiling" in which he locates the fundamental duplicity of the linguistic sign.[35]

> All these propositions merely veil over the fact that the phallus can only play its role as veiled, that is, as in itself the sign of the latency with which everything signifiable is struck as soon as it is raised to the function of signifier.[36]

Meaning is only ever erected, it is set up and fixed. The phallus symbolises the effects of the signifier in that having no value in itself, it can represent that to which value *accrues*.

Lacan's statements on language need to be taken in two directions—towards the fixing of meaning itself (that which is enjoined on the subject), and away from that very fixing to the point of its constant slippage, the risk or vanishing-point which it always contains (the unconscious). Sexuality is placed on both these dimensions at once. The difficulty is to hold these two emphases together—sexuality in the symbolic (an ordering), sexuality as that which constantly fails. Once the relationship between these two aspects of psychoanalysis can be seen, then the terms in which feminine sexuality can be described undergo a radical shift. The concept of the symbolic states that the woman's sexuality is inseparable from the representations through which it is produced ("Images and symbols *for* the woman cannot be isolated from images and symbols *of* the woman. . . . [I]t is the representation of sexuality which conditions how it comes into play"), but those very representations will reveal the splitting through which they are constituted as such.[37] The question of what a woman is in this account always stalls on the crucial acknowledgement that there is absolutely no guarantee that she *is* at all. But if she takes up her place according to the process described, then her sexuality will betray, necessarily, the impasses of its history.

Sexuality belongs for Lacan in the realm of masquerade. The term comes from Joan Rivière for whom it indicated a failed femininity.[38] For Lacan, masquerade is the very definition of "femininity" precisely because it is constructed with reference to a male sign. The question of frigidity (on which, Lacan recognised, psychoanalysis "gave up") also belongs here, and it is described in "The Meaning of the Phallus" as the effect of the status of the phallic term.[39] But this does not imply that there is a physiology to which women could somehow be returned, or into which they could be freed. Rather the term "frigidity" stands, on the side of the woman, for the difficulty inherent in sexuality itself, the disjunction laid over the body by desire, at the point where it is inscribed into the genital relation. Psychoanalysis now recognises that any simple criterion of femininity in terms of a shift of pleasure from clitoris to vagina is a travesty, but what matters is the fantasies implicated in either (or both). For both sexes, sexuality will necessarily touch on the duplicity which underpins its fundamental divide. As for "normal" vaginal femininity, which might be taken as the recognition of the value of the male sign (a "coming to" that recognition), it will always evoke the splitting on which its value is erected ("Why not acknowledge that if there is no virility which castration does not consecrate, then for the woman it is a castrated lover or a dead man . . . who hides behind the veil where he calls on her adoration").[40]

The description of feminine sexuality is, therefore, an exposure of the terms of its definition, the very opposite of a demand as to what that sexuality should be. Where such a definition is given—"identification with her mother as desiring and a recognition of the phallus in the real father," it involves precisely a collapse of the phallus into the real and of desire into recognition— giving the lie, we could say, to the whole problem outlined.[41]

3

Negativity in the Work of Melanie Klein

> Analytic theory has treated the two instincts in an unusual manner: the libido is the first-born and privileged child, the destructive instinct is the latecomer, the stepchild. Libido was recognised as such from the first; the other instinct, its adversary, went under various disguises, and had several names before its identity was established.
>
> —Paula Heimann, *Freud-Klein Controversies 1941–45*

> If we stick to Freud's elaborated categories . . . we are able to conceive the primitive psychical make-up of an infant and the elaborate organisation of an adult personality as a lawful continuity.
>
> —Hedwig Hoffer, *Freud-Klein Controversies 1941–45*

For anyone attempting to follow the tracks of the psyche across the terrain of contemporary political life, it is hard to avoid Melanie Klein. The new brutalism of Thatcherism in the 1980s and the Gulf War, with its renewed and absolute moral antinomies for the West, are just two instances where some seemingly irreducible negativity, bearer of a violence sanctioned—if only momentarily—by State and subjects, appears to rise up to the surface of political consciousness, setting the parameters of our being-in-the-social, confronting us with something at the limits of psyche and social alike. High priestess of psychic negativity, Melanie Klein pushed the institution of psychoanalysis in Britain—and, some would argue, her child patients—close to the edge. In the tradition of Freud, she saw her task as one of excavation, as the retrieval of something which even Freud, she argued, had barely been able to approach. Thus outmaneuvering the father of psychoanalysis, while claiming her unswerving loyalty to and continuity with his project, she assigned to him as much the role of represser as uncoverer of the hidden repressed. And yet, in the recent and continuing turn to psychoanalysis in the humanities,

Klein—compared with Freud—has received relatively little attention. Why, then, has there been no rereading of Melanie Klein?[1]

In the context of the humanities, the idea of rereading has become something of a commonplace. Without assuming that a writer has necessarily been read before, it refers instead to a strategy of reading which heads past the most immediate or professionally received meanings of the writer, straight for the points of creative tension in her or his works. This way of reading "otherwise" is interested in the moments when writing slips its moorings, when it fails—as all writing must fail, it is suggested—its own tests of coherence, revealing—the analogy with analysis is intentional—its "other" scene. In relation to psychoanalysis, this way of reading, often described as "deconstructive," takes on a particular weight. Less interested in a general instability of language, it places itself instead *inside* the psychoanalytic project, aiming to demonstrate the triumph of the unconscious over all attempts at hermeneutic or therapeutic control. In a recent discussion on "Melanie Klein Today," organized in London as part of a series aiming to promote dialogue between psychoanalysis in the clinic and psychoanalysis in the academy, Elizabeth Bott Spillius, editor of two volumes of contemporary analytic essays on Klein, argued that Klein was not a theorist in the strict sense of the term.[2] What happens if we read her comment not as a statement *against* theory, but as suggesting that Klein does theory *otherwise*, that Klein produced a theory which, because of what it was trying to theorize, could not, by definition, contain or delimit itself? Another way of putting this would be to ask whether Klein's writing is a monolithic, singular text; or, can she be read as producing in her writing something as intractable, as creatively unmasterable, as what many readers have become accustomed to discovering in Freud?

In the humanities, a post-Lacanian orthodoxy has blocked access to Klein. In a reading of which it should theoretically, according to its own tenets, be more suspicious, this orthodoxy has accused her of taking apart—but only to re-solder more rigidly—body, psyche, and speech; it has imputed to her something of a psychic and sexual fix. Klein's ego is too coherent; it eventually takes all conflict and phantasy under its control. Her concept of the instinct is reductive; deriving all mental operations from biological impulses, Klein leaves no gaps, no space for the trials and errors of representation, in the mind. Her account of sexuality is coercive; sexual difference, and hence heterosexuality, is given in advance by the knowledge which the bodies of girl- and boy-children are assumed, from the beginning, to have of themselves.[3] And yet, alongside these criticisms, we have to place the no less fervent rejection of Klein for proposing something so negative that it is incapable of assimilation by human subjects, by theory. Especially in the United States, Klein's work has been rejected on account of its violence and negativity. It is a critique which, as we will see, was at the centre of the fierce dispute which, in England too, was originally aroused by her work.

Far from offering reassurance, these reactions suggest, Melanie Klein disturbs. That disturbance, largely responsible for the rejection of Klein in analytic circles in the United States, has been mirrored in recent feminist debate. Searching for an alternative femininity free of the dictates of patriarchal, oedipal law, one feminism has turned to the pre-oedipal relation between mother and girl-child only to find Klein's account of early psychic processes standing in its way.[4] Too negative, this account blocks the new identification, troubles the ideal. Against the idyll of early fusion with the mother, Klein offers proximity as something which devours. Is there a way of linking the two criticisms—Klein as too safe and too dangerous, Klein as taking too much under, letting too much slip out of, control?

It is in the context of these issues that I want to return here to the earliest disagreement over Melanie Klein's work in England, which threatened to divide the psychoanalytic institution and has left its traces on the organization of the Institute of Psycho-Analysis to this day. The focus for this was the "Controversial Discussions," relatively unknown outside analytic circles, which took place at the scientific meetings of the British Psycho-Analytic Society between 1943 and 1944, centering on the disagreement between Anna Freud and Melanie Klein. In this instance, the theoretical issue reveals itself unmistakably as an issue of the psychoanalytic institution and its continuity. As if in response to the dictates of unconscious time—amnesia as the first stage in allowing something to return—this moment of psychoanalytic history has gradually and recently come back to the fore of debate. In 1991, the full edition of the "Controversial Discussions" was published as volume 11 of the New Library of Psychoanalysis, a monumental feat of editing running to over 900 pages and including all the original papers and the ensuing debates (prior to this, only a selection of the papers had been available in a 1952 edition itself reprinted in 1989).[5] Articles have been written on the subject; two books have appeared on the institutional vicissitudes of psychoanalysis in Britain—*Freud in Exile* and an anthology of articles, *The British School of Psychoanalysis: The Independent Tradition* (the independents were those who chose to affiliate with neither party to the dispute).[6] Within feminism, a sometimes celebratory (Klein as "mother" of a new second-generation psychoanalysis), sometimes critical (Klein as sexually normative) attention has produced something, if not quite, in the order of a "return" to Melanie Klein.[7]

More oddly, this originating moment of local institutional dispute had its highly successful passage across the London stage. Nicholas Wright's play *Mrs Klein* played to packed houses in 1988 at the Cottesloe Theatre, and then transferred to the West End.[8] Vicariously, the play offers the spectacle of three women—Melanie Klein, her daughter Melitta Schmideberg, and Paula Heimann—battling it out over the legacy of Klein's work. Femininity becomes the site on which the vexed question of affiliation and institutional continuity is explored. It is a shocking play, not least of all, as one student commented, because of the terrible way analysts are seen to behave. Now this story of dreadful behaviour on the part of analysts has of course been told over and over again in relation to Freud; for some thinkers, it has become the key to the analytic institution itself (Roazen, Roustang, Derrida, Grosskurth).[9] But this has been seen to date as an affair strictly between men. The affair involved here, by contrast, is strictly between women, between mothers and daughters (literally and metaphorically), which might suggest another reason for looking at it again.

It is a point worth making in relation to a book like François Roustang's *Dire Mastery*, one of the more nuanced, less simply accusatory readings of the historic trials of psychoanalytic affiliation and descent. Roustang traces what he sees as the psychotic fantasies underpinning the institution and its (patri)lineage, and locates these fantasies on more than one occasion in an unconscious image of femininity which, he argues, that same institution refuses and on which it relies. Yet, he never makes the link from there to the work of Melanie Klein—theoretician of the psychotic in all of us and, together with Anna Freud, the first woman inheritor, contester, and transmitter of the legacy of Freud. When Jacques Derrida asks in a final essay in his book on Freud, "Who will analyse the unanalysed of Freud?" ("Qui paiera à qui la tranche de Freud?"; more exactly, "Who pays the price for the unanalysed slice of Freud?"), it is tempting to answer, "Melanie Klein."[10] Similarly, Julia Kristeva has argued that Freud's obsessional return to the oedipal narrative was a way of rationalizing his own more psychotic discovery of a negativity which he both theorized and effaced. Freud, she suggests, thus repeated in his own intellectual trajectory that process of flight from, disavowal, and semi-recognition of something murderous and unmanageable which, at the end of his life, he read in the story of Moses.[11] What all this points to is a residue—theoretical, institutional, sexual—of the Freudian institution, in which Melanie Klein, or more specifically the controversy over her work, occupies a crucial place.

Two issues arise centrally from this moment of analytic history, both with relevance for how we think about psyche and the social (the psyche as social) today. First, the concept of psychic negativity in Klein: What is it? Is it an instinctual reductionism, with biology the final court of appeal for what is most troubling in the mind? Or is it something else, perhaps closer to, even if crucially distinct from, the negativity which Lacan places at the heart of subjectivity—not as instinctual deposit, but as the price that all human subjects pay for the cruel passage of the psyche into words? Secondly, what was at stake in the row over child analysis between Anna Freud and Melanie Klein? Central to the psychoanalytic institution is the problem of how to transmit knowledge of—which must mean educating—the unconscious without effacing the force of the unconscious as such. What happens when this problem turns into the question of whether one can, or indeed should, analyse a child? It is the point where the institution comes up against its own subjective origins, or rather the fantasy of its own origins, its own infancy—an infancy which, according to its own theories, it must both relinquish and repeat. It is also one of the points where the issue of power in the analytic scenario reveals itself most starkly, since the analyst's intervention in the mind of the child seems to be disputed according to the alternatives of education or violation, moral control or abuse. Clearly a matter of psycho-politics, because it touches on the limits of the psychoanalytic institution in its dealings with its own outside. But if the issue of psychic negativity can be included under the same heading, it is because it also seems to bring us up against a limit: the limit of what a society, of what a subject, can recognize of itself. It does so, however, in a way which is absolutely unassimilable to that idea of transgressive liberation which has been the most frequent radical political version of Freud (what would a "liberation" of unconscious negativity mean?).

In the context of Klein's work, the dialogue between psychoanalysis and politics therefore shifts. As it does, we can see just how tightly the institutional and disciplinary boundaries and points of affiliation have recently and restrictively been drawn. Instead of the dialogue between psychoanalysis and literature or film, for example, we find psychoanalysis in confrontation with pedagogy and the law. Instead of the unconscious as the site of emancipatory pleasures, we find something negative, unavailable for celebration or release. One could argue that it has been too easy to politicize psychoanalysis as long as the structuring opposition has been situated between an over-controlling, self-deluded ego and the disruptive force of desire; that this opposition has veiled the more difficult antagonism between superego and unconscious, where what is hidden is aggression as much as sexuality, and the agent of repression is as ferocious as what it is trying to control. Much of the psycho-political colouring of the past decade suggests that the political import of psychoanalysis may reside in what it has to say about the passage across the social of thanatos as much as eros (not the unconscious which the social denies, but the unconscious which it sanctions and pursues). By seeing the unconscious as the site of sexual or verbal free fall, the humanities have aes-theticized psychoanalysis, bypassing other points of (greater) friction, both internal to psychoanalytic thinking and in the historically attested confronta-tions between psychoanalysis and its outer bounds. Could it be that the humanities, inadvertently repeating a legacy of which they have been un-aware, have, like psychoanalysis itself, preferred the "legitimate heir" over the "stepchild"?

The "Controversial Discussions" were originally published in 1952 in a collec-tion edited by Joan Rivière under the title *Developments in Psycho-Analysis* (volume 43 of the Hogarth International Psycho-Analytical Library). The book included three of the original papers: "The Nature and Function of Phantasy" by Susan Isaacs, "Certain Functions of Introjection and Projection in Earliest Infancy" by Paula Heimann, and "Regression" by Paula Heimann and Susan Isaacs. It also included an introduction by Rivière, additional papers by Heimann and Rivière, as well as four papers by Klein, including a revised version of the paper which she herself delivered to the scientific meetings in March 1944.[12] In what follows, I concentrate on the papers by Isaacs, Rivière, and Heimann. Apologias for, and defences of, Klein's work, they speak for Klein, although not in her voice, hovering in that hybrid space of identification where bodies and psyches at once recognize each other as separate and get too close (whether identification as incorporation neces-sarily destroys its object will be one of the issues of theoretical dispute). Less well known than Klein's own writings, these papers offer perhaps the clearest account in Kleinian writing of negativity in the process of emergence of the subject, as the passage through which subjects come to be. What is also remarkable about them is their degree of theoretical self-elaboration, or self-consciousness about theory, which means that they read very differently from that extraordinary direct lifting of theory out of the act of interpretation which more than one commentator has remarked on in relation to Klein.[13]

Taken in conjunction with the responses now made available with the 1991 publication of the full text of the debates, these documents provide a unique opportunity to examine *in statu nascendi* the founding, theoretically, of a school. It should be stressed, then, that this is an analysis of one key moment of self-representation in a body of evolving thought, not an account of what Kleinianism has become, in theory and practice, today.

One reason for the self-elaboration of these papers is that they are presented, had to be presented, in terms of an argument for their own legitimacy, their right to contest areas of Freudian orthodoxy even as they claim to be developing from the true letter of his text. In Britain, Melanie Klein was to find herself at once the heiress and usurper of Freud—brought to England by Ernest Jones in 1926, twelve years before Freud himself arrived, in 1938, accompanied by Anna Freud. Recently published correspondence shows Freud, long before his arrival, troubled by a number of Klein's theoretical innovations (on the superego, on the sexual development of the girl), but even more concerned about the critiques of his daughter by Klein and her supporters, which he took as a personal affront.[14] When Anna Freud arrived, therefore, she took up a position which was at once laid down—she was the daughter of the founding father of psychoanalysis—and occupied or contested in advance. Who, we might ask in this context, is the legitimate child?

It follows that Klein and her followers could only partially base their claims for authority on their fidelity to Freud. In his preface to the 1952 collection, Ernest Jones writes: "What is certainly illegitimate is the Procrustean principle of assessing all conclusions with those reached by Freud, however great our respect for the latter can and should be."[15] Joan Rivière opens her general introduction with this quotation from Freud: "I have made many beginnings and thrown out many suggestions. . . . I can hope that they have opened up a path to an important advance in our knowledge. Something will come of them in the future."[16] Given what we know of Freud's vexed relation to filiation and legacy, we already have to view this with caution, as something of a rhetorical strategy, a calling up of Freud against Freud. Freud is being invoked here as permitting—demanding even—a future for his discipline which goes beyond his own name (something of a self-cancelling proposition in itself). But it allows Rivière to argue that, while Freud's central discovery was the world of unconscious phantasy, "there are many problems to which he did not apply it," which have subsequently been brought nearer to a "solution" by Klein ("her consistent awareness of its significance").[17] And she continues: "The circumstances under which his work began and was carried through, i.e., its origin in medicine, no doubt affected his outlook," leading him to concentrate on the differences between "normal" and "morbid" mentality at the expense of general laws and to an overestimation of the "force of the reality principle."[18]

The case for Melanie Klein rests, therefore, on this image of her as inheritor of the Freudian "truth" (Rivière's word), one which the limits of Freud's own scientific training made him unable fully to pursue. What is already clear is that this truth, in the name of which Rivière speaks for Klein, does not belong to an order of scientifically verifiable knowledge. In the heat of the discussions, Susan Isaacs replies to her critics: "Dr Friedlander refers to the fact that Mrs. Klein's views as to mental life is 'inferred knowledge' as of course it is."[19] Critiquing the Kleinian concept of phantasy, Marjorie Brierly states: "If we persist in equating mental functions with our subjective interpretations of them, we forfeit our claim to be scientists and revert to the primitive [sic] state of the Chinese peasant who interprets an eclipse as the sun being swallowed by a dragon."[20] To which Paula Heimann replies: "The science of psychology is not to be equated with the science of astronomy. What we are studying is not the solar system, but the mind of the Chinese peasant, not the eclipse but the belief of the peasant concerning the eclipse. How do such beliefs arise? . . . And further, how does the knowledge that the sun is not swallowed by a dragon develop in the mind of peasants and philosophers?"[21] For Heimann, psychoanalysis makes no distinction between peasants and philosophers. The unconscious conditions of all knowledge and belief systems are what need to be explained. As Rivière later puts it, citing Bacon: "There is a superstition in avoiding superstition."[22] The dispute about the transmission of the Freudian legacy thus appears as a dispute about the possibility of objective knowledge and (thinly veiled behind the first) the scientific supremacy of the West.[23]

These, then, are the grounds of the first opposition to Klein; the second Rivière attributes to Klein's idea of a destructive instinct and a psychotic part in all human subjects: "The concept of a destructive force within every individual, tending towards the annihilation of life, is naturally one which arouses extreme emotional resistance; and this, together with the inherent obscurity of its operation, has led to a marked neglect of it by many of Freud's followers, as compared with any other aspect of his work"; "[in] the very early phases of mental life . . . she finds in operation mental mechanisms (splitting, projection, etc.) closely similar to those of the psychotic disorders, another aspect of her work which arouses strong emotional resistance."[24] Thus the argument about fidelity to, and divergence from, Freud carries the weight of psychosis and death—precisely the discoveries which Kristeva argued were rationalized by Freud. (Note too the link between destruction and obscurity as if destruction were conceivable only if it can be fully—scientifically—mastered or grasped.) It is, however, another classic rhetorical move, where opposition or resistance to a theory is seen to belong inside, or be tributary of, what it is that the theory itself invokes. But we should perhaps ask what a legacy can be in this context, how an institution can perpetuate itself, when what it offers as the true content of that legacy is death? Death, after all, as Paula Heimann puts it in her paper on introjection and projection, is the one thing which the mind cannot expel.[25] It is in this context with all its institutional ramifications that the "Controversial Discussions" offer their account of what is meant by the destructive impulse or the death instinct in the work of Melanie Klein.

The first thing that becomes clear is that the concept of the death instinct or impulse is in no sense a biologistic concept in the work of Klein.[26] It was the Anna Freudians who insisted on the biological status of the concept (the principle of conservation and the return to the inanimate state) in order precisely to keep it outside the range of analytic work. The objections to the centrality accorded to the concept by Klein rested, therefore, not on her biologizing of the concept (instinctual reductionism) but on the opposite, on the way she assigned to it psychic significance, made it part of the phantasy life of the child. Whether the child could inhabit a world of meanings would be another central issue in the dispute over Klein's work. To cite Isaacs: "The word 'phantasy' serves to remind us always of this distinctive character of meaning in mental life"; Michael Balint: "'Phantasy' suggests 'meaning'"; Barbara Lantos: "This pleasure we call auto-erotic . . . organ pleasure . . . and intellectual pleasure—they all are the same in so far as they are pleasures in themselves, that is to say: pleasures without meaning"; Edward Glover: "And so we come back once more to the dispute over 'meaning' and 'implicit meaning.'"[27]

Death for Klein was *meaning*, which also meant that death *had* meaning for the infant. When Freud argues that the infant could have no knowledge of death, this does not preclude the possibility, Rivière argues, that the child "can experience feelings of the kind, just as any adult can feel 'like death,' and in a state of great anxiety often does."[28] What seems to be going on here, if we look closely at the passage, is not an undiluted appeal to feeling, but rather the suggestion that feeling itself is simile ("feel '*like* death'"), that the most severe anxiety the child can feel opens up the path of indirect representation by putting it at a fundamental, at *the* most fundamental, remove from itself. Thus the child's anxiety becomes the foundation for the first experience of "as if": "We surmise that the *child feels as if*"; "'He behaves as if,' to my mind, is the same thing as saying 'He has phantasies. . . .'"[29]

It is this fundamental negativity which these papers put at the basis of subjectivity. This is a moment of infancy when, if an ego can be postulated, its powers to integrate mental processes are weak. The problem for Klein's critics was that conflict was seen to arise before there was an ego there to manage it: "According to the theory of the English school of analysis, introjection and projection, which in our view should be assigned to the period after the ego has been differentiated from the outside world, are the very processes by which the structure of the ego is developed."[30] Edward Glover, in his long critique of Klein published in the first volume of *The Psychoanalytic Study of the Child*, in 1945, argued that, unlike the customary teaching which over-estimates the primitive ego, there is an underestimation of the primitive ego in Klein.[31] Two common recent theoretical assumptions about Klein therefore fall to the ground: her biologism and the pre-given category of the ego. If Klein was objected to, it was precisely because she was seen as bringing the death drive under the sway of a subject, as making the death drive constitutive of a subject, who is not yet enough of a subject for death to be mastered or controlled.

The third point of dispute was the early relation to the object (these are the three basic points of disagreement which Rivière lists in her introduction). For the Anna Freudians, the infant—again posited in essentially biological terms—is narcissistic and autoerotic, pure pleasure-seeker under the sway of the erotogenic zones. One way of describing the Freudian position, then, would be as a plea to keep pleasure out of the reach of meaning, to leave pleasure *alone*: "Does Isaacs think—as we do—that there are activities just carried out for the sake of auto-erotic pleasure without any phantasies being attached to them . . . just for the sake of the organ-pleasure which is gained?"[32] For the Kleinians, the child relates to the object from the start, meaning not that the child has some inherent capacity for relatedness, the version of object-relations which has become best known, but that even in the state of autoeroticism there are bits and pieces of objects—fragments of introjects, objects that are not quite objects—inside the mind. Objects without propriety, neither fully appropriated nor whole: "Miss Freud speaks of object relationship 'in the proper sense.' I do not think there is a 'proper' sense."[33]

No ownership, therefore, and no agent of control. At each stage, the infant and its world seem to emerge *in absentia, or at a loss.* It is by withholding that the external world comes to be. Rivière writes: "Painful experience does much to bring about the recognition of an external object."[34] The infant oscillates between "seeking, finding, obtaining, possessing with satisfaction" and "losing, lacking, missing, with fear and distress."[35] In this scenario, and despite references to satisfaction obtained, the emphasis is far more frequently on the negative pole. For the loss of the object forces a breach in the primitive narcissism of the subject, a breach which, in a twist, then produces the object as its effect: "The ego's need to dissociate itself from the unpleasure is so great that it *requires an object* upon which it can expel it. . . . For such an experience of unpleasure is too intense to be merely 'killed,' hallucinated as non-existent. Narcissistic phantasy would thus in itself lead to object-relations, and these object-relations will at first be of a negative order."[36] Note again that reference to death in the instigation of the object, an experience of unpleasure so intense that it cannot be "killed," cannot be negatively hallucinated. And note too how different this is from the more familiar idea of hallucination ("narcissistic phenomenon *par excellence*")—not in this case something desired, but something instead which fails to be effaced.[37] The lost object is not, therefore, only the hallucinated object of satisfaction; it is also and simultaneously an object which, because of this failure of negative hallucination, is required—is actively sought after—*in order to be bad.* In these papers from the "Controversial Discussions," the genesis of the famous Kleinian bad object is nothing less than the genesis of the object itself.

Rivière will qualify her account in her 1950 footnotes to her essay: "The view that the earliest relation was negative and hostile was expressed by Freud. Later work leads to a correction of this hypothesis," referring to two later papers by Klein included in the 1952 collection; and in her introduction to the book: "It will be seen from Chapters VI and VII that this is not Melanie Klein's view."[38] Likewise she will answer those who objected to the weakness of the Kleinian ego by insisting on its integrative powers. But in the overall context and feel of the papers, these qualifications sit oddly—symptomatic presence of something which it became too difficult to sustain? Another way of putting this would be to ask how an unconscious identification with death *could*—theoretically, institutionally—be sustained. This would be just one way of reading the editing, the start of a theoretical shift between the original discussions and the 1952 publication of the book.

In these earlier papers, it is stated over and over that the subject first comes to experience itself negatively. Self-alienation gives the colour of the subject's coming-to-be: "Nothing good within *lasts* . . . the first conscious idea of 'me' is largely coloured by painful associations"; "It would seem with every infant that we have to give far more experimental weight to the felt hostility of the external world over a considerable period in early development than we had thought"; "the relation of hate to objects is older than that of love."[39] The persecutory object-relation rises up as the first defence against something without "definite name and shape" (like the patient Klein describes in *Narrative of a Child Analysis* who dreamt of an "indefinite object" stuck to a car, something which "she both wished to see and not to see").[40] Object-relations are "improvements on" and "protections against" primordial narcissistic anxiety; distrust of the object is better than despair.[41]

More than primitive instinct, therefore, the Kleinian concept of negativity appears as a psychic activation of the *fort-da* game as famously described by Freud, an answer of a sort to this question which, as Klein and Heimann both point out, was left in suspense by Freud: "When does separation from an object produce anxiety, when does it produce mourning and when does it produce pain? Let me say at once that there is no prospect in sight of answering these questions."[42] Freud did not believe that absence of the mother could be connoted as loss of love or anger, whereas for Klein the mother rapidly comes to be experienced as bad. "This fundamental fear of loss of the loved object," Klein states, "seems to me psychologically well-founded"—"predetermined, one may say, in the infant from the experience of birth."[43]

It is at this point that the account offered here of psychic beginnings starts to sound uncannily like that of Jacques Lacan; so it is perhaps not surprising to discover Klein and Lacan converging on Freud's paper on "Negation" (the link is not wholly coincidental, since this was the time when Lacan was working on his never to be completed translation of Klein).[44] "Negation" was the key text for Rivière, Isaacs, and Heimann, who took it as the model for their theory of the subject's relation to its object-world.[45] Given the awkwardness as we have seen it of their relation to Freud's legacy, the terms with which Rivière declares this affiliation are at least worthy of note: "One of the richest and most highly condensed productions that he ever composed . . . Melanie Klein's theories dovetail with exquisite precision into its tight and rigorous propositions."[46] Easy or forced entry? What more fitting image for an intimacy uncertain of the legitimacy of its own claims. As if it were being acknowledged that the only passage for these doubtful inheritors was to come up on Freud from behind (sphincter theory, we might say).

The problem of beginnings, it would seem, is at least partly tributary to the problem of descent. What "Negation" offers is a way of theorizing a subject who comes into being on the back of a repudiation, who exists in direct proportion to what it cannot *let be*. If there is no presupposed category of the subject in Kleinian theory, then the subject can emerge only in a moment of self-differentiation, as a difference from itself: "When exactly does the ego, the differentiation from the amorphous id, begin?"[47] It is through the category of negation, the category in which Lacan locates the fundamental negativity of the symbolic function, that Klein and her followers find the reply. Let's consider first what Lacan reads in this famous—and famously cryptic—text by Freud.

Lacan's discussion of Freud's article takes up three chapters of the full version of his 1966 *Ecrits*—an analysis by the Hegelian scholar Jean Hyppolite with an introduction and commentary by Lacan.[48] All three were originally part of Lacan's first seminar of 1954 on the technical writings of Freud—the only works by Freud, interestingly, not included in the Pelican Freud, a comment in itself on the severance between psychoanalysis as clinical and as wider cultural discourse in Great Britain today.[49] Hyppolite focuses on this sentence from the end of Freud's paper: "Affirmation—as a substitute (*Ersatz*) for uniting—belongs to Eros; negation—the successor (*Nachfolge*) to expulsion—belongs to the instinct of destruction (*Destruktionstrieb*)."[50] He reads in Freud's distinction between "substitute" (or "equivalent") and "successor" a crucial difference in the way affirmation and negation relate to the instincts from which they are said to derive. For Hyppolite that "successor" (as opposed to "equivalent") opens up a gap between negation and destruction; they are precisely not equivalents, not the same thing. Hence, he argues, we can read in Freud two concepts of negation: on the one hand, a pleasure of denying which results simply from the suppression of the libidinal components under the domination of the instincts—this already suggests, in a way that troubles some cherished boundaries, that the instinct of destruction is attached to the pleasure principle (Rivière: "Many psychic manifestations show that a threat from the death instinct produces a strong uprush of Eros"[51])— and, on the other, negation as the basis of the symbolic function: "a fundamental attitude of symbolicity (symbol-making capacity) made explicit."[52] What Freud's article shows is that this capacity emerges in a "space of suspension," from a "margin of thinking" where thinking—and being—can only emerge through what they relegate to non-being, to the not-thought: "what one is in the mode of *not* being it."[53]

It is this second emphasis which is picked up by Lacan: "Negativity of discourse, insofar as it brings what is not into being, sends us back to the question of what non-being, manifested in the symbolic order, owes to the reality of death."[54] Negation, for Lacan, is death in the structure, or what he also calls the "real," which, for symbolization to be possible, has to subsist outside its domain. Negation shows the subject, and its world, arising in an act of demolition. For the subject to enter into the possibilities of language and judgment, something has to be discarded, something falls away. For Lacan, therefore, negativity resides on the edge of speech. In an account which is strikingly resonant of this vision, Ella Sharpe reinterprets Melanie Klein: "[The breasts] become the symbol of that undecomposed world which was once the baby's before knowledge entered to start him on the path of detachment."[55] Knowledge, as much as—inseparably from?—aggression, breaks up the unity of the world. We could say that Lacan goes furthest in detaching negation from the destructive impulse—"successor" precisely, but not "equivalent"—because the moment of negation posits the end of equivalence, the end of unity, as such. As Hyppolite puts it: "Primordial affirmation is nothing other than to affirm, but to deny is more than to want to destroy."[56] For those accustomed to reading Freud in terms of the concept of "after-effect" (Nachträglichkeit), it is easy to read in that Nachfolge or "following after" the idea that what precedes has not necessarily come before.

In this commentary by Lacan, the reference to Melanie Klein, moreover, is explicit. A discussion of Klein's 1930 paper on symbol formation ("The Importance of Symbol-Formation in the Development of the Ego") follows immediately after Hyppolite's commentary when it was originally presented to Lacan's seminar, in 1954, and the discussion ends with a link between Hyppolite and Klein for what they each demonstrate regarding "the function of destructionism in the constitution of human reality."[57] In his reply to Hyppolite, Lacan makes a passing reference to a paper by Melitta Schmideberg, identifying her as the first analyst of a patient of Ernest Kris whose acting out of a prematurely cut short orality might explain, he suggests, the relative failure of that earlier analysis with Schmideberg.[58] Thus Lacan's commentary on Freud's "Negation" leads, in a beautiful circularity, back to Melanie Klein.

In fact, the reference to Schmideberg could be seen as the vanishing-point of Lacan's commentary, as well as of the history and theory being discussed here—a part of analytic literature which, as Lacan says, has "unfortunately become very difficult of access," and an orality embedded somewhere in a paper by an analyst, the daughter of Melanie Klein, who, one could argue, as an effect of its unbearable intensity, its acting out inside the analytic institution, will finally reject all such concepts and sever her links with the psychoanalytic world.[59] Ella Sharpe: "I assume hopefully a possibility of discussing Mrs. Klein's theory, of being critical in the constructive meaning of that word, of accepting some things without its being interpreted that one has swallowed Mrs. Klein and her work whole."[60]

It is through orality that Isaacs and Heimann read Freud's paper on "Negation." For them, this is the key passage:

> Expressed in the language of the oldest—the oral—instinctual impulses (*Triebregungen*—impulses of the drives), the judgement is: "I should like to eat this," or "I should like to spit it out"; and, put more generally: "I should like to take this into myself and keep that out."
>
> That is to say: "It shall be inside me" or "it shall be outside me." As I have shown elsewhere, the original pleasure-ego wants to introject into itself everything that is good and to eject from itself everything that is bad. What is bad, what is alien to the ego and what is external are, to begin with, identical.[61]

For Isaacs what this passage reveals is that the function of judgment is derived from the primary instinctual impulses. This is the famous "instinctual reductionism" for which Klein is often criticized.[62] Indeed, Isaacs stresses the concept of derivation, and dismisses Freud's phrase "expressed in the language of the oral impulses" as "picturesque."[63] But, as her commentary on this passage makes clear, it is the mechanisms of introjection and projection which are crucial, and the role of phantasy as the operational link between the two, "the means by which the one is transmuted into the other": " 'I want to eat that and therefore I have eaten it' is the phantasy which represents the id impulse in the psychic life; it is at the same time the subjective *experience* of the mechanism or process of introjection," an interpretation in turn, therefore, of the symbolic process of taking in.[64] Judgment devours and expels its objects: it derives from an orality which in turn becomes a metaphor for judgment itself. This, as I read it, is less derivation than circularity: "One of the 're-sults of the phantasy of introjection' is the process of introjection."[65] No less than Lacan's commentary, which turns on the concept of foreclosure, the ability of the psyche under pressure of denial to wipe something out, this is a process which can have as its logical outcome the effacement, or scotomization, of the world.

The mechanism of denial is expressed in the mind of the subject in some such way as "If I don't admit it [i.e., a painful fact] it isn't true." Or: "If I don't admit it, no one else will know that it is true." And in the last resort this argument can be traced to bodily impulses and phantasies, such as: "If it doesn't come out of my mouth, that shows it isn't inside me"; or "I can prevent anyone else *knowing* it is inside me." Or: "It is all right if it comes out of my anus as flatus or faeces, but it mustn't come out of my mouth as words." The mechanism of *scotomisation* is experienced in such terms as: "What I don't see I need not believe"; or "What I don't see, other people don't, and indeed doesn't exist."[66]

What is striking about this passage is the way it seems to undermine the very causal sequence from which it claims to derive. For, if the body can become a mechanism of disavowal for language ("It is all right if it comes out of my body as flatus or faeces, but it mustn't come out of my mouth as words"), then the body is already being inscribed in a linguistic process, is being called up as metaphor even as it is metaphor—the passage of bodily process into language —that the subject resists. So the more Isaacs carries out her derivation of phantasy from impulse, the more the impulse becomes after the fact ("successor" we might say) the metaphoric correlate of the phantasy it supports. Thus the Kleinians flesh out the structure of negation. At one level it is without doubt a more literally—vulgarly—corporeal reading than that of Lacan; but no more than his can it guarantee the reality of the world which it constitutes but can equally efface. Orality appears here as the transcription or metaphor of itself. What primacy is being given here to the concept of the impulse—"mythological beings superb in their indefiniteness" as Heimann and Isaacs put it, citing a famous remark of Freud's?[67]

It is, I think, worth stressing this question of transcription because, in relation to Klein, it is most often misread. Thus Nicolas Abraham and Maria Torok criticize what they call Klein's "panfantastic instinctualism"; while Jean Laplanche and J. B. Pontalis takes Isaacs's definition of phantasy as the "mental expression" of the impulse as evidence of a potential reductionism in Klein, one which Klein herself resisted but which has been exacerbated by other interpreters and followers of her work.[68] In her introduction to the 1952 collection, Rivière cites Isaacs's definition together with the lines from Freud on which it is based: "Freud said: 'We suppose that it [the id] is somewhere in direct contact with somatic processes and takes over from them instinctual needs and gives them mental expression.' Now in the view of the present writers, this *mental expression* is unconscious phantasy." But, Rivière continues, the passage goes on: "There is no impulse, no instinctual urge or response which is not experienced as unconscious phantasy."[69] The two propositions are clearly not symmetrical: to say that one thing is the *expression of* another is not the same thing as to say that one thing *has to find another* in terms of which it can be expressed. As Isaacs summarized in her original paper, "Instinctual urges . . . cannot operate in the mind without phantasy."[70] The second implies translation, mediation, or, as Isaacs puts it, "operative link"; that is, it implies interpretation, or rather misinterpretation, the word used explicitly by Rivière: "On Freud's own hypothesis, the psyche responds to the reality of its experiences by interpreting them—or rather *misinterpreting them*—in a subjective manner."[71] Subjective experience involves the child in perpetual misreadings of the world: "[The child's] misunderstanding of the situation is precisely that subjective interpretation of his perception."[72]

Phantasies, Isaacs writes, are the "expression of wishes and passions": "It is primarily because he *wants* his urine to be so very powerful that he comes to believe it is so."[73] The destructive impulse therefore turns on a tautology—destructive because of the omnipotence with which the child wields and translates it to or her or his own ends. This is the impulse "pressed into the service of need" of phantasy as the "mental expression of" instinctual need;[74] not a reduction of phantasy to a biological instinct, but a massive inflation of the power of phantasy to make, and break, the world.

What emerges most strongly from these papers is the impossibility of assigning some simple origin to destruction. Hate may be older than love, but Melanie Klein's conclusions: "do not stand or fall on the concept of the death instinct."[75] What seems to be outrageous—paradoxically harder to manage than death as a pure force, as something which assaults the subject from outside—is this internalization of death into the structure. If death is a pure point of biological origin, then at least it can be scientifically known. But if it enters into the process of psychic meanings, inseparable from the mechanisms through which subjects create and recreate their vision of the world, then from where can we gain the detachment with which to get it under control?

It is clear that for the critics of Klein and her supporters, it was the priority accorded to subjective experience and the implications of this for knowledge which was at stake. (Recently Meltzer has suggested that this is *the* philosophical problem posed by Klein.)[76] Klein, Isaacs, and Heimann were confusing "the mental corollary to instinct" with "what we are used to call phantasy,"

subjective definition with mental mechanism—"The mixing-up of concep-
tions impresses all of us as most undesirable"; "What happens when the
distinction is lost?"[77] Each time, Isaacs and Heimann respond by insisting on
the impossibility, within the logic proper to psychoanalysis, of holding the
elements apart: "*What I believe is that reality-thinking cannot operate without
concurrent and supporting Ucs phantasies*"; "a rigid separation between 'mechanism' and 'content' is a danger to psychological understanding . . . [I]t springs
from a basic fallacy: a rigid divorce between the id and the ego"; "perception
and image-formation cannot be sharply separated from unconscious phantasy"; "the suggestion that we should discuss 'the nature of the process itself'
rather than its content seems to rest on a false assumption. The nature of
mental process, as well as of the structure and mechanisms of the mind, is
partly determined and characterized by phantasies, that is to say, by the
subjective content of the mind."[78] Compare Anna Freud from her 1945 paper
"Indications for Child Analysis": "All through childhood a ripening process is
at work which, in the service of an increasingly better knowledge of an
adaptation to reality, aims at perfecting these functions, at rendering them
*more and more independent of the emotions until they become as accurate and
reliable as any non-human mechanical apparatus.*"[79]

What seems to be involved, therefore, is something in the nature of a
boundary, or category, dispute. How much is subjective experience allowed to
take in (can the category of cats be a member of itself)? Marjorie Brierly
proposes that "introjection" be kept as the term for the mental process,
"incorporation" for the experience of taking things in: "When a baby is trying
to put everything into its mouth, it comes across many things that won't go in.
Image formation as a function of mind will not go in to incorporation."[80] To
which Heimann replies: "Mentally, anything can go into anything."[81] But if
anything can go into anything—both mentally and theoretically—then what
is there to distinguish psychoanalysis, as a form of mental activity, from the
all-devouring, all-incorporating child?

Or, to put it in another way, what is left of identity and its (self-)definition
if these distinctions cannot be sustained? If incorporation cannot be distinguished from introjection, or introjection from identification (as Sharpe
points out, Freud often blurred the distinction between the two), then the
idea of identity as distinct from, even if created through, its objects becomes
unclear. How can incorporation be the foundation of identity when it seems
to imply as a concept a dissolution of the separateness on which identity
relies?[82] The issue here is not whether these distinctions can, or cannot, be

theoretically mounted, but the form of loss that seems to threaten when they fail. What do these uncertainties imply for an adult subject (an adult science)?

Brierly makes it explicit that the distinction between subjectivity and mechanism carries with it the distinction between first and third person, between identification and object-relationship, between knowledge and science.[83] If psychoanalysis cannot distinguish between knowledge and phantasy, it becomes an infant incapable of taking its measure of reality, incapable of stepping out into the world. So when Glover insults his adversaries—accusing, for example, Klein of projecting into children, Heimann of playing with Freud's theories like a "kitten plays with a ball of wool"—I read this as more than personally symptomatic.[84] He has, like others of Klein's critics, spotted one of the most far-reaching and troubling implications of her theories: not just the point convincingly made by many recent commentators of Freud—that psychoanalysis can be only a speculative form of knowledge, that it must, if it is to remain loyal to its object, undo its claims to authority as it goes—but that, in relation to the project of child analysis, that same undoing propels the analyst *and her theories* back into the realm of the child.[85] Psychoanalysis cannot ignore, cannot separate itself from, the unconscious conditions of knowledge. Could it be the force of this recognition during the "Controversial Discussions" that led, in reaction, to what today is often seen as the opposite—the rigidity of Kleinian interpretation, the fierceness with which Kleinian thinking now lays claim to its status as science? Walter Schmideberg: "I listened to [the papers] in silence and some of them made me think that the accusations of our enemies that it is impossible to distinguish between the phantasies of the patients and those of the analyst contained more than a grain of truth"; Karin Stephen: "Do we really know what we are doing?"[86] What happens if we read this as the insight and not the failure of the dispute?

Clearly, then, it is the status of psychoanalysis as scientific knowledge which is at stake—what might be called its coming of age. Is psychoanalysis an adult science? Do children develop from point A to point B, or do they evolve according to a different sequence, one which throws into crisis our idea of what a sequence should be? Thus the question of development arises logically out of the question of knowledge and science. It is, writes Brierly, "to put the cart before the horse" if you make introjection, based on bodily behaviour, responsible for image formation.[87] If mental mechanisms are partly determined by phantasy, then "expressed in theoretical terms this would mean that the end results of mental processes determine the processes themselves which is absurd."[88] Complicated emotional attitudes are assumed to be in existence before instinctual urges; the infant interprets its experience in terms of a superego not yet in force: "Coming events cast their shadow before."[89] What has happened to sequence and causality? What priority—theoretically—is being given to unconscious time?

Once again the theoretical point takes its colour from the psychic processes being described. What Brierly and Glover have identified is that Klein's account of beginnings, of the infant's first being in the world, inaugurates circular rather than sequential time. This is how Rivière describes the "vicious circle" which is the child's first apprehension of cause and effect: " 'You don't come and help, and you hate me, because I am angry and devour you; yet I *must* hate you and devour you in order to make you help.' "[90] The child is caught in an impasse, "the fear of destroying the mother in the very act of expressing love for her" and of "losing her in the very process designed to secure her possession."[91] Incorporation does not only take everything in; it also abolishes its object. If we go back, to those moments of primordial absence and negation and put them together, we can watch this scenario emerge. What is lost is a persecutor; the only way of being of the object is as something devoured or expelled; the lost object is bad *because* the only way of being the object is as something devoured or expelled. If this is a vicious circle, it is also, in these early papers, a process without end; inherently contradictory, these mechanisms serve the very impulses against which they defend, and they founder on the "problem of preservation" as emptiness, aggression, and sadistic impulses all return: "The omnipotence of phantasy is a weapon which cuts both ways."[92] Similarly, what is seen to resolve the cycle belongs no less in circular time: "Here we have a benign circle."[93]

One of the most interesting things about these papers, therefore, is that they lay out so clearly the problem of generating an account of positive development out of the processes they have described—positive as in psychic, positive as in linear time. Not that Klein does not add, as Rivière insists, a new emphasis on the mother as good object, on the early love relation, on the depressive phase in which the child takes everything back (as opposed to "in") and subjects it to a meticulous and loving repair. "Even during the earliest stage," Klein writes, "persecutory anxiety is to some extent counteracted by the experience of the good breast."[94] And yet, even inside this account (and on the same page), the experience of gratification turns into idealization, which then sets up the object as "perfect, inexhaustible, always available, always gratifying."[95] As Klein puts it in the discussion following her paper in 1944: "Even when the feeding situation is satisfactory, hunger and the craving for libidinal gratification stir and reinforce the destructive impulses";[96] and again in an earlier paper: "Some measure of frustration is inevitable . . . what the infant actually *desires* is unlimited gratification."[97] Gratification therefore sets up the terms of its own demise. Or, where it repairs, it also repeats: "The experience of gratification at the mother's breast after frustration" develops the infant's confidence that "bad things go and good things come"; it enters into the logic of expulsion and projection that it is also intended to subdue.[98]

Klein's contribution to the debate can be read at least partly as a reaffirmation of love against what has come before. But this love, she insists, is complex; it is not a value or thing itself. If it is present from the earliest stages, it nonetheless comes at least partly in reply to the mother's demand ("An infant knows intuitively that his smile and other signs of affection and happiness produce happiness and pleasure in the mother"); turning on her pleasure, it seeks out her desires and her words. Klein provides a graphic image of this early relation in the five-month-old patient who puts his fingers in Klein's mouth in "an attempt to fetch the sounds out" (introjection, as Lacan would put it, as "always introjection of the speech of the other").[99] These feelings, Klein states in reply to Brierly, are not a "primary simple affect."[100]

Likewise, reparation can reinforce omnipotence. (Although Klein herself had insisted on the distinction from 1935, one point of dispute was whether it simply derived from Freud's concept of reaction formation and obsessional undoing.)[101] In these discussions the concept of reparation appears less as part of a naturally evolving development, more as a *requirement*, something enjoined—internally and externally—on the child. It is, in fact, striking the way it appears as a concept in the imperative mode: "The object within, feelings about people *must* be put right"; "The external objects, real parents, brothers and sisters and so on, *must* be pleased and made happy"; "The full internalisation of real persons as helpful loved figures *necessitates* abandoning this defence-method of splitting feelings and objects into good and bad"; "Good and bad feelings *have to be* tolerated at one and the same time."[102] Manifestly replying to criticisms from the earlier debate, Rivière states: "The significance of the phantasies of reparation is perhaps the most essential aspect of Melanie Klein's work; for that reason her contribution to psychoanalysis *should not* be regarded as limited to the exploration of the aggressive impulses and phantasies."[103]

To what *necessity* we might ask—theoretical and institutional as well as psychic—does the concept of reparation correspond? Two recent Kleinian commentators have described the development of the concept as something of a mystery in Klein's work. For Meltzer, at the point where Klein starts to distinguish between manic reparation "as defence against persecutory or depressive anxiety" and "something more genuinely in the service of the objects," it begins to take on a "more mysterious meaning"; in the discussion cited at the start of this chapter, Elizabeth Bott-Spillius described as "mysterious" the shift of attention from sadism to love in Klein's later work: "I don't know where it came from."[104] It is as if reparation can theorize itself only as absolute necessity and/or absolute unknown. What these papers suggest is that reparation cannot be detached from the issue of knowledge. Indeed, one might say that, as psychic process, reparation requires a suspension of absolute knowledge if it is not to turn into pure omnipotent defence. It is not, therefore, to deny the validity of the experience of reparation to note that it has often come to serve in the Kleinian corpus as a solution to difficulties—of negativity, causality, and knowledge—which, in this earlier debate, seem to be without end. The point is made, although from very different perspectives, by both Glover and Lacan.

For it is central to Kleinian theory that the anxiety which leads to fixation and regression in both sexes also plays its part in precipitating the libido on its forward path: "Each of the fixations and pathological symptoms apt to appear at successive stages of development have both a retrogressive and progressive function, binding anxiety and thus making further development possible."[105] Which is to say that development is in some sense pathological—Heimann calls this the "negative aspect of progression."[106] Klein herself states repeatedly, with reference to the depressive position, that each step in unification leads to a renewed splitting of the imagos—of necessity, since the depressive position genetically derives from the paranoid state that it is meant to surpass. What Heimann and Isaacs refer to as a "benign circle" follows the same logic: "These ego achievements . . . are prime factors in the fight against anxiety and guilt. A certain degree and quality of guilt and anxiety stimulate reparation and thus encourage sublimation."[107]

Thus, when Isaacs writes that "the established principle of genetic continuity is a concrete instrument of knowledge," "the essence of Freud's theory lies in just this fact of detailed continuity," this is not a developmental paradigm in any straightforward sense.[108] The movement is constantly in two directions— progression being constantly threatened by the mechanisms which move it on. Hence the well-known paradox that, in Klein's account, homosexuality arises out of the anxieties of heterosexual phantasy; that if heterosexuality is somewhere pre-established for the subject, it is so only as part of an unmanageable set of phantasies which are in fact incapable, in the theory, of ensuring heterosexuality itself.[109] As much as the idea of a developmental sequence, this could be argued to be the logic proper to Kleinian thought: "Anxiety and guilt at times check and at other times enhance the libidinal development"; "while in some ways these defences impede the path of integration, they are essential for the whole development of the ego."[110] Thus, as Lacan points out in his commentary on Klein's paper on symbol formation, the ego appears twice over and in the space of a single sentence as precocious or overdeveloped and as what, through its weakness, is preventing normal development from taking place: "The early operation of the reactions originating on the genital level was the result of premature ego development, but further ego development was only inhibited by it" (Lacan: "She says that the ego was over precociously developed . . . and then in the second part of the sentence that it is the ego which is preventing development from taking place").[111]

Too much and too little of an ego whose role it is to master the anxiety out of which it has itself been produced. Anna Freud objects: "According to the theory of the English school of analysis, introjection and projection, which in our view should be assigned to the period after the ego has been differentiated from the outside world, are the very processes by which the structure of the ego is developed."[112] Only if the ego comes first is development assured. Those who criticize Klein, for developmental normativity (the idea that subjects progress naturally to their heterosexual goals) would do well to note that, at least as much as regards Freud's own normative moments, it is not in these terms that Klein's writings can theoretically sustain themselves.[113] The value of the stress on negativity would then reside in the trouble it poses to the concept of a sequence, the way that it acts as a bar, one could say, to what might elsewhere (and increasingly) appear as normative and prescriptive in the work and followers of Melanie Klein.

For Glover, in his long critique of Klein, a central problem—if not *the* central problem—was that "the author cannot tell a developmental story straight."[114] (For those in the humanities seeking after the trials of writing, this would be the ultimate accolade.) The "subversive nature" of Heimann's and Isaacs's paper on "Regression" is precisely that "if fixation can be regarded as a reaction to (result of) regression and if regression itself works backwards through a developmental aggression series, it follows that progression must be attributed to the same factors."[115] For Glover, this is to undermine—or deviate from—the "biological progression of an instinct-series"—that is, the whole conception of libidinal development as laid down by Freud: "It subverts all our concepts of progressive mental development."[116] Only "if we stick to Freud's elaborated categories," writes Hoffer, are we "able to conceive the primitive psychical make-up of an infant and the elaborate organisation of an adult personality as a *lawful continuity*."[117] Thus Melanie Klein, in the eyes of her critics, theoretically disinherits herself.

The objections to these papers thus make it clear that the emphasis on negativity operates not as a primordial, biological pre-given from which an orderly sequence ("an orderly series and correlations") can be derived, but as the subversion of sequence and biology alike. And Glover is explicit that this subversion is the direct consequence of the emphasis on phantasy in the work of Klein. It is at that moment of primitive hallucination when, she argues, the child misinterprets its experience "against the whole weight of the biological evidence of survival" that the instinct loses the "realistic aim" on which such a concept of orderly progression relies. And what, Glover asks, does this make of the infant if not "fantast" and "fool"?[118]

It seems to me that this is the problem which then works itself out inside the analytic institution and specifically in relation to the analysis of children. Let's note that the genesis of the persecutory object in Kleinian thinking casts a shadow over interpretation, since, according to the logic of negation, interpretation comes as a stranger from the outside. And let's note too that if Klein makes of the analyst a fool and a fantast, it is from this place that the analyst has to try to speak, bridging the gap, as Rivière puts it at the end of her introduction, between the baby ignorant of the external world and the scientist aware of nothing else. For the baby derives and imputes meanings which, because they do not relate to external or material reality, the scientific worker cannot appreciate. And the analyst can bridge the gap only insofar as "she can assume the baby's condition."[119] What is this, other than to require psychoanalysis to enter into what Kleinians seem to theorize, to the consternation of their critics, as an infinite regress? A place which Rivière assigns to those "gifted and intuitive mothers and women" who know that the child inhabits a world of psychic significance and who are "almost as inarticulate as babies themselves."[120] Leaving aside this extraordinary image of women's relationship to language in an introduction to a book in which only women in fact speak, the question has to be asked: what problems must it pose for an analytic school to situate itself in the place of an infant to whom interpretation is by definition unwelcome and who is fantast and fool?[121]

A point finally about the wider political resonance of this dispute. The discussions, as is well known, were staged at the height of the Second World War. The emphasis on negativity, the ambivalence about reparation (reparation as ambivalent), takes its reference from, even as it casts light on, the conflict going on all around. Ella Sharpe comments: "For a belief in the actual good object the actual bad one results in world affairs with a Hitler-ridden Germany and pipe-smoking optimists elsewhere who say 'God's in His Heaven, all's right with the world.'" And again: "The 'status quo' is a frequent phrase heard today. The full phrase is 'the status quo ante.' How many people still hope that the end of the war may mean a restoration of the pre-war conditions for which they are most homesick, although progressive minds on every hand warn us that restoration of old conditions could only lead to renewed disaster."[122] What clearer statement of the political provenance of theory? What clearer indication that, for this analyst at least, if psychoanalysis concentrates on the good and the restorative, it heads straight into a theoretical and political blind?

Mass Psychology

It is a commonplace assumption that psychoanalysis only deals with individuals. More, or worse—loyal to its origins in the social milieu and mind of its founder, Sigmund Freud—the only individuals it deals with are an unrepresentative minority of the respectable, bourgeois, and well-to-do. And yet, as Freud points out in the opening paragraph of *Mass Psychology and the Analysis of the "I,"* without the presence of others, there can be no mental life. "On close examination," he writes, "the antithesis between individual or mass psychology, which at first glance may seem to us very important, loses a great deal of its sharpness."[1] We only exist through the others who make up the storehouse of the mind: models in our first tentative steps towards identity, objects of our desires, helpers and foes. The mind is a palimpsest in which the traces of these figures will jostle and rearrange themselves for evermore. From the very earliest moment of our lives—since without the rudiments of contact, the infant will not survive—we are "peopled" by others. Our "psyche" is a social space.

With one, short, exception, all the texts discussed in this essay were written after the First World War, while the last one, *Moses the Man and Monotheistic Religion,* was composed while the clouds of the Second were gathering across Europe. In fact, you could argue that the whole of Freud's writing life was shadowed by the catastrophe biding its time, waiting in the wings, which will finally come to its cruel fruition with the outbreak of hostilities in September 1939, barely two weeks before he died. In 1897, two years after the first German publication of *Studies on Hysteria,* the Emperor of Austria, Franz Josef, reluctantly confirmed the anti-Semite Karl Lueger as mayor of Vienna (he had refused to do so no less than four times).[2] From that point on, no Jew in Austria could ignore the fact that the collective, or mass, identity of Europe was moving against the emancipatory tide. Enlightenment, the belief that a cool-headed reason could rule the world, was a dream, while the despised and dreaded unreason of the night would soon be marching on the streets. In a way this should have been no surprise to Freud. Such inversions were the hallmark of his craft. Nonetheless there are moments where Freud appears to be struggling to catch up with his own insights. From *Mass Psychology* to *Moses the Man*, his last major work, all Freud's writings on collective life share a question. What drives people to hatred? Even in their dealings with those to whom they are closest, Freud muses, people seem to display a "readiness to hate," something "elemental" whose roots are "unknown."[3] As if Freud had made two utterly interdependent discoveries that also threaten to cancel or wipe each other out, taking the whole world with them. No man is an island: you are the others who you are. But the mind is also its own worst enemy; and there is no link between individuals, no collective identity, which does not lead to war.

In 1914, Freud had set out the basic terms of what has come to be known as his second "topography." A previous distinction between love and hunger, the drives of desire and those of self-preservation, between the other and the "I," breaks down when he alights upon the problem of narcissism, the subject's erotically charged relationship to her- or himself. If you can be your own object, the neat line between impulses directed towards the self and those tending towards the other starts to blur. But it is no coincidence that this discovery of subjects hoist on their own self-regard should bring him up so sharply against the question of how we connect to the others around us. How indeed? No longer is it the case that what we most yearn for in others is the satisfaction of our drives; what we are no less in search of, and passionately require, is to be recognised, acknowledged, seen. Freud is often wrongly taken to be interested only in the sexual drives (or, for the truly reductive version, only in "sex"), but that is half the story. If we need others, it is not so much to satisfy as *to fashion* ourselves. And in this struggle to conjure, and hold fast to our identities, there is no limit to what we are capable of. From the outset, identification is ruthless; we devour the others we wish to be: "Identification . . . behaves like a product of the first *oral* stage of libido organisation in which the coveted, treasured object was incorporated by eating and was annihilated as such in the process."[4] Overturning his model of the mind in the face of war, Freud thus arrives at the problem of collective life. But he does so on the back of an analysis that has made such life, in anything other than a deadly form, all but impossible.

What is a mass? At first glance, Freud's answer to this question would seem to be contemptuous. " 'The people,' " he writes to his fiancée, Martha Bernays, in August 1883, "judge, think, hope and work in a manner utterly different from ourselves" (if the scare quotes indicate a caution about his own category, they also suggest his distaste). In a letter to her sister two years before he had described them as a "different species," "uncanny," knowing the meaning of neither "fear nor shame." And yet even here there is a subtext. Anti-Semitism gives a different historical substance and context to what might otherwise appear as no more than a familiar and conservative revulsion against the mob. As a Jew, Freud knows what it is like to be the target of collective hate. In an altercation about an open window during a train journey to Leipzig in the same year, someone in the background shouts out: "He's a dirty Jew!" "With this," he writes to Martha in December, "the whole situation took on a different colour. . . . Even a year ago I would have been speechless with agitation, but now I am different. I was not in the least frightened of that mob." They were just a group of travelers sharing a train compartment. But, under the pressure of race hatred, the voice of one turns into a "mob."[5]

Even when Freud's remarks cannot be softened by such historical allusions, his revulsion seems to be at odds with a far more compassionate, politically nuanced, critique. As he continues his letter of August, it becomes clear that the "people" are "utterly different," not due to some inherent failing in their nature, but because they are so beset. The "poor people," who become just "*the poor*," are "too helpless, too exposed, to behave like us"; in their "lack of moderation" they are compensating for being "a helpless target for all the taxes, epidemics, sicknesses, and evils of social institutions." By 1921, when *Mass Psychology* appears, the "people" have become the "masses." Certainly the shift of vocabulary might suggest that any traces of empathy have been lost. The masses are gullible, suggestible, out of touch with reality, blind. Although Freud rejects Gustave Le Bon's idea of a specific herd-instinct, he accepts most of his characterisation of a mass as at once all-powerful and a mere straw swaying in the wind. Gathered-together individuals become both too heavy (the mass comes into being as *critical mass*) and too light; threatening—"ready, in its awareness of its own strength, to be dragged into all sorts of atrocities such as might be expected only from an absolute, irresponsible power"—and prone: "It wants to be dominated and suppressed and to fear its master."[6] Freud acknowledges that masses are capable of "great feats of renunciation in the service of an ideal"; they can rise as well as sink.[7] But, whether lofty or base, people en masse are only inspired to an *extreme*. Averse to innovation, conservative; always—since time immemorial—the same.

Above all, the mass, lacking all inhibition, exposes the unconscious of us all: "The unconscious foundation that is the same for everyone is exposed."[8] Like the pervert and the hysteric, the mass, from which the bourgeoisie no less fiercely like to distinguish themselves, is showing us something that we all need to see (the mass is also contagious, which means that none of us is immune). Ugly, the mass lifts the veil of the night, releasing humans from cultural constraint—in the mass, man is allowed to do what no individual would dare. At moments, it is as if the mass *becomes* the unconscious— without logic, knowing "neither doubt nor uncertainty," living a type of collective dream. Freud may be repelled; he may be frightened (despite the bravura of his letter to his fiancée in 1883). But he has also made man in the mass the repository of a universal truth: that human subjects suffer under the weight of repressive cultural imperatives that force them against their nature. By the time he writes *The Future of an Illusion*, in 1927, that early insight into the poor as the bearers of the worst "evils" of social institutions has become even more political and precise:

> If a culture has not got beyond the point where the satisfaction of some participants requires the oppression of others, maybe the majority (and this is the case with all contemporary cultures), then, understandably, the oppressed will develop a deep hostility towards a culture that their labour makes possible but in whose commodities they have too small a share.

"It goes without saying," he concludes, "that a culture that fails to satisfy so many participants, driving them to rebellion, has no chance of lasting for any length of time, nor does it deserve one."[9]

Although Freud calls his text "Mass Psychology" (from the German "*die Massen*"), the core of his work centres on two great social institutions, the army and the church, and two intensely intimate conditions—being in love and hypnosis, in which, to use his own formula, we are dealing with "if the expression will be permitted" a "mass of two."[10] Faced with such moments of awkwardness, most translations prior to Jim Underwood's for the new Penguin Freud, notably Strachey's *Standard Edition*, have chosen to translate "mass" as "group," giving us a "group of two members," which no doubt causes less of a conceptual stir. But it is not for nothing that Freud, having first charted his path through the most threatening aspect of behaviour in the mass, lands us in the middle of two of society's most prized and refined collectivities, and at least one of its most cherished states of mind. In our normal run of thinking, there are "groups" and there are "masses"—the first of which it is assumed, unlike the second, always keeps its head in bad times. In fact we could say that it is the role of church and army, great policing institutions both, to channel the one into the other, to offer—against any menace in the wider world—the sanctuary of the group. In an ideal world, so this logic might go, there would be no masses, which however fiercely bound together, always seem unruly, as if threatening something loose. Freud's view is more radical, cutting through such precious distinctions. For all their gravitas and grace, church and army, in their very ability to generate unquestioning, sacred, loyalty, are microcosms of what they most fear. They seed what they are meant to contain.

It is central to Freud's thinking on this topic that what binds people together, for better and worse, is their commitment to an internal ideal. Because we are narcissists, we will only relinquish, or even circumscribe, our self-devotion for something or someone that we can put in the same place. Something that makes us feel good about ourselves. Something that tells us, even if we are a multitude, that somewhere, somehow we are also the only one. And that whatever we do—and this is the killer, so to speak—we are a cut and thrust above the rest. To be part of a group is to push everything hated to the outside (which is why for Freud, along with the more mundane, territorial reasons, nations go to war). Freud's originality, however, is to add to this insight the idea that rivalrous hostility towards the other is integral to the very formation of the group. I will suspend my hatred of the other, and bind my fate with his, if you—mentor, leader, father, God—recognize *me*. Clearly there is something amiss. How can rivalry be redeemed by the clamour for such exclusive attention? In one of his most trenchant, and clinically deceptive, formulas, Freud states: *"A primary mass is a number of individuals who have set one and the same object in the place of their 'I'-ideal and who have consequently identified with one another in terms of their 'I.'"*[11] That is what it means to become as "one." I will identify with you, but only on condition that the ideal you take for your own has become my internal psychic property. The group is an orchestrated flight into inner superiority, which everyone is then presumed to share. In a paradox Freud never succeeds in unravelling, hostility is suspended by narcissistic acclaim. But what this means is that when men—since it is most often men—band together to go to war, another state of war, barely refined, is most likely to be going with them.[12]

Two things, Freud insists, distinguish his account from the previous literature on which he so copiously draws (only chapter 1 of *The Interpretation of Dreams* can rival *Mass Psychology* for the lengths to which he goes to incorporate other theories on his topic): love relationships: "Let us remember that the existing literature makes no mention of them"; and the tie to the leader: "For reasons that are as yet unclear, we should like to attach particular value to a distinction that the existing literature tends to underrate, namely that between leaderless masses and masses with leaders"; again, only a few pages later: "We would already venture to level a mild reproach against the authors of the existing literature for having done less than justice to the importance of the leader as regards the psychology of the mass"; and even more forcefully towards the end: "The nature of the mass is incomprehensible if we ignore the leader."[13] "The essence of a mass," Freud writes, "consists in the libidinal attachments present within it."[14] Love, then, and devotion to the leader are what binds. If the mass is held together by some force, "to what force could such an achievement be better ascribed than to Eros, which holds the whole world together?"[15]

Leaving aside for a moment the fact that the world does not obviously "hold together," as Freud of course knows well, it is worth pausing here, and asking what Freud means by love. For psychoanalysis, as he explains, "love" has a very wide range. It includes "self-love, parental and infant love, friendship, general love of humanity, and even dedication to concrete objects as well as to abstract ideas."[16] To deny the libidinal component of these attachments is only for the "feeble-hearted."[17] So, Freud concludes, "we shall try adopting the premise that love relationships (to use an inert expression: emotional ties) also form part of the essence of the mass mind."[18] It is on this basis that Freud takes us into the analysis of church and army. Love, it turns out, follows the path of identification when the loved object, requiring like a leader total surrender, *usurps* the place of the "I" (all roads, it seems, lead back to the "I"). So what are these love relationships or emotional ties which bind subjects en masse? They are precisely the experience of *being loved*; or to put it in more clichéd terms, not what I give to you, but what you give, or do for, me. To ignore the role of the leader, Freud writes, is not just a theoretical shortcoming but a practical risk. Under cover of a leader's love or benevolent knowing, even the world at its most perilous feels safe. Thus, he argues, it was not the realities of the battlefield, but ill-treatment by their superiors, that caused the breakdown of Prussian soldiers during the Great War.

And yet Freud is aware that this love of the leader is a precarious gift. Barely concealed behind any leader is the father who was hated as much as he was revered. In *Mass Psychology*, Freud slowly moves back to the theory first advanced in *Totem and Taboo*, in 1913: that society originally came into being on the back of a primordial crime. The brothers banded together to murder the father who controlled all the women of the tribe. Once the deed was done, only guilt, plus the dawning recognition of the danger each brother now represented to the other, caused them to bind together and lay down their arms. Whether you accept the historical account or not—and there are no historical grounds to do so—Freud's myth, as always, is eloquent. Trying to explain how love averts hatred, his intellectual trajectory here, the very movement of his text and of his argument, takes a strikingly different path (regressive as he would say of the mass mind), as slowly but surely, he moves away from mutuality to murder. How solid can any group identification possibly be if the leader we love and who loves us all as equals is also, deep in the unconscious, the tyrant who must be killed? It would seem that the mass is only held together, like those first brothers, because it is aghast at its own history, its own actual and potential deeds. A mass freezes into place at its own dread. At the heart of Freud's analysis of the mass entity is a self-canceling proposition. We love the other most, or need most to be loved by the other, when—from that other and from ourselves—we have most to fear. It is a "miracle," Freud writes, that the individual is willing to "surrender his 'I'-ideal, exchanging it for the mass ideal embodied in the leader."[19] A miracle like love, one might say; or like the belief that love conquers all.

It is almost too easy to see in Freud's portrait of the leader the outlines of his own personal drama as the founder of psychoanalysis. More simply, to see him as issuing a demand: Love me. Ever since the split with Jung, in 1914, the year after he wrote *Totem and Taboo*, Freud had reason to fear that the love his followers bore him was laced with a hostility that could threaten his movement. What if his group, instead of being a free association of like-minded individuals, were one of those "artificial masses," like church and army, in need of "a certain external compulsion . . . to prevent them from falling apart"?[20] The only thing preventing a mass from behaving like an "ill-mannered child," "impassioned, unsupervised savage," or worse, like a "pack of wild animals" is the agreed conditions laid down for it to function.[21] When Freud draws on W. McDougall's *The Group Mind* to lay out these requirements—a measure of continuity, a specific conception of the group's "nature, function, attainments and aspirations," contact with related but differing collective entities, traditions, customs, and institutions particularly such as bear on the relationship of its members with one another, a careful grading and differentiation of functions—it reads at least partly as a countdown against bedlam, his own wish to bind the chaos he might himself have unleashed.[22] As if he were describing a model for a psychoanalytic institution that would be a cross between a secret society and a bureaucratic machine. In *Mass Psychology*, we can see Freud already struggling with a dilemma that psychoanalysis as an institution has not solved to this day, even while it is the one institution that recognized that dilemma as foundational to what any subject, any institution, might be. How to aim for perfected organized continuity given the cruel ambivalence lurking within our most cherished forms of allegiance?

In his 1907 paper "Compulsive Actions and Religious Practices," Freud suggests that religious ceremony shares its nature with compulsive or obsessional neurosis, in which subjects ritually perform actions designed to ward off the intolerable burden of a guilt-ridden mind. Condemned to the endless repetition of meaningless gestures, lacking the symbolic weight of the sacred, the compulsive neurotic, with his "half-funny," "half-sad" distortion of a private religion, is a clown.[23] Or perhaps a parodist, who mocks the petty rituals that in the modern day and age are thrusting the deeper content and meaning of religious faith to one side (one objection of enlightenment, *Haskalah* Jewry to the Orthodox in Freud's time was that they were burying the spirit of Judaism under a tide of observational constraints).[24] If religion apes neurosis, being part of a religious collective also assuages the mind. "Even one who does not regret the disappearance of religious illusions in today's cultural climate," Freud concludes *Mass Psychology*, "will concede that, while they still held sway, they afforded those in thrall to them their strongest protection against the threat of neurosis."[25] Mass formation, and none so powerfully as religious mass formation, is therefore one of the most effective systems a culture creates to keep its subjects sane. It does this by deluding them with the false consolations of belief, but above all by allowing them to repeat, in the daily actions required of them as testament to that belief, the behaviour of a subject who knows he has a great deal to atone for. It keeps them sane but only by mimicking, and thence preserving, the very form of neurotic obsession. "One might venture to construe" neurosis as "individual religiousness," Freud writes in the 1907 paper, and religion as a "universal compulsive neurosis."[26] The neurotic—this is from the last pages of *Mass Psychology*—creates his own "fantasy world, religion and system of delusion," but in so doing he is merely "echoing the institutions of humanity in a distorted form."[27] Once again, man's most revered institutions hold at the heart of their being the forms of disturbance from which they are intended to protect mankind.

In the move from *Mass Psychology* to *The Future of an Illusion* and *Moses the Man*, the question of faith gradually usurps that of mass formation only to

rejoin, slowly but surely, the man in the crowd. To the end of his life, Freud
was convinced that his view of faith as deluded, worse as a reaction formation
akin to a neurotic disorder, was the view that set him most at odds with the
surrounding culture. Translations prior to that of Jim Underwood have lost
the link between religion as *compulsion* (as in *Zwangsneurose*) and Freud's
later death drive or repetition compulsion (*Wiederholungszwang*), a link that
drives religious sensibility firmly towards the demonic. Less repellent than
sexuality, less radically disorienting than the idea of the unconscious, such a
vision of religious belief nonetheless threatened to breach the most strongly
fortified symbolic ramparts of Heimliche man. Even when he was writing
Moses the Man across the Anschluss of Austria and his exile to London in 1938,
Freud persisted in thinking that his critique of religion placed him at risk. He
was a target of persecution first as disbeliever, only then as Jew: "I should now
be persecuted not only for the way I think but on account of my 'race.' "[28]
"The only person this publication may harm," he writes at a particularly
defensive moment in *The Future of an Illusion*, "is myself."[29]

In many ways, Freud's critique of religion, laid out most ruthlessly in *The
Future of an Illusion*, appears as something of a footnote to his view of the
mass. After all, in *Mass Psychology*, the masses discard reality in favour of
"affectively charged wishful feelings"; they never "thirst after truth"; they
"demand illusions."[30] Although *The Future of an Illusion* is also the text in
which Freud most loudly acknowledges their oppression, from its opening
section, the masses appear as the concentrate of their worst attributes (le-
thargic, unreasonable, unpersuadable, incapable of restraint). For anyone
wanting to limit the damage, Freud's response to the acrimony unleashed by
The Future of an Illusion in *Civilisation and Its Discontents* two years later only
makes matters worse. "The whole thing is so patently infantile, so incongruous with reality, that to one whose attitude to humanity is friendly, it is
painful to think that the great majority of mortals will never be able to rise
above this view of life."[31] This does not sound friendly. Galled, humiliated ("it
is even more humiliating")—Freud loses patience like an irascible father trying to correct the homework of his child. Unless they happen to be the child
whose tale he recounts in *The Future of an Illusion*, precociously distinguished
by his love of "objectivity," who, when told that a fairy story was not true—a
story to which other children had been listening "with rapt attention"—
"assumed a scornful expression and withdrew."[32] Who, we might ask, is most
to be pitied in this story—the boy trapped in his deadening "matter-of-
factness," or the other children, whose reverie he will presumably have torn

apart with his contempt? For Freud, engaging with the opponent he conjures for the sake of argument throughout *The Future of an Illusion*, this anecdote is meant to be decisive. Like the child, humanity will stop believing when it grows up: "A turning away from religion must be expected to occur with the fateful inexorability of a growth process" (note how that "fateful" places our cool emancipation from faith in the lap of the gods).[33] Nothing in the twenty-first century to date suggests this is the case.

The Future of an Illusion is a diatribe. In many ways it is also, I would suggest, Freud's most un-Freudian text, and one which will return to haunt him in the final years of his life. Religion infantilises the people, consoles them for the inconsolable, suppresses their wholly legitimate and unanswerable fears. The world is brutish and nature does not care. When we most think to have controlled her, she strikes ("coldly, cruelly, without a qualm").[34] The elements mock our restraint, the earth heaves and splits open, waters drown, storms blow everything away. This is Freud in imitation of Lear. Add the contingency of human diseases, the random inevitability of our own deaths, and we have every reason to despair: "There remains an uncomfortable suspicion that the bewilderment and helplessness of the human race is beyond remedy."[35] To add insult to injury, we heap suffering upon each other: "Passions rage in the elements as they do in the human heart."[36] Enter religion, which tells us that none of this—in the final, cosmic, order of things—matters. We are protected by a benevolent God who redeems our helplessness even when we are unaware (although believing in Him of course helps). Most simply, we are watched over. Someone is looking. The values of our ideals are, Freud repeats here from *Mass Psychology*, narcissistic in nature. Even more than our saviour, God is our spectator. The citizens of America, which proclaims itself "God's own country," share with the Jewish people, although Freud coyly does not name them here, the belief that God has made their nation his own: "And for one of the forms in which humans worship the deity that is indeed true."[37] How deep must be the narcissistic wound of humanity, if the only way to redeem it is to feel yourself swelling to the measure of the heavens?

The Future of an Illusion offers Freud's most passionate defence of the order of reason. There is, he insists, no "higher authority."[38] *Vernunft* in German, which means reason or even more prosaically "good, common, sense," has none of the ambiguous flexibility of *Geistigkeit*, central to *Moses the Man*, which hovers between "intellectuality," but with none of the negative connotations of aridity attaching to it in the English, and "spirituality," as an

internal quality with no specifically religious meaning (a term therefore eloquently suspended between heart and brain). "Reason," on the other hand,
brooks no argument (as in "it stands to reason"). Freud is pitting "reason"
against "illusion," pitting, at its crudest, the educated elite against the mass—a
"split," as his opponent in the text argues, between the "philosophical thinker"
and the "uneducated mass."[39] Once again Freud's view of the people en masse
is uncharitable. As Freud describes them, the arguments for religious belief
are self-defeating, "oddly out of harmony with one another": our forefathers
believed them; we possess proof from distant times; no justification of belief is
permitted or required.[40] But, according to Freud's own analysis, this is the
logic of the unconscious or what he defines in a famous passage in *The
Interpretation of Dreams* as "kettle logic," the logic of a man defending himself
against his neighbour's charge that he has returned his kettle in a damaged
state: I never borrowed it; it doesn't have a hole; the hole was there when you
lent it to me. Freud therefore knows that the illogic of this form of reasoning is
a sign that a particularly deep vein of psychic investment *(Besetzung)* has been
tapped. Strachey translated *Besetzung* as *cathexis*, the Latin inappropriate, the
technicality off-putting for a term meant to indicate our most heartfelt and
obdurate attachment both to others and to parts of ourselves. Underwood's
more recent version offers instead "charging," as in an electrical current, which
is far closer to the urgency of Freud. Of all people, Freud should know better
than to think that you can walk into this part of the mind and try to *reason
with it*. No one enters here without being burnt.

Freud allows his fictional opponent to articulate many of these criticisms
(this is the only text, apart from his 1926 *The Question of Lay Analysis*, in which
Freud personifies one half of the argument he is almost always having with
himself). But he does so only the more stubbornly to argue him to the
ground. Freud believes not only that religious belief is deluded and infantile,
but also that it deprives human subjects of freedom (it is the ultimate form of
surrender). Because religion ultimately fails to console humans for death, so it
shifts increasingly and inexorably into the domain of human affairs, arrogating
to itself the ethical life, whose precepts are meant to keep subjects in their
place. It is therefore a way of subduing their legitimate internal revolt against
the constraints and injustices of culture, on which Freud was so articulate
from the time of the First World War. At moments, Freud's defence of his
position reads like Bertolt Brecht's Galileo, whose discoveries, as the Church
well knew, were a threat as much to secular as religious authority. "Truth,"
states Galileo in Brecht's play, "is the child of time, not of authority"; "I believe

in the gentle power of reason, of common sense over men."[41] Compare Freud: "The voice of the intellect is a low one, yet it does not cease until it has gained a hearing"[42] (Freud compared himself directly with Copernicus, as well as with Darwin, for dethroning man from the center of all things).

What Freud desires most fervently in this work is that man should generate his ethical precepts out of himself, that he should "leave God out of it entirely," and "frankly concede the purely human origin of all cultural institutions and rules."[43] He does not therefore want the constraint of culture abolished. Unlike some of his later followers, such as Herbert Marcuse and Wilhelm Reich, he was no libertarian; indeed he believed that religion was failing to make man moral, was not taming the "anti-social drives" *enough*. If man knew himself to be the source of his own authority, he would not seek to overturn the precepts of culture; he would try to *improve* them. Presumably— if we recall Freud's statement that a culture based on flagrant inequality does not deserve to survive—he would make them more just. Freud's biographer Ernest Jones is convinced that Freud's positive interest in religion, which the reader would be forgiven for not picking up here, stemmed not from theological concerns but from "the ethical teaching," particularly "on the theme of justice."[44] "By withdrawing his expectations from the Beyond and concentrating all the forces thus released on earthly existence," Freud concludes near the end of his text, "he will doubtless manage to make life bearable for all and ensure that culture quite ceases to oppress."[45] In this he anticipates many of today's critics of fundamentalism. A secular polity would make the world a better place.

And yet there remains something unpersuasive about this text. By the time Freud wrote it, he had become convinced that religion preserved deep inside its unconscious archive a forgotten or repressed historical truth. God is the direct descendant of the primal father; that is why, in our petitions to the deity, our dreadful helplessness is our strongest suit. By reiterating here his belief in a primary parricide at the origins of all culture, Freud is allowing therefore that religion is a form of reminiscence, and that this historical reality is what endows it with much of its powers. And yet he sweeps past this recognition with remarkable haste. Not to say panic. Of course "acknowledging the historical value of certain religious teachings increases our respect for them," but that, he insists, in no way invalidates the desire to do away with them. "Quite the contrary!" It is "thanks to these historic residues" that the analogy between religion and neurosis can be made; as with the neurotic patient it is time to replace repression with "ratiocination." In any case, "we need make no apology" for departing from "historical truth" in providing a rational motivation for culture as this truth is so distorted as to be unrecognized by the mass of humanity.[46] This is indeed kettle logic and to see it you do not have to accept Freud's view of primary murder at the origins of mankind: there is a truth in religion; it is so distorted the masses cannot see it anyway; reason is more important than historical truth.

As with *Mass Psychology*, it is as if murder returns to haunt the barely acquired, fragile, rational civility of the tribe. Freud does not know where to put this murder, because he loves his new theory and in *Moses the Man* he will place it at the very core of the Jewish tradition and faith; indeed murder will become what most intensely ties the Jewish people to their law. The question, as Freud knows only too well, is not whether religion is true but why it has the power to bind its adherents (a fact to which he will ascribe the Jew's ability to survive). What matters, we might say, is not reason and reality, but—to refer again to *Mass Psychology*—the force of human identifications, whether lethal or redemptive (indeed often both). Or, going back to the very beginning of Freud's work, people—and the force of this later writing is to show how that includes "peoples"—invent themselves out of their memories; what counts is not the accuracy, but the productivity, not the strictness, but the movement, of the meanings we make. Near the end of *The Future of an Illusion*, Freud agrees that reason can do nothing when religion proclaims a "superior spiritual essence whose properties are indeterminable and whose purposes are unknowable."[47] The German here is *"geistigen Wesens"*; a term untranslatable into English as we have already seen, meaning spirituality or intellectuality or both. In the end, Freud leaves us with the glowing residue of his own conviction—something that cannot be fully determined, grasped or known (like the unconscious we might say). What if religion were determined by tradition, memory, murderousness, by indefinable qualities of being and of the mind? What if—as one of the twentieth century's most famous godless Jews was perhaps best placed to discover—this, or at least some of this, is what it means to belong?[48]

On 6 May 1926, an address by Freud was read to the Vienna lodge of B'nai Brith (Sons of the Covenant), an order representing Jewish cultural, intellectual and charitable interests originally founded in the United States, to which Freud, outcast as he had felt himself to be in the beginning, had addressed many of his early papers. "Whenever I felt an inclination to national enthusiasm," he states, "I strove to suppress it as being harmful and wrong, alarmed by the warning examples of the peoples among whom we Jews had lived." "But," he continues, "plenty of other things remained over to make the attraction of Jews and Jewry irresistible—many obscure emotional forces all the more powerful the less they could be expressed in words, as well as a clear consciousness of an inner identity, the intimate familiarity of the same psychic construction" ("die Heimlichkeit der gleichen seelischen Konstruction," translated by Reik as "the secrets of the same inner construction").[49] This identity, which Freud here as elsewhere scrupulously detaches from national passion, was not simple; and, even though he will refer to it on occasion as an essence, in many ways as we shall see it was not "clear." It was after all the whole burden of his 1919 paper on the uncanny—"Das Unheimliche"—that what is *heimlich* or "homely/familiar," the term he uses here, is intimately, not to say eerily, related to its opposite. Nonetheless, what Freud is describing is undoubtedly a sense of belonging. Crucially, that sense stems from those same dark, obscure "emotional forces" ("all the more powerful the less they could be expressed in words") that Freud will turn on so ruthlessly in *The Future of an Illusion* the following year.

In "A Religious Experience," written in the same year as *The Future of an Illusion*, Freud tells the story of a young American physician who first discards all religious belief and then is promptly reconverted by an inner command, after witnessing the corpse of an old woman laid out on the dissecting table. Freud, in one of his most reductive moments, traces the conversion to deferred obedience to the man's Christian father, against whom the young man, appalled by the sight of the "sweet-faced old woman" (for which read the mother), had momentarily but violently rebelled. And yet he knows that the very simplicity of his own analysis—"so simple, so transparent"—deceives: "One cannot avoid asking whether . . . anything at all has been gained as regards the psychology of religious conversion."[50] What, to repeat his own question in *The Future of an Illusion*, are the obscure emotional forces— "whose properties are undeterminable and whose purposes are unknowable" —on which religious affiliation relies?[51] Or in the words of *Moses the Man*: "From what springs do some ideas, particularly religious ideas, draw the strength to subjugate individuals and nations alike?"[52] In the final years of his life, under the threat of impending exile, *Moses the Man* erupts as the unfinished business of *The Future of an Illusion*, as the return of its repressed. "We find to our surprise," Freud writes in the first Viennese foreword to the last essay of *Moses* (the second was written in England), "that progress has forged an alliance with barbarism."[53] Freud knew he had not answered the question of his earlier work; something, in his words, "remained over." But it was another ten years, in the last major work of his life, before he offered his final unexpected reply.

If *Moses the Man* returns Freud to the question of religion, it also returns him to that of mass psychology. The Jewish people become the testing ground of how viable it is to insert the notion of the unconscious into collective life. Much will hang on this, but if anything Freud is now more cautious: "It was not easy, I admit, bringing the concept of the unconscious into mass psychology"; and increasingly unsure as he proceeds: "We do not find it easy to transfer the concepts of individual psychology to mass psychology."[54] By 1938, this "mass" has become as much a national, as a religious, entity; at issue now is the strength of religion to subjugate "individuals *and nations* alike."[55] Religion, Freud more or less states, forges nations. Nationhood is, or can be, a religious passion. Freud may have wanted to believe that religious beliefs would go away; but instead he seems to be issuing a rather different warning —against the power of national identities, as everything in more recent times confirms, to endow themselves with the aura of the sacred.

Faced with the rise of Nazism and the growing prospect of invasion and exile—although until February 1938 he persisted in thinking that the Anschluss could be averted—Freud found himself up against nationalism in two of its most radically disconcerting shapes. Both can be felt pressing on his study of Moses. On the one hand, a ruthless and expansive German nationalism, its masses in thrall to their leader (Nazism as hypnotic collectivity in its purest, most deadly guise); on the other, the nationalism of a dispossessed people, arising at least partly in response to the excesses of the first, but whose history and inner identity offers—or at least this is Freud's hope and claim here—the possibility of another, more nuanced, form of belonging. Freud does not mention Hitler in this work; he could hardly do so of course as long as he remained in Austria, where the bulk of the work was written. But it is, surely, impossible not to see the German leader, traced in a type of grotesque reflection, behind the man held—as Freud puts it in his opening lines—to be the "greatest son" of the Jewish people. Remember too that Freud up to now has offered no portrait of the leader; in *Mass Psychology*, there was no sign of the figure on whom, as he repeatedly insisted, his whole analysis relied.

In his address to B'nai Brith, Freud spoke of "national enthusiasm" as "being harmful and wrong, alarmed by the warning examples of the peoples among whom we Jews had lived." Jewish national belonging must be different. In his famous letter of 1930, after the Arab riots in Palestine, he refused an appeal from Dr Chaim Koffler of the Jewish Agency to add his voice to those of prominent European intellectuals calling for a reversal of British policy on access to the Wailing Wall and on Jewish immigration to Palestine. Writing to Ferenczi in 1922, Freud had spoken of "strange secret yearnings in me— perhaps from my ancestral heritage—for the East and the Mediterranean"; but these yearnings aroused his own suspicion, and when Arnold Zweig returned from a visit to Palestine in 1932, he described it as this "tragically mad land" that has "never produced anything but religions, sacred frenzies, presumptuous attempts to overcome the outer world of appearance by the inner world of wishful thinking."[56]

Yet despite this anxious recognition and recoil (in which we can recognize a barely concealed orientalist revulsion towards the East), in his letter to the Jewish Agency, Freud does not rule out the creation of "a Jewish homeland." By 1935, he describes the World Zionist Organisation as "a great and blessed" instrument in its endeavour "to establish a new home in the ancient land of our fathers."[57] By then what is at issue for Freud, and not only for Freud, is "our invincible will to survive."[58] In *Moses the Man*, Freud attempts the almost impossible task of squaring the circle of this tragic historical moment. Can there be a form of survival for a people that does not fatally—fatally, that is, for itself and for the others against whom it stakes its claim to existence— entrench and sanctify itself? Freud does not seem to believe for a minute, as he does for religious faith, that "national enthusiasm" can be reasoned away. What is the likely fate of a longing that you can only, in his words, "suppress"?

It may seem odd to suggest that the thesis of *Moses the Man and Monotheistic Religion* is simple; after all the book is, as Yosef Yerushalmi describes it in his magisterial reading—*Freud's Moses: Judaism Terminable and Interminable*— possibly the most opaque of Freud's works.[59] It was published piecemeal and with anxiety, the first two parts in *Imago*, the third with two "mutually contradictory" prefaces—the first of which stating that it will never be published— while the complete text was not published until after he died.[60] The work is repetitive and uneven, bearing all the signs of a hesitation only partly explicable by the length of time it took him to write it and the unique historical conditions under which it was composed ("internal misgivings coupled with external constraints").[61] Freud was never at ease with it: "I miss the sense of oneness and solidarity that ought to exist between the author and his book"; he could see how it might appear as "a cast-iron figure resting on feet of clay";

or "a dancer balanced on the tip of a single toe."[62] To read Freud's *Moses*, writes Lydia Flem, "is to read Freud writing *Moses*."[63] It is in *Moses the Man* that Freud famously describes historical writing, on which he is himself at least partly engaged here, as a corrupt and murderous craft: "The corruption of a text is not unlike a murder. The problem lies not in doing the deed but in removing the traces."[64] By the time Freud arrived in England, the work was haunting him "like an unlaid ghost."[65] Accompanying him on his last journey, *Moses the Man* is, we could say, Freud's phantom limb (the hysteric of his earliest work returns at the end of his life). In the words of the Russian Formalist Viktor Shklovsky, this is writing as "*attenuated tortuous speech*," whose point, as he puts it in words remarkably resonant of psychoanalysis, is to "examine the object, *to dismember it*, to represent it not only as they [the artists] saw it, *but as they knew it*."[66]

And yet, despite this oddness ("unorthodoxy" or "eccentricity" in the words of Strachey), it is one of Freud's most fiercely determined texts. Freud believes that Moses was an Egyptian, a prince, priest, or high official belonging to the ancient monotheistic cult of Aton that was swept away with the death of its founder, the Pharaoh Amenthopis or Akhenaten, in 1358 B.C. Whereupon, Moses seized a semitic tribe, slaves of Egypt, as his people and led them to freedom in Canaan on condition that they adopt the religion to which his own people had proved so pitifully inadequate. The people rebel against Moses and murder him (not this time because he owned all the women, but because of the dreadful severity of his law). From that point onwards, monotheism and the crime fade in the life of the nation until, generations later, they meet up with a second Moses, son of the Midianite priest Jethro, who belongs to the cult of the volcanic god Yahweh, to which—in an act of partial historical remembrance and atonement—the religion of the first tribe is slowly but surely assimilated.

Freud takes his thesis of the murder of the first Moses from a then famous work by Sellin, published in 1922 (when Freud was told that he had later recanted, he famously replied that Sellin was mistaken and should have stuck to his original idea). He takes the account of the second Midianite priest from the historian Eduard Meyer, and several of his contemporaries who argued that the Jewish tribes "from which the people of Israel eventually emerged" took on a new religion at a certain point in time, not at Sinai, as the Bible has it, but in the locality of Meribah-Kadesh in a stretch of country south of Palestine.[67] Freud's crucial move—in a theoretical gesture that mimes the story he tells—is to *merge* them. Barely concealed behind the unity of the

Jewish people, inside its most intimate, *heimlich*, "inner identity" is an un-canny, *unheimlich*, doubling (for Freud doubling is one of the most effective vehicles of the uncanny). Nothing simply belongs. Once again the issue is not the—much contested and indeed dubious—accuracy of his narrative, but its effects. Like a compulsion, Freud's account and his history repeat themselves: "constant repetitions and recapitulations" to use Strachey's terms.[68] What does it mean to insist, as Freud does here, that a people were founded, their divine election established, not in one unanswerable moment of recognition between the people and their God, not once, but twice? Freud was not alone in pointing to this duality in Jewish history, but he adds and embroiders, making it the driving force of the people. *Moses the Man*—the original title only recently restored in Underwood's translation—is therefore something of a misnomer. What type of historical novel was Freud envisaging that cuts its hero into two?

> Putting our conclusion in the shortest possible form of words, to the familiar dualisms of that history (*two* peoples coming together to form the nation, *two* kingdoms into which that nation divides, *two* names for god in the source writings of the Bible) we add two new ones: *two* religious inaugurations, the first forced out by the second but later emerging behind it and coming victoriously to the fore, *two* religious inaugurators, both of whom went by the same name Moses.[69]

It is, as Freud was only too aware, an embarrassment of riches that is also the cruelest act of dispossession.[70] Imagine a child from a broken home with a father and a stepfather, stating in all innocence, as pure matter of fact: "I do not have one" (meaning "I do not have *one* father, but *two*"). Freud is sowing dissension in the tribe. He does not want his people unified. Or if he does, he wants them unified differently. Not singular, created once in an act of divinely sanctioned recognition, which henceforth will brook no argument, but torn internally by the fragments of a complex, multiple past.

Above all, he wants the Jewish people, and through them all people, to imagine the unimaginable—to contemplate the possibility that the most binding social ties are forged through an act of violence. "All these distinc-tions," Freud writes, "are inevitable consequences of the first, namely that one component of the people had been through what has to be defined as a traumatic experience that the other had been spared."[71] Trauma therefore first splits, and then forms, *fuses* the group. What binds people to their leader is that they killed him, although remembering the deed takes time. When

Yerushalmi criticises Freud for suggesting that the Jews repressed this memory, given that "the most singular aspect of Jewish tradition [is] its almost maddening refusal to conceal the misdeeds of the Jews," he is, however, missing the psychoanalytic point.[72] It is the characteristic of any compulsion (*Zwang*) that you endlessly berate yourself, that you atone, with unflagging and elaborate ceremonial, for everything apart from the one thing you most fear you might have done. For Freud, the subsequent emergence of Christianity, in which the son lays down his life for humanity, should be read as the next verse of this epic of denial and atonement (it must have been a dead father if only the death of a son can redeem it; and if a voluntary death is the penance, then murder must have been the original crime).

But if this narrative has a logic, one which we by no means have to accept at every turn, Freud's boldest move is to place at the heart of the group what it would most like to dispose of. The original, lost, faith returns to the group, slowly and tentatively, after a first ruthless rejection. Only after the encounter with the second Midianite priest does monotheism become the defining feature of religious belief. Right at the heart of the best, most fervently held conviction, Freud places doubt (we believe because we are not sure). Right at the centre of group adherence, he places killing. In "The Disillusionment of the War," he had stated that we had not "sunk so low as we had feared" because we had "never risen as high as we believed."[73] Now he spells it out. We are all killers or capable of being so, if only unconsciously. This is not, however, the soft insight that it might first appear to be, as in: we are all murderers at heart. By binding this insight into group life, Freud drives a stake through collective self-idealisation. As if he were asking nations to consider a very different, less glorious, form of reckoning with themselves. To be a member of a group is to be a partner in crime. You are guilty by association.

As the new millennium already bears witness, war is almost invariably justified in terms of an outside danger or threat: the other is the aggressor; it is only in order to survive that you kill. Freud offers a counter-history. He takes slaying, at which subjects en masse excel, and hands it back to the people. Even the most innocent of people (and for Freud there are no pure innocents) believe somewhere that they are also culprits. What effect might it have on modern-day rhetoric against terrorism, or on its accompanying refrain of good versus evil, if it were acknowledged that what binds a people together, what drives a nation self-righteously across the globe, are the unspoken crimes and failings of its own past?

Moses's Egyptian provenance is central to this narrative, not just because it announces and crowns the losses and dislocations to come (in the opening line Freud acknowledges that he is denying, robbing, depriving the Jewish people of their founder, or, as he puts it, "their greatest son"—the German *abzusprechen* means more literally to "take back the saying of").[74] But because, as Edward Said stresses in his vital rereading of the work for Israel/Palestine at the present time, it inscribes the Jewish people in a non-European heritage, "carefully opening out Jewish identity towards its non-Jewish background" (while also attesting, as the Egyptologist Jan Assman puts it in his 1997 study, *Moses the Egyptian*, to the fundamental importance of Egypt in the history of mankind).[75] This is a plea for a model for nationhood that would not just accept the other in its midst, nor just see itself *as other*, but that grants to that selfsame other, against which national and political identities define themselves, a founding, generic status at the origins of the group. Freud knows that this is a form of sacrilege as well as a huge risk, and not just to himself. After all, it was he who insisted in *Mass Psychology* that panic or breakdown in the mass is the result of loss of belief in the leader, not of legitimate fear even in the face of real danger. At the very moment when the Jewish people have most reason to fear, when they are faced with the rise of a leader who will set as his aim the destruction of the mass of European Jews, Freud removes their most ardently possessed figurehead at a stroke. Why, if not, surely, to suggest that it is time for groups to look for less rigid, potentially abject, forms of psychic and spiritual cohesion?

In fact it is possible to read *Moses the Man* as a critique of monotheism *tout court*. The gift that Moses bestows on his people is one that cannot be borne. This monotheism is "rigid," intolerant, expansive, and imperialist.[76] Claiming universality, it demands—in a gesture that has nothing to do with a critique of national identity—that "godhood give up its national confines."[77] As it gained in strength under Amenhotep, it achieved "ever-greater clarity, consistency, brusqueness."[78] The father-god it introduces is "boundlessly dominant," "jealous, strict and inexorable."[79] In a word, monotheism is awful (the U.S. policy of "shock and awe" in the 2003 invasion of Iraq could be said to take its cue from just such monolithic forms of psychic coercion). Monotheism ushers religious intolerance into the world. For Assman, it is a counter-theology because it renders idolatrous ancient polytheisms whose principle characteristic was that of being infinitely *translatable* into each other. Prior to monotheism, peoples worshipped different gods, but no one contested the existence of foreign gods or the legitimacy of foreign forms of worship. When monotheism cries false to strange gods, it shuts itself off and, with it, a whole galaxy of potential connections: "False gods cannot be translated."[80]

This was, as Assman calls it, the "Mosaic distinction," and "the most outspoken destroyer of the Mosaic distinction was a Jew: Sigmund Freud."[81] In the long tradition that made Moses Egyptian, either historically (Manetho, Strabo, Toland) or in affinity, initiated into "hieroglyphic wisdom and mysteries" (Spencer, Warburton, Reinhard and Schiller), it is always the rigid difference between monotheism and a more copious religious profusion that is stressed.[82] Jews were hated. Freud's stated objective in his work was, not as might have been expected, to understand anti-Semitism in the mind of the hater, but "how the Jew came to attract this undying hatred."[83] By making Moses an Egyptian, Freud liberates his people from the beginnings of their own theocracy. The founding moment of an oppressive law and intolerant faith fall outside Jewish jurisdiction. "Who," Freud asks in a footnote, "prompted the Jewish writer Heinrich Heine in the nineteenth century to complain about his religion as 'the plague we dragged along with us from the Nile Valley, the unhealthy ancient Egyptian faith'?"[84] Judaism, to use the expression of Martin Buber in his essay "The Two Centres of the Jewish Soul," "itself is not of the Law."[85] Freud is releasing Judaism from its own obduracy, its rigid orthodox strain. It is then perfectly possible to move from here back into the mystical counter-tradition inside Judaism itself. Writing to Jung in 1909, after a numerological discussion of the number 62, Freud states: "Here is another instance of the specifically Jewish character of my mysticism."[86] Kabbalah shares with psychoanalysis its belief in hermeneutics and the infinite permutations of words (Freud discusses the plurality of God's name in *Moses*). It also always contained an anarchic streak. Like the seventeenth-century mystical messiah Shabtai Svi, Freud can be seen as an iconoclast, leading his followers and his people, against the Law, into apostasy and freedom. (And in the *Zohar*, major document of the kabbalistic tradition, Moses is an Egyptian.)[87]

The Law will not strike. Thus Freud reads Michelangelo's "wonderful," "inscrutable" statue of Moses in San Pietro in Vincoli in Rome, as the prophet frozen in the moment before he breaks the tablets, restraining his anger, reining back his wrath as he descends from Mount Sinai to the spectacle of his backsliding people. He reads him, that is, as curtailing, even if only for a moment, the punishing component of his own God-given Law. There is no higher "mental achievement," Freud concludes, than such restraint (we can feel the strength of Freud's own efforts to control himself in the face of his increasingly dissident followers). Freud visited the statue, which must have played its part in his later study, whenever he was in Rome as a type of pilgrimage, creeping out of the "half-gloom" to "support the angry scorn of the hero's glance," "as though I myself belonged to the mob upon whom his eye is turned." He is therefore Moses *and* the people (split in two like the history of the Jews that he will much later recount). But it is surely note-worthy that the only moment in all his writing when Freud identifies himself with the mob, he does so as *idolater*.[88]

If this were all, then *Moses the Man* might become prime evidence in the case for Freud's rejection of his own Jewish legacy (the book was criticised by some as anti-Semitic). As critics like Marthe Robert who take this line have pointed out, Freud did on occasion refer to his Jewishness as the bearer of hereditary illness, or "taint."[89] But, if we read through the text again, it seems that Freud is far more equivocal than this. Monotheism, together with the violence of its earliest history, is not just "ruthless," "intolerant," "inexorable"; it is also the foundation of ethical life. If anything Freud makes even stronger in this last work the tie between guilt and justice: "the act of patricide with which social order, the moral law, and religion had first come into being."[90] Or in the words of Bluma Goldstein: "Violent acts can serve as a source not only of spirituality and intellectual achievement, but also of ethical codes for a just and virtuous life."[91] As we have seen, in Freud's account, the Jewish people become so forcefully a group because of the murder that first bound them together. Only an unconscious identification of this depth and virulence will work. Because they are always unconsciously atoning, so they are always watching and being watched to make sure that the treatment they mete out to others is fair. Freud famously claims in *The Future of an Illusion* that justice arises out of envy: if I cannot be privileged, no one must.

But if the Jews are a just people, it is also because the Egyptian Moses gave to them a god "as all-loving as he was all-powerful," who "held out for men, as their highest goal, a life lived in righteousness and truth."[92] (Akhenaten de-scribed himself in his inscriptions as "living in *ma'at*"—"truth, righteous-ness".)[93] "Is it not about time," asks the author of the article on anti-Semitism that Freud cites in his short piece, "A Comment on Anti-Semitism" of 1938, "we stopped tossing [the Jews] favours when they have a right to justice?"[94]

It does not matter, therefore, that the first Moses was slain; what was finest in his tradition survived and slowly but surely it usurped the law of the volcanic Yahweh who might appear, according to the more obvious sequence of events, to have replaced it. Amenhotep had been a pacifist. According to tradition, he rejected "in his ethics all hatred and all acts of violence," sublimating all aggression, in the words of Freud's contemporary, the psychoanalyst Karl Abraham, to an "unusually far-reaching degree," allowing his religion to languish because, out of touch with reality, he lived in the peaceful idyll of his own dreams (Abraham was one of Freud's inner circle but the article is strangely not referred to by Freud).[95] Yahweh was, on the other hand, a conqueror, "violent and bloodthirsty."[96] "For a people on the point of taking violent possession of fresh places to settle," Freud writes, "the god Yahweh was undoubtedly more suitable."

Now we can perhaps see more clearly the advantages, as well as the fully political import, of having two Moses. Not just to disrupt the crushing monolith of national identity, but also so that Judaism, saved from its most exacting features (and one might add any conquering ambitions), can still be the fount of wisdom in the world. "No one doubts," Freud states near the beginning of the final essay, that "it was only the idea of this other god that enabled the people of Israel to survive all the blows of fate and has kept it alive to this day."[97] Freud, we could say, takes the Jewish people's greatest son away with one hand, and gives him back with the other. The people, or rather the best of the people, survive. Freud's saga is a political narrative for our times. The Jewish people had two possible paths that they could take, and their history—in ways borne out so dramatically today—would be the struggle between them. In Freud's narrative, justice, not settlement, ethics, not land, enables the Jewish people to survive. But he hardly could have anticipated that this split between his two figures of Moses, between conquering settlement and a people living in justice, would have such an afterlife, that, ten years after he wrote his work, it would become the most disturbing and intractable legacy to the Jewish people of the founding, in 1948, of the Israeli nation-state. On 19 March 2004, Rabbis for Human Rights took out a full-page advertisement in Ha'aretz to express their support for their colleague Rabbi Arik Ascherman, on trial in Jerusalem for trying to prevent the demolition of two Palestinian homes: "Zion will only be redeemed through justice and those who return to her through acts of righteousness."[98] The first Moses, writes Freud, "held out for men, as their highest goal, a life lived in righteousness and truth."[99]

In *Moses the Man*, therefore, the question of faith is slowly but surely displaced by that of tradition: "In what form is effective tradition present in the life of peoples"?[100] (This is Yerushalmi's basic argument.) The point, then, is no longer to dissipate faith with a blast of reason, but to understand, even respect, the unconscious transmission of mass or group. To understand why people, from generation to generation—with no solid ground and in the teeth of the most historically unsympathetic conditions—*hold on* (the ties of the mass have shifted into the descent of a people). Individual and collective join at the seam of historical identities transmitted over time—the analogy between the two, Freud insists here, is "complete."[101] If not Judaism as Law, then Jewishness as tenuous but tenacious remembrance, in the unconscious memory traces of the people, passes down through the ages. Freud never stopped believing in the inheritance of acquired characteristics even when science had moved on to genetics, even while he acknowledges here that biology has rejected this belief. It is, we could say, through Jewishness or *for Jewishness* that Freud's Lamarckianism also survives—in his discussion of *Moses*, Ernest Jones describes it as the "weakest link." Something is passed down even if we do not know how. As Freud wrote to Arnold Zweig: "Our forebears lived there. . . . [I]t is impossible to say what heritage from this land we have taken over into our blood and nerves."[102] However much you try to destroy the law of the father, you are obedient to him at least in the unconscious interstices of inherited memory and time. For ever. Pushing it, you could argue that the very concept of "deferred obedience," not to mention the primal murder of the father and indeed the whole oedipal structure—all reiterated here—are intended to secure this legacy, this recognition of something all-enduring inside the mind, which was as violently repudiated as it was clung to by Freud. After all, his myth of Oedipus simply states that man kills his father and then must identify with the father he kills (the dead father enters the soul).

Turning to the future, we could say that the question of his Jewish identity propels Freud towards the idea of "transgenerational haunting," a concept forged by the Hungarian émigré analysts Maria Torok and Nicolas Abraham, significantly in the aftermath of this historical moment, as they tried to understand the silent persistence of the Holocaust in the minds of second-generation Jews. A child can be the bearer of the unspoken and often unspeakable legacy of her or his parents (the legacy passes in the unconscious not in the bloodstream).[103] You do not need Lamarck to believe that the sins and suffering of the fathers are visited on the sons. "The deeper motives for hatred of the Jews," Freud writes, "are rooted in the remote past. They operate out of the unconscious of nations."[104]

What cannot be known or spoken now becomes key. In 1930, in the preface to the Hebrew edition of *Totem and Taboo*, Freud made this, his perhaps most famous statement about his Jewish identity.

> No reader of [the Hebrew version of this book] will find it easy to put himself in the emotional position of an author who is ignorant of the language of holy writ, who is completely estranged from the religion of his fathers—as well as from every other religion—and who cannot take a share in nationalist ideals, but who has never repudiated his people, who feels that he is in his essential nature a Jew and who has no desire to alter that nature. If the question were put to him: "Since you have abandoned all these common characteristics of your countrymen, what is there left to you that is Jewish?," he would reply: "A great deal and probably its very essence."[105]

No faith, no language, no nationhood—as Said stresses, Freud defines himself here as Isaac Deutscher's non-Jewish Jew; but for all that, or even *because of that*, he is Jewish in essence.

In the third and final essay, written across the passage into exile, things take a new turn. It is in this essay that Freud argues that the Jewish people are the bearers, and originators, of *Geistigkeit*, an intangible quality that, as we have already seen, represents the best of intellectuality (without the aridity), the best of spirituality (without religious constraint). Unquestionably an advance or progress—*Fortschritt*, the *fort* is the mark of the irrevocable, as in "from this time on" or "no turning back"—*Geistigkeit* stands for that moment when man's beliefs achieved a level of abstraction without which there would never have been ethics, justice, truth. It rides the distinction between paternity and maternity, the one a logical inference, the other an unavoidable empirical fact (motherhood is something affirmed by the evidence of the senses). The supreme achievement is to worship a god "one cannot see."[106] *Geistigkeit* leads humans to acknowledge "spiritual powers" which, although they cannot be grasped by the senses, manifest "undoubted even super-powerful effects."[107] Freud writes this without so much as a backward glance to *The Future of an Illusion* in which, as we saw, any such powers were deeply suspect (although the question of emotional forces of "indeterminable properties" and "unknowable purposes" was already there).

Now to define a force as intangible or unknowable is to accord it the highest praise: ask Freud what was left to him that is Jewish and he would reply: "A great deal and probably its very essence," although he continues that "he could not now express that essence clearly in words." "We are as a group a mystery," Wulf Sachs, Lithuanian Jew and first practicing psychoanalyst in South Africa, writes to Freud from Johannesburg on 1 August 1939 in response to reading *Moses the Man*, "to ourselves and others."[108] In the middle of writing the work, Freud writes to his sister-in-law Barbara Low on the death of the psychoanalyst David Eder: "We were both Jews and knew of each other that we carried this miraculous thing in common, which—inaccessible to any analysis so far—makes the Jew."[109] *Geistigkeit*, we could say, is Freud's attempt to give substance, though that is not quite the right word, to this essence; or to solve the mystery, while preserving it, keeping its miraculous nature intact.

Above all, this achievement of *Geistigkeit* makes the Jewish people of value *to themselves*. The Jews were not just chosen by their leader, the qualities his faith bestowed on them gave them infinite worth in their own minds: "The 'I' feels elated, it takes pride in renouncing the drives."[110] Moses, and through him his god, chooses the people. As Yerushalmi points out, by retaining this from the Bible Freud turns his back on modern secular Jewish liberalism for which such an idea had become an embarrassment. In fact Moses does not just choose his people; he *creates* them—Freud is pushing to its furthest conclusion the argument of *Mass Psychology* that without a leader the mass cannot exist. Not for nothing does Freud entitle one section of his work "The Great Man" (his "implacability" in dismissing everything told about other gods as "lies and deceptions" now becomes "superb").[111] Like all good leaders, but going one better, Moses raises the masses in their own eyes: "All such advances increase self-esteem, making people proud."[112] Through Moses, "the self-esteem of the Jews" became, uniquely among faiths, "anchored" inside their religious belief.[113] We could say, tautologically, that their proudest possession becomes their pride. This is what gives the Jewish people their "toughness."[114] *In extremis*, the Jews take as their mantle the narcissism of the group. They become, so to speak, the supreme embodiment of culture's good opinion of itself: "The satisfaction that the ideal gives to those involved in a culture is of a narcissistic nature."[115] In the process they become a people in whom Freud himself can likewise once again take pride. That Yahweh was finally usurped by the god of Moses is "evidence of a special psychic aptitude in the mass that had become the Jewish nation."[116] By the end of *Moses the Man*, the Jews, who make their first appearance as "a bunch of culturally backward foreign immigrants," have completed the transformation from mass into people; they have become an *elite*.[117]

Freud therefore turns Moses into an Egyptian, lets the stranger into the tribe. He castigates the ruthlessness of monotheism, breaks apart the unity both of the people and their faith. He places murder at the origins of the group. But this is, finally, no simple iconoclasm. The integrity, the narcissistic unity and at-oneness of the group, *returns*. Identity, as Jewish identity, re-affirms itself. How could it not in 1938? In this final essay, Freud leads the Jewish people into their true inheritance (*Moses the Man* can be read equally as betrayal or as boast). But he has done so at a time and in the framework of an analysis which suggests that identity, while it may indeed be necessary for the survival of subjects and peoples, is no less a danger to both. The problem, not least for the Jewish people, will not go away. Writing to Gershom Scholem in reply to his criticisms of her study of Eichmann in 1963, Hannah Arendt argues: "The greatness of the people was once that it believed in God, and believed in him in such a way that its trust and love towards him was greater than its fear. And now this people believes only in itself? What good can come out of that?" She was responding to an assertion by Golda Meir: "Of course I do not believe in God; I believe in the Jewish people."[118]

It seems therefore futile to try and decide whether Freud's essay on Moses puts him on the inside or outside of Jewish tradition. The only viable answer must surely be both. Freud defined himself as Jewish in "essence" even as he feared—and not just for the obvious historical reasons—that psychoanalysis was being seen as a "Jewish national affair" (ironically given their falling-out, it was only Jung's appearance on the scene that he believed would allow psycho-analysis to escape this danger). What Freud does teach us, however, in a struggle present on almost every page of his own text, is how hard it is for any collectivity to avoid the potentially militant self-possession of the clan. Per-haps Freud was trying to do the impossible. How do you save a people at one and the same time from the hatred of others *and* from themselves?

Freud's ideal was Jabneh, the first Torah academy, where the life of learning became the highest aim. "The fact that Rabbi Jochanan ben Zakkai imme-diately after the destruction of the Temple obtained from the conqueror permission to establish the first academy for Jewish knowledge," he wrote in a 1938 letter to Dr Jacob Meitlis of the Yiddish Scientific Institute in Vilno, "was for me always one of the most significant manifestations of our history";[119] Jabneh also appears in *Moses*: "Henceforth it was holy scripture and the spiritual effort that held the scattered nation together."[120] But Freud also identified with Moses the hero, seeing his life as the founder of psychoanalysis in terms of conquest in a hostile world (the "Man Moses" in the title restored in this translation redeems the faith). Psychoanalysis offers us the spectacle of a Janus-faced discipline or way of thinking, at once combative and, as it turns to what Freud terms here "the darkness of the inner life," in retreat.[121]

"A Note on Anti-Semitism," which appeared in a German journal in Paris in November 1938, was, as a gloss appended to the title stated, the first of Freud's works to be published since his exile from Vienna. It consists almost entirely of a long quotation from an article—"so extraordinary that I selected excerpts from it to use myself"—about whose source, as the last lines of the piece establish, Freud is completely unclear.[122] Commentators have therefore speculated that Freud himself is the author of a critique of anti-Semitism that he has chosen to place in the mouth of a non-Jew. As if to say: in his analysis of Moses he could only do so much; in the end the persecutor must look to himself. But whether these are Freud's own words or not, the effect is the same. Either way, by copiously citing or by inventing, the distinction breaks down, the two fuse. As they must if race hatred is ever to end, Jew and non-Jew speak with one voice, cross over to the other's place. Wonderfully encapsulating the hardest part of his endeavour, this last piece thus performs in the very form of its writing the task whose difficulty Freud proclaims more or less on every page of all these works. Issuing its challenge to the crisis of the times and beyond, the journal in which the article appeared was called *The Future: A New Germany, a New Europe*.

In each of the writings discussed here, psychoanalysis steps outside its own doors, claims its status as fully social analysis, whether between people (empathy, identification, hypnosis, and loving) or across the generations (memory, tradition, faith). Even when we dream, we are not alone. Our most intimate psychic secrets are always embedded in the others—groups, masses, institutions, and peoples—from which they take their cue, playing their part in the rise and fall of nations. Not to recognise this is, finally, the greatest, most dangerous, illusion of them all.

PART II   Nation

Nation

Central to Jacqueline Rose's contribution to critical theory has been her concerted redeployment of technical psychoanalytic categories in a feminist political frame. As we have pointed out in our introduction, the concept of "fantasy" has proven particularly fruitful in this regard. It enables, above all, a nonreductive examination of the relationship between representations, their authors, and their contexts that can productively illuminate, on the one hand, the intricate ambivalences of personal identifications, and, on the other, the massive (and often seemingly intractable) rituals of national identity. The word *nation* derives from the Latin for "to be born" and can encompass the meanings of "breed," "stock," "kind"; although it is now usually applied to state-formations ("United States," "England," "Australia," "Japan"), it is also used to designate groupings of indigenous peoples. We have used the word as a rubric for this section in order to give a sense of the problems of the relation between the contingencies of birth, elective affinities, affective practices, transgenerational transmission, and governmental structures—and it is indeed these problems that Rose examines in the sequence of essays reprinted here. A "nation" is always divided against itself, and it is to such (often disavowed) divisions of state that Rose attends. The essays—"States of Fantasy," "Just, Lasting, Comprehensive," "Apathy and Accountability," "The Body of Evil," and "Zionism as Psychoanalysis"—all target liminal and ambiguous political phenomena, which Rose approaches, as always, from oblique yet revelatory angles, at once personal and global. Literature here plays a crucial function in mediating between unutterable private fantasies and unspeakable state actions.

The essay "States of Fantasy," which opens the collection of the same name, is probably as close as Rose gets to a manifesto. Opening with a meditation on her 1980 trip to Israel to visit a sister living in a Bedouin community in Sinai, Rose proceeds to render problematic the ruses of "belonging." As a

Jewish woman, Rose is—as one Israeli discourse has it—returning to her "new homeland" ("Altneuland," Theodor Herzl, the progenitor of modern Zionism, might have said), although neither she nor her family have had any connection to the land itself in living memory. That Rose feels anxious about such a "return-for-the-first-time," and, moreover, that this anxiety is a sign of refusing a desire she "ought" to have, is itself a noteworthy geopolitical phenomenon. As Rose writes, "This is a nation which desires its potential citizens—exiled, diaspora Jewry—to come home, with as much fervor as it banishes the former occupants of its land from their own dream of statehood" (124 herein). The peculiar nature of this contemporary ethnonationalistic interpellation leads Rose to a meditation on the vicissitudes of "belonging." One's "belonging" is never a simple identity or identification at the best of times, and, indeed, one way of belonging is precisely to feel uncomfortable, resentful even, about the fact that one is to be coerced into feeling one ought to belong. Yet the fantasies that fuel the injunction "You must belong!" are hardly susceptible to being wished away or abandoned; moreover, political entities cannot function without such fantasies, establishing defensive bulwarks both internally and externally. Drawing on a typically wide range of materials—such as her personal experience, George Eliot's *Daniel Deronda*, Freud's letters to Fliess, a nineteenth-century psychology handbook, the work of Olive Schreiner and Max Weber, among others—Rose weaves the motifs of violence, fragility, and intransigence into her account of the inseparable imbrication of "fantasy" and "state." As W. B. Yeats wrote, in one of the poems that comprise "Meditations in Time of Civil War" (1923),

> We had fed the heart on fantasies,
> The heart's grown brutal from the fare,
> More substance in our enmities
> Than in our love.

Yeats was of course an Irishman, living in Ireland, with a long-standing, complicated, and often fraught dedication to Irish nationalism. Yet if Rose and Yeats both share a conviction of the integral role that fantasy plays in the nationalist psyche, several of the problems that Rose poses hinge specifically on the Jewish diaspora's relationship to Israel. As Rose puts the problem of criticism, or, more pointedly, of *critics*, in this context, "The status of diaspora intellectual cannot be invoked as a solution when, for the nation in question, the diaspora is the source of the problem, the place where historically it begins" (000 herein). The very position from which a critique might be enabled is, in this case, precluded by the peculiarities of the state of Israel itself; a state that offers itself up as the salve for diasporic Jewish woes thereby discounts in advance the legitimacy of those who refuse it.

The problems of address that arise in any discussion about the Middle East become Rose's focus in "Just, Lasting, Comprehensive," an essay which extends the questions broached in "States of Fantasy" to the key words of contemporary global politics. Here Rose considers the term "Justice" as a "fantasy," that is, a term with the strongest internal lock in our minds, that "shapes the contours of our political worlds." But of course it also shapes our private worlds, just as it does, quite directly, those genres of representations called "literature" and "literary criticism." Rose notes that the reading of prose texts and the reading of political situations are inevitably related, despite the familiar disregard of political actors for literary pursuits, and the muscular distaste that many prominent literary critics show for the "confusion" of literature and politics. Against such descriptions, which entail that one cannot be just or do justice in or by literary means, Rose proffers an eminently literary *question* that is also eminently political: "Can you ever speak for justice on somebody else's behalf?" Following the implications of this question leads Rose to interrogate such problems as "intentional vagueness" in political formulations, the excessive cruelty of superegoic morality, the necessity of often unjustly discriminating in love, and the links of these problems to the imposition of boundaries, on land as in minds.

The questions Rose raises in these essays regarding the psychopolitical uses of key words are further explored in "Apathy and Accountability: The Challenge of South Africa's Truth and Reconciliation Commission to the Intellectual in the Modern World," first delivered at a conference in 2000 and then published, in 2002, in a collection edited by Helen Small. Here Rose pinpoints further peculiarities in the putative effectiveness (and ineffectiveness) of political action—and *inaction*. Not only bad actions (e.g., violence upon others) and botched or failed actions (e.g., the thwarting of intentions, the interruptions of others, etc.), but inaction, or the variety of forms of failure to act, become her critical focus. In 1995, following the destruction of apartheid as an official state policy of racial segregation, the new government set up an incredible public experiment in truth-telling, the aforementioned Truth and Reconciliation Commission, chaired by Archbishop Desmond Tutu. One of the commission's central aims was to solicit testimony from both victims and perpetrators of abuses under the apartheid regime, to enable experiences and events to come to light that would otherwise be obliterated (indeed, the previous government had set in motion a concerted process of destroying relevant documents). Of the three committees that comprised the commission—the Human Rights Violation Committee, the Reparation and Rehabilitation Committee, and the Amnesty Committee— the last named of these is the one that most concerns us here. Partly to encourage full disclosure, partly in an experiment in nonpersecutory reconciliation, the commission was empowered to deliver amnesty to perpetrators of abuses under apartheid. If one can immediately imagine the procession of torturers petitioning for amnesty under such conditions, Rose picks out an anomalous petitioner: "In perhaps one of the strangest moments in the extraordinary document that makes up the report of the Truth and Reconciliation Commission of South Africa, an application for amnesty, described as 'intriguing,' is recorded from an unnamed Indian woman applying for amnesty for what she described as her 'apathy'" (156 herein). Following the implications of such an unexpected application leads Rose to analyze the problems it poses to political governance: "This unnamed Indian woman . . . is suggesting, in a way that was clearly baffling to the Commissioners, that what you don't do as a political subject can have effects, might be as important in the transformations of the world as what you do" (159 herein). Not only that, the Indian woman's claim raises the question of the role of women in sustaining apartheid, given that the special section of the commission dedicated to women remains the "most depleted" part of its entire report. Once again, as Rose so often does, it is by focusing on little anomalies that enables her to identify and draw out some essential features of political situations and actions (or inactions) that might otherwise go unnoticed. Yet what can one do when confronted by seemingly unaccountable "evil"—and how does such a confrontation itself implicate its witnesses? Accountability is not justice, and yet some kind of accountancy and reparation in the service of reconciliation in the wake of evils done cannot be evaded.

The theme of "evil" returns in "The Body of Evil: Arendt, Coetzee and 9/11," an essay whose very title introduces the new shorthand for the new millennium's signature act of geopolitical terrorism: the September 11 attacks on the United States. Rose begins by quoting Osama Bin-Laden, Tony Blair and Ariel Sharon, and comments, "People using the term 'evil' all sound the same" (170 herein). Like those parts of language called "shifters" by linguists, the word *evil* enables rapid movements between heterogeneous registers of discourse, and, in doing so, itself "moves," creating intense affects of revulsion. Evil is always what the Other does; even if one commits comparable acts, these acts turn out to be mere expedients, even necessary responses in the face of such evil. Rose proceeds to track the mutability of "evil" by way of a close reading of *Elizabeth Costello*, a novel by the South African novelist J. M. Coetzee, and Hannah Arendt's famous formula of the "banality of evil." Coupling the paradoxes generated by literary texts—texts that stage fundamental political problems without resolving them—with propositions drawn from political philosophy, Rose examines identifications around evil. Evil is not just a shifter, or an absolute, but also a kind of "nothing" too (the thesis of the nonbeing of evil having deep roots in Western theology, for example, with St Augustine). More disturbing still, does this nothing, Rose asks, not also seem to be "the violent, intransigent—obscene—embodiment *of*, the highest law?" Rose quotes the English psychoanalyst Christopher Bollas on serial killers: evil seems to have a deep bond with transcendence.

It is to the problem of transcendence, with its deep historical and theological roots, that Rose returns in *The Question of Zion* (2005), from which we have extracted " 'Imponderables in Thin Air': Zionism as Psychoanalysis (Critique)." We have already discussed some of the controversies that erupted around this book on its publication, but here we just wish to place this extract in its context. Contemporary Israel, Rose argues, is sustained by a form of Zionism with deep mystical, indeed messianic, roots. Drawing on the work of Gershom Scholem, the great twentieth-century Kabbalistic scholar, Rose wishes "to try to grasp what it is about Zionism that commands such passionate and seemingly intractable allegiance."[1] In line with the psychoanalytic principle that current events cipher a secret prehistory—a prehistory that may well precede the birth of the subject itself, and draw its power from ancient traumas—Rose returns to the early-modern prehistory of messianic Judaism that emerged after the expulsion from Spain in 1492 and, in particular, to the deeply ambivalent figure of Shabtai Zvi, the notorious seventeenth-century "false messiah." Shabtai Zvi, whose declaration as the Messiah led to extraordinary scenes of Jewish enthusiasm all over Europe (many people sold their businesses and belongings in their desperate scramble to return to the Holy Land) and who died a convert to Islam due to an ultimatum of the Ottoman Sultan, becomes an exemplary figure of Zionist prehistory. In his own book on Zvi, Scholem poses the crucial question.

> What, we may ask, did the messianic idea imply for the simple Jew whose hopes were nourished, in addition to the biblical prophecies, by a number of popular and well-known legends and apocalyptic midrashim? Tradi-

tional popular messianism was characterized by catastrophe and utopianism, and both elements play an important role in the dynamics of the
messianic faith. Both have their roots in biblical prophecy, the one in the
vision of the end of days (as in Isaiah), the other in the notion of a day of
the Lord (as in Amos).[2]

Picking up on Scholem's analysis, Rose wants to show how such messianic
elements continue to work through Israel today, even in the secular forms of
Zionism that purport to reject them, in a state in which, in Rose's words,
"catastrophe has become an identity."[3] Yet Zionism is not, as Rose also wants
to show, necessarily a catastrophic formation bound to these troubling forms
of vision; indeed, it has historically been able to harbor a far more expansive
set of diverse discourses. There are brands of Zionism Rose seeks to recover
which, precisely, could function as countervailing tendencies to the apocalyptic fervor that dominates the present. In the extract here, she links Herzl with
Zvi—to go quickly, by way of their "manic-depressive" characters, not as
disparagement but as a sign of the links of these key figures to the deepest
subterranean components of their histories—in order to then ask as to Zionism's relationship with its unconscious dimension (Zionism and psychoanalysis are, so to speak, contemporaries). Here, Rose locates the great figures of
Martin Buber, Hannah Arendt, Hans Kohn, and Ahad Ha'am, who in the
period leading to, and after, the establishment of Israel, all continued to
promote the value of a Jewish home in Palestine, but nonetheless found
themselves less than elated about the form that that alleged "homeland" was
taking. It is here that Rose's own affiliations are perhaps clearest: to affirm that
older, unactualized possibilities of acting otherwise are still capable of being
reinvented for the present, and thereby direct us toward less catastrophic
possibilities for life.

—*Justin Clemens and Ben Naparstek*

5

States of Fantasy

Fantasies moved within her like ghosts . . . dark rays doing their work invisibly in broad light.
—George Eliot, *Daniel Deronda*, 1876

[Pathological phenomena] are, one might say, a State within a State, an inaccessible party, with which co-operation is impossible, but which may succeed in overcoming what is known as the normal party and forcing it into its service.
—Sigmund Freud, *Moses and Monotheism*, 1934–38

During those terrible nights of the June war, Arab men flocked there to fish. . . . [T]hey were searching in the sea for the reassurance that there was something stronger than our state.
—Emil Habiby, *The Secret Life of Saeed, the Ill-Fated Pessoptimist: A Palestinian Who Became a Citizen of Israel*, 1974

. . . feelings heard,
But every time articulate
Scarcely a word.
But you have too long deferred
Your visit to the modern state.
—Muriel Spark, *The Mandelbaum Gate*, 1963

In 1980, I was visiting a sister in Israel who was living at the time with a Bedouin community in occupied Sinai—land which, on the terms of the 1979 Camp David treaty, was to be returned to Egypt the following year. I had never been to Israel before. Until this sister's personal journey spared me the need for a justification which I had been unable to find, it had felt impossible.

There is something bizarre about travelling to a country where you do not belong, in the sense of having no lived connection, not for me, not in my family's past, a country to which I was not therefore returning, but where to say that much is already, in the eyes of the country itself, grounds for reproach. Not to return as a Jewish woman to Israel, not to feel a sense of belonging, not to recognize the very fact and existence of Israel as in itself a historic return, is to break on each count the symbolic parameters of the nation. It is a willed refusal, a rejection of proffered desire. Going to Israel is to enter a country in yearning, one whose passions flow not only from people to homeland but also and just as powerfully the other way. This is a nation which desires its potential citizens—exiled, diaspora Jewry—to come home, with as much fervour as it banishes the former occupants of its land from their own dream of statehood.

I think it is for this reason that talk of the postmodern predicament—belonging everywhere and nowhere at the same time—has never felt quite right. There is something about this vision of free-wheeling identity which seems bereft of history and of passion. As if the anxiety of belonging, itself the product of stories which stretch back in time, could be redeemed in the present by dispersal, the heart miming, shadowing, beating to the tune of a world whose contours can no longer confidently be drawn. Loss of confidence may be welcome, especially where it was misplaced, coercive, or oppressive (you might want to argue that confidence is always one of these three). But it is far from clear that the mind leaps from here into freedom. Hearts can retrench; the body which feels weak rearms itself. The carapace of selfhood and nations cannot be willed—does not fall so easily—away.

In common parlance, fantasy is what you get up to when the surveying mind and surveying society are both looking the other way. Fantasy is supremely asocial. Doubly licentious, it creates a world of pleasure without obligation to what it is either permissible or possible, outside the realm of fantasy, to do. You might think, however, that these two forms of profit cancel each other out. If fantasy is private only, reveling in its own intimacy out of bounds, then however outrageous its contents, it will be powerless to affect or alter the surrounding world.

Although psychoanalysis is often associated with this version of fantasy (the dirty tricks of the mind), it in fact begins somewhere else. In his earliest correspondence with Wilhelm Fliess, Freud distinguished fantasies (*Phantasien*) from dreams on the grounds that unlike the latter, which travel back from perception to unconscious, disintegrating and reordering themselves as they go, fantasy is always progressive.[1] Never completely losing its grip, fantasy is always heading for the world it only appears to have left behind. For some, it is only when Freud credited fantasy with its own unique, psychic reality that psychoanalysis proper could begin (for others this was his grossest act of betrayal, as he shifted his focus from the accounts of real seduction of his female patients which he had seen as the cause of their disorder up to then).

But this moment, while crucial to the history of psychoanalysis, is one step to the side of the aspect of fantasy which interests me here. In the quarrel over Freud's relinquishment of the "seduction theory of neurosis," almost no attention has been paid to what Freud was saying about fantasy before his famous theoretical turn. Continuing his discussion with Fliess, Freud turns from fantasy to morality: "Another presentiment, too, tells me, as I knew already— though in fact I know nothing at all—that I shall very soon discover the source of morality."[2] Tentatively (both sure and unknowing), Freud passes from fantasy to the question of how subjects tie themselves ethically to each other and enter a socially viable world.

What he came up with was guilt for crimes not committed, unconscious wishes, troubled identifications which—although it would take him a quarter of a century to formulate it—formed the basis, the emotive binding, of social groups. Mourning was the key. No other experience captures the ambivalence of love and recrimination, allegiance and triumph, exoneration and guilt; no other condition reveals in the same way a tie which binds most powerfully at the very moment when, objectively speaking at least, it has set you free. As early as 1897, therefore, Freud links fantasy to what makes group identifications possible and impossible at one and the same time (only in 1915, in the middle of the war, will he return to this link between mourning and ethics). Fantasy is not therefore antagonistic to social reality, it is its precondition or psychic glue. But fantasy surely ceases to be a private matter if it fuels, or at least plays its part in, the forging of the collective will. More simply, you don't have to buy into Freud's account of hidden guilt to recognize the force in the real world of the unconscious dreams of nations.

Once it is seen in these terms, fantasy sheds its private, illicit nature and goes to work in the world at large. "For a revolution not to latch onto an inner cycle," writes Ammiel Alcalay, "is to remain forever removed from every turn."[3] He is writing about the Palestinian *intafadah*, but his comment can be stretched beyond its immediate context to take in all those moments when a historical desire, drawing its energy from the legacy of ages, emboldens and actualizes itself. Although, as the target of the *intafadah*, Israel was on the opposite side of this conflict, it could itself be seen as one such desire, a nation built by its own account out of sand and dreams. In the words of the twenty-ninth Zionist Congress of 1982, "Zionism is the uniquely Jewish movement for national liberation and redemption based upon our messianic dreams and upon practical action for self-realisation."[4] Israel, as Amos Oz put it in a 1992 lecture, is "a dream come true."[5] Perhaps one reason why Israel is often felt to be so awkward politically for both supporters and critics is that it wears its heart so transparently on its sleeve.

There is no way of understanding political identities and destinies without letting fantasy into the frame. Far from being the antagonist of public, social, being, fantasy plays a central, constitutive role in the modern world of states and nations, in which Israel since 1948 (longer if you include the *idea* of Israel) has played such an important and difficult part. The fierce and traumatized intensity of longing that went into its creation seems so recalcitrant, so unable or unwilling—for those in power at least—to soften or modulate itself. Not all Israelis feel this, of course; there is a significant minority who for some time now have supported the idea of a bipartite state. But if you listen to one dominant rhetoric, it seems as if Israel cannot grant statehood to the Palestinians, not just because of felt real and present danger, but also because so great is the charge of fantasy against such a possibility that, were it to be granted, the nation would lose all inner rationale and psychically collapse in on itself.

Fantasy, then, belongs at the heart of our political vocabulary, but with a qualification. If it can be grounds for license and pleasure (the popular meaning is not of course completely out), it can just as well surface as fierce blockading protectiveness, walls up all around our inner and outer, psychic and historical, selves. Political passion might take on the colours of resistance— Ammiel Alcalay's quote—but there is no guarantee that it will travel that way. In fact in psychoanalytic language, resistance as a concept is far closer to defensiveness than to freedom; you resist when you don't want to budge. There is a common assumption that fantasy has tended to be excluded from the political rhetoric of the Left because it is not serious, not material, too flighty and hence not worth bothering about. My starting premise works the other way round. Like blood, fantasy is thicker than water, all too solid— *contra* another of fantasy's more familiar glosses as ungrounded supposition, lacking in foundation, not solid *enough*.

For one line of thinking, the concepts of state and fantasy are more or less antagonists, back to back, facing in opposite directions towards public and private worlds. But fantasy, even on its own psychic terms, is never only inward-turning; it always contains a historical reference in so far as it involves, alongside the attempt to arrest the present, a journey through the past. In the opening epigraph from *Daniel Deronda*, Gwendolen Harleth is struggling to shed her knowledge of her husband's guilty secret, his past mistress and children who—in the chapter called "Revelations" from which the quote is taken—appear along the railings to stare at her as she rides with him in the park. Rejoining the Greek meaning of fantasy as "spectral apparition" or "phantom," Lydia Glasher stands witness for a history which might have been Gwendolen's (might have been any woman's), and for the most tangible of claims—her felt right to a legacy of which Gwendolen, by marrying, has deprived her. Shake the cobwebs from your vision, look the apparition straight in the eye (twice this moment is recalled as a "Medusa-apparition"). What petrifies is an age-old story of the unequal and punishing sexual-cum-legal history of women: "As if some ghastly vision had come to her in a dream and said 'I am a woman's life.' "[6]

Behind any fantasy, there is likely to be some such potential narrative. "Fantasies," Freud writes to Fliess, are "*protective fictions*," "psychical façades which bar the way to memories" (this is fantasy as pure defence and the version Freud is considered to have left behind).[7] But fantasy is also a way of re-elaborating and therefore of partly recognizing the memory which is struggling, against the psychic odds, to be heard. In 1897, the examples Freud gives could all be grouped under what has come to be known today as "transgenerational haunting," forms of remembrance—most often of hidden and shameful family secrets—which hover in the space between social and psychic history, forcing and making it impossible for the one who unconsciously carries them to make the link.[8] (Contrary to the normal argument, therefore, in this early account Freud was theoretically way ahead of himself.) Like the young woman afraid of becoming a prostitute who was, without knowing it, reliving in fantasy her father's seduction of serving-girls (unconscious solidarity we might say); or the agoraphobic woman whose refusal to go out was her way of asserting her mother's unfaithfulness (an unconscious bid for freedom so unacceptable that it could only be experienced as terror).[9]

Go back to *Daniel Deronda*, and transgenerational haunting would also be the appropriate term to describe the other strand of fantasy coursing through the text: Zion, whose possible actualization is the only way for the hero to redeem his Jewishness in the face of the concerted denials of those around him, and of his absent mother behind them. Like the hysterical patient whom Freud described as "in the peculiar situation of knowing and at the same time not knowing—a situation, that is, in which a psychical group [is] cut off,"

Deronda finds himself enacting a history which exceeds his conscious grasp.[10] Hence one might argue Deronda's grandiosity, his wild and omnipotent belief in himself as the saviour of his people. To argue that George Eliot simply concurs with the Zionist vision is to ignore the extent to which she represents Deronda's passion as his symptom (states of conviction tend to be involved in an invisible quarrel with themselves). Israel willing itself into being sounds solipsistic and a bit crazed. There are moments when Deronda's zeal could be put alongside this comment of Moshe Dayan's reported after the 1967 Six-Day War: "If we believe [in it] and want it, the map of Israel can be determined by ourselves."[11]

In Eliot's novel, Gwendolen Harleth and Daniel Deronda are haunted in very different ways and with very different consequences; only Deronda is allowed to settle his ghosts by giving historical substance to his dreams (Gwendolen returns to her mother). But both of their inner landscapes, hers no less than his, are peopled with the burdens of history. For both of them a history not of their choosing unfolds in the deepest recesses of the mind.

If fantasy reaches out to the unspoken components of social belonging, "state" also has a set of meanings which move back from public being into the heart. Most likely, it is this connotation which my title—"States of Fantasy"— will immediately evoke. If the expression "states of fantasy" does not appear to yoke opposites together, it is because state—in thrall to fantasy, one might say—has gone over to the private side of its semantic history and shed its public face. In fact the word "state" has a psychological meaning long before its modern-day sense of polity, or rather one which trails beneath the shifting public and political face of the word. To take a relatively modern instance: in his 1854 psychology book, *Unsoundness of Mind*, J. C. Bucknill commented of one insane: "He was *fully conscious of his state*, and had great hopes of being cured in an asylum."[12] Here "state" is almost a synonym for "insanity." Thus idiotism and madness were "states of mind" distinguished by their passivity from other mental acts and operations in which the mind was assumed to retain a grip on itself. It would therefore be pointless to ask of Bucknill's example: if he is fully conscious, exactly how far gone, or indeed partly redeemed, is his state?

Think of the modern expression "in a state"; it has the same feel—you never have to spell out, especially if you are the sufferer, what exactly it means. As if to be "in a state" is precisely to lose the capacity to travel with any clarity through the world of words. "States of confusion," "states of panic," "state of dissociation": they could all be seen as tautologies. In each case, the mind simply falls apart, lets go of itself. To describe "a state" as involving a *relinquishment* of authority would not in this context be a contradiction in terms. But in this, the word "state," unexpectedly perhaps, exactly rejoins that of fantasy in one of its modern, psychoanalytic, definitions: "The intrusion of fantasy causes the ego to give up its own self-government for a moment. . . . While remaining the seat of its actions, the ego momentarily refuses to be its author."[13] It is because fantasy arrogates an authority which properly belongs to the ego alone, threatens the ego's supremacy, and forces it to step down, that—like Freud's pathological phenomena in the second epigraph above—it could be described as a "State within a State" (*ein Stat im Staat*).[14]

One of the reasons the idea of fantasy has a hard time getting into the political argument is, I believe, because it is seen as threatening political composure. In politics, at least, we can be sure of our psychic ground, shedding if only for the brief moment of our political being all tortuous vagaries of the inner life. For some time now, feminism has reproached politics as he is fought for having precisely such an imaginatively restrictive vision. Thus Olive Schreiner, whose 1883 *Story of an African Farm* was the first novel to bring South Africa home to the British, argued in her later feminist tract, *Woman and Labour*, that a politics which gave due place to women would not feel threatened by being fragmentary, provisional, but would precisely carve out an agenda closer to the shape of the mind (the feminist manifesto *Beyond the Fragments* would reproduce this argument almost verbatim in 1979).[15] Although none of them were alluding to the unconscious, what Schreiner and the authors of the later text were getting at was that politics cannot divest itself of its affective colours, it cannot step free of its subjective undercurrents— its psychic states. As Beatrix Campbell once famously commented, the difference between male Left politics and feminism is that men tend to enter the former armed with the truth, whereas women are more likely to become feminists when everything, starting with truth itself, has collapsed. But it is a form of redemptive fantasy in itself to believe that, in the world of publicly engaged action, you can step forth free of mental embarrassment (enter the grown-up world). This is, note, a point distinct from the recent argument that modernism's aesthetic project, also pseudo-redemptive, was to repair the horrors of the real world with words.

Look a little more closely at the word "state" in its political significance as polity, commonweal, commonwealth. Place it alongside that other meaning of "state" (and of "fantasy") as loss of authority, and it appears that the private and public attributes of the concept "state" are not opposites but shadows—

outer and inner faces precisely—of each other. In a sense this is obvious, since wherever there is authority there is always the possibility of its demise. Hence Machiavelli's famous assertion, which some see as the beginnings of modern statehood, that the prince must set about "conquering *and maintaining* his state."[16] The prince's state was a front; it relied on deceiving the people and on cowing them into submission (far better for a prince to be feared than to be loved).

Likewise Max Weber, listing the factors which secure allegiance to the modern state—tradition, charisma, legality—ends by commenting that "*in reality*" (his words, my emphasis), the obedience of the people rests on hope and fear: "fear of the vengeance of magical powers or of the power-holder, hope for reward in this world or in the world beyond."[17] A state may be sovereign (in this context "sovereign state" is the tautology), but that doesn't dispense with, it intensifies, the requirement to make *sure* of itself. Over and above its monopoly of legitimate violence, the modern state's authority passes straight off the edge of the graspable, immediately knowable world. "When and why do men obey? Upon what inner justifications and upon what external means does this domination rest?" (the first being the question Freud was led to in his consideration of fantasy in that early correspondence with Fliess).[18]

In fact, as the first pages of *Economy and Society* make clear, it is particularly difficult for the state, as a collective entity, to get into Weber's basic frame of rationally purposive action (actions which the individual himself can explain). It can do so only in terms of the inner meaning it holds for its subjects or the subjective belief they attach to it. But these are factors which, precisely because of their intangible, speculative component, cannot be held to reason. They immediately threaten to run into the arms of all the other "borderline" factors which Weber lays out as most recalcitrant to sociological explanation of the type being proposed: ends which defy intellectual grasp, hidden "motives" and "repressions," mystical experience which cannot be fully communicated with words. If the state has meaning only "partly as something existing," if it rests on the belief of individuals that it "exists or should exist," then it starts to look uncannily like what psychoanalysis would call an "as if" phenomenon.[19] You mould your acts and gestures to a persona that deep down you know isn't really there.

Something irrational—not as in unreasonable, but as in relying on a power no reason can fully account for—has entered the polity. For social theory, the decisive shift occurs at the point where the ruler, instead of "maintaining his state," serves a separate constitutional and legal state which it is his "duty to maintain." Once real authority is no longer invested in the prince and his trappings, it loses its face and disembodies itself: "With this analysis of the state as an omnipotent yet impersonal power," Quentin Skinner concludes his study of the foundations of modern political thought, "we may be said to enter the modern world."[20] The modern state enacts its authority as ghostly, fantasmatic, authority. But it would be wrong to deduce from this—like those who misread Freud's attention to fantasy as essentially trivializing—that the state is any the less real for that.

In fact there is a paradox here, for it is this transmutation—the impersonality of the modern state—which guarantees the possibility of freedom (a democratic order into which everyone formally can enter) even if in reality the state has more and more been reduced to serving ruthless competition in the modern world. In this split between state and civil society, the individual's collective being is unrealized—in Marx's words, "abstract," "artificial"; detached from the ideal, it becomes no less fantasmagoric, the mere shadow of itself.[21] Pure phantom—"Individuals are only phantoms like the spectrum" (Schelling)—the individual yearns for true embodiment in the state. "I want," writes Fichte in *Foundations of Natural Law*, "to be a human being. . . . [I]t is the aim of the state fully to procure this right for man" (Deronda could be seen as enacting the frantic, willed, form of such self-incarnation).[22]

It should perhaps then come as no surprise to notice the curious but striking proximity between this account of modern statehood and the superego, that part of the mind which Freud eventually theorized as the site of social law. For Freud, the superego exerts an authority beyond all reason, implacable to the precise extent that it draws on all the unconscious energies it is meant to tame (it therefore endlessly punishes *and* recycles the crime). Which is why inside the head, the law always feels a bit crazy and why, although it never stops trying, it can never quite justify itself. Like the state, the superego is both ferocious and a bit of a fraud.

It has often been argued that Freud's concepts owe more to the society surrounding him than he allowed, but it has not been suggested, as far as I know, that it is not the contents of social being that Freud imported into the psyche so much as its *form*. This ruthless superego looks very much like Weber's vision of the modern state, binding its subjects to a violence which—Weber makes this central to his definition—is pure *means* without end (there is no way of defining the state in terms of its ends given that there is no end which "*some* political organization has not at some time pursued").[23] It also borrows something of Weber's account of charismatic authority, which he invites us into via the image of heroic frenzy, manic seizure, and mad dogs.[24] But it is not only Weber who has analyzed this punishing, alien component of the state's putative reason. "It seems to me," writes Gramsci, "that one cannot start from the point of view that the State does not 'punish.' . . . [T]he State must be conceived as an 'educator,' in as much as it tends precisely to create a new type or level of civilisation."[25] It is because the state has become so alien and distant from the people it is meant to represent that, according to Engels, it has to rely, more and more desperately, on the sacredness and inviolability of its own laws.[26]

I would like to suggest that the terrifying fragility and intransigence of modern statehood can be illuminated by placing it into this dialogue with Freud: not just insofar as his concept of the superego tracks the modern theorization of statehood; nor just to the extent that psychoanalysis might help to elucidate the subjective component of political being (extending Benedict Anderson's famous "imagined community" of nations); but in this further sense, that psychoanalysis can help us to understand the symptom of statehood, why there is something inside the very process upholding the state as a reality which threatens and exceeds it. As Weber lays it out so clearly in that opening chapter of *Economy and Society*, you cannot call up the subjective dimension and expect to keep it in place. For while it may be in the unconscious that you most profoundly submit to the law, the unconscious is also, according to psychoanalysis, the place where all your other and better ideas can be found. If the modern state is a fantasy—if it relies on fantasy for an authority it can ultimately neither secure nor justify—then fantasy will always be there to one side of it, like Emil Habiby's fishermen of the third epigraph, calling its bluff, knowing better, wanting something more, something else: "During those terrible nights of the June war, Arab men flocked there to fish. . . . [T]hey were searching in the sea for the reassurance that there was something stronger than our state."[27]

As "A Palestinian Who Became a Citizen of Israel," Saeed the Pessoptimist does not in fact, other than purely formally, have a state in the full meaning of the term. In response to this dilemma, he moves liminally through his political world. He hails the narrator and reader on the first page from outer space and starts the chapter of this quotation from deep within the catacombs of Acre (in a crucial later scene, the freedom-fighter Walaa walks into the sea with his mother). In this novel it is at least an open question whether you should ever take the risk, politically or psychically, of *grounding* yourself.

When Freud took his metaphor for pathological phenomena from the state—"a State within a State"—he was a stateless person (it would be wrong to see psychoanalysis in its first generation as untouched by these historic concerns). Not for the first time, one might say, he was unconsciously analysing himself. Living in England, Freud was working on *Moses and Monotheism*, his great "Jewish" work completed in the shadow of the impending war and written across his own passage into exile. It would not appear until after his death in 1939, but he had started it in Vienna in 1934, four years before he had been forced to leave. The living—and dying—representative of the crisis which would eventually lead to the creation of the state of Israel, Freud did not offer a heroic account of Jewish history (for that reason many saw it as not only inaccurate, which it was, but inopportune). Instead he told the story of a people violently willing themselves into a nation. Freud believed that Moses was an Egyptian, that there was not one Moses but two, and that the first had been murdered by his followers. It was the stubborn persistence and later reemergence of that trauma in the form of deferred obedience to the first dead Moses that led to Freud's analogy with the symptom ("a State within a State")—something defiant and potentially destabilizing that will not go away.

If there is something wild about Freud's story then its form of extravagance is of special pertinence to what I am trying to evoke here. Slowly and through the passage of his own history, Freud makes his way back to the traumatic theory of neurosis which, according to the dominant account, he had definitively relinquished in 1897. In terms of *history*, trauma reappears; the journey of the concept through Freud's opus thus beautifully imitates its content (trauma always returns). The story, and the analogy, are there to remind us of that part of historical being, passionate and traumatized, which runs backwards and forwards, never completely in the grasp of its subjects, through psychic time. This famous quote from Gramsci is cited by Edward Said on the question of Palestine:

> The starting point of critical elaboration is the consciousness of what one really is, and is "knowing thyself" as a product of the historical process to date which has deposited in you an infinity of traces without leaving an inventory.[28]

To paraphrase: these are traces which persist and colour the present to the exact extent that everything inside people and psyche are willing themselves not to remember, not to know. Like Gramsci, Freud too called up the Delphic oracle "Know thyself" (he was writing about the slips which reveal us to others better than we know).[29] But his starting premise was that such knowledge would have to pass through the defiles of the unconscious.

Read through the filter of the present, this last work of Freud's seems like an advance warning, a caution against the belief that statehood could ever be the total psychic redemption of its people. Freud was sympathetic to Zionism and by 1935, when Nazism was established, he was in favour of a Jewish nation-state in Palestine, but earlier in the 1930s he had spoken out against the idea.[30] Driven into exile, it is as if he were almost demonstrating in his person how loss, historic deprivation, transmute themselves into necessity, one which soon—he did not live to see it—would entrench itself beyond all negotiable reach. The state, lost in reality, turns into metaphor and takes refuge deep within (it is a truism in psychoanalysis that the lost object is the one that never lets go). Run the line from Freud's analogy to his own historical condition and I read him as diagnosing statehood as the symptom of the modern world. Run the line from here back to 1897 and the Moses narrative can be read as the last chapter in Freud's attempt to link public, collective life to the unconscious, fantasmatic, life of the mind.

The final epigraph of this chapter is taken from Muriel Spark's 1963 novel, *The Mandelbaum Gate*, set in Jerusalem and Jordan in 1961, the year of the Eichmann trial.[31] The novel tells the story, mainly, of an Englishwoman— Barbara Vaughan—who puts herself and all those who seek to pursue or protect her at risk by crossing over to Jordan through the Mandelbaum Gate. Every Christmas up until 1967, Palestinian Israelis with relatives in Jordan, when permitted and under restriction, would do the same. There is of course no real symmetry here. In the 1986 novel *Arabesques* by Anton Shammas, the Palestinian Israeli author writing in Hebrew, such paltry and diminished forms of contact are represented as the point where all real connection and memory slip away.[32]

Spark's novel appears as a way of situating the issue of modern statehood at the heart of Englishness. It shows the English on location in refined and semi-farcical panic, confronted by a legacy which in some deep sense, since Balfour at least, could be said to be theirs. But the novel, and epigraph, are also there because of their hesitancy: the question, only partly answered by the book, as to whether this Englishwoman, Jewish through her mother's side, should in fact be in this part of the world at all. For the Israeli guide who confronts her, Barbara Vaughan's presence is acceptable only if she is willing to shed the non-Jewish part of her identity, only on condition that—without reservation or qualification—she identifies. She must make the imaginative project of Israel her own.

During my visit to Israel in 1980, I encountered something of the same demand. It was matched by the contrary recrimination from one Palestinian woman—assuming from the fact of my being Jewish that I saw Israel as my homeland—of identifying or belonging, not too little, but too much. Out of that double reproach, and the dilemma it focused for me of how to participate in a history not exactly of my own making (I was born the year after the creation of Israel when the United Nations Armistice lines were laid down) but to which I feel an intense and continuing connection, emerged much of my concern with the Middle East today.

When Virginia Woolf wrote that women are fortunate to be denied the full "stigma of nationhood," that a woman wants no country, "as a woman my country is the whole world," she offered a vision of feminized migrancy which it is tempting to lift as a solution to the political ills of the contemporary world (tempting perhaps, too, as the solution to the personal dilemma just described).[33] The epigraph from Spark is therefore also there as a caution, for its reminder that the encounter with modern statehood cannot be indefinitely deferred: "You have too long deferred / Your visit to the modern state." You can't, even as a woman, just float off. Woolf was not reckoning with the postwar legacy which engendered Israel/Palestine.

There is a point of more general significance. It has often been remarked that when the white critic talks of postcolonial culture, there is always the risk that she will simply reappropriate that culture back into her own language, repeating the original (colonial or imperial) offence. Two alternatives, it is suggested, confront her: either the barrier is insurmountable, or it can—perhaps—be challenged, rendered precarious, by the migration of all identities in the postmodern world. But Israel came into being to bring the migrancy of one people to an end. Uniquely, perhaps, it saw its task as the redemption, not just of that people, but of the horrors of modernity (which is not to ignore the equally strong impulse to give the Jew her place as fully modern citizen). Displacing the Palestinians, it then produced on the spot a new people without statehood, not just by oversight or brutal self-realizing intention, but as if it had symptomatically to engender within its own boundaries the founding condition from which it had fled.

In this context, the Jewish critic who wishes to address Israel as an outsider marks herself immediately as a participant by default: even more so today when, in the words of Israel Shahak, the issue for Rabin's generation is no longer, as it was for the first generation of leaders, the benefit of the Israeli state for the Jews, but the benefit of the Jews for the security of the state.[34] But the status of diaspora intellectual cannot be invoked as a solution when, for the nation in question, the diaspora is the source of the problem, the place where historically it begins. And if in defiance—it is impossible for this not to be partly a gesture of defiance—she invokes this status as freedom, as releasing a permission to identify with the oppressed group (as many Jews outside and inside Israel do), she immediately hits the buffers of statehood once again. For the Palestinians, statehood is the demand. It is the only condition of freedom for the group with which she has chosen so undutifully to identify (a device for talking "peace without statehood" was how one commentator defined the 1993 Oslo Accord).[35]

In recent literary discussion, the terms "culture" and "identity" have been the common currency. In fact they are inseparable, since it is assumed that culture, as opposed to, say, class, is the process through which lines of identity, especially in the field of sexuality, are drawn. But culture has a tendency to become its own history; as the place where identities are not just formed but contested, it seems at times to acquire a political valency which allows it to set off all on its own (politics as culture and nothing else). And identity, most famously in what has come to be known as identity politics, challenges the dominant but without changing the rhetorical or psychic rules; recognized for a moment as unstable, it then immediately reasserts itself as counter-identity, and starts to mirror the forms of unswerving conviction it was meant to have left behind (question everything but identity itself).

If we replace the terms "culture" and "identity" with "states" and "fantasy," it seems to me that we avoid both of these problems at once (since sexuality is often what is being talked about, "identity" seems too "hard," "culture" too "soft"). However far it travels, the term "state" always holds its reference to the founding political condition of the modern world. And "fantasy," however much it threatens subjects with the prospect of its own and their dissolution, keeps sight of the peculiarities with which identities, not only consciously but also unconsciously, make and unmake themselves. To place "state" and "fantasy" together is not only to propose a new theoretical turn but is also, as I have tried to suggest here, to uncover the history of their intimate relation. Long before psychoanalysis got the idea—although Freud's involvement with these matters has been mostly overlooked—fantasy has been where statehood takes hold and binds its subjects, and then, unequal to its own injunctions, lets slip just a little. We cannot bypass modern statehood; we are still living in its world. Fantasy allows us first to acknowledge that as a more than external matter. But we should not forget, either, that fantasy's supreme characteristic is that of running ahead of itself. There is something coerced and coercive, but also wild and unpredictable, about it. If fantasy can give us the inner measure of statehood, it might also help to prise open the space in the mind where the worst of modern statehood loses its conviction, falters, and starts to let go.

6

Just, Lasting, Comprehensive

The title of this essay is taken from the repeated formula for political settlement in the Middle East. It has also been chosen because justice is so
difficult—one could say "impossible," but that would be too easy—to talk
about. Justice is one of those terms which excites the most passionately
committed investment but which, almost in proportion to that investment,
seems hardest to actualize on the ground. Nowhere does this seem more vivid
or pertinent than in South Africa and Israel/Palestine. As I finished writing
these pages in their original form, begun as lectures in April 1994, within days
of each other the first nonracial democratic elections took place in South
Africa, and Israel and the PLO signed their accord. It is not to underestimate
the historic significance of both of these events to say that, in both cases,
justice had only—and in the case of the Middle East Agreement, I would say,
barely—begun.

Justice could be called an ideal, but the word is too bland; it settles the
tension between wish and actuality, desire and embodiment, in advance (an
ideal is only ever an ideal). We could call it rhetoric, but that would be to
ignore or override too quickly the whole tradition, starting with *The Republic*,
which pits justice against rhetoric as the mere play of empty verbal form. It
might be called a performative, but it is rather the opposite: talking won't do
it; say it and its substance seems just as likely to vanish or drift away. Justice
may not be mere rhetoric, but there is no term quite like it for forcing our
attention onto the possible gap between word and deed; no word which
threatens so dramatically to empty itself of content at the very moment when
it is declared. Whenever the word justice is spoken, you always have to look
again. Justice always makes us suspicious. Whoever speaks it, chances are
someone else is being conned.

I would prefer to call justice a fantasy, but on condition that fantasy is not
understood as daydream, delusion, degraded desire. If the argument of this

essay is that the best way to think about justice is as fantasy, it is not because justice is something we cannot aim for, something by definition impossible to achieve. Nor is it because fantasy is something locked into private territory: your secret, my shame. Like morality or virtue, fantasy shapes the contours of our political worlds. It breaks through the boundary separating inner and outer space. To think of fantasy as private *only* is a form of possession; holding on to our fantasy, we blind ourselves to the way it circulates and empowers itself in other more public, collective domains. This essay therefore reverses the psychoanalytic dictum that the patient acts out her or his fantasy in real life as a way of disowning the private, guilty fantasy-life of the mind. For you could just as well say the opposite (the two are in a sense the obverse of each other)—that the fantasy *of* fantasy as mine and mine alone is no less denial; going back in the other direction, we flee our potential and actual political selves. Frozen, on hold, in retreat. That fantasy is only a private matter is perhaps the supreme fantasy, fantasy par excellence.

The issue of justice hovers on the edge of literary debate. Changing the canon, voicing the silenced, becoming visible, tearing the veil (two of these are the tides of early feminist anthologies)—each move, each formula, models itself at least partly on the discourse of rights.[1] To whom have we denied a hearing? With what history of oppression have we been complicit by not noticing, not allowing the ghostly political subtext of this hitherto revered piece of writing to be read? When critics respond by arguing that politics should be kept out of literature, aren't they nonetheless, one way or another, sharing the same language, entering the same terrain? Studying literature, as one argument goes, is no way to redeem injustice—the wish is inappropriate, the activity unequal to the task (much of Stanley Fish's case in his 1993 Clarendon lectures could be encapsulated in the slide between these two).[2] Let literature and justice go their separate ways. Above all, when you read a piece of literary writing, do not *judge*. Judgment and judicious reading are incompatible. Writing of the feel for language essential to the second, Iris Murdoch states: "Developing a *Sprachgefühl* is developing a *judicious* respectful sensibility to something which is very like another organism."[3] How do you take the just measure of a text?

Somewhere in all these questions, there hovers another, perhaps founding, distinction—the conviction that you can only give literature its due (justice for literature) by detaching it from the sphere of rights. Along not wholly dissimilar lines, Derrida describes justice as an "experience of the impossible": "A will, a desire, a demand for justice whose structure wouldn't be an experience of aporia would have no chance to be what it is, namely, a call for justice."[4] As a call, justice is always suspended along the path of its anticipation, which means that it is incalculable (requiring us to "calculate with the incalculable") whereas law (*droit*) "may find itself accounted for."[5] But if you follow this path and set the incalculable infinity of justice against the regulated and coded prescriptions of rights, you run the risk of reinforcing the link between literature and justice, by placing them together beyond all measure, out of all legal and historical bounds.

What are the links between justice, rights, and literature? Amos Oz writes in judgment of his nation—by his own acknowledgment the more it fails the more he writes; but in the name of a founding ideal of justice which, for all its violations, Israel never ceases in his eyes, at least potentially, to represent.[6] Oz's characters fall ill, sink into despair, go mad on Israel's behalf. Their pathos is Israel's saving grace. Cradling the nation's unconscious, however ugly, in his writing, Oz redeems its soul. But justice on these terms is partial; it can never go across fully to the other side. Solipsistic, non-exchangeable, the very agony of justice means that it cannot fully be shared. Only the Israelis have the privilege of justice as an object of mourning; as if for the Arabs, justice is never desire or dilemma, only pure need or demand. In this sense, Oz's passion, what *moves* the writing in both senses of the term, undermines his own claim for justice by letting it do only half its work. In *Black Box*, Michael Sommo writes to his stepson: "In their Koran it is written: the faith of Mohammed by the sword. And in our Torah it is written: Zion shall be redeemed by justice. That's the whole difference. Now you choose which of the two suits you better."[7] Or in Oz's own words: "We have become specialists in Arab mentality. . . . Force is the only language the Arabs understand."[8]

For Wulf Sachs, writing in South Africa in the 1930s and 1940s, psychoanalysis is a discourse of justice, since it can be used against scientific racism to show that the black and white unconscious are the same.[9] Even more, as his narrative *Black Hamlet* progresses, psychoanalysis crosses completely over and, via *Hamlet* (which you might have thought would have saved it from so crude a political destiny), passes into the service of a revolutionary ideal. "Curing" the native diviner, John Chavifambira, means for Sachs releasing him into political agency on behalf of his race. Sachs's difficulty is, in a sense, the mirror of that of Amos Oz. Too little identification in the first instance which in the second becomes too much; even if Sachs is on the side of black liberation, it is still his psychic agenda, still therefore an appropriative gesture, which is involved.

Who, then, speaks for justice? Or to put it another way, what happens to the language of justice, is it in fact viable, when it appears in the mouth of someone other than the one claiming their own rights? Can you ever speak for justice on somebody else's behalf? When Kazuo Ishiguro adopts the voice of the English serving class and lets the butler tell his story in *The Remains of the Day*, he makes this issue the formal wager of his writing. The servant who was silent in the face of appeasement—who appeased the appeaser, we might say—now speaks. Speaks for his own class: the very fact that he achieves self-representation is an answer of sorts to the threat to democracy posed by the Second World War (it is much clearer in the book than in the film that, while the master spoke of justice, the rights of the servant were threatening to slip away). But—and here's the catch—he also speaks for the dishonoured class which right to the end he continues so honourably to serve. This is the irony, or what could be called the "illocutionary" paradox of democracy for the oppressor class. Give voice to the oppressed, the hitherto unrepresented, and the risk is that they will endlessly reiterate your own shame.

So can you ever speak for justice on someone else's behalf? This might give another colour to the opposition between justice and rights in relation to contemporary literary debate. Perhaps one reason why there has been so much resistance to letting rights into writing is because it opens up this zone of uncertainty. If we take on the new agendas of literary studies, it is not in "our" name or for "our" own cause that "we" speak (I use "our" and "we" advisedly and in quotations to mean not in the name of the critics who until recently had the monopoly of the profession). It is the classic dilemma of liberalism that however crucial the gesture of solidarity, your voice might be the last one in need of being heard. Another way of putting the question— who speaks for justice?—would be to ask instead how, or whether, the language of justice can be shared. This seems to be the question, or lesson, to be drawn from the Middle East Peace Process whose reiterated formula—just, lasting, comprehensive—provides the title of this essay. Take the three terms together as they now often appear ("just" and "lasting" first appear in the 1967 Security Council Resolution 242, the third in a 1977 joint declaration on the Middle East by the U.S. and U.S.S.R.), and it is their combined weight and finality which is so striking.[10] Let justice be done—completely, once, for all. You can read them as equivalents ("just" *and* "lasting" *and* "comprehensive"), as progressive qualifiers (an all-inclusive justice that will endure), or as tautological (if justice is not comprehensive how could it be just?). In the words of the 1977 Joint Statement, comprehensive means "incorporating all parties concerned and all questions." "Incorporate" seems apt. As one psychoanalytic account has it, you incorporate something by devouring it; unlike introjection, where you take someone in as part of yourself but recognize them as separate, still let them be.[11] As if it were being inadvertently acknowledged that so total a justice, instead of leaving the world standing, would simply swallow and abolish all differences, wipe out all parties to the deal.

It is a point often made in Critical Legal Studies that the language of contract is inherently self-deceptive. Roberto Mangabeira Unger, key proponent of the movement, sees the language of contract as containing a fundamental contradiction between freedom and power: "The mechanisms of egalitarian, self-interested bargaining and adjudication cannot be made to jibe with the illiberal blend of power and allegiance."[12] The modern law of contract "preaches equality in distrust."[13] Unger's point is part of a larger historical argument about rights. In prerevolutionary aristocratic and corporatist Europe, rights were meant to "exhibit on its surface the gross structure of society, like those Renaissance buildings whose façades transcribe their internal design."[14] Modern legal thought begins when rights detach themselves from the social structure and become a universal category for describing the possible relations between citizens (the transition from special to equal rights). To these two founding moves in the history of rights, critical legal theory adds a further twist. No longer a reflection of social hierarchy or its transcendence, the discourse of rights today serves above all to *deny* the constitutive forms of social inequality on which it rests. In critical legal parlance, the language of rights is most likely to do cover for evasion; at the very least it is unequal to the forms of inequality which it attempts to mediate, travel across, or resolve. As Judith Shklar puts it, in *The Faces of Injustice*, in an unequal society the law falls unevenly on the desperate and the powerful, hence justice serves injustice "which has an exuberant life of its own."[15] Or in the words of Sir Thomas Bingham, Master of the Rolls: "We cannot forever be content to acknowledge that in England justice is open to all, like the Ritz Hotel."[16]

Far from being an argument for abandoning the discourse of rights, Unger's manifesto is more a plea for exposure (a psychoanalytic argument, one could say). Whenever someone or something—resolution, declaration—says "rights," look for what is not being said (ever since Pierre Macherey at least, this is something that critics and students of literature have been trained to do). Go from here back to UN Resolution 242 on the Middle East.[17] This is the resolution which calls for Israel's withdrawal from the occupied territories, hence its importance for so long. But read its silences. You will then find that "rights" means the right of every state in the area to "live in peace within secure and recognised boundaries free from threats or acts of force"; but the word "Palestinian" does not appear. The expression which does appear, "just settlement of the refugee problem," does not specify *who* are the refugees. There is in fact no mention whatsoever of political rights in the sense most commonly understood.

If Palestinian rights are not named, then the phrase "every state in the area" cannot include, not even potentially, a state of Palestine. Since the law against deportation under the Geneva Convention can be invoked only by states and not individuals, this has meant, amongst other things, that no stateless Palestinian can make use of it.[18] "Every" is therefore a totalizer that veils an exclusion. In this case, the term "just" does cover for injustice; the term "lasting" is there as the gesture towards a possibility which, because it is ruled out by the language, cannot even begin.

Only in 1974, a week after Yasser Arafat gave his historic address to the United Nations, does the expression "inalienable rights" of the Palestinians, including self-determination, national independence, and sovereignty, appear in General Assembly Resolution 3236.[19] Not until the 1993 Declaration of Principles is the compound "Palestinian people" used for the first time.[20] According to Israel Shahak, talking in 1975, if you used the word "Palestinian" in Israel you were "already half a rebel" ("Usually you say 'Arab' ").[21] The 1993 Declaration states that elections in Jericho and Gaza "will constitute a significant interim preparatory step toward the realization of the legitimate rights of the Palestinian people and their just requirements."[22] "Interim," "preparatory," "toward"—how many qualifiers of "realization" can you find? (It is now acknowledged that at this point neither Rabin nor Arafat want the elections to take place.) As many commentators have pointed out—Edward Said was foremost among them in the West—all mention of the "occupation" has been dropped.[23] By omission, the declaration also spells the end of the right to return of the 1948 refugees (a right confirmed annually since the 1948 adoption of Resolution 194 by the UN): "Their plight seems to be forever deleted from the lexicon of the Middle East. . . . [I]t's time now to master the art of forgetting."[24] In fact, as Rabin announced to the Knesset in May 1994, the final terms of agreement ensured the return neither of the 1948 nor of the 1967 refugees.

Like Resolution 242 which was, according to Noam Chomsky, left "intentionally vague," the Oslo Declaration is formulated, in the words of Hanan

Ashrawi, so that "every side interprets it in his own way."[25] Even vagueness, however, can be unequally distributed: "In order to comprehend the real meaning of the Oslo accords . . . refer to its text, which is purposely vague on issues of Palestinian rights while precise on issues of what power Israel will retain."[26] Or in the words of one of the Kibbutzim interviewed by Oz in 1987 on the possible outcome of the Lebanon war (Israel invaded in 1982): "We might just come out from this deal with a comprehensive, total peace, on our own terms."[27]

None of this is to ignore, it should be stressed, the real issue for Israel, although not only for Israel, of secure and recognizable boundaries. But look again here and another version of the same problem appears. How, as Abba Eban, Israel's Foreign Minister put it in 1968, can you base the possibility of peace on secure boundaries when dispute over the boundaries is the major obstacle to peace?[28] How can you withdraw to the *status quo ante* when "there is nothing normal or established or legitimate to which to return"?[29] How can peace be "juridically expressed, contractually defined, legally binding" when the foundations of contract—two parties to a deal—could only be the effect, and not the presupposition, of peace?[30]

Above all, running under all of this there is a fundamental problem which no language—not of rights or of justice—can resolve. It is one which has a particular resonance not only in the Middle East but also in central Europe today. And that is the problem of how the grounds of national entitlement can ever be definitively secured. For if national assertion is precisely *self*-affirmation, it rhetorically and ritually blinds itself to the other on whose recognition its claim finally depends. In his 1976 essay "Rights, Law and Reality," Yeshayahu Leibowitz writes: "Fortunate is the people whose conception of its tie to its country is recognised by others, for should this connection be contested, no legal argument could establish it. . . . Considerations of historical 'justice,'" he continues, "are irrelevant. The conflict is not one of imaginary 'rights.' Nor is it a clash 'between Justice and Justice'—since the legal (or moral) category of justice does not apply."[31] (Oz, who has often described the Israel/Palestine conflict as one of "right" against "right," qualifies this in 1992 as "claim" against "claim" precisely because of this problem of recognition.)[32]

Leibowitz's comment does not, in fact, in his terms, spell the end of justice. His remark is specifically addressed to those who justify Israel's existence in terms of a historico-religious or immemorial right to the land: "an eternal right that cannot be called into question," in the words of the Knesset Fundamental Policy Guidelines of 1981 (the ultimate unnegotiable right, one might say).[33] Nor does it prevent him from proposing his own solution; he ends his article by calling for the partition of the country into two nations. Rather, what I take from his comment is the way it underlines the subjective, imaginative component of national belonging. Not just in the sense of imagined communities as famously defined by Benedict Anderson, but in terms of recognition.[34] Whether I—or we—can be a nation depends on your desire. The viability of a nation does not rest with its own self-imagining, but on whether the other can (chooses, wants to) recognize *me*. We have entered the terrain of political fantasy, or rather of fantasy as it works its way underneath the political terrain. Above all, we have entered a realm where justice cannot be protected from the vagaries of conscious and unconscious desires. As Unger puts it in his discussion of legal indeterminacy, "Complexity, especially in the form of ambivalent or conflicting desires, must be kept under control."[35]

So we might put the last question—"Can justice be shared"—differently again. What is a just subject, or rather, what does justice assume or require a subject to be? It might be only at this level that justice could be called a performative, because of the image of subjectivity which has to be mobilized or called immediately into action whenever justice is evoked. Does justice have to assume a subject who is already somewhere just? The insane man, Socrates argues in *The Republic*, is beyond the bounds of justice: if a sane friend lends you a gun, goes mad, and asks for it back, you don't comply; nor do you tell the whole truth to anyone who is out of his mind.[36]

Critics have often commented that John Rawls's famous theory of distributive justice relies on a very specific concept of the mind. In a recent article in *Critical Inquiry*, he extends the theory to the law of peoples.[37] As with his earlier theory, the participants are to operate under a veil of ignorance—they do not know in advance "the size of the territory, or the population, or the relative strength of the people whose fundamental interests they represent."[38] An unlikely scenario but one which precisely introduces an element of the speculative, or indeed fantasmatic, into justice. Justice, Rawls seems to be suggesting, has first of all and before anything else to take a purely disembodied place in the mind (critics who reject the whole project on the grounds that the starting premise is unimaginable have therefore missed the whole point).

Seen in these terms, the problem with Rawls is not that he starts way out in the blue, but that he does not go far enough. Once you usher the subjective component into justice, recognize its already constitutive place, why on earth should anyone be *reasonable* about it? Look at that starting premise again.

Rawls's actors may be suspended in space and time, but they are absolutely self-identical, utterly *sure* of themselves. His so-called ignorance is disingenuous, not to say knowing, at least about what is going on inside everyone else's head. Everybody is "reasonably situated and rational," "deciding in accordance with appropriate reasons"—hence no ugly surprises, no mistakes.[39] The problem, however, is that, if this is true, then the people have already submitted to the moral law and this is already a perfect world: "More than any other doctrine," Rawls states, the doctrine of this law "ties together our considered political convictions and moral judgements at all levels of generality, from the most general to the most particular, into one coherent view."[40] Compare Socrates: "Hardly anyone acts sanely in public affairs."[41]

Could there be something crazy about justice? This may sound like a somewhat crazy suggestion, but it is a way of drawing attention to the almost maniacal insistence on reasonableness that justice as a concept seems to provoke. "The special assumption I make," Rawls states in his original *Theory of Justice*, "is that a rational individual does not suffer from envy." (A big assumption if you are talking about the law of nations since envy and nationalism are often blood-brothers: "a panacea for nagging doubts, a way of coping with envy.")[42] Justice has to—how could it not?—aim for reason; but the fact that it is something we yearn for suggests that it belongs as much to our passionate as to our enlightened selves. "They are in the right because I love them," Jean Genet writes of the Palestinians, "which is not to say," he adds, "that justice has no 'role.'"[43] But once that much has been granted, then we are up against the vagaries of desire for which contract has no place, and the partial insanity of our own self-relation which distributive justice inside nations and between peoples has to disallow. So, to put the question another way, what kind of object is justice inside the mind? What does justice (remember what does a woman) want?

Ironically, it might be that justice becomes harder to actualize the more the emotive, refractory, subjective dimensions of justice are denied (this would be the opposite of, although not unconnected to, the injunction—most often issued to feminism—that the best way to advance a cause is to "keep emotions out of it"). But the point here is not that human beings are really unjust and selfish, an assumption which Rawls in a sense starts from and which is also the unspoken bastion of Conservative ethics. This is not an argument about the necessity, in the service of justice, of taming human desires (which assumes those desires to be more or less consistently aimed at my own advantage or good). What is at issue here is a far less cohesive, more slippery idea of subjectivity, one which starts from the assumption that subjects can be, and nowhere more than in the sphere of morality, riven—or driven, even—against themselves. Are we always on our own side? Are we, indeed, always just to ourselves? Arguing against what she calls Aristotelian common sense, Judith Shklar writes: "We blame ourselves for acts we did not perform and feel guilty for imaginary faults. We punish ourselves irrationally." (She is also arguing against Aquinas, who said that no one ever willingly hurts themselves.)[44]

By calling her book *The Faces of Injustice*, Shklar places the whole issue of justice in the framework of desire. Set justice, not in opposition to rights, but to injustice, and you are up against an "irreducibly subjective component that the normal model of justice cannot easily absorb."[45] To ask what injustice feels like seems obvious—in fact injustice is often unrecognizable except as a subjectively registered state. But it feels weird, to say the least, to ask the same question of justice ("How was it for you?"). If there is always a risk that revenge will get the better of justice, it might be, she suggests, because in the case of justice there is nothing like the same kind of pleasure involved.[46] Justice and injustice are not "psychologically complementary or symmetrical"; they neither fully cancel each other out, nor quite add up.[47] Justice may be sought after, but it is also eminently forgettable; unlike injustice, which nobody asks for but which never goes away. Nothing establishes the psychic component of injustice more clearly than racism because of the factor of humiliation involved—a factor supplementary even if attached to the issue of rights.[48] (By trying to make pornography a civil offence against the rights of women, Catharine MacKinnon, I would argue, confuses the two: systematic degradation does not necessarily involve the deprivation of rights.) Many of Nelson Mandela's speeches both before and after the 1994 election could be read in these terms, as his bid to stop the legacy of past injustice in South Africa from playing effective and affective havoc with the attempts, however partial and tentative in the first instance, toward a more just and equal world. Forgive, but above all do not humiliate the enemy—however unjust he once was (it is this which Desmond Tutu refers to as the "miracle" of post-apartheid South Africa and one of Slovo's obituarists as the "astounding metanoia and reconciliation which South Africa was to undergo").[49]

By stressing the passionate, subjective dimension of justice, I am, however, trying to point to something beyond, or not fully graspable by, the moral philosopher's vision of desire. To call subjects self-driven can imply stubborn but endearing contrariness; or it can imply, as with psychoanalysis, a far more radical cleavage of the soul. What does justice look like if you introduce into this discussion the idea of the unconscious? So far fantasy has been used in this chapter to signal those moments where the language of justice follows the path of the super-rational supra-sensible ego, magically inflating and fulfilling itself (in the words of Stephen Greenblatt, talking of the earliest colonial ventures: "a self-authorizing, self-authenticating representation . . . that intensifies imaginative possession of the world").[50] But fantasy also has an almost exactly opposite meaning; it can just as well refer to the point where the subject "vanishes" or "fades" into the unconscious (to use Lacan's terms), to all those dimensions of subjectivity which most dramatically escape the ego's thrall. What happens, in the field of justice, if you use this second meaning of fantasy to call the bluff on the first, as a way of countering fantasy's masterful delusion of itself?

For many involved in recent literary and cultural theory, it has become customary to turn to psychoanalysis for a radical critique of sexual norms. The idea of a bisexual unconscious can serve nicely to upset the stifling language of heterosexual normality which does service for virtue in so much of the bankrupt, moralizing discourse of the modern world. It might be, however, that all that (welcome) attention to the throes of sexuality has meant that those of justice have been left curiously unexamined and exposed: "The requirement . . . that there shall be a single kind of sexual life for everyone," writes Freud in *Civilisation and Its Discontents,* "cuts off a fair number from sexual enjoyment, and so becomes the source of serious *injustice*" ("*Ungerechtigkeit*").[51] And yet, as he himself puts it only a few pages earlier, for a law to be just ("*Gerechtigkeit*") it *must* be universal, that is, broken in no one's favor; although this tells us nothing, he adds, about the ethical value of such a law.[52]

Sexual "injustice" (his word) thus becomes the supreme illustration of the gap between law and ethics; it shows universality as justice *and* injustice at one and the same time. This is a paradox internal to the concept of justice, but one which it seems to me that, in our keenness to use psychoanalysis to champion an "other" sexuality against the dominant, some of us have overlooked. Or to put it another way, in turning to psychoanalysis as a potential discourse of justice, might we have inadvertently ignored what psychoanalysis itself has to say about the difficulties—no less complex than those relating to sexuality—of justice itself?

A long time ago, a friend suggested that it was so much easier to be a Marxist than a Freudian because whereas, whatever your social origins, you could wake up one morning and more or less decide to be on the side of the working class, you couldn't quite in the same way decide one morning that from that day on you would throw off all inhibition and be sexually free (or rather you put a somewhat different set of demands on yourself if you did). There is a strange belief underlying moral injunctions that inappropriate desires, whose entire "rationale" is that they defy best intentions, can be sweet-reasoned away. "Be good sweet maid and let who will be clever"—as I look at that formula today (one whole strand of my life could fairly be summed up as a rebellion against it), it is not just its discouraging chauvinism which seems so offensive, but its assumption, no less fraudulent, that being good is something easy or straightforward to be.

From where does the inner sense of morality arise? This would seem to be a rather important question for women, since if you are a girl it is somehow assumed that it arises spontaneously from the inside; whereas what is involved for boys is obedience to an external social law they will themselves finally appropriate and represent (this is one reason why any feminist argument that starts by assuming women are inherently more virtuous makes me so uncomfortable). In this context it becomes a strength rather than a weakness of Freud's writing that he finds it so difficult to give an adequate account of how any of this comes about. Morality and justice, he writes in *Moses and Monetheism*, "came about with a *renunciation of instinct*."[53] But, as has often been pointed out, this begs the question, since presumably you will only renounce instinct if you have already bought into societal values and accepted a non-instinctual ideal. We can dismiss this as a flaw of psychoanalytic reason, but it might also help to explain why the moral life is so hard to achieve. It is because there are no grounds, no good, earthly reason to obey you, that you bring your weight to bear on me with such unjustified—unbearable—force.

For psychoanalysis, this is a problem structural or inherent to moral law. Failure is never therefore just individual failing; it is always at the same time a measure of the impossibility of what is being required. Failure in this context is suggestive and provocative. Rather like the impossibility of femininity, or indeed of Jewish national identity (indeed it could be argued that both these forms of pained but strategic failing take their orders from the first). "The cultural superego ... does not trouble itself enough," Freud states, "about the facts of the mental constitution of human beings."[54] It doesn't bother to ask whether its commandments are possible, psychically, to fulfill. Listen again, he suggests, to one of the "ideal demands" of "civilized society": Love thy neighbour as thyself. Adopt a naïve attitude as though you were listening to it for the first time, and "we shall," he predicts, "be unable then to suppress a feeling of surprise and bewilderment": "Why should we do it? What good will it do us? But, above all, how should we achieve it?"[55] My love is precious to me, the result of the finest discriminations, selections, and histories, without which, in some sense, I cease to be. I diminish it, and myself with it, if I offer it to every corner on the ground. "A love that does not discriminate [does] an injustice ["*ein Unrecht*"] to its object."[56]

Furthermore, it is only on the basis of such fine and self-defining discriminations that collective identities are made: "My love is valued by all my own people," Freud continues, "as a sign of my preferring them, and it is an *injustice* ["*ein Unrecht*"] to them if I put a stranger on a par with them."[57] "The commandment, 'Love thy neighbour as thyself' is . . . an excellent example of the unpsychological proceedings; of the cultural superego. The commandment is impossible to fulfil."[58] Or in the words of the Umbro football poster which appeared all over London in the summer of 1994: "God says Love Thy Neighbour. Sorry God."

This superego is a cruel taskmaster (necessarily, given the Sisyphean nature of its task). You cannot dispense with the problem of cruelty by obeying it because of the ferocity with which it imposes its ideals. Like Kant's categorical imperative, it is something of a fanatic ("Kant's imperative reeks of cruelty," "it is a hanging judge seated within the mind").[59] Writing on the moral sense, the feminist moral philosopher Annette Baier proposes Aristotelian cultivation of virtue in the young as an alternative to a moral law which "has to be burned in, and which tends to provoke return aggression, or more strongly working poisons" (in fact she places Freud alongside Aristotle on the side of more benign, albeit costly, forms of correction, but this is in fact a perfect description of the superego at work).[60] A line from the notes of Alexander Gideon, a character in Amos Oz's *Black Box*, captures something of the tone: " 'Thou shalt love thy neighbour as thyself'—at once or we'll fill you full of lead" (he is writing about fanaticism, but only just).[61] As if in reply, the young Israeli poet, Sami Shalom Chetrit, cited by Ammiel Alcalay as representative of the new generation of "Oriental" Jewish writers, ends his twenty-nine-stanza poem on the *intafadah*—"Hey Jeep"—with "but thou shalt love thy neighbour as thyself" reiterated, dully, pointedly, vacuously, thirteen times.[62]

Furthermore, the superego dispenses its moral favours unevenly, without ratio, since the more you obey it the more you feel answerable to its judgments (conscience torments the saint far more than the sinner, virtue not its own reward). The superego draws its energies from the same unconscious

impulses it is intended to tame; it turns against the ego the very force with
which the ego strains to reject its commands (this gives a whole new meaning
to the idea of a punishment that fits the crime). Superego and unconscious
are antagonists, but they also have the most intimate, passionate relationship
with each other: dedicated combatants, tired and devoted cohabitees. There
is, as has often been pointed out, something sadistic about this version of
morality. Enter this zone of punitive pleasures, and who, we may ask, is
punishing, who pleasuring, whom?

Certainly, there is nothing in this account that will submit to a language of
contractual negotiation which presupposes the rationality of the rules, or of
the participants, in advance. Playful, perverse, savage—to call justice a fantasy
in this context is to say no more or less than that it is the supreme target and
embodiment of our social aspirations, our most exacting ideal. Or, to put it
another way, there is no ideal without fantasy, no shortcut through the trials of
fantasy to the realization of our political dreams.

When justice attempts such a short-circuit, it threatens to destroy everything, including justice itself. These lines are from the Israeli poet Bialik, cited
in *The Land of Israel* by Amos Oz:

> If there is justice, let it be seen at once.
> But if after I am desolated under the heavens,
> justice should appear,
> let it be destroyed for ever.[63]

He then makes the link to the slogan "Redemption Now" of Gush Emunim.
Redemption, justice, now, or redemption and justice can go to hell. Justice on
these terms is apocalyptic. Like the cities of the old Mediterranean described
by Alcalay: "bracketed off in expectation of either perfect time and the final
correspondence of words and things, or the aftermath of global disaster."[64]
Perfection courts disaster ("peace everlasting . . . take the world by storm").[65]
As soon as justice becomes its own ultimatum, it gets vicious, hell-bent on
fulfilling itself (the only frame, perhaps, in which the idea of an "end of
history" makes sense). During the 1983 Jerry-Falwell-sponsored tour of the
Holy Land, Grace Halsell interrogated one of the Christian Zionists about the
"new Jerusalem" they anticipate and yearn for, the final Armageddon in the
plain of Esdraelon when two-thirds of the Jews living in the region will be
"purged"; she was told that once eternity begins, "after that there are no more
sequences of events."[66] In the words of Max Weber,

the adherent of an ethic of ultimate ends suddenly turns into a chiliastic prophet. Those, for example, who have just preached "love against violence" now call for the use of force for the *last* violent deed, which would then lead to a state of affairs in which violence was annihilated. . . . The proponent of an ethic of absolute ends cannot stand up under the ethical irrationality of the world.[67]

For similar reasons, totalitarianism cannot be placed on the other side of justice as if it had no investment in it, as if justice was not one of its main concerns: "Totalitarian lawfulness," writes Arendt in *The Origins of Totalitarianism*, "pretends to have found a way to establish the rule of justice on earth."[68]

In this context, the point of the turn to psychoanalysis is that it tears a rift in this vision of justice, opening up an aporia in our social, moral being no less radical than that affecting our sexual identities, the ones which the culture most coercively presumes to know. Against that presumption, that knowledge, we have been happy (some of us) to take on the concept of the unconscious, to tie sexuality to perversion, or rather to break down the distinction between the two. But the perverse component of justice? What good—to echo Freud's query about "Love Thy Neighbour"—will it do? Unless we turn that question round—the classic psychoanalytic move—and ask instead: what might an account of justice look like that included that perverse component in its terms, one which allowed the most difficult psychic dimension of justice to be entertained? Can we demand justice without making a virtue of it? Could there be a theory of justice that doesn't require us all, miraculously and coercively, to be good (a recipe for disaster in my mind)? I desire justice; but not if it rules out the scrutiny of desire.

Everything in the literature examined here would seem to suggest that it is only when you try to expel desire from justice and start to believe in its absolute and total perfectibility (the second move only possible on condition of the first) that justice turns nasty and starts punishing the very world it was meant to save (it is not a belief in the possibility of reason, but overinvestment in one's own sure possession of reason which is the trap).

There is a passing moment in *Whose Justice? Which Rationality?* when Alasdair MacIntyre argues that only psychoanalysis, notably that of Freud and Lacan, offers a cogent account of the "schism" of the self which the liberal order has to repress and disguise (his words) in order to produce its "false and psychologically disabling unity of presentation" (each individual a "single, well-ordered will").[69] This is part of MacIntyre's overall project which started with *After Virtue*, his critique first of liberalism's assumption that there is a neutral ground from which competing claims to justice can be assessed; and then of the assumption behind that one, that justice and rationality can be understood independently, that theories of justice don't always bring a very specific, historically variant account of what makes a reasoned subject in their train (hence his move from *After Virtue* to the project and title of this second book). But, as he sees it, psychoanalysis retreats from its insight into cure, patching up the liberal self by offering therapeutic solutions to an essentially historical problem: the demise of a liberal order, in itself the effect of a breakdown in consensual being to which it vainly tries to offer a solution, blind to the fact that its history has come to an end.

But supposing it is in the field of justice, far more than in the field of individual pathology, that the rational pretensions and curative aims of psychoanalysis could be shown most definitively to break down? As Freud himself acknowledged, the problem with the analysis of so-called social pathology is that, unlike the individual symptom, there is not even the pretence of a norm. You can at least argue as to whether the aim of psychoanalytic practice is the fortification of the ego as agent, or the release of the subject, against society's best (worst) moral intentions, into the vicissitudes of desire. But in Freud's account of how subjects take up their social identities, there is nothing to support what MacIntyre sees as happy, if misguided, liberal-social communing. Nothing to buttress a conviction that conflict in the modern world can be resolved in the sphere of pure reason alone ("each individual a single well-ordered will"). "Ethics," Freud writes, "is thus to be regarded as a therapeutic attempt—as an endeavour to achieve, by means of a command of the super-ego, something which has so far not been achieved by means of any other cultural activities."[70] (This is to put the *placebo* delusions of therapy on the other, societal, foot.)

Psychoanalysis might then be seen as the unconscious of one specific liberal tradition, the one that by requiring—to use another of MacIntyre's own formulas—that we "conceal the depths of our conflicts," social no less than psychic, makes it impossible for those conflicts, and above all for their *relationship*, to be acknowledged, let alone understood. When Henry Louis Gates Jr. delivered the lecture "A Killing Rage—Black-Jewish Relations" in London in April 1994, his topic was strikingly pertinent to my interest in following some of the lines between Israel/Palestine, South Africa, and England, in tracing the historic and imaginative links between English culture, black,

Palestinian, and Jew.[71] Gates's lecture was a plea for an end to black anti-Semitism and Jewish racism. It began with the problem of how collective guilt gets transmitted across generations, fixing and damning our political futures in advance, and ended with a call for the politics of identity (I know who I am) to be replaced by the politics of identification (I want to know you).

The politics of identity, one could say, shares all the problems of the particular version of liberalism just discussed. It is because the self it asserts against prior injustice remains forged in the image of reason, of false self-consistency—which is what it means to assert an identity—that it finds itself powerless in the face of identity's unreason, powerless to resolve the conflicts of allegiance, the incommensurable and often antagonistic demands that such a politics provokes. It is a problem which was invisible until the politics of identity actualized it so vividly (this is the opposite, note, of reacting to these new voices as if they had all the power and were on the point of taking over the world). But if you respond to this difficulty by calling for a politics of identification, then the question of what permits and forbids identifications, of what makes recognition (love of neighbour, for example) possible and impossible has to come next. Gates's crucial demand has to go further; his call for new forms of affinity, recognition, and identification ends exactly where, psychically speaking, we need to begin.

In May 1990, in an address to three hundred corporate businessmen, Nelson Mandela cited this famous speech of Shylock from *The Merchant of Venice*.

> Hath not a Jew eyes? Hath not a Jew hands, organs, dimensions, senses, affections, passions? fed with the same food, hurt with the same weapons, subject to the same diseases, healed by the same means, warmed and cooled by the same winter and summer, as a Christian is? If you prick us, do we not bleed? If you tickle us, do we not laugh? If you poison us, do we not die? And if you wrong us, shall we not revenge? If we are like you in the rest, we will resemble you in that. . . . The villainy you teach me, I will execute; and it shall go hard, but I will better the instructions.[72]

It was a stunning rhetorical move. Jews will undoubtedly have been present in his audience. Business and radicalism were the two main destinies of Jewish immigrants to South Africa (sometimes, as with Ruth First's family, both at the same time). But there is also a long tradition of anti-Semitism in the country. When Daniel François Malan, founder of apartheid, introduced his Quota Bill in 1930, limiting immigrants from "non-scheduled" countries (Greece, Latvia, Lithuania, Poland, Russia, Palestine), it was generally recognized as an attempt, which proved successful, to halt the immigration of Jews. Since this was 1930, eighteen years before the official inauguration of apartheid, his speeches on this topic can be read as a rehearsal for what was to come: "Nations desire to preserve homogeneity, because every nation has got a soul, and every nation naturally desires that its soul shall not be a divided one."[73]

That, then, is the identification to which Mandela, citing those lines of Shylock, made his appeal: the line that links black to Jew as members, equally although distinctly of a persecuted race. A plea to remember, an attempt—in the words of Ammiel Alcalay—to turn "the texture of memory ahead."[74]

But Mandela's use of this speech was also a warning. It has another, more deadly potential future tense. From suffering to revenge, Shylock traces a curve which puts a stop, no less dramatically, to the very redeeming identification it seems to propose: "And if you wrong us shall we not revenge? If we are like you in the rest, we will resemble you in that." Mandela then took out these lines: "If a Jew wrong a Christian, what is his humility? Revenge. If a Christian wrong a Jew, what should his sufferance be by Christian example? Why, revenge." He took out the lines of the speech which show virtue—humility and then sufferance as ethos—turning violently inside-out on themselves. It would undoubtedly have complicated the argument. By leaving virtue standing, as it were, Mandela could communicate far more powerfully to this audience the extent to which their future actions would determine just how far it is at risk.

Of course, it has been the case for a long time that critics trying to defend Shakespeare's *Merchant of Venice* against the charge of anti-Semitism have turned to these lines. But they tend to ignore the dark side of the message and of the humanity to which the Jew stakes his claim: that it is through self-perpetuating violence that oppressed and oppressor most often identify. It is too soon to say whether this political scenario has been averted in South Africa, although much of the energy is going towards making sure that it is. In Israel/Palestine, the conditions seem so unpromising that it is not even clear if the question can begin to be put. English life and letters have, of course, tended to purify themselves of all this. It has been the main purpose of this discussion to make the connection unavoidable for us all.

Apathy and Accountability:
The Challenge of South Africa's Truth
and Reconciliation Commission to the
Intellectual in the Modern World

> Another man will never be able to know the degree of my suffering, because
> he is another and not me, and besides a man is rarely willing to acknowledge
> someone else as a sufferer.
> —Dostoevsky, *The Brothers Karamazov*

In perhaps one of the strangest moments in the extraordinary document that
makes up the report of the Truth and Reconciliation Commission of South
Africa, an application for amnesty, described as "intriguing," is recorded from
an unnamed Indian woman applying for amnesty for what she described as
her "apathy." The application stated that those appealing for amnesty on these
grounds recognised that they

> as individuals can and should be held accountable by history for our lack of
> necessary action in times of crisis. . . . [I]n exercising apathy rather than
> commitment we allow(ed) others to sacrifice their lives for the sake of our
> freedom and an increase in our standard of living.[1]

In this case amnesty was not granted. Although the applicants argued that
apathy fell within the brief of the commission as an act of omission, the
commissioners decided that it did "not disclose an action or omission
which amounts to an offence or a delict in respect of which amnesty can be
granted." Amnesty—the most controversial, the last added, and legally challenged clause of the Mandate of the Commission—could only be granted for
acts whose motivation was political, which occurred between the Sharpeville
massacre of 1960 and the inauguration of Mandela as president in 1994, on the

basis of full disclosure of relevant information and if the rubric of proportionality—ends to means—was observed. A declaration or confession of apathy falls at the first of these conditions. No political organisation asked for it.
Apathy receives no official sanction. Indeed, only rarely and reluctantly—
hence the strangeness of this moment—do people admit to it, although they
are very ready to diagnose it in others (it has in fact become one of the
favourite recent political diagnoses of the West).

But if apathy does not come on political instruction, one could nonetheless argue that the system of apartheid, and not only of apartheid, relied on it,
or something close. That inhuman political structures depend, for as long as
they last, not just on the power of the oppressors and the silent complicity of
the beneficiaries, but also on numbers of the oppressed being struck with an
inability to connect, or give themselves, to their own cause, as well as on those
beneficiaries who may have hated the system but did not—by their own
repeated account in the report—do enough: "At the very time when we
should have continued to speak out clearly for the truth and against injustice,"
the spokesperson for the Stellenbosch Presbytery of the Dutch Reformed
Church submitted at the human rights violations hearing in Paarl, "we grew
tired and gave up protesting" (5:384). History, the precise formula insists, will
hold individuals accountable for "a lack of necessary action in time of crisis."
For apathy, since the commission did not recognise the offence, history is the
only court.

In fact, the charge falls before the conditions of amnesty on more than the
first count. What is the time of apathy? How would you date it? What are the
means and what the end? Is it in fact an intention at all? And what could
count as full disclosure? Is apathy something communicable, is it something
we have a language for talking about? Or does it, more like a disease or
shameful secret, rely on doing work invisibly in the dark? How can you fully
disclose something whose chief property is deficiency, to be in some sense
absent from history and missing to yourself? In today's political climate, in
Great Britain at least, apathy tends to be talked about as something which has
been done to civic and political responsibility ("eighteen years of Conservative rule"). As if you could only be *made* apathetic—a kind of double passive,
an act of grammatical bad faith which mimics or repeats the problem it is
claiming to diagnose. But the idea of apathy as purely passive should make us
suspicious—as Freud once famously commented, it requires a great deal of
activity to achieve a passive aim.

For anyone reading the report of the commission, it is hard not to be "overwhelmed," to use the word of the commissioners, not by apathy but by the opposite, that is, by what people are actively capable of. The commissioners were "almost overwhelmed," the chapter on Recommendations in the last volume, begins: "by the capacity of individuals to damage and destroy each other" (5:306). As we look back on the last century, this has become the recurrent and chilling refrain. To use a recent formula of the historian Eric Hobsbawm, we are faced with the paradox that the twentieth century "has killed more people than any other century, but at its close, there are more people living and living better."[2] We are faced, that is, with the fact that in the second half of the century we have barely taken leave of, the human capacity for destruction and the human capacity for improvement have—arm in arm as it were—reached new heights. It must be, then, one of the roles of the modern intellectual to try and understand this paradoxical fact of modern times, one half of which must be to try and understand what makes it possible for people to act in this way (it was part of the mandate of the commission—part of its aim of "restorative justice"—to understand the "motives and perspectives" of the perpetrators [1:130]). At what has become a famous moment in the hearings, former Security Branch officer Jeffrey Benzien demonstrated wet-bag suffocation on a dummy in front of the court and when asked by former victim, Tony Yengeni, what kind of man could do this, replied: "I, Jeff Benzien, have asked that question to such an extent that I voluntarily—and it is not easy for me to say this in a full court with a lot of people who do not know me—approached psychiatrists to have myself evaluated, to find out what type of person am I" (5:370).

Some of the students on a course I teach on South African literature saw this as the supreme moment of fraudulence in the proceedings, whereas—despite the "pride" Benzien also expressed in his method: "Mr Yengeni, with my absolutely unorthodox methods and by removing your weaponry from you, I am wholly convinced that I prevented you and your colleagues . . . I may have prevented you from being branded a murderer nowadays" (5:263), and even the chilling repetition only a moment later in court: "Do you remember, Mr Yengeni, that within thirty minutes you betrayed Jennifer Schreiner?"—I am more inclined to take this question at its word.[3] Not least because it brings us close to one of the defining features of atrocity in the modern world. Something akin to disbelief. In which part of your mind are these testimonies to be stored? How can these narratives be held in the mind at all?—a question which seems to me to go way beyond the issue of remembrance or forgetting. In his extraordinary book on Rwanda—to move for a moment to a very different part of Africa—Philip Gourevitch writes: "All at once, as it seemed, something we could only have imagined was upon us—and we could still only imagine it. This is what fascinates me most in existence: the peculiar necessity of imagining what is, in fact, real."[4]

Among many other things, the Truth and Reconciliation Commission will take up its place historically for its relentless charting of the horrors of our age. Early in the report we are, however, given a warning: "This focus on the outrageous has drawn the nation's attention away from the more common-place violations," producing a failure on the part of ordinary South Africans to recognise "the 'little perpetrator' in each one of us" (1:133). The implication is not only, as the paragraph continues, that "only by recognising the potential for evil in each one of us [can we] take full responsibility for ensuring that such evil will never be repeated," but also that the hearings themselves, the explicit dwelling on atrocity, have let huge swathes of the white population off the hook, those who in Njabulo Ndebele's words dwell in "the interstice between power and indifferent and supportive agency": "Yes, they [the bleeding-heart liberal, English-speaking South African] have a story to tell. . . . In that interstice the English-speaking South African has conducted the business of his life."[5]

But what this unnamed Indian woman is talking about is something rather different. She is suggesting, in a way that was clearly baffling to the commissioners, that what you don't do as a political subject can have effects, might be as important in the transformations of the world as what you do. To read the report of the commission is to be confronted on almost every page with how difficult it is to speak of atrocity, whether as victim or perpetrator of the act, although the difficulty is radically different for each. It has been at the centre of the commission and the source of its greatest difficulty that language—in the words of Antjie Krog, the Afrikaans poet commissioned by the South Africa Broadcasting Association to report on the hearings—does not easily "bed" the truth.[6] But we are presented here with the strange suggestion that the ways in which we do not implicate ourselves in the burdens of history might be something which it is even harder to talk about. Intellectuals are of course always accused of talking too much, not acting enough—hence also the relevance of the Commission Report, which presents the problem of speech, and its relation to acting, and failure to act, in such uniquely focused terms.

Although Hobsbawm places most of Africa outside the reach of Western modernity and democratisation—there are, he states boldly, no democracies in Africa—no country perhaps has enacted the paradox he describes as fully as South Africa: the very existence of the commission is testimony to the violent gestation of a democracy which puts the Western world to shame. Hobsbawm contrasts the mile-long queues of the 1994 election in South Africa with the dwindling numbers of voters in the democracies of the West, and takes this fact to be one of the clearest signs of failure in the polity ("at the cost of the integrity of the political process"; 34–38 percent of the electorate voted in the last U.S. election).[7] The chairman of the commission, Archbishop Desmond Tutu, makes a similar point. "In normal [his word] countries," he comments on the second page of his own book on the commission, trying to convey the exhilaration of April 1994, "the concern was usually about voter apathy."[8] What's normal? we might ask. True to the spirit of one strand of modern intellectual life, Tutu has given to abnormality a positive, celebratory, political gloss.

The Indian woman's testimony is given at the end of the report of the Special Hearing for Women which came about when a workshop on gender pressured the commission to acknowledge that it might be "missing some of the truth through lack of sensitivity to gender issues" (4:282). This may at a superficial glance seem surprising, for there is a sense in which the Truth and Reconciliation Commission was dominated by the voices of women. It is they who predominantly speak. But they mostly testify as the often sole surviving relatives and dependents of the mainly males who had suffered violations of human rights. The aim of the special hearing, then, was to create a space in which women might talk of the violations they had undergone, might therefore speak for themselves. The Indian woman appears at the very end of this section of the report concluding the fourth volume—concluding in a sense the whole report since the fifth and final volume gives the Findings—under a section entitled "Women as Perpetrators." Barely five pages long, it is perhaps the most depleted section of the report (the report runs to nearly 3,000 pages overall). Of the 7,128 applications for amnesty received by the commission only fifty-six were known to come from women. Under apartheid, the message seems to be, there is very little women were guilty of.

It is in this blurred and almost empty context—like a frame with no painting—at a moment of the hearings which might, but for pressure from below, have not even existed, that a woman steps forward and claims for apathy a fully political status. Presenting the commission with something which it had by its own account neglected (it lists apathy as a feature under the "Neglected Factor" of "Secrecy and Silence": "Much of the country's population went silent through fear, apathy, indifference or genuine lack of information" (5:250, 299, although in the chapter on the perpetrators, the commission does allude to what it defines as "diminished affective reactivity" [5:259])—something intriguing, unexpected, disturbing perhaps, certainly bizarre. What—her appearance dramatically focuses—are the limits of accountability? How far does it spread? If the idea of apathy is so disquieting in this context, it is because it brings the issue of accountability, for the last person who might seem to be accountable, home to roost. It seems to me that it is not a coincidence—nor the first or last time—that a woman, tucked away almost in the back pages of history, speaks—if not *the*—certainly a truth. One of the things her testimony forces us to acknowledge is that we cannot claim apathy as the exclusive political property of the West.

I always start the course I teach on South African literature by asking the students to say, as economically as possible—a word, image, character—what, when they think of South Africa, comes into their minds. It gives us a sense before we begin of an engagement which is going to be, for most people in the room, partial, tentative, and refracted in space and time. In one year, the course almost didn't get going when a white student, in response to this query, said "guilt." She was challenged by another white student who claimed, outraged, that in relation to South Africa, whites in Britain had nothing whatsoever to feel guilty about. Should this happen again, I will refer the students to the Truth and Reconciliation Report, which, in the spirit of fullest reconciliation (hence of course the title), nonetheless does not mince words when it comes to naming the British. In addition to providing a full historical account for each region whose stories of human rights violations it tells, the report opens, after the chairman's foreword, with a chapter on history which regresses accountability for apartheid into South Africa's British-dominated past. This is just one example from the very first pages of the report:

> It is important to remember that the 1960 Sharpeville massacre (with which the mandate of the Commission begins) was simply the latest in a long line of similar killings of civilian protestors in South African history. It was, for example, not a National Party administration but the South African party government, made up primarily of English-speaking South Africans, that in July 1913 crushed a series of miners' strikes on the Reef—sending in the army and killing just over one hundred strikers and onlookers. Thrice in 1921 and 1922, this same governing party let loose its troops and planes. . . . Thus, when the South African Defence Force (SADF) killed just over 600

men, women and children, combatant and non-combatant, at Kassinga in Angola in 1978, and when the South African Police (SAP) shot several hundred black protestors in the weeks following the June 16 events at Soweto, they were operating in terms of a well-established tradition of excessive or unjustifiable use of force against government opponents. (1:26)

A simple act of historical recollection which contains a gentle rebuff to the temporal mandate of the TRC (Sharpeville, the start date, was not the start). And while South Africa entered a permanent winter with the Native Land Act of 1913—"There is winter in the Native Land Act. . . . [T]he trees are stripped and leafless"—this too is not the beginning.

> But if this was an act of wholesale dispossession and discrimination, so too was the 1909 South Africa Act which was passed, not by a South African legislature, but by the British Parliament. (1:28)

In relation to British accountability, the report—from its very opening pages —chooses to jog the mind. To use the words of Gerry Hugo, former intelligence officer of the South African Defence Force and torturer (the interview in *Index on Censorship*'s special issue on Truth Commissions and War Tribunals is entitled "Confession of a Torturer"): "Accountability doesn't stop" (he is in fact talking about de Klerk).[9]

But it is not as simple as this (you might think that there is nothing easier for the white liberal intellectual in Britain than to point to historical accountability in this sense). For in fact the report of the Truth and Reconciliation Commission can also be read for the immense difficulty with which it surrounds the issue of accountability—historical and political, collective and individual—in the modern world. The Indian woman's appeal gives one particularly bold, or striking, instance of this. Accountability, the commission itself and the controversies it has generated clearly demonstrate, is not just a matter of answering the question: who? It is not just a matter of burrowing into corners to find responsibility, or indeed guilt, lulling in the dark—even apathetic—night of the soul. On this issue, although it takes up a strong position, the commission is not so much judge (it was not of course a criminal hearing) as the active, troubled, sometimes uncertain, not always unified participant in the changing face and climate of what it describes. Hence the "challenge" of my title: "The Challenge of South Africa's Truth and Reconciliation Commission to the Intellectual in the Modern World." I read the report as a document which testifies not only to the horrors of the modern world but to a problem integral to the very recognition of such horror, a recognition which it has perhaps done more than any other modern process to achieve (the only truth commission of our time to have held its hearings in public, no other hearing has managed to combine truth-seeking with quasi-judicial power [1:54]). How do you at once recognise the fullness and extent of historical accountability and draw boundaries around it, how do you let it flow (in the words of Roelf Meyer of the National Party: "Wrongs . . . flowed from apartheid" [5:403]), while also keeping it in, if not its proper, then at least a definable, precisely *accountable*, place?

To take perhaps the most important and controversial decision of the commission on this topic: It is only recently in international law that non-state actors have been indictable for gross violations of human rights (1:69). Drawing on decisions of the International Criminal Tribunal in relation to the former Yugoslavia as recent as 1997, the report states: "The Act establishing the Commission adopted this more modern position. In other words it did not make a finding of a gross violation of human rights conditional on a finding of state action" (1:70). If this was crucial to pull in all the abuses committed between the release of Mandela and his election in 1994, when "the great majority of human rights violations were being carried out by persons who were not bound to a political authority" (2:5), it also means that all human rights violations, regardless of their provenance, whether carried out by resistance movements or by the apartheid state, become not ethically, but effectively, equal: "A gross violation is a gross violation, whoever commits it and for whatever reason" (1:12). What matters is the nature of the act. Justification, the central plank of legal accountability, is therefore set aside.

> The position adopted by the Commission was that any killing, abduction, torture or severe ill-treatment which met the other requirements of the definition, amounted to a gross violation of human rights, regardless of whether or not the perpetrator could be held accountable for the conduct. . . . There is legal equivalence between all perpetrators. (1:72, 12)

The commission therefore holds to the distinction, older in international law, between the justice of the means and the justice of the cause of war: "The Commission concurred with the international consensus that those who were fighting for a just cause were under an obligation to employ just means in the conduct of this fight" (1:69). On the justice of the cause, the report is of course unequivocal: apartheid was a crime against humanity, and the struggle against it a just war.

Within these terms, confusing as it may seem, and for some critics unjust, the ANC—in the finding that almost stopped the publication of the report—becomes wholly accountable. Not legally—legal accountability has been set aside (the commission is not a court, it is a hearing). Something more like answerable. And ironically, all the more so because, unlike those at the summit of former power, specifically de Klerk, the ANC accepted responsibility for the actions of its members.

> The Commission takes note that the political leadership of the ANC and the command structure of MK have accepted political and moral responsibility for all the actions of its members in the period 1960–1994 and therefore finds that the leadership of the ANC and MK must take responsibility and be accountable for all gross violations of human rights perpetrated by its membership and cadres in the mandate period. (2:685)

(All the findings of the commission are presented in small bold capital letters which makes them look on the page like an inscription on a tomb.)

A great deal of attention has been paid to this finding of the commission; it is, depending on from where you are looking, the finding on which the ethical viability of the commission either falls or rests. But there has been less focus on what it says about the issue of accountability, the fraught and fine distinctions, in and out of law, on which it is based. For one set of critics, which includes the present Minister for Education, from the moment the commission chose to define violations of human rights in terms of individual acts, it ceased—politically and historically—to be viable: "There is," write Kader and Louise Asmal and Ronald Suresh Roberts, in a follow-up article to their book on the commission, "simply no proportionality between the two sides of the struggle, a fact that is lost in the Commission's decision to individualise its definition of a gross human rights abuse" (interestingly, in view of this, all individual explanations of atrocity are rejected in the chapter on "Causes and Motives" in favour of an analysis in terms of the group). They continue: "This is a failure deriving from a lack of political and ethical understanding."[10]

How can everyone be equally answerable when the means available to the opponents, given in advance, are so unequal? How can you hold in the same measure, consider both as perpetrators, an illegal state and the combatants of a just war? For Asmal, Asmal, and Roberts, in response to apartheid and as its appropriate legacy for international human rights law, the distinction between just cause and means of war has become—or rather, it *should* become—redundant: "Given the convention-dependent nature of the morality of war, and apartheid's wholesale breach of those conventions, the question of *jus ad bellum* cannot be arbitrarily separated from the latter question of justice in the conduct of the cause, *jus in bello*."[11] Ironically, however, if this path had been followed, the Truth and Reconciliation Commission might never have started. Although called into being to effect the transition to democracy (without the possibility of amnesty in some form, the transition could not have been peaceably guaranteed), it nonetheless had its germ in the decision by the ANC itself to investigate its own human rights abuses. In fact, it was Kader Asmal who mooted the idea, on behalf of the ANC, on his installation as professor of human rights law at the University of the Western Cape on 25 May 1992.

Spread accountability too wide by flattening out the differences between the state and its opponents, then oddly, symmetrically, it will also start to shrink, as the crimes of apartheid become more and more the acts of individuals, less and less the machinery of the unjust and illegal apartheid state ("the violence of the law"—in the report's own words—pushed over the legal edge [1:40]). Once it has been individualised, the act stands out in bold, plucked out of its context. In fact, the more inhuman and outrageous the act— remember the commission's own self-critique for its stress on the "outrageous"—the more drastically it curtails the commission. The report acknowledges as one of its failings its inability to bring under its sway the basic, daily humiliations, inequalities, and fundamental social injustice—mostly still unredeemed—of the apartheid state: "Our mandate was not the policies of apartheid" (5:48).[12] When Commissioner Dr Ramashala, referring to those who fall outside the commission's mandate, especially the orphaned children of the struggle, says to Roelf Meyer of the National Party: "I really have never heard any discussions from the political parties about these children and our future, because these are our future South Africa," Meyer responds: "If we can't find an answer to the very question that you have put, then the work of the Commission, with all respect, is not going to be in the long term worth anything" (5:403).

A similar point was made by Lewis Nkosi when judge Albie Sachs, also central in the founding of the commission, came to Queen Mary College at the invitation of the Law Department in 1998 to lecture on the history and justification for the commission (a lecture he has given worldwide). Nkosi simply asked him what the present government was planning to do about redistribution of land (the issue which has of course emerged so explosively in Zimbabwe in the past year).

So what comes first? Which form of transformation—psychic and subjective, or material and redistributive—will provide the real, sure, foundation for the other? For you could of course argue—as the rationale for the whole commission and as Asmal himself argued when putting his original proposal for the commission in 1995—that a nation aiming to build a new future for its people, whatever concrete measures it enacts, without a reckoning with its own past violence will be building the whole edifice on sand.

> We must take the past seriously as it holds the key to the future. The issues of structural violence, of unjust and inequitable economic social arrangements, of balanced development in the future cannot be properly dealt with unless there is a conscious understanding of the past.

(His words are cited on the first pages of the Mandate chapter [1:49]).

Accountability as an issue is therefore inseparable from that of justice. Justice, of course in the most familiar sense, was set aside by the act establishing the commission. "There would have been no negotiated settlement and so no new democratic South Africa," Tutu writes, "had the negotiators on one side insisted that all the perpetrators be brought to trial. While the Allies could pack up and go home after Nuremberg, we in South Africa had to live with onto another" (this chapter of his book is called "Nuremberg or National Amnesia? A Third Way").[13] No trials also because they would simply have been too long and too costly, and because with the burden of absolute proof— "beyond all reasonable doubt"—falling on the investigators, too many of the guilty would have escaped the net (although the commission itself was enormously hampered by the Corbett decision, which stipulated that anyone against whom a detrimental finding was being contemplated should be given forewarning and a reasonable opportunity to respond). "We discovered in the course of the Commission's investigations," Tutu observes as part of this case, "that the supporters of apartheid were ready to lie at the drop of a hat. . . . They lied as if it were going out of fashion, brazenly and with very considerable conviction."[14] He doesn't, however, pause to ask whether his comment casts the whole basis of a Truth Commission into doubt.

But if justice, as in full-scale criminal proceedings, is set aside, it reappears as redistributive justice all the more forcefully through the commission's back door. I have already given one example in the exchange between Ramashala and Roelf Meyer. This is from the Minister of Justice, cited in a section called "Amnesty and Social Justice" in the chapter on Concepts and Principles from volume 1 of the report.

We have a nation of victims, and if we are unable to provide complete justice on an individual basis . . . it is possible for us . . . to ensure that there is historical and collective justice for the people of our country. If we achieve that, if we achieve social justice and move in that direction . . . at that level we will be able to say *that justice has been done.* (1:124, original emphasis)

And on this matter, there is, as it were, a fault line running through the commission more or less by its own account. For if the commission, or rather its associated amnesty hearings, has the quasi-judicial power to grant amnesty, on reparation and rehabilitation it has solely the power to recommend. It was one of the chief principles of the commission to restore the dignity of victims (the discussion of whether indeed they should be called "victims" turned on this concern): "restoring the human and civil *dignity* of [such] victims by granting them an opportunity to relate their own accounts of the violations of which they were the victims" (1:55). Dignity in the act of speech— this the commission could enact, in this sense the commission is one of the great performatives of modern times; dignity of a continuing life is something else: "And by recommending reparation measures in respect of them . . . the individual reparation grant provides resources to victims in an effort to restore their *dignity*" (5:184).[15]

One of these forms of dignity is measurable, calculable; one is not. The strength and uniqueness of the commission is to have thrown itself into the realm of the incalculable, speech upon speech for victims for whom speech— pained, sometimes reluctant, by no means always healing—was the only thing left to say. But you could argue that these two forms of dignity—of speech and of daily life—are not so much incommensurable as critically reliant on, or even subtractable from, each other. That the speech of the victim, the speech to which at one level the whole of the hearings was devoted, cannot reach its destination, unless economic equality, social justice is achieved (the minority, dissenting commissioner, Wynand Malan, even argues that liberal rights can act as an obstruction to social rights—the granting of social rights by the previously elite minority costs, as in hurts, more). The last paragraph of Findings and Conclusions states,

Ultimately, however, because the work of the Commission includes reconciliation, it needs to unleash a process that contributes to economic developments that redress past wrongs as a basis for promoting lasting reconciliation. This requires *all those who benefited* from apartheid, not only those whom the Act defines as perpetrators, to commit themselves to the reconciliation process. (5:258)

The differential of accountability, lost in one sense in the body of the report, returns therefore on the issue of redistributive justice; as does its infinite, one might say, interminable extensibility: "*all those who benefited*" is in italics.

Wole Soyinka—in a wonderfully theatrical moment in an already theatrical speech on "Reparations, Truth, and Reconciliation"—gives the comic—black comic—version.

> Just to let one's fantasy roam a little—what really would be preposterous or ethically inadmissible in imposing a general levy on South Africa's white population? This is not intended as a concrete proposal, but as an exercise in pure speculation. . . . [S]uch an offer could originate from the beneficiaries of Apartheid themselves, in a voluntary gesture of atonement—it need not be a project of the state. Is such a genesis—from within the indicted group itself—truly beyond conception? . . . [Should] some external prodding prove necessary, the initiative could be taken up by someone of the non-establishment stature of Archbishop Desmond Tutu. The respected cleric and mediator mounts his pulpit one day and addresses his compatriots on that very theme: "White brothers and sisters in the Lord, you have sinned, but we are willing to forgive. The scriptures warn us that the wages of sin are death but, in your case, they seem to be wealth. If therefore you chose to shed a little of that sinful wealth as a first step towards atonement . . . etc. etc."[16]

The suggestion that perpetrators should make a financial contribution to the families of victims is also made by Cynthia Ngewu, mother of one of the Gugulethu Seven, at the forum on Reconciliation, Reconstruction and Economic Justice in Cape Town in March 1997 ("the best way to demonstrate a truthful commitment to peace and a truthful commitment to repentance" [5:402]). But it says something that outside that context, Soyinka can only conjure up the possibility of such material accountability on the part of the white community as fantasy.

There is therefore, by its own account, a hiatus in the commission, a double deal on either side of the truth in which one justice is exchanged for another, neither of which are exactly there. Justice, as in criminal proceedings, set aside for the commission to do its work; justice as in social justice suspended beyond its remit into an unknowable future. In the middle sits "restorative justice," the foundation of the commission's daily work, but only "if the emerging truth unleashes a social dynamic that includes redressing the suffering of victims will it meet the ideal of restorative justice" (1:131). If the commission presents us more starkly than any other modern document with the difficult relationship between truth and language it also forces a no less crucial and fraught connection between the registers of justice and truth. As Wole Soyinka puts the question: "Is knowledge on its own of lasting effect?"[17]

It is not then, quite, that making accountability a matter of individual acts fails to discriminate appropriately, veiling the state behind its agents; if anything it is the opposite, as each individual act described, along with all the acts which surrounded it and made it possible—the "interstice between power and indifferent or supportive agency"—are, in a still unredeemed future, held to indefinite account. To read the report is to watch accountability contract and expand, pulsing under the pressure of a set of crucial but barely sustainable distinctions. "Accountability doesn't stop." There is no upper limit—hence the devastating effect on the commissioners of the denials and fudges of de Klerk; there is no outer limit—the interstice between "power and indifferent or supportive agency" is very, very wide; not before, not after—the commission makes its recommendations, halfway between a pledge and a plea. . . .

The original meaning of the word "apathy" was to be without "pathos," insensibility to suffering, the highest virtue for the Stoics, only gradually degrading itself to listless, stolid indifference. It could be, however, that in the setting of South Africa, apathy includes something of the earlier meaning, in which suffering—actively—is held at bay. A state of mind racing away from itself. Apathy in the modern sense would then contain, working away inside it, the germ of its own undoing, a kind of internal dissent. The implication would be that, for anyone struck with apathy in a situation of historic injustice, there is a partial recognition, not just of the suffering of others, but of what it would do to you, just how far you might have to go, to make the link. If making those links is, as I see it, one of the tasks of modern intellectual life, one of the things South Africa's Truth and Reconciliation Commission teaches me is that it has never been more important or harder to do so.

The Body of Evil: Arendt, Coetzee, and 9/11

The wind of faith is blowing to remove evil from the peninsula.

—Osama Bin Laden, statement broadcast on al-Jazeera television,
7 October 2001

Out of the shadows of this evil should emerge lasting good.

—Tony Blair, Labour Party Conference, 2 October 2001

The way of the wicked will be defeated, those who profess evil will not prosper.

—Ariel Sharon, cited in the *Sunday Times*, 10 March 2002

Evil, as these quotes suggest, is a moveable feast. It has the strange characteristic of being at once an absolute, and something far closer to what linguistics calls a "shifter." Pronouns, famously the pronoun "I," are purely indexical signs which refer only to the moment they are spoken. They only work for any one of us because they can be appropriated by everyone else. Hence "shifter." Their meaning resides in their capacity to move. There is of course something deeply unsettling about this—after all the pronoun "I" is the word in which we invest our most fundamental sense of self. Evil has something of the same aura. When people use the word "evil," it is very unusual to question whether they in fact know what they are talking about. And yet, in the above quotes, "evil" refers alternately to the United States, to Al-Qaeda, and to suicide bombers in Israel/Palestine. Read them out without identifying the sources, as I did at a debate organised by the *London Review of Books* in May 2002: "The War on Terror—Is There an Alternative?," and people are hard pressed to say, not only who is being referred to as evil but, more interestingly, who is *speaking*. People using the term "evil" all sound the same.[1]

In considering evil, we should perhaps start by noticing this contradiction. Surest of terms, invariably invoked with the most passionate if at times desperate conviction, evil also spins on its axis, loses its way. It behaves like that part of language which fatally, if invisibly, undermines the certainty of our speech. Evil is also mobile in another sense. Like all words for "immediately" which gradually degrade into meaning something like "in a while," "evil" has a remarkable capacity for extending and diluting itself. The *Oxford English Dictionary* lists as the meanings for "evil": "wickedness, moral depravity, sin," then "whatever is censurable, painful, malicious or disastrous," and finally "any particular thing that is physically or morally harmful." Provided it is unwelcome, evil can be *any particular thing*. A void opens waiting to be filled. During his first election campaign (so before 11 September), Bush commented on the enemies of America: "We're not so sure who they are, but we know they're there." More recently, Defense Secretary Donald Rumsfeld explained the Pentagon's shift from a "threat-based strategy" to an offensive "capabilities-based approach" in terms of the need "to defend our nation against the unknown." (As Frances Fitzgerald puts it: "[This] means simply that the Pentagon can ask for whatever it wants without having to justify its requests by the existence of even a potential enemy.")[2] In this essay, I want to pursue the radical instability, or vacuity, of evil—as distinct from the "banality of evil"—to take and remake Hannah Arendt's famous phrase.

Since 11 September 2001 evil, as one might say, is in the air. In an interview I conducted with Noam Chomsky for a television film on Israel, he described how Turkey, Israel, and the United States are referred to in the Egyptian press as the "axis of evil": "plenty of evil," he continued, "in this case a real axis, not an invented one." Similarly, as the Russian Formalist Boris Tomachevsky pointed out in 1925, new literary schools, opposing an older aesthetic, nearly always proclaim themselves, one way or another, more "realistic" or attuned to reality than the one that went before. The issue here is not who has the greater right to make the claim, but the contested nature of its grounds. Sometimes vocally, more often silently, there is an argument going on whenever "evil" is proclaimed. Chomsky is in fact making a very simple point. He is suggesting that those who brandish the epithet "evil" post–11 September, notably Bush in his "axis of evil" speech, ignore the uneven distribution of power (it was not, Bush has repeatedly insisted, America's power that was the target but her freedom). Choosy and yet indiscriminating, evil becomes the supreme and unjust equaliser between men. When you accuse someone of evil, history disappears. In the great and uneven distribution of the world's resources, it becomes strictly irrelevant where or who they are.

In the report of South Africa's Truth and Reconciliation Commission, the commissioners point to a striking disparity—the "magnitude gap"—between the perception of violations of human rights under apartheid by the victims and by the perpetrators of the crime.[3] For the victims, such action either exceeds the range of the comprehensible, enters a realm of mystery, or it is "deliberately malicious," "sadistic," "an end in itself" (Gillian Slovo's account of the amnesty hearings of the man responsible for her mother's death was entitled by the *Guardian* "Evil Has a Human Face").[4] "Each party," writes Susan Neiman in *Evil in Modern Thought: An Alternative History of Philosophy*, "insists with great conviction that its opponents' actions are truly evil, while its own are merely expedient."[5] Either way, the act deemed evil is beyond the pale; it fails to enter a world in which anyone would choose to recognise him- or herself. In South Africa, for the perpetrators their acts were the rational consequence of historical necessity, the nation defending itself by all available means from a Communist threat. As Archbishop Desmond Tutu puts it in his introduction: "The supporters of the previous regime have been at great pains to insist that the reason they did many of the unsavoury things that have since some to light was largely because they were fighting an evil and predatory Communism."[6] The disparity is eloquent of the way evil "shifts" in another sense—more "shifty," as one might say. "I" am never evil; only "you" are. In this respect the term "evil" perversely mimics the first-person pronoun in reverse. No one wants to wear it; unlike the "I" which each human subject spends a large part of their life rushing—however ruthlessly—to claim. But it may be too that the South African experience can help us understand one of the reasons why Arendt's "banality of evil" was such a controversial phrase. If evil, it must be total. No part of the personality must escape. "Evil," states Elizabeth Costello in J. M. Coetzee's essay/short story on this topic—"The Problem of Evil"—which will be the focus of much of this essay, "would not be true evil if it can be exited and entered at will."[7] Evil accepts no qualifiers. You can't do evil partly (it is never something you "sort of" do). Reduce the force of evil one iota, and the perpetrator of atrocity has won the argument. His actions just might be reasoned, necessary. Or, simple, banal, they make up the colours of the day. For the victims, the commissioners comment, the experience was sheer "horror"; for the perpetrators, more often, "a very small thing." "Perpetrators," they continue dryly, "tend to have less emotions about their acts."[8]

What seems to be at stake then is the issue of how much, or rather how little, it is permissible to feel. The worst outrage is for someone to have committed an atrocity without the requisite affect. In Gillian Slovo's memoir,

Every Secret Thing, she describes her encounter with the man who organised the murder of her mother as a moment of mutual dissociation: "Our meeting," she writes, "had been an exercise in dissociation from which I'd emerged in a stupor that had sent me straight into a dreamless afternoon sleep."[9] Craig Williamson is incapable—syntactically incapable—of recognising what he has done. Read the pronouns in this sentence when Slovo presses whether Ruth's death weighed on him.

> "Yeah," he said grudgingly, "I said that you'll never get rid of. You can wish it or regret it or do as much as you like but you can't change it. What's done is done and if you try to analyse why it was done and how it was done and what the strategy and belief behind it was . . . it's difficult to believe that it could have been done but it was."[10]

The "I" hardly figures here, nor indeed the crime: "*that* you'll never get rid of." I spend some time arguing with my students in a course I teach on South African writing, whether that last sentence—"it's difficult to believe that it could have been done but it was"—indicates a subject struggling to enter his statement, acknowledging that he is faced with something too dreadful to be thought, or is merely the voice, in Slovo's words, of "a huge mountain of a man, all oil, and lies, and half-excuses."[11]

We could perhaps ask, then, whether it is the action that is the worst evil or the perpetrator's refusal to recognise the horror, to identify psychically with his victim or, in simpler language, to "connect." It was Arendt's insistence that neither the intention of the perpetrator nor his affectivity should be deemed relevant in measuring the magnitude of the crime (Eichmann's apparent lack of evil intent should not exonerate him). One of the wagers of South Africa's Truth Commission was to make victims and perpetrators go the distance and recognise each other across what the commissioners themselves describe as an almost insurmountable abyss. In the trial of Ruth Ellis, who murdered her lover in 1950s Britain (she was the last person to hang in this country), or in the response to social worker Marietta Higgs, who had scores of children she suspected of being victims of abuse in Midlands Britain in the 1980s withdrawn from their homes, the worst outrage was the lack of emotion both women displayed. Higgs was of course wresting children from a crime many would classify as "evil," Ellis was technically on the other side. And yet the screaming outrage against these two women, partly one suspects because they were women, put something graphic on display. Anyone brushed with "evil" must, for *us* to survive *their* encounter, lose or appear to lose control of their minds. "Evil" is unbearable or it is nothing. Like death, it is something from which you don't return.

In 2002, I attended a conference in Tilburg entitled "Evil," the second of a series organised by the Nexus Institute called "The Quest for Life." J. M. Coetzee accepted the invitation on condition that he could deliver his paper in fictional form. Returning to the format of his Tanner Lectures of 1998, published as *The Lives of Animals*, now republished as *Elizabeth Costello*, Coetzee chose this occasion to revive the character of Elizabeth Costello, feminist, vegetarian, and campaigner who, in her first appearance, had given a prestigious series of literary lectures on the somewhat unexpected topic of animal slaughter (she was invited as the famous author of a 1969 novel about Molly Bloom, the wife of Leopold Bloom, "nowadays spoken of in the same breath as *The Golden Notebook* and *The Story of Christa T* as pathbreaking feminist fiction").[12] In this instance she has been invited to Amsterdam to address a conference on evil. Once again Coetzee doubles his character with his own position as speaker (although the immediacy of this is lost in the published version of the text). The story turns on a crisis. Costello has come to speak about a book—Paul West's *The Very Rich Hours of Count von Stauffenberg*—a book whose depiction of evil has deeply repelled her and led her to question the ethical limits of the writer's craft and task, only to discover that Paul West is attending the conference. For Costello, the issue is precisely how or where to place evil in her mind. *The Very Rich Hours of Count von Stauffenberg* tells the story of Hitler and his would-be assassins in the Wehrmacht, above all of their execution which is described in a physical and mental detail which she finds obscene. West goes too far into a realm where she now feels, as a result of the effect on her of reading this book, writers perhaps should not tread: "In representing the workings of evil, the writer may *unwittingly* make evil seem attractive and thereby do more harm than good" (that "unwittingly," in italics in the text, is a concession—Costello knows by now that West is in the audience).[13]

The story is wonderfully self-defeating, because its central proposition will only work if we enact in relationship to Elizabeth the very form of fictional identification she is now cautioning against. That is to say, it only works if we find ourselves, without let or inhibition, entering Elizabeth's own mind. A mind which includes, not just the horror of reading the book and the ethical protest it provokes on her behalf, but also the memory—reluctant but overwhelming—of a scene of sexual violence to which she was subjected as a young girl. As well as, in perhaps the most powerful moment of the essay, an instant where, in a shocking identification, Elizabeth looks at her own naked body and imagines herself as one of those women victims of the Nazis "at the lip of the trench into which they would, in the next minute, the next second, tumble, dead or dying with a bullet to the brain."[14] In an ironical twist which makes her objections more not less poignant, it is Elizabeth, not Paul West, who—we might say—does the best line in forced identifications, throwing the reader into the arms of evil, or into the pit.

The point is that her critique of the power of writing only works because of the power of her own; because she does to the reader—through the strength of her ability to convey her experience—exactly what she objects to having had done to her by Paul West's book. Of course, being in a story by Coetzee, she is only too aware of this. Costello argues with herself: "Yet she is a writer too. She does the same kind of thing, or used to" (that "used to" is sleight of hand since Costello—Coetzee as writer—is doing it to the reader *now*).[15] Writing forces unexpected, often unwelcome identifications, or it does nothing. Coetzee knows well that scenes like the one where Elizabeth was assaulted, however repugnant, will be compelling to the reader. Designed to shock, they make the reader intimate with fear. In this case there is an added pull because the violence is conveyed as an almost reluctant memory, the narrator's private musings on an event which she has never communicated before. We are the hidden, privileged, party to a confession of something so devastating it has never, until now, made the passage into words. Nineteen years old, she has just been picked up by a docker and goes back to his room.

> "I'm sorry," she said, "I'm really sorry, can we stop." But Tim or Tom would not listen. When she resisted, he tried to force her. For a long time, in silence, panting, she fought him off, pushing and scratching. To begin with he took it as a game. Then he got tired of that, or his desire tired, turned to something else, and he began to hit her seriously. He lifted her off the bed, punched her breasts, punched her in the belly, hit her a terrible blow with his elbow to her face. When he was bored with hitting her he tore up her clothes and tried to set fire to them in the waste-paper basket.[16]

And so on. . . . "It was," Costello comments, "her first brush with evil."[17] She is convinced that he liked hurting her more than he would have liked sex. "By fighting him off, she had created an opening for the evil in him to emerge."[18] I should perhaps add, as it will be relevant later, that while I am happy—although "happy" is not the right word—to reproduce these lines here, I found it very difficult and then impossible to read them out at the annual Conference of the Council for College and University English in Oxford and then at the conference honouring Gillian Beer on her retirement in Cambridge in 2003 (it gets worse).

It would, I think, be fair to describe such a moment as obscene (in the sense of what it wants to be). In fact Costello saves this epithet for the description of the bodies of the plotters on the point of execution, above all for the way the executioner humiliates and terrifies them, taunting them with the physical details of what is to come. Can there really, she asks, have been witnesses who wrote this down in such detail? Or is it West's fantasy: his passionate identification with the victims, but no less—of necessity if he is to render the scene faithfully—with the executioner, "the butcher with last week's blood caked under his fingernails," whom he brings so intensely to life? ("Terrible that such a man should have existed, even more terrible that he should be hauled out of the grave when we thought he was safely dead.")[19] This is, for Costello, "obscene." Although it is not clear in the following sentence whether it is the grim abjection of the plotters or the no less grim perversity of the executioner which oversteps the bounds: "*Obscene*. That is the word, a word of contested etymology that she must hold on to. She chooses to believe that *obscene* means off-stage. To save our humanity, certain things that we may want to see (*may want to see because we are human!*) must remain for ever off-stage."[20] To rephrase: obscenity must remain offstage because, as humans, we want to see it so much. This, I would suggest, comes very close to making evil, if not the essence of writing, then no more than an exaggerated, or a kind of worse-case, embodiment of what compels us to read. Like evil, writing is enticing: "He made her read, excited her to read."[21] We want to get inside other people's skins even if they are about to be fleeced alive. In the throes of identification—with victim *or* executioner—there is no limit to how far people are willing to go. What Costello seems to be objecting to is not evil so much as its *temptation*: "She had gone on reading, excited despite herself."[22]

The idea of evil as tempting has a long history (from the beginning, as one might say). One of the ways of thinking about the horrors of the last century —to leave aside for the moment those unfolding today—is as a transmutation in the age-old connection between these two terms. "Evil in the Third Reich," writes Hannah Arendt in her famous *Eichmann in Jerusalem: A Report on the Banality of Evil* of 1963, "had lost the character by which most people recognise it—the quality of temptation" (she is writing about the same history as West's book).[23] In civilised countries, she continues, the law assumes that the voice of conscience instructs its citizens: "Thou shalt not kill": "even though man's natural desires and inclinations may at times be murderous." But under Hitler, when the law changes sides, temptation follows suit: "Many Germans and many Nazis, probably an overwhelming majority of them, must have been tempted *not* to murder, *not* to rob, *not* to let their neighbours go off to their doom . . . and not to become accomplices in all these crimes by benefiting from them, but, God knows, they had learned how to resist temptation."[24]

Imagine then a situation where the law instructs you to commit acts you would barely entertain in your wildest dreams. In Freudian terms, the law is always a problem because our psychic enforcer, the superego, draws its energy from the unconscious it is meant to tame; which is why the superego's edicts often seem fierce or cruel. Laced with perversion. But this is something else. Now the superego is instructing you to let the most terrifying components of your own unconscious go stalking. Faced with such an edict, the voice of conscience pales, becomes a ghost of its former self. Tempting, but impotent. Like the memory of someone you might once have been. But it would be wrong to think that this is anarchy, a release into freedom, no holds barred. The strength of Arendt's analysis is that she recognises that there is something deadly in the law. Hence her repeated emphasis on the "reason of state" and its inherent violence: "The rule of law, although designed to eliminate violence and the war of all against all, always stands in need of the instruments of violence in order to assure its own existence."[25] Likewise Chomsky, against the dominant rhetoric on terrorism, relentlessly charts acts of Western-sanctioned state terrorism in the modern world.

Perhaps we are tempted by evil, find its literary representation so compelling, because evil is not just an outsider, nor just our guilty secret—the word "transgression" won't do here—but belongs at the heart of the very mechanisms we deploy in order to restrain it. Violence is never more terrifying than when it believes itself justified by the highest law (Bush has stated quite clearly that he has known his divine mission since 11 September). In Coetzee's story, it is the law—brazen, mocking—that produces the excessive energy which Costello describes as obscene: "In his gibes at the men about to die at his hands there was a wanton, an *obscene* energy that exceeded his commission."[26] This energy is contaminating, "like a shock, like electricity."[27] If it weren't, Costello as reader would have no reason to object. West has thrust her, not just into the horror of what is still for many the worst atrocity of the twentieth century, but into its *mind*. Fiction's greatest offence becomes its ability to turn us into perpetrators, each and every one.

In their chapter on "Concepts and Principles," the South African commissioners feel the need to justify their exploration of the "Causes, Motives, Perspectives" of the perpetrators which appears in the final volume of "Findings and Recommendations." Understanding can be seen as exonerating. Trying to get into the mind of the perpetrator is too risky: "Without seeing offender accountability as part of the quest for understanding, the uncovering of motives and perspectives can easily be misunderstood as excusing their violations."[28] Far from fiction, even in the most somber conditions of political assessment and analysis, to allow a mind to the perpetrators of atrocity is, it seems, to risk one identification too far (as I have argued in relation to suicide bombing).[29] In fact in the chapter itself, the perpetrators emerge as oddly without character. Psychological analysis is more or less eschewed: "In such situations, people act primarily in terms of their social identities rather than personal attributes."[30] "Political frameworks provide the fuel for atrocities."[31] One by one, the report rules out the argument from human nature (regression into atavistic behavior), the argument from psychopathology (no psychological dysfunction), the argument from authoritarianism (a collective phenomenon, not a personality type). In fact in a report that has been severely criticised for its emphasis on individual actors at the expense of a critique of state power, it is striking how in this chapter the whole analysis scrupulously, repeatedly, swerves in the direction of what Freud famously called group (or "mass") psychology. Under apartheid, crime became the law: "[To paraphrase Hannah Arendt]," write the commissioners at the end of the opening chapter on the historical context, "twentieth-century law in South Africa made crime legal."[32] The perpetrators are best understood in terms of social coercion or "binding" ("compliance," "identification," "internalisation").[33] Only acts, not individuals, can be described as "evil": "While acts of gross violations may be regarded as demonic, it is counterproductive to regard persons who perpetrated those acts as demonic."[34] In a strange mimicry of what collective identification is presumed to do to individuals (take away their personalities), it is as if there is nobody there.

And yet, by the account of the commissioners themselves, these explanations are unsatisfactory. There is a factor that escapes. On authoritarianism: "But does this offer an explanation for a predisposition to commit atrocities? Evidence is really rather thin"; on social identity: "It may be noted that social identity theory does not explain violence itself, but the preconditions of violence"; on group identification: "while these processes begin to explain why we become bound into groups, institutions and authorities, they do not yet suggest violence."[35] "Do not *yet*"—something has to wait. Without final cause, atrocity resists explanation, draws a blank. Attempting to explain the demonic, the commissioners find something invisible, unnegotiable, sinister (demonic?) at play. Evil, it seems, is not just an absolute, not just a shifter; it is an empty place. This may seem like a failure of explanation. Or it may take us, I want to suggest now, to the heart of the matter. In her famous exchange with Gershom Scholem over her book on Eichmann, Arendt writes,

> It is indeed my opinion now that evil is never "radical," that it is only extreme, and that it possesses neither depth nor any demonic dimension. It can overgrow and lay waste the whole world precisely because it spreads like a fungus on the surface. It is "thought-defying," as I said, because thought tries to reach some depth, to go to the roots, and the moment it concerns itself with evil, it is frustrated because *there is nothing*.[36]

To describe evil as a "fungus" is to remove from it even the faintest trace of sublimity. It also means, as Susan Neiman suggests, that the sources of evil do not reach to a depth "that would make us despair of the world itself."[37] But might there also be a connection, I want to ask for the rest of this essay, between evil as nothing, and evil as subject to, or even as the violent, intransigent—obscene—embodiment *of*, the highest law?

Arendt's analysis of Eichmann suggests there might be. She is best known for describing him as petty, banal (her phrase is cited by the commission). Arendt continues the quote above: "That is its 'banality.'" But in a less commented moment early in the book when she is introducing her main character, she tells of how he saw his birth as an "event to be ascribed to 'a higher Bearer of Meaning,' an entity somehow identical with the 'movement of the universe.'" She writes: "The terminology is suggestive. To call God a *Höheren Sinnesträger* meant to give him some place in the military hierarchy, since the Nazis had changed the military 'recipient of orders,' the *Befehlsempfanger*, into a 'bearer of orders,' a *Befehlsträger*, indicating, as in the ancient 'bearer of ill tidings,' the burden of responsibility and of importance that weighed supposedly upon those who had to execute orders."[38] Eichmann is dismissive of metaphysics—the moment is passed over—but it is nonetheless central to Arendt's analysis that Eichmann's "'boundless and immoderate admiration for Hitler'" (in the words of a defence witness) played a major part in his accepting that Hitler's *word*, without having to be written, had the force of law.[39] Hitler, or rather love of Hitler, comes close to the sacred. Evil is tempting because the devil, however despicable to the sanguine mind, takes on the aura of a god. There may be something mysterious, resistant to final explanation, in people's ability to commit evil acts, although to say that is already to run the risk of mystification—hence Arendt's insistence that evil must be understood (Neiman identifies two traditions on this issue, one from Rousseau to Arendt for which morality demands we make evil intelligible, the other from Voltaire to Jean Amery for which morality demands that we don't). But mystery might also be intrinsic to the process which enables individuals to violate, even in the name of legality, the bounds of all human law. In *The Brothers Karamazov*, the Grand Inquisitor says to Ivan Fyodorovich,

> There are only three powers, only three powers on earth, capable of con-
> quering and holding captive for ever the conscience of these feeble reb-
> els, for their own happiness—these powers are miracle, mystery and
> authority.[40]

Without depth—Arendt continues her letter: "Only the good has depth, can be radical"—evil relies on transcendence. This is of course to invert the normal order of things in which the devil is presumed to exert all his power from below.

To pursue this a little further, I shall take a detour, before returning to Coet- zee, via a moment which for many has become the new century's embodiment of evil. "Fear is a great form of worship, and the only one worthy of it is God"—these words are from "Atta's Document," the document released by the FBI that was found in the baggage of Mohammed Atta, the suspected ringleader of 11 September, thought to have piloted the first of the two planes into the Twin Towers. The original Arabic text has not been released, and only four of five original pages have been made available for translation.[41] Although its authenticity has been questioned by some (why wasn't his baggage on the plane?), and critiqued as a violation of Islam by others, it is such a bizarre mixture—in the words of the *Observer*, who published it on 30 September 2001—of the "apocalyptic," "dramatic," "sometimes downright banal," that it is hard to imagine it invented even by someone, post-9/11, intent on the most violent slandering of Islam. In fact three copies were found—one more in the wreckage of the plane that crashed in Pennsylvania, another in a car aban- doned by the hijackers outside Dulles Airport. "It is [therefore] unlikely," write the commentators Kanan Makiya and Hassan Mneimneh, "that many of the hijackers did not know the suicidal nature of their mission."[42] The document is, as they put it, "an exacting guide for achieving the unity of body and spirit necessary for success."[43] That God is the instructor is unsurprising. Returning to the spirit of the Prophet, to the brief period of his rule between 622 and 632, the manual calls for a return to the path of *ghazwah*, to be understood as a raid on the path of God.

> Consider that this is a raid on a path. As the Prophet said: "A raid . . . on the path of God is better than this World and what is in it."[44]

Most striking, however, is the way the words work, as divinely sanctioned performatives to be repeated at every stage: "Recite supplications," "Remind yourself and your brothers of the supplications and consider what their meanings are," "Recite repeatedly the invocations to God (the boarding invocation, the invocation of the town, the invocation of the place, the other invocations)," "When you arrive and see [the airport], and get out of the taxicab, recite the invocation of place," "Recite the supplication," "Wherever you go and whatever you do, you have to persist in invocation and supplication." Like the God to whom they are addressed, these supplications are infinite but invisible: "It should not be noticeable," "If you say it a thousand times, no one should be able to distinguish whether you were silent or whether you were invoking God."[45]

The preparation for the body is no less crucial than that of the mind: "Shave excess hair from the body and wear cologne," "Shower," "Tighten your shoes well, wear socks so that your feet will be solidly in your shoes," "Tighten your clothes"—in square brackets we are told by the *Observer* translator, Imad Musa: "a reference to making sure his clothes will cover his private parts at all times."[46] ("A ritual act of self-purification," as Bruce Lincoln puts it, "that helps secure salvation"—the process brings to mind the link Freud posited between religious observance and the compulsive actions of the obsessional.)[47] The body must be perfectly in place so that it can most perfectly forget or let go of itself: "True selflessness," comment Makiya and Mneimneh, "requires an acknowledgement of the flesh-and-blood self in order to become estranged from it."[48] If slaughter is, chillingly, a gift, it is not an act of aggression because there is precisely no-body there, only God: "Fight for the sake of God those who seek to kill you, and do not commit aggression. God does not favour those who aggress."[49] This is for the commentators the most frightening aspect of the document because it inserts into the Muslim tradition the idea of the martyr who, void of any communal purpose, acts solely to please God (there is no mention anywhere of any wrongs to be redressed).

> Martyrdom is not something bestowed by God as a favour on the warrior for his selflessness and devotion to the community's defence. It is a status to be achieved by the individual warrior, and performed as though it were his own private act of worship.[50]

Instead of which, they observe, martyrdom in the Muslim tradition is always subject to stringent forms of judgment about the communal benefit at stake (the tradition is "being turned on its head").[51]

Later developments of Islam relegate the most extreme forms of fear as worship to mystical experience, but here the martyr is driven by a fear of God which empties him of any personal intent. The document tells the story of Ali Bin Abi Talib (companion and close friend of the Prophet Mohammed), who, when spat on by a nonbeliever in battle, did not kill him immediately but raised his sword: "After he spat at me, I was afraid I would be striking him in revenge, so I lifted my sword." Only when sure of his purity of purpose did he go back and kill the man. Without qualities—remember Arendt on Eichmann: "He had no motives at all"—the document offers us an image of someone who purifies mind and body in the cause of slaughter: "You must make your knife sharp and must not discomfort your animal during the slaughter," and then heads, in both senses, for the skies.[52] If Eichmann, in Arendt's account, lacked intention, in the case of 11 September, the intention on the contrary could not have been more absolute—"a maximalist intention" in Lincoln's phrase (the hijackers are instructed to endlessly renew their plans).[53] "The description of evil as thoughtless," writes Susan Neiman, "captured so many cases of contemporary evil, that we were unprepared for a case of single-mindedly thoughtful evil."[54] But in both cases, something has to be emptied for a higher, deadly, purpose to be fulfilled.

"It is tempting," writes Lincoln, "in the face of such horror, to regard the authors of these deeds as evil incarnate. . . . Their motives, however, were intensely and profoundly religious."[55] Jane Smith, professor at Hartford Seminary, Connecticut, and author of *Islam in America*, comments: "Apparently one can assume that what was done was done by people out of a genuine and sincere belief that they were helping bring about the will of God. And that, in turn, may be the most frightening thing about it."[56] Or in the words of John Esposito, director of the Center for Muslim-Christian Understanding at

Georgetown University, "We have a certain need to explain what somebody does as totally irrational. . . . [T]he fact that they might come out of a pious background stuns us."[57] In fact, if martyrdom has become an individual path to transcendence, then piety has deformed itself (one reason among many for not seeing 11 September as the embodiment of Islam).

As we have seen in the essay on "Mass Psychology," Freud was eloquent on the subject of group insanity. But what would he have had to say about a superego carved so closely to the features of a monotheistic God that it would destroy half the world in His name? (It is a question, one should add, as relevant to Evangelical America as to fundamentalist Islam.)[58] Or was he already sentient of the dangers: "[In the history of religion] human beings found themselves obliged in general to recognise 'intellectual [geistige]' forces—forces, that is, which cannot be grasped by the senses (particularly by the sight) but which none the less produce undoubted and extremely powerful effects"?[59] In Civilisation and Its Discontents, he gave what remains today perhaps the most persuasive account of fear as the driving force of social life. The child lives in fear of a superego whose aggression knows no bounds simply because it has inherited all the aggressiveness which the child would like to use against it. There is something unavoidably craven, abject, masochistic —self-abolishing—in every subject's relationship to the law. When we read Atta's Document alongside Freud's text in an M.A. class in 2001, it seemed as if there was only one step from his analysis to the idea of obedience as a form of divinely sanctioned fear. "Fear," Freud writes, "is at the bottom of the whole relationship."[60] In the link between superego and ego, the link we rely on for entry into our social identities, fear is key. At the very least Freud seems to be suggesting that our worst acts—in the West as much as anywhere else—are driven by a tendency to worship what we are most frightened of.

In his essay on "The Structure of Evil," the British psychoanalyst Christopher Bollas describes evil as a form of transcendence. "The killer finds a victim who will die his death." The killer murders his victim, as it were, on his own behalf. Enacting death, he avoids his own subjection to its law. Every time the killer strikes, it is his own death that he avoids. In this analysis, murderousness is based on a passionate if involuntary identification. Like the term "evil" itself, killing serves to get rid of something felt as too threatening; you hand it over to someone else and then destroy it so that you can wipe your hands of the affair. Evil represents "the unconscious need to survive one's own death."[61]

184 THE JACQUELINE ROSE READER

Onto the other you slough off this mortal coil. If we go back to Costello, we could therefore say that every time fiction ushers us into a world of evil, it is at least partly our own death that we escape.

Transcending one's own death might be a fair description of Atta's Document. But Bollas's article can also take us back to Elizabeth Costello. If we return to the passage where she finds herself identifying with the women victims of Nazism at the edge of the pit quoted earlier, we see that it is a very specific body—the aging, flagging body—that Costello finds herself in identification with.

> If there were a mirror on the back of this door instead of just a hook, if she were to take off her clothes and kneel here before it, she, with her sagging breasts and knobbly hips, would look little different from the women in those intimate, those over-intimate photographs from the European war, glimpses into hell, who knelt naked at the lip of the trench.[62]

In "The Problem of Evil," aging and its humiliations are something of a refrain: "Twenty million, six million, three million, a hundred thousand: at a certain point the mind breaks down before quanta; and the older you get— this at any rate is what has happened to her—the sooner comes the breakdown"; "She does not know how old Paul West is. . . . Might he and she, in their different ways, not be old enough to be beyond embarrassment?"; "She does not like to see her sisters and brothers humiliated, in ways it is so easy to humiliate the old, by making them strip for example, taking away their dentures, making fun of their private parts."[63] This is at the heart of the most offending, *obscene*, chapter from West's book.

> Fumbling old men for the most part . . . their false teeth and their glasses taken from them . . . hands in their pockets to hold up their pants, whimpering with fear, swallowing their tears, having to listen to this coarse creature, this butcher with last week's blood caked under his fingernails, taunt them, telling them what would happen when the rope snapped tight, how the shit would run down their spindly old-man's legs, how their limp old-man's penises would quiver one last time?[64]

If this is the ultimate degradation, whose writing, it seems fair to ask—Paul West's, Elizabeth Costello's, or J. M. Coetzee's—is repeating the offence?

Is the ultimate evil then a dying body that no ablution or supplication can save? Is such a body—which of course means all bodies—the real disgrace? In Coetzee's prizewinning novel of that title, the central character, David Lurie, meets with his estranged wife after his sexual harassment of a young student has driven him from his university position: " 'Do you think,' she asks, 'a young girl finds any pleasure in going to bed with a man of that age? Do you think she finds it good to watch you in the middle of your. . . .' " Lurie muses: "Yet perhaps she has a point. Perhaps it is the right of the young to be protected from the sight of their elders in the throes of passion."[65] Again it is a refrain. Lurie takes tea with his daughter when he has just arrived at the farm: "He is aware of her eyes on him as he eats. He must be careful: nothing so distasteful to a child as the workings of a parent's body."[66] Explaining to her later why he will not appeal against his dismissal: "After a certain age one is simply no longer appealing, and that's that."[67] And perhaps most tellingly in the first chapter of the book:

> He ought to give up, retire from the game. At what age, he wonders, did Origen castrate himself? Not the most graceful of solutions, but then ageing is not a graceful business. A clearing of the decks, at least, so that one can turn one's mind to the proper business of the old: preparing to die.[68]

We might note too in passing that in *Disgrace* Lurie—following a violent assault by a group of black youths during which his daughter, Lucy, is raped—is forced to ask, when Lucy will not speak to him: "Do they think that where rape is concerned, no man can be where the woman is?" and then later to take his own question further: "He does understand; he can, if he concentrates, if he loses himself, be there, be the men, inhabit them, fill them with the ghost of himself. The question is, does he have it in him to be the woman?"[69] In *Disgrace*, the answer is that he doesn't. Lurie is never allowed to enter Lucy's violated experience and space.

But in the story of Costello on evil, Coetzee defies his own caution. He gives us Elizabeth's scene of sexual violence, puts us in the room with her, goes—one might say—to places where, by his own previous account in the earlier novel, the man should not, or cannot, tread. Is the worst offence of this story, therefore, not West's forcing us to enter—body and mind—into Hitler's executioners and the hangmen, not Costello letting us into a moment of sexual violence from her past, but Coetzee as author entering this time the mind of his female character at the very point which, in *Disgrace*—and it is not an aside, it is absolutely central to the dilemma explored by the novel—was not possible or permissible for the man? Is Coetzee, advertently, or perhaps in this instance inadvertently, indicting himself? Coetzee's preoccupation with the aging dying body gives us the other face—or underside—of transcendence. It suggests that the issue, in *Disgrace*, but not only in *Disgrace*, is not just one of moral turpitude but also of physical turpitude, a turpitude of the body, utterly effaced in Atta's Document, taken on—tremulously, obscenely—by Coetzee, to which one morality, *in extremis* as it were, may be a possible reply. *Disgrace* ends with Lurie, having dedicated himself to the care of abandoned and stricken dogs, handing one of them over to die. Lurie's connection to these dogs is the key to his transformation in the book. Earlier, in a crucial moment of dialogue with Lucy, Lurie—with obvious allusion to white treatment of the blacks in South Africa—had made his view of the place of dogs in the scheme of things very clear: "By all means let us be kind to them. But let us not lose perspective. We are of a different order of creation."[70] Lucy on the other hand is willing to envisage herself returning in her next life as a dog. (She is a Rawlsian—she knows that if there is to be any chance of justice in the world, then you are obliged to imagine yourself in the weakest place.)

Previously, like many other readers, I saw the last moment of the book as an act of compassion or mercy on the part of Lurie towards a degraded species: "Are you giving him up?" "Yes, I am giving him up."[71] Now I am more inclined to see it as an act of mercy towards himself. Nor do I think we can read this as simply a metaphor for a dying white South Africa and its language, although both can be read into the book (a reading confirmed by the fact that on his retirement in 2002 Coetzee left South Africa). Through Lurie and Costello, I see Coetzee as giving us one of the barest accounts, for someone for whom transcendence is no option, of the dilemma of a body—an aging, dying, body—that is repelled by itself. They are on a continuum: if you cannot secure a path to God, travel down the chain of being in the opposite direction. Lie down with the animals (the first book in which Costello appears, making her plea against animal slaughter, was called *The Lives of Animals*).

Coetzee is not alone. Jean Amery, author of one of the most harrowing accounts of life in Auschwitz, went on to write a book on aging, *On Aging: Revolt and Resignation*. Aging appears as an experience of horror—"*horror* and *angor*," "fear, *angor, angustiae*, constriction, anguish"—that, shockingly he insists, nothing of his experience in the camps can match.[72] To die in the camps would have been to be brought down by an enemy—"the good death by murder that didn't want to know me at all"—whereas aging comes from within, a sheer degradation that alienates us from our bodies while bringing us closer to their "sluggish mass than ever before."[73]

At a seminar organised by the University of Pittsburgh for its visiting students in London to mark the first anniversary of 11 September, seven minutes of footage were screened, footage only shown once on American and British television and then pulled as too disturbing by CNN. It consists mainly of bodies—visible, almost recognisable—plunging from the burning buildings to their deaths. There is, commented one participant in the seminar, a taboo on death in American culture. (In Russia, the image shown repeatedly was of people in the building waving white flags, an image never shown on U.S. television, presumably because it could be seen to signify surrender.) Above all a body must not be seen to die. Bodies that fail and fall. To efface, or preempt, such images George Bush—with the full backing of Tony Blair— went to war against Iraq. The infinitely superior killing machines of the West took to the skies. Another way of saying, perhaps, that the greatest evil lies within ourselves.

9

"Imponderables in Thin Air":
Zionism as Psychoanalysis (Critique)

There is a strand to Zionism to be found in writers like Martin Buber, Hannah
Arendt, Hans Kohn, and Ahah Ha'am that provides the profoundest analysis
of dangers which—it is my argument—have to be understood as much in
psychic as political terms. These dissenters were articulate, vocal, throughout
the crucial period leading up to the formation of the nation, although inside
Israel their voices have been mostly silenced since. Arendt's ideas, writes
Amnon Raz-Krakotzkin, "became irrelevant when what she foresaw came to
be real"; they were deemed "unrealistic" in proportion as "reality" proved her
correct.[1] National passion, as we have already seen, defies reality, since reality
is rarely the yardstick of the group. It is for me therefore one of the strengths
of Zionism—one of the reasons why it should not be dismissed, even or
especially by its critics—that it could have produced this dissenting analysis
from within. Like Gershom Scholem, all these writers witnessed in their
lifetime the triumph of the Jewish nation that none of them could have
confidently predicted, but the shape it assumed before their eyes made this a
cause less for elation than for lament. This did not stop them from espousing
the Jewish cause, nor indeed from advocating a Jewish home in Palestine. But
they each believed that Zionism could have taken a different path from the
one it proclaimed, and still proclaims, as its destiny. All of them except Arendt
took up residence in Palestine. Imagine how hard it must have been to pull
against the drift, to have been anything other than euphoric in 1948. Today
theirs is the still resonant, melancholic, counternarrative to the birth of a
nation-state.

At the heart of Zionism, writes Martin Buber in his article "Zionism and
'Zionism,'" published on 27 May 1948, two weeks after the establishment of
Israel, there is an "internal contradiction that reaches to the depths of human
existence."[2] Two notions of national rebirth. Both require a return to Palestine.

But whereas one desires to become a "normal" nation with "a land, a language and independence," the other, outside political time, aims to restore the spirit: "The spirit would build the life, like a dwelling, or like flesh."[3] These two tendencies, which have been "running about next to each other from ancient times," represent the division between the task of truth and justice, and the wish—"all too natural"—to be like other nations.[4] Like Arendt, Buber takes Zionism to task for being the real form of assimilation. "The Zionists were the only ones who sincerely wanted assimilation," writes Arendt, "namely, 'normalization' of the people ('to be a people like all other peoples')."[5] "Of all the many kinds of assimilation in the course of our history," Buber had written in 1939, "this nationalist assimilation is the most terrifying, the most dangerous."[6] The ancient Hebrews did not succeed in becoming a normal nation: "Today," he writes in 1948, "the Jews are succeeding at it to a terrifying degree."[7] Zionism should not have created, or tried to create, a normal nation.

Buber's distinction between the spirit building the life and the normality of nations is therefore mapped onto a distinction between truth and justice, on the one hand, and terror or fear: "Today the Jews are succeeding to a terrifying degree" (that a nation's triumph, as much as external threat, can be a cause for fear is not something we hear in Israel today). "Where," he asks, "do truth and justice determine our deeds?"[8] Most simply, crucially, Buber is objecting to the injustice being perpetrated against the Arabs: "What nation will allow itself to be demoted from the position of majority to that of minority without a fight?"[9] But Buber's argument contains a complex psychic dimension. His question "Where do truth and justice determine our deeds . . ." in fact continues "either inwardly or outwardly?" "I said 'inwardly,'" he then adds in parentheses, "because unruliness directed outwards inevitably brings on unruliness directed inwards."[10] Buber is warning that the outward injustice towards the Arabs not only harms them but will also have damaging consequences inside the new nation. Far from securing its future and safety, it will threaten its inner cohesion, bringing havoc, or "unruliness," in its train. Not only will the nation be the object of attack ("What nation will allow itself to be demoted without a fight?"), but, *by the mere fact of becoming a normal nation*, it will corrupt its inner life and will not survive.

Almost before the first shot was fired in 1948, Buber is suggesting both that Israel will be the object of aggression *and* that it will fail in its attempt to locate the aggressor purely on the outside. There is a crucial lesson here— criticising Israel does not involve denying that it has enemies. Violence will come home to roost. In psychoanalytic parlance, the nation will fail to project.

Seeing the enemy as outside threat only, Israel was sowing the seeds of long-term damage within. "Everything that did stay to challenge Israel," writes Edward Said in his essay "Zionism from the Standpoint of Its Victims," "was viewed not as something *there*, but as something *outside* Israel and Zionism bent on its destruction—from the outside."[11] One effect of course has been to render virtually invisible, or nonexistent as equal citizens, the Israeli Palestinians inside the nation. In September 2003, the Or Commission Report recommended, "The State of Israel has an interest in acting to erase the stain of discrimination against the Arab citizens."[12]

This is not, it should be stressed, the kind of criticism that bemoans the nation's subsequent betrayal of itself (a betrayal represented for many by the occupation of 1967). It is a far more radical critique. For Buber, the soul of the nation was forfeit from the day of its creation: "We have full independence, a state and all that appertains to it," Buber writes even more urgently in the following year, "but where is the nation in the state? And where is that nation's spirit?"[13] Which is not to say, it might need stressing, that Israel should cease to exist, but that the nation will perhaps survive only if it takes the fullest measure of this founding dilemma. Today, David Grossman makes the same link as did Buber between inward and outer havoc, between blindness and injustice. He makes a similar plea. The average Israeli, he writes in his dispatches from Jerusalem, refuses introspection, dreading the "disconcerting and menacing emotions it might provoke": "He dreads that they will kindle disquieting questions about the justice of his actions."[14]

It seems to me that what Buber is saying is that an intangible, unconscious dimension, spiritual and ethical, should give to this new collective being its shape. "Setting a true political goal," he writes in "Politics and Morality" in 1945, "always plumbs the depths of history and taps the primary forces which determine the life and death of peoples."[15] Again, this ethical dimension has nothing to do with Ben-Gurion's trumpeting the unique moral mission of Israel (which leads in its worst forms to the insistence voiced repeatedly by a number of those I interviewed in 2002, such as Zalman Shoval, former Israeli ambassador to the United States, that America supports Israel because as nations they share a unique moral character).

As I see it, Buber is lifting into the realm of politics the complex relations that hold between unconscious and conscious life. Freud had a formula for the aims of analysis—"Wo es war soll ich werden"—that James Strachey notoriously translated in the *Standard Edition* as "Where Id was there Ego shall be."[16] To which Jacques Lacan offered the counter-translation "There where *it* was so should, must, *I* come to be."[17] For Lacan, far from aiming to raise the unconscious into the realm of the all-knowing ego, which believes itself to be the sole measure of the universe, psychoanalysis should expose any such mastery as delusion. The "I" (no Ego) should cede before the unpredictable movements, the intangible processes, of the unconscious. Strachey's formula tries to normalise the mind. The ego, like the normal nation, carves out its identity. Buber quite explicitly makes the link: "The typical individual of our times," he wrote in his 1939 lecture "The Spirit of Israel and the World of Today," "holds fast to *his expanded ego, his nation*."[18] Similarly Hans Kohn would argue that Zionism, which should have offered a new model of nationhood, has fallen prey to the *"naïve and self-limited egoism* of sacred faith."[19] The nation should not be normal. Instead of owning others or itself, instead of battening down, fixing itself, knowing and owning too much, let it slip between analogies: the spirit, Buber writes, should build the life "like a dwelling or like flesh."

What would a nation look like constituted on some such terms? If this is messianism, it is a far cry from the messianism on which the nation has predominantly fashioned itself.[20] Utopian but resolutely anti-apocalyptic, Buber's Zionism was not political Zionism but Zionism devoted to the life of the spirit, and, drawing on the Hasidic tradition, to the sanctification of everyday life. "The grand Eastern Jewish creation of Hasidism," writes Arnold Zweig in 1920, "pours into the most prosaic of daily activities, into the most immediate call of the day" (on this Buber and Scholem parted ways—for Scholem, Buber's vision was too mundane, too much a dilution of messianic belief).[21] Much follows from this. Although Buber was undoubtedly proposing intensive Jewish settlement of Arab land, such a Zionism does not require the ever increasing ingathering of the exiles: "We need for this land as many Jews as it is possible economically to absorb, but not in order to establish a majority against a minority."[22] Nor the denial of the Arab's political rights: "Jewish immigration must not cause the political status of the present inhabitants to deteriorate."[23] Famously Balfour had spoken of the civic and religious but not political rights of the "existing non-Jewish communities in Palestine," whereas the program of the Ichud, or League for Arab-Jewish Rapprochement to which Buber was a signatory, listed as its first aim "government in Palestine based upon equal political rights for the two peoples." Nor the conquering of the land: "We are not obliged to conquer the land, for no danger is in store for our spiritual essence or our way of life from the population of the land."[24]

Concretely, what Buber proposed was not partition, which he saw as a "slicing" or breaking apart of the land, but a "covenant" of two independent nations with equal political rights, "united in the enterprise of developing their common homeland and in the federal management of shared matters."[25] The only thing to be sanctified for Buber is "work in common," by which he means in common with the Arabs—not the land, not the state (there should not be a sovereign state), only the slow pacings of daily tasks. For Buber, writing in 1948, the fact that Zionism failed this opportunity, made itself sovereign so as to enter into the world of nations, is nothing short of a political and spiritual catastrophe: "This sort of 'Zionism' blasphemes the name of Zion."[26]

Compare Herzl: "I have already drafted . . . the entire plan. I know everything required for it. Money, money, money, and more money; means of transportation, provisions for a vast multitude, maintenance of discipline, organisation . . . treaties with heads of state . . . the construction of new and splendid dwelling places. And beforehand, a prodigious propaganda . . . pictures, songs . . . a flag."[27]

Or compare Weizmann, in whose discourse the plea for normality is thunderous: "The greatest challenge to the creative forces of the Jewish people, its redemption from the *abnormalities* of exile"; "scattered among foreign cultures . . . our life displays something *abnormal*"; "a decisive step towards *normality* and true emancipation"; "our relations to the other races and nations would become more *normal*"; "we shall revert to *normal* . . . 'like unto all the nations.' "[28] For Buber, on the contrary, the nation becomes normal—in this he is very close to psychoanalysis—at the cost of perverting itself.

Hans Kohn, one of Buber's closest disciples and friends, had been a devoted Zionist since 1909, when he had joined the Bar Kochba student organisation in Prague; he had arrived in Palestine in 1923. Explaining his decision to resign from the Zionist Organization after the Arab riots of 1929, he writes, "Such events are eye-openers and call for decisions, the urgency of which we fail to appreciate in 'normal' times."[29] For Kohn, normality veils the truth. It is a cover for the incipient violence of the burgeoning state: "We pretend to be innocent victims. Of course the Arabs attacked us in August. Since they have no armies, they could not obey the rules of war."[30] "We are obliged," he insists, "to look into the deeper causes of this revolt," such as the fact that we have not "even once made a serious attempt at seeking through negotiations the consent of the indigenous peoples" (compare Sharon, refusing even the possibility of a negotiated settlement and unilaterally withdrawing from Gaza today).[31] Even more strongly, Buber had stated, "on several occasions when peace seemed to come within our reach, we did much to prevent it"; although this did not stop him from criticising the Arab "blindness" on the same issue of peace.[32]

Writing of the suppression of the Arab revolt, Kohn then warns against a falsely triumphant "victorious peace": "Just like the powers in the [First] World War, we have declared that we would gladly make peace if only we were strong enough."[33] Such strength, he suggests, is illusory. It will have to feed on itself. Politics in this guise is both superficial (fails to look into the "deeper cause" of this revolt) and endless. Interminable, violence will inscribe itself into the heart of the nation: "I believe that it will be possible to hold Palestine and continue to grow for a long time. This will be done first with British aid and then later with the help of our own bayonets—shamefully called *Haganah* [i.e., defense]—clearly because we have no faith in our own policy. But by that time we will not be able to do without the bayonets."[34] Looking back in the 1960s, Kohn explains, in an essay called "Zionism," that it was from A. D. Gordon that he drew his critique of the militarism of what was to become the Israeli state: "A people cannot be 'redeemed,' Gordon taught, by political success, even less by military victory, but only by the spiritual and moral rebirth of the individual."[35] Kohn has predicted that a nation investing itself in military power will be unable to restrain itself.

Like Buber, from whom he takes his inspiration—his essay "Nationalism" is dedicated to Buber—Kohn wants *another* type of nationalism, one that reaches, in his words, "for the stars"; neither "deadly drug" nor "hypocritical camouflage" for state needs and collective power, it will be "more loving," "more attached to the life of the individual" ("the most private and hidden essence of mankind").[36] Kohn arrives at his vision after the dark night of the First World War, which he saw as the "witch's orgy" of the nation-state.[37] He therefore invested in Zionism a belief in a new form of nationhood that would make national war "as impossible as the religious fanaticism of Saint Bartholomew's Night."[38] Similarly Virginia Woolf proclaimed in 1927, "Can't you see that nationality is over?" As Hermione Lee, Woolf's biographer, comments in parentheses after this quotation, "They would all spend the next fourteen years seeing the flaws of this argument."[39] But the analysis, even if not the utopian prediction, still holds today. For Kohn, nations were lifting from religious creeds the dangers of territorial expansion and authoritarian violence. In an ideal future, nations must therefore shed the aura of the sacred: "The sacred rights of the nation . . . will be as incomprehensible as the military and murderous fury released by a disputed interpretation of a Biblical word or form of the sign of the cross."[40]

Like Woolf, Kohn was wrong in his hopes of what was to come. But it is one of the ironic strengths of his analysis that all its central terms—sacred, violent fury, militarism, religious fanaticism—should return to the heart of Israel's future struggle both with its neighbours and with itself. At a roundtable meeting of Israelis and European Jews, organised by the Jewish organisation Hanadiv and held in Canisy, northern France, in January 2003, the leading *Ha'aretz* journalist Daniel Ben-Simon observed that up to the outbreak of the second intifada a crucial discussion was taking place inside Israel about the relationship between a secular and a religious future for the country—or, as he put it, between democracy and clerical fascism. Now it has simply stopped.

If Kohn's vision is, as for Buber, a form of messianism that "redeems the world," it is also—again like that of Buber—resolutely anti-apocalyptic, seeing its destiny, not in the apotheosis, but in a sacrifice, of self.[41] Like Buber, Kohn distinguishes between a nation as something "inwardly experienced" ("a group of people linked together through a common descent and common or similar historical destinies") and the nation as a state "bound to the external principle of territory by politics and government" ("A relentless slash cuts away everything that is politics, state, or economy").[42] But Kohn goes even further than Buber in plumbing the psychic dimension—the compelling and dangerous force—of nationalism in its modern guise. This passage, worth quoting in full, could almost have been lifted out of Freud's *The Future of an Illusion*:

> The enormous suffering of existence, the enigma of life staring at us eternally, the plethora of all things and connections assaulting us with a destructive gesticulation, the dark beast that inexplicably threatens, keeps arising within us—all these things would be unendurable if a faith, a sustaining world principle, did not bind them into unity and give them meaning and purpose, making the remote and the unsure more familiar through the threads of myth.[43]

Nationalism, the wrong kind, the kind that has become "absolute," "an idol," allows you the illusion of mastering the unmasterable: the enigma of life, destructive gesticulations, the dark beast (for Freud, the terrors of nature, the cruelty of Fate, the sufferings imposed by civilisation).[44] It allows you, like the ego, to believe you could be sufficient unto yourself. Similarly, Judah Leon Magnes, first president of the Hebrew University of Jerusalem, another dissenting voice, warned in 1930 in an article interrogatively entitled "Like All the Nations?": "There is the *Wille zur Macht*, the state, the army, the frontiers. . . . [N]ow we are to be masters in our own home."[45]

"Must not," Freud asks, "the assumptions that determine our political regulations be called illusions as well?"—for Kohn, one of the worst illusions is that of "national sovereign independence," the belief that a nation could be based on the "non-intervention of the 'foreigner' in 'our' affairs."[46] Freud had famously argued in *Moses the Man*, his last major work, that the founder of the Jewish people had been an Egyptian. Edward Said's recent analysis of Freud's text as offering to the modern world the idea of a nation created by a foreigner would then place Freud in this early Zionist lineage of critique.[47] The vision of an isolated nationhood, Kohn writes, is an aberration, a "ghostly phantom."[48] We can gauge just how radical this is by comparing it with Leon Pinsker, for whom it is the Jews without a homeland who are the "ghosts," "the dead walking among the living": "We wish to be a nation like the others."[49] For Kohn, the far greater danger comes when a nation, cut off from the world around it, tries to wrap itself anxiously, defensively, around its own core: "We will not be able to do without the bayonets." In 1948, the army of the new state united the Haganah, which drew its troops from the Zionist movements devoted to pioneering and communal living, and the Irgun, the paramilitary organisation that aspired to Jewish control over all of Transjordan and Palestine. Buber was aghast: "The Israeli army, elements that are [physically and spiritually] rooted in the land and those that are not, mingle with each other," wrote Buber, "*stand up as a wall, conquer, vanquish*."[50]

From the beginning, writes Arendt in her 1944 essay "Zionism Reconsidered," Zionism wanted, more than anything, "utopian national independence."[51] But nations are not independent. To be a law (race, faith) unto yourself is a myth. Dramatically, Israel has offered the spectacle of that illusion—the belief and its necessary failure—playing itself out on the world's stage. Not for the first time, there is something fundamental about nationhood that Zionism, so determined and yet fumbling in the dark, allows us to see. "He did not realise," Arendt writes of Herzl, "that the country he dreamt of did not exist, that there was no place on earth where a people could live like the organic national body that he had in mind and that the real historical development of a nation does not take place inside the closed walls of a biological entity."[52]

"Paradoxical as it may sound," she argues, "it was precisely because of this nationalist misconception of the inherent independence of a nation that the

Zionists ended up making the Jewish national independence entirely dependent on the material interests of another nation."[53] If nationalism is "bad enough" when it trusts in "nothing but the rude force of the nation," a nationalism dependent on the force of a foreign nation is "certainly worse."[54] Arendt warns, "The anti-Semitism of tomorrow will assert that Jews not only profiteered from the presence of the foreign big powers in that region but actually plotted and hence are guilty of the consequences."[55] "Only folly," she concludes, "could dictate a policy which trusts a distant imperial power for protection, while alienating the good will of neighbours."[56] Israel, as Arendt also predicted, would become utterly reliant on America. "We feel our battle is with America," the Ramallah politician Ramadan Safi told me in 2002: "The tanks are American, the guns are American, the fighters are American."[57]

It is one of the defining problems of Zionism that it imported into the Middle East a Central European concept of nationhood in the throes of decline. This was a concept of organic nationhood, founded on ethnicity and blood (or "land, descent and the dead"). For Moses Hess, ancient Judaism had in fact been the first such group in human history—romantic nationalism was therefore at once the legacy and destiny of the Jewish people. It was of course a myth, and as the century unfolded, the Jews, above all other people, would be its victim. Writing seventy years after the publication of *Der Judenstaat*, J. L. Talmon, professor of history at the Hebrew University of Jerusalem, commented, "Little did Hess, Mazzini, Mickiewicz and their like know that in endowing nationalism with the dimension of a Salvationist religion, and in transferring to it so much of the Socialist appeal, they were unwittingly offering a rationale to that type of racial, exclusive nationalism, which Hess so abhorred among the Germans, and indeed to anti-Semitism, in both its racial and social versions."[58] Israel inscribes at its heart the very version of nationhood from which the Jewish people had had to flee.

Furthermore, at the very moment when Israel was created to secure the future of the Jewish people, this version of statehood revealed, not only its inherent dangers, but its radical inability to defend the very principles on which it had once been built. Like Kohn, Arendt traces the beginning of this failure, which reaches its climax for the Jews in the Second World War, to the catastrophe of the First: "As for nationalism," she continues, "it never was more evil nor more fiercely defended than since it became apparent that this once great and revolutionary principle of the national organisation of peoples could no longer either guarantee true sovereignty of the people within, or establish a just relationship among different peoples beyond, the national borders."[59] This is nationalism, in the words of Tom Nairn, trapped in "the essentialist cage of regimented identity, flag-worship and armour-plated community."[60] National faith of this kind becomes belligerent and expansive because it is so vulnerable and so raw, defending boundaries of the body and mind that do not exist. For that very reason, it "permits and excuses anything" (the words of Hans Kohn, who could just as well be describing the politics of the preemptive war on terror today).[61]

Picking up her pen like Buber in May 1948, Arendt predicts with uncanny prescience the future of the new nation after its victory in the coming war.

> The "victorious" Jews would live surrounded by an entirely hostile Arab population, secluded inside ever-threatened borders, absorbed with physical self-defense to a degree that would submerge all other interests and activities. The growth of a Jewish culture would cease to be the concern of the whole people; social experiments would have to be discarded as impractical luxuries; political thought would center around military strategy; economic development would be determined exclusively by the need of war.[62]

Explaining his refusal to serve in the occupied territories, Lieutenant Yaniv Iczkovitz states: "The Labor party is coming apart, and Meretz, the Israeli social democratic peace party, can be neither seen nor heard. . . . The chairman of the opposition is the chairman of silence. The biggest mistake of the left is its preoccupation with security issues. . . . It's a sin that began with the establishment of the state."[63] "Our country is going into a decline, nearing a catastrophe in all areas of economy, politics and social services and security," Yaakov Perry, who ran Shin Bet from 1988 to 1995, commented recently. "If we continue to live by the sword, we will continue to wallow in the mud and to destroy ourselves."[64]

The nation cannot secure its own future. Surely, it is often asked, Jewish nationalism is justified by the need of the Jewish people to have a place in the world where they can feel safe? Or physically and mentally at ease—a place where, as Gordon wrote to Ahad Ha'am in 1912, "a Jew does not need to feel his national pulse beating every hour." But Jews are not safe in Israel today. Nor indeed at ease with themselves. Exactly as Arendt predicted, the ethos of survival "at any price" has become brutalised and now, after thirty-seven years in the occupied territories, is placing not just the safety but the sanity of the nation at risk. "I was carried away by the possibility of acting in the most primal and impulsive manner," Staff Sergeant Liran Ron Furer says of his experience in Gaza in his book *Checkpoint Syndrome*. "Over time the behaviour . . . became normative . . . without fear of punishment and without oversight . . . a place to test our personal limits—how tough, how callous, how crazy we could be."[65]

"The question that looms," writes Ze'ev Schiff in *Ha'aretz* after the assassination of Hamas leader Sheikh Yassin in March 2004, "is whether Israel has been attacked by the virus of a crazy state."[66] According to Amir Rappaport, writing in the newspaper *Ma'ariv*, Israel's air strikes on Gaza, which came in response to eight Qassam rockets fired by the Palestinians in October in 2003, were deliberately disproportionate to convey the message to the Palestinians that "Israel has gone mad."[67] "I see terrible graffiti—racist and Kahanist—that we accept offhandedly," writes Avraham Burg, former speaker of the Knesset and member of the Labour Party; the settlers and the right wing have left no "place that is not affected by the nationalist consciousness."[68]

In their different ways, in the dialogic space that runs between Buber, Arendt, and Kohn, I hear all of them arguing that Zionism might have created a form of nationhood that would slash away politics, face its own dark beast, make room for the foreigner in its midst (or, even more radically perhaps, see itself as the stranger for the Arabs in Palestine). For a brief moment, Zionism had the chance of molding a nation that would be not an "expanded ego" but something else. At the opening of his essay "Nationalism," Kohn describes how "shifts of consciousness" are always accompanied by "deep shocks," creating a time of "disquiet, tension, isolation, dissociation"; such processes are "obscure," "ambivalent," "uncertain."[69] He could be describing glimpses of the unconscious, those moments—dreams, slips, symptoms—when the unconscious is allowed to steal past the wires, past the defences of the conscious mind, and makes its presence felt. Precisely because of the tragic peculiarity of Jewish history, because Jews have indeed in some sense been lost to the world—we do not have to reject Pinsker's "ghosts"—Zionism, as a unique national movement, had the opportunity to forge a model of nationhood, neither belligerently nor preemptively, but ambivalent, uncertain, obscure, something closer to this disquieting and transformative space. But did not take it.

Meanwhile, the vision they all sustained for a life and nationhood held in common for Jews and Arabs is one that has returned to the centre of debate inside Israel today. Partly out of fear—if Israel holds on to the territories, Jews "risk becoming a minority in their own land" (this fear is seen by many to be the only driving force behind Sharon's Gaza plan); partly, however, because it is felt that the settlements have rendered a two-state solution nonviable, and that the only way forward is for Israel to become the state of all its citizens.[70] The idea of a binational solution is by no means widely accepted—for its opponents it precisely spells the destruction of a Jewish state. But it has some barely known historic precedents, moments of cohabitation and cooperation between Jews and Arabs in Mandate Palestine, against the drift of their hardening respective nationalisms, recently uncovered by Ilan Pappe: "From a historiographical point of view," he writes, "the impression left is of an alternative history."[71] In 1948, Herbert Samuels wrote to Jan Smuts of South Africa, "The right alternative [to partition] is a provision for Jewish and Arab representative bodies based upon the actual facts of the situation, that is to say, upon the existence of communities that cannot be segregated geographically either into states, provinces or cantons."[72] Today the binational idea finds some unlikely adherents. For Daniel Gavron—"mainstream, orthodox Labour Zionist," as he describes himself, whose book *The Other Side of Despair: Jews and Arabs in the Promised Land* appeared in Israel in 2003—such a vision follows logically from the multiethnic character of the ancient world: "King David, if the Bible is to be believed, conquered Jerusalem from the Jebusites and then shared the city with them. He made use of Canaanite officials, had a Hittite general, enjoyed good relations with the Phoenicians, and (after some bloody conflicts with them) deployed Philistine units in his army, the Cherethites and Pelethites."[73]

When Hannah Arendt expresses her fears for the growth of Jewish culture, or Martin Buber talks of an organic centre, they may well have been thinking of Ahad Ha'am, for whom Jewish culture was the sole raison d'être of a homeland in Palestine. Ahad Ha'am, who took the pen name "one of the people," was born Asher Ginzberg in Skvire, in the Russian Ukraine. Although little known today outside Israel, inside the country some of his writings are still taught at school. They were also read by Noam Chomsky in his youth. Most famous for his plea for Palestine to become a "spiritual centre" for world Jewry, he was, like Buber and Kohn—the latter edited a selection of his writings—deeply suspicious of the idea of statehood. On publication of the Balfour Declaration, which as Weizmann's "intimate adviser" he had played a part in formulating, he commented,

> The British Government promised to facilitate the establishment in Palestine of a National Home for the Jewish people, and not, as was suggested, the reconstitution of Palestine as the National Home of the Jewish people.[74]

Much hangs on that distinction between "for" and "of." If Balfour meant that the Jews had the "historic right" to build their national home in Palestine, it also meant *"a negation of the power of that right to override the right of the present inhabitants, and to make the Jewish people the sole ruler in the country."*[75] Kohn had warned of incipient Arab nationalism: "The Arab national movement is growing and will continue to grow."[76] But Ahad Ha'am was one of the rare critical voices to speak of Arab national aspirations in positive terms: "This country is their national home," he wrote to Weizmann in 1918, "and they too have the right to develop a national power to the best of their abilities" (the topic was rarely broached even by Brit Shalom).[77]

Ahad Ha'am's reputation as Jewish nationalism's major internal critic dates from his first 1891 visit to Palestine. "What I have seen," he wrote in his article "The Truth from Palestine," is the "concrete truth . . . of which I wish to reveal a bit—the ugliest bit."[78] Ahad Ha'am presents himself as the purveyor of the (ugliest) truth. Variously described as the "first philosopher of Zionism," "foremost exponent of a humanistic, liberal Zionism," and "disturber of the peace," Ahad Ha'am was also the first Jewish nationalist to recognise the darker side to the relationship between Arabs and Jews in Palestine.[79] How, he asked, in a scathing review of Herzl's *Altneuland*, could the New Society obtain sufficient land for Jews from all over the world if the arable land that previously belonged to the Arabs remained in their hands as before?[80] Each paragraph of "The Truth from Palestine" began with the phrase "We are accustomed to believe"; for instance, that Palestine is empty, whereas in fact arable land is at a premium and there is very little left. "We are accustomed to believe that all the Arabs are desert savages."[81] It was a role he maintained. In 1913, he answered a letter from the Hebrew writer Moshe Smilansky on the settlers' treatment of the Arabs, specifically on the boycott of Arab labour: "If it is so now, what will be our relation to the others if in truth we shall achieve 'at the end of time' power in Eretz Israel? If this be the 'Messiah,' I do not wish to see his coming."[82]

"One of the people," Ahad Ha'am sets himself up as a type of prophet (or analyst) speaking truth to a power in gestation, to a state, not already established and glib in its empowerment, but in the very throes of creating itself. In Ahad Ha'am's writing, as I see it, Zionism diagnoses or *reads itself.*

Ahad Ha'am was Herzl's most articulate critic. To invoke the title of one of his earliest and most influential pieces of writing, he thought Herzl was going about things "the wrong way" (too much money, too many flags). It was not just that Ahad Ha'am promoted a spiritual rather than political embodiment of nationalism; it was also that, like Buber, he thought that the path to nationalism involved a complex negotiation of historical and psychic time. Things started to go wrong when a new, revived, belief in the right of the Jews to be a "single" people transformed itself, with seemingly miraculous efficiency, into deeds: "The friends of the idea raised a shout of victory, and cried in exultation. Is not this a thing unheard-of, that an idea so young has strength to force its way into the world of action?"[83] But the "shout of victory" and cry "of exultation" were mistaken. Triumphalism is always a form of magical thinking or self-deceit: "Every victory involves a defeat and a death."[84] Similarly, Scholem had written to Walter Benjamin in 1931, "We were victorious too early."[85] Impatient, Jewish nationalism, finding it had the strength to force its way, became incapable of deferring itself. It is, he writes, a peculiarity of the Hebrew language that it has no present tense of the verb *to be*: "Israel has never lived in the present."[86] In their rush to the future, the Jewish people were failing to subsist in the slow interstices of everyday time (where Buber located the sacred).[87]

Moses was his hero. It is impossible not to read his long essay on the Jewish leader as a critique of Herzl: "He knows that signs and wonders and visions of God can arouse a momentary enthusiasm, but cannot create a new heart. . . . So he summons all his patience to the task of bearing the troublesome burden of his people and training it by slow steps."[88] In a way Moses's greatest quality becomes his failure. That he did not enter the Promised Land, that he had to face the "utter, fathomless, degradation of his people" and "tear out of his heart a splendid hope."[89] Today, although the future, as utopian promise, is on everyone's lips, Ahad Ha'am believed that the possibility of a real, more difficult future had been "forgotten," as the Jewish people sped towards their felt destiny in unseemly haste. Instead nirvana had taken its place. For Ahad Ha'am, the danger facing the Jewish people from political Zionism was a ruthless self-idealisation that will brook no disappointment and knows no bounds (in Magnes's terms, the "*Wille zur Macht*," in Arendt's, Herzl's "will to reality" or "furious will to action at any price").[90] "Everything must be done immediately!" Herzl had written to Moritz Güdemann in 1895; "That too is part of my plan."[91]

In *Der Judenstaat*, Herzl had deliberately raised the expectations of the earliest pioneers by insisting that only those would depart for Palestine who "are sure thereby to improve their position."[92] "To attract the Jews to the land," he stated in conversation with Baron Maurice de Hirsch in 1895, "you would have to tell them a fable about how to strike gold. By way of fantastic example, you might say: whoever ploughs, sows and reaps will find gold in every sheaf.

Nearly the truth in fact."[93] For Ahad Ha'am, in this scenario, the "demon of egoism," the flush of individual self-interest, substitutes for the more complex historical and cultural affinities of the group, which became vulnerable when, as was often the case with the earliest emigrants to Palestine, personal expectations were not met.[94] Losing touch with its historical memory—"the chain" uniting "all the generations"—political Zionism wrongly promised too much: "a complete and absolute solution of the Jewish problem in all its aspects."[95] In the process, it made the mistake of demanding actualisation, for each and every one of its actors, in the here and now (I want results). Note how in this case the idea of a chain of ancestral memories forging a link to the land—the idea so often voiced to justify the occupation of "Eretz Israel"—leads to the opposite of a violent claim upon it. What matters are the group's inner or, as Buber would put it, "inward" relations. Jewish nationalism must take out the ego. Overanxious to realise its ambitions, the ego always tends to get carried away, to move too fast. Paradoxically, Jewish nationalism will come into being only if—as a dream of seizing the land, ruling the Arabs, economically prospering—it abolishes itself. Ahad Ha'am's proposal is both modest and slow (this is not Weizmann calling for the long, but finally proprietorial, cultivation of the territory). Offering himself as the group analyst of Zionism—to the various descriptions already offered, I would like to add one more—he puts a question. How do you make a nation pause for thought?

"The human mind," he writes, "has laws of its own not always consistent with logic."[96] It is a central part of Ahad Ha'am's project to trace those laws, which dominate "not only the judgement but the memory," as they impact on collective life.[97] "A people," he recognises, "cannot live on logic"; they are indeed guided, in the words of Herzl, by "imponderables" that float "in thin air."[98] Ahad Ha'am can be seen as taking up Herzl's formula—for Herzl a political opportunity to relish—where he left off. If not a redemptive, or even apocalyptic, fulfillment of self, then it must be asked: what alternative version of Jewish selfhood should Zionism be trying to promote? In what does, or should, a political identity consist? What allows a man, or a group, to believe in itself? All questions, Ahad Ha'am's writings reveal, that are at the heart of the most fundamental political disagreements about the future of Palestine.

"When a man says 'I,'" Ahad Ha'am writes in "Past and Future," "he is thinking of that inner spirit, or force, which in some hidden manner unites all the impressions and memories of the past with all his desires and hopes for the future, and makes of the whole one single, complete, organic entity."[99] The organic "I," which is not, note, the same as the individual ego, matches the organic centre of Judaism, which the homeland in Palestine will bring to life. Ahad Ha'am takes this vision of psychic unity from the works of the French psychiatrist Frédéric Paulhan—whose study of the growth of Darwin's creative personality he used as the basis for his own discussion of Moses: "a mind which reached an almost perfect unity."[100] "The mind," writes Paulhan, "is or tends to be a unified and coordinated whole."[101]

But the mind is also a palimpsest, its inheritance imperishable. Latent within us, we carry the traces of those parts of the personality that our predecessors inhibited and that never completely disappear: "We are always to some extent what we once were before or what our ancestors were before us."[102] Ahad Ha'am's vision of an organic centre for Judaism is therefore mapped directly onto a theory of the mind as at once unified and multiply shaded, a mind filled with the inhibitions of our forefathers, the traces of our ancestors, the fragments of the past. You would be hard pressed to draw from this vision of the psyche or inner life any foundation whatsoever for the too hasty, surefire political will. There is a continuity here—Jewishness cannot survive without it—but it is precarious, treading on ghostly, unmasterable, ground. "Unity," writes Paulhan in his analysis of Darwin, "remains only an ideal."[103] Even the harmonious mind bears the scars of its former struggles.

In Paulhan's model, the mind is endlessly at work. At every instant, psychic phenomena awaken inside us, develop, and disappear, giving rise to others in their place, entering into play often despite ourselves and without our knowledge. "There is," he writes in his 1905 *Lies of Character*, no part of our soul "that is not disputed, fought, denied by another."[104] In our ideals we constantly lie to ourselves. "Do not seek precision and stability in psychic life; the facts of the mind are more mobile, fluctuating, and restless than the waves of the sea."[105] A truly organic centre of Judaism would not make the mistake, like a declaration of statehood, of thinking that either the mind or the soul could come to rest.

At moments Ahad Ha'am's view of subjectivity is truly, and often disturbingly, psychoanalytic before its time. "Every civilised man who is born and bred in an orderly state of society," he writes in his 1892 essay "Two Masters," "lives all his life in the condition of hypnotic subject, unconsciously subservient to the will of others."[106] The opening of the essay is worth quoting.

Familiar as we now are with the phenomena of hypnotism, we know that under certain conditions it is possible to induce a peculiar kind of sleep in a human being, and that, if the hypnotic subject is commanded to perform at a certain time after his awakening some action foreign to his character and wishes, he will obey the order at the appointed time. He will not know, however, that he is compelled to do so by the will and behest of another. He will firmly believe . . . that he is doing what he does of his own freewill and because he likes to do so, for various reasons which his imagination will create, in order to satisfy his own mind.[107]

The question Ahad Ha'am puts to political Zionism could be put to any form of political selfhood, any nationalism, carving out its space in the world. It is as if he were questioning the idea that the only way to forge a political life and future is to believe, unreservedly, in the force of identity, to believe that identity—this would be one version of Jewish identity—is exclusive, and, as a people, exclusively your own. Bit by bit Ahad Ha'am takes apart our pride of possession in the components that make up a self. Language and literature, religion and morality, laws and customs—these are the "media" society uses to put the individual "to sleep."[108] Inside every individual member of society, there are "thousands of hypnotic agents, whose commands are stern and peremptory"—"Such and such shall be your opinions; such and such your actions"—and which the individual "unconsciously" obeys.[109]

Nearly forty years before Freud's *Civilisation and Its Discontents*, Ahad Ha'am has produced an account of the superego ferociously issuing its edicts to the unconscious mind. The fiercest edicts—"arch-hypnotisers, the all-powerful masters of the individual and society alike"—are the "men of the distant past."[110] Because they are unconscious, these voices are unanswerable. If they carry the dynasty of the ages, they are also the bearers of some of its most sinister calls. Hatred of the Jews is one of the "best-established commands of the past to the nations of Europe."[111] Our most forceful legacy comes from voices of the past that we cannot even necessarily hear speaking.

What would happen to a political or religious identity, even the most binding, if it could see itself as contingent, as something that might have taken another path? Can you be devoted to an identity—or would you be differently devoted to your identity—if you knew it was also unsure? The priest Mortara "thunders" from his pulpit against the enemies of the Catholic faith, striving out of the depths of his "inner consciousness" to prove its righteousness and truth, but if Catholic priests had not snatched him from the arms of his Jewish mother in childhood, other "hypnotic" agents would have been "speaking through his lips with precisely the same warmth of conviction."[112] It is because deep down they are not wholly convinced, that people have to deceive themselves and lie, as Paulhan put it, in the service of their ideals. Following the Arab riots of 1936, a group of schoolchildren at the agricultural school Ben Shemen were set the question "How do you explain the troubles arising in the country over the past few weeks?" Dr Siegfried Lehmann, director of the school, summarises the essays: "Right is on our side; good can come out of evil; the whole world and the Arabs [sic] will know that we wish for peace." He comments, "As in a dream, one notes the complete lack of any unpleasant reality which might risk thwarting our aspirations."[113]

Like Freud, Ahad Ha'am, citing the American philosopher John Fiske, uses Copernicus to underscore the radically decentred nature of this account of subjectivity.

> It is hard to realise the startling effect of the discovery that man does not dwell at the centre of things, but is the denizen of an obscure and tiny speck of cosmical matter quite invisible amid the innumerable throng of flaming suns that make up our galaxy.[114]

For Freud, man had suffered a triple blow to the hubris of the ego: not the centre of the universe, nor the origin of the species, nor master in his own psychic home. "Man does not dwell at the centre of things." In fact, as much as Freud, the passage could be Robert Louis Stevenson, who famously postulated in *The Strange Case of Dr Jekyll and Mr Hyde*, "I hazard the guess that man will be ultimately known for a mere polity of multifarious, incongruous and independent denizens."[115] The ego crumbles. In the name of *another* Judaism, neither orthodoxy nor statehood, Ahad Ha'am brings pretty much the whole apparatus of psychoanalysis—the deadly and deceptive lure of the ego, the ferocity of the superego, the unconsciously commanded subject— blazing in his train.

As if the only path open for Jewish nationalism's strongest internal critic is through the defiles of the unconscious. Jacques Lacan once said of the hysteric that the screen of the ego is strangely transparent, "there being nowhere else, as Freud has said, where the threshold between the unconscious and the conscious is lower."[116] If the hysteric is compelling, Lacan also suggests, it is because she never stops asking the most basic questions—like, for example, "Do I exist or not?" Likewise Zionism—so fragile *and* dogmatic, so ruthless with its own doubts that are yet so transparently there to see. "I am tormented by an abrupt question that will not leave me in peace," wrote early Zionist, Russian student, Haim Chisin in his diary in 1882, " 'Who are you?' I try to convince myself: 'Do I really have to be somebody?' "[117]

When I interviewed the settlers Aaron and Tamara Deutsch, they insisted, as of course many settlers insist, that Israel is the land God promised to the Jews. "We wanted to join our people and our destiny, our history and our nation."[118] In his pathbreaking book *Zakhor*, first published in 1982, Yosef Hayim Yerushalmi pointed out that it was a peculiarity and creation of Jewish thought that human history reveals the will and purpose of God ("the fathers of meaning in history were the Jews").[119] For the rabbinic tradition that dominated Jewish historiography for centuries, history was not a continuous and continuing chronicle of deed or event, but lifted above time as a vehicle of the sacred. It is precisely against this tradition that David Hartman makes his plea for Israeli society to end the vision of its history as divinely sanctioned and reenter the slow accommodations of political time.[120] For the Deutsches, the world today, Israel today, fulfills the covenant of the past: "These are the roads where Abraham walked. This is where Jacob married Rachel."[121] "The Bible," as Ben-Gurion put it, "is our Mandate." Following Ahad Ha'am's account of hypnotic agency, we could describe this as ancestral belonging with a vengeance (it was precisely in their most fervent moments that the Deutsches seemed to be talking by rote). "To this day," writes the journalist Nadav Shragai, the residents of Kfar Darom "feel the 'ancient voices' are a part of their daily life, and not just something to be thought of as metaphor or heritage."[122] To Yerushalmi's investigation of historical time, we might therefore add another question. Whose voice is speaking when they speak?[123]

Like all Zionists, Ahad Ha'am was troubled by the assimilation of the Diaspora Jews. If he opposed political Zionism, it was not because he thought dispersal was the only possible Jewish identity and fate (he entered into lengthy dispute with Simon Dubnow, who advocated that the Jews should become a national entity inside their respective European nations). But when he criticised assimilation, it was not, he insisted, in the name of an identity that should see itself as self-sufficient and pure. As well as hypnotic, identity was for Ahad Ha'am fundamentally mimetic (we discover ourselves by imitating the others who we are). Imitation, he wrote in his 1893 essay "Imitation and Assimilation," is wrongly taken as the sign that a man is not "speaking out of his own inner life," whereas it is in fact the very foundation of society, without which its birth and development would not take place.[124] It is only when imitation slides into self-effacement that it leads to assimilation, a state of "neither life nor death" in which all national or communal consciousness is lost: "No community can sink to such a position as this without danger to its very existence" (the soul is "burnt out").[125]

Ahad Ha'am is struggling to produce a version of Jewish identity that, even in the Diaspora, will preserve itself. This was for him one of the main purposes of establishing a "spiritual centre of our nationality," or Jewish spiritual centre in Palestine.[126] He was at pains to stress that this did not mean the centre in Palestine would be spiritual only, but that it would be a spiritual centre for Jewry worldwide (not all Jews, he also insisted, would have to come to Palestine). And he wants this identity free of the stifling dictates of rabbinic Orthodoxy, which produce slavish imitation in another guise. He would have been appalled by Tamara Deutsch's call for a Torah State.

I like to think that Ahad Ha'am is calling on his forebears to soften or modulate their voice (rather like psychoanalysis aiming to reduce the ferocity of the superego in the mind of a child). Jewishness, he believed, must be saved, or rather reforged in the crucible of the new homeland. But if you are meant to imbibe the spirit of the ancestors, you are not meant to be slavishly mouthing the dead. Furthermore, as evidenced by the tale of the thundering Catholic priest snatched in childhood from his Jewish mother, you may feel secure in your cultural, religious, or ethnic selfhood, but you could in fact have been anyone. People who thunder, psychoanalysis would merely add, are generally those who are least sure of themselves. We can watch Ahad Ha'am trying to create a new identity for the Jewish people, at the same time as he acknowledges with equal force that your identity is never simply your own but always comes from somewhere or somebody else. Can there be—this is a question for modern times—a form of identity that is what it is *and* everything else at once?

Out of the creative instability of Ahad Ha'am's psychological vision, something even more provisional, suggestive, starts to emerge. If identities are formed mimetically, coercively, hypnotically, they are also on the move ("more restless than the waves of the sea"). They travel. Across communities in the present as much as to the ancestors of the past. Imitation is promiscuous. As soon as different societies are brought into "closer intimacy," "fuller acquaintance" with one another, identities start to spread and to blur.[127] Imitation "widens its scope," becomes "intersocial or international."[128] No man, no nation can isolate itself. Moses "makes no distinction between man and man" but goes to the aid of strangers.[129] Remember Kohn and Arendt, for whom the greatest and most dangerous illusion was the sovereign, independent nation closing in on itself: "The non-intervention of the 'foreigner' in 'our' affairs is a dangerous phantom."[130] What would Israel look like if it acknowledged its intimate affinity with its neighbours? We are, stated Weizmann, in many respects "their cousins."[131] What would happen if Israel could recognise its links to the people who—whether in refugee camps on the borders (the putative Palestinian state), or inside the country (the Israeli Palestinians), or scattered, like many Jews still today, all over the world (the Palestinian diaspora)—are in fact, psychically as well as politically, in its midst?

What finally emerges from Ahad Ha'am's writing is a type of psychic manifesto, not just for Zionism, but for modern times. We need, he insists, to be open. We need, not just to imbibe, but to *understand*, the spirit of the ages (we should study and read). "The student of the spiritual life of mankind," he writes in "Ancestor Worship," "has no concern with good and evil, wisdom or folly."[132] He becomes the "spiritual incarnation of the souls of all the ages," a conduit to everything in the past.[133] We are not "better" than our ancestors; we are "different." We do not rush to judgment. We allow the capacity for evil its place in our own minds: "There is nothing so barbarous, so evil, that the human mind cannot accept it and foster it, given suitable conditions."[134] Compare again Freud: "No one can really know how far he is good or wicked."[135] Once you say this, you stop thundering from the pulpit. Identity ceases to be a creed. We have a monopoly on neither righteousness nor truth, "and consequently many of the sacred truths of every generation must become falsehoods and absurdities in the next."[136] Nor, perhaps above all, on judgment: "They who judge today will not escape scot free from the tribunal of tomorrow."[137]

It is important not to idealise Ahad Ha'am. He was notoriously elitist, autocratic—Bnei Moshe, the organisation that he founded in Odessa in 1889 to foster Jewish spiritual self-development, foundered under pressure of his exacting requirements. Unlike Buber, he did argue that the Jews must be a majority in Palestine. He could be racist. He objected, for example, to the suggestion in *Altneuland* that a homeland for the Jews should lead to liberation and nationhood for the "negroes" of Africa. But he throws out a set of urgent questions to Jewish nationalism that still need, or need perhaps even more, to be thought about today. What effect would it have on the dominant rhetoric of the Israeli state if it allowed its own capacity for evil? What would happen if it allowed that it was being hypnotised, coerced, by the ancestral voices from which, it insists, the nation's authority stems? Or if it allowed that it might once have been snatched from the arms of a mother of another faith? Or that it was sleepwalking? Or that its boundaries should not be fixed against the enemy but should loosen to allow a place for the stranger whom Moses went to save? Or that it might be answerable for its activities in the occupied territories today before the tribunal of tomorrow? "People listened to the victim and they listened to the politicians," writes Staff Sergeant Liran Ron Furer, "but this voice that says: I did this, we did things that were wrong—crimes actually—that's a voice I didn't hear."[138]

Speaking of Operation Defensive Shield, in which the army responded to suicide bombing by razing the refugee camp of Jenin and the historic casbah of Nablus, army chief of staff Lieutenant General Moshe Ya'alon "told some of his soldiers that he did not care if the army 'looked like lunatics.' " Ya'alon is not consistent, at moments calling for a change in Israeli policy on the grounds that its treatment of Palestinian civilians is fomenting terror, at others giving public seminars arguing that Hamas, Islamic Jihad, and other organisations should be lured into a clash with the IDF and killed en masse.[139]

At the heart of the army, voices—the refuseniks now include Black Hawk helicopter and F-16 fighter pilots, as well as members of the elite Sayaret Matkal, Israel's special forces—are crying out that Israel's belief in its own moral destiny, under pressure of the occupation, is slowly turning inward and imploding.[140] "No one," writes ultra-Orthodox Yehuda Shaul—who, after serving in Gaza, curated an exhibition of photographs of human rights abuses by the army in Hebron—"returns from the territories without messing up his head."[141] "The moment I drove the tractor into the camp, something switched in my head. I went mad," writes Moshe Nissim, the D9 tank operator in Jenin in 2003, "I wanted to destroy everything."[142] "It's a sin," writes Lieutenant Iczkovitz, "that began with the establishment of the state."[143] In the new homeland, the Jew—as Herzl, Gordon, and so many believed—would be a "natural wholesome human being who is true to himself."[144]

In his essay "Politics and Morality" of 1945, Martin Buber spoke of the Jewish need for an "organic centre," a desire and indeed a phrase he shared with Ahad Ha'am, and then proceeded to draw an ethical boundary around what was permissible to achieve it: "I seek to protect my nation by keeping it from false limits."[145] Remember Buber always called himself a Zionist, unlike Kohn, who ceased to do so, and Arendt, who did so only with immense qualifications (by the 1960s, Buber's involvement in the publication *Ner*, which fought against military rule in the Arab areas, further sharpened his critique). If, Buber writes, one has the "intention of driving people who are bound to the soil out of their homeland," then the limits of the permissible have been breached: "I shall never agree that in this matter it is possible to justify injustice by pleading values or destinies." And he continues, "If there is a power of righteousness that punishes evildoing, it will intervene here and react."[146]

Buber was right but also wrong. What he names explicitly as a "transfer of population," the expulsion of the Palestinians, took place with no answering intervention, no retribution, from above. I read Buber as saying that what leads nations astray—what would lead the new Jewish nation astray—is false conviction. As soon as destinies and values become secure possessions, they serve to legitimate power. Omnipotent, they start to corrupt themselves. When he wrote this essay in 1945, the full extent of the destruction of European Jewry was known—not the easiest of moments to set limits when all human limits had been crossed. But perhaps for that very reason it was all the more imperative to do so. In its statement of July 1945, published in *Herut* (Freedom), the Irgun attacked Buber's organisation, the Ichud.

> We reject the morality of the observers [*ha-tzofim*], the professors of Mt. Scopus [*Har-Hatzofim*]. We the flesh of the flesh of the slaughtered [Jews of Europe], we the blood of their blood. And what is more important, we the spirit of the spirit of the martyrs of Israel in the past, the present and the future. . . . In matters of supreme importance we do not and will not know compromise.[147]

Perhaps the most dangerous historical moments are when a destiny seems unanswerable (the nation will not survive if it has to compromise or criticise itself). "Today reality has become a nightmare," Arendt wrote in May 1946, "horrible beyond the scope of the human imagination."[148] The Jewish people now see themselves, as Herzl had always seen them, as surrounded by eternal enemies. "Our failure to be surprised at this development," she continues, "does not make Herzl's picture truer—it only makes it more dangerous."[149]

Naomi Chazan was until 2002 deputy speaker of the Knesset and is a member of Meretz, the party described by refusenik Lieutenant Iczkovitz as "neither seen nor heard" in this time of greatest need. When I interviewed her in Tel Aviv in 2002, she issued a caution resonant of Martin Buber in 1945. "Survival," she said, "is not a value . . . tolerance is, peace is, equality is. But survival is not a value. Survival is the means to something else."[150] I was, I admit, astounded to hear an Israeli say this. After all, Jewish survival can be seen as the cause of Israel and, in the dominant rhetoric, of everything that has happened since. My cast of characters in this chapter—Buber, Kohn, Arendt, and Ahad Ha'am—all believed, however, that survival, however urgent, indeed desperate for those who lived to 1945, should become not the rationale of statehood but the means to something else.

Then, as now, the issue was justice. As early as 1932, Buber had offered his warning to a Zionism that would achieve its aims "at any price": "It may however be characteristic of Zion that it *cannot* be built 'with every possible means,' but only *bemishpat* (Isaiah, 1:27), only 'with justice.' "[151]

In his book *Israel and Palestine Out of the Ashes: The Search for Jewish Identity in the Twenty-First Century*, Marc Ellis suggests that Jews often do not know that there was this history of dissent which has been "forgotten or deliberately buried."[152] Most simply, I have wanted to revive it. To show that Zionism was not one thing, that it knew itself better than it thinks. To read these writers, alongside the dominant voices of Israeli statehood, is to be confronted with something like a split between lethal identification and grievous disenchantment; as if the State of Israel were offering its citizens and the rest of the world only the options of idealisation or radical dissent. It is also to be struck with an overwhelming sense of a moment missed, of voices silenced, of an argument, at terrible cost, re-repressed. Today we are all still suffering the loss of their critical, insightful, vision.

PART III   Representations

Representations

The problem of "representation"—in both aesthetic and political senses of the term—is determining for Rose. It is precisely because there is no "power without glory" (to invoke a theological vocabulary) that representations must be integral in the constitution, maintenance, and transmission of power. There is also no power without resistance to power. Such "resistance" is itself ambivalent, however. Resistance can certainly take on a heroic coloration, as with the French Resistance to Nazi occupation in the Second World War, and it can designate an entire range of behaviors, ranging from passive resistance to armed struggle against oppression. But "resistance" can just as easily denote a resistance *to* needed change. Hence, psychoanalysis posits resistance-to-self as a fundamental operation of the psyche. Power can extend and bolster itself through resistance, and some forms of resistance are, perhaps despite appearances, indices of power's consolidation and triumph, not its imminent collapse. Such autoresistance is inevitably accompanied by primordial affects, such as those of rage, disgust, shame, and guilt. And, as we know, the generation and control of affects is integral to the question of representation. Literature is one place where such relations between power, resistance, and affect are not only freighted, but rigorously analyzed—and it is these powers of literature to which Rose is notably sensitive. These issues are treated explicitly in the essays reproduced in this section of the reader: "Sexuality in the Field of Vision," "*Hamlet*: The 'Mona Lisa' of Literature," "Virginia Woolf and the Death of Modernism," "Daddy," "Peter Pan and Freud," and the sections from Rose's novel *Albertine*. It is also noteworthy that criticism in Rose's hands is rarely, if ever, an organ of judgment; it is far more often an experiment in translation and in transformation.

"Sexuality in the Field of Vision," written as a catalogue essay for the exhibition *Difference: On Representation and Sexuality* in 1984, and reprinted in the collection of the same title in 1986, starts by identifying a defining moment in Freud's commentary on a drawing by Leonardo da Vinci. Freud thinks that the drawing in question (today only partly attributed to Leonardo) of heterosexual intercourse in anatomical section is a *failure*. Not a failure of talent or capacity, of course, but one which rather, in Rose's words, suggests "that there can be no work on the image, no challenge to its powers of illusion and address, which does not simultaneously challenge the fact of sexual difference" (222 herein). Rose follows this line of questioning to the point where received distinctions between "image" and "word," "language" and "culture," "meaning" and "theory" begin to betray their own motivated (if unavoidable) refusals of the problems of sex.

Sexuality is clearly big trouble in one of the canonically central plays of world literature, William Shakespeare's *Hamlet*. Rose enters the debate obliquely, by showing how sexuality unexpectedly yet centrally inflects the literary theory of T. S. Eliot. The phrase that serves as the title for Rose's essay "The Mona Lisa of Literature" (published in *Critical Quarterly* in 1986) is drawn from Eliot's essay in which the famous concept of "objective correlative" emerges. Rose comments, "The question of femininity clearly underpins this central, if not indeed the central, concept of Eliot's aesthetic theory" (228 herein), precisely because it appears "in the form of a reproach" against the status of the mother, Gertrude, in Shakespeare's play. Rose follows the surprising yet revealing thread in Eliot's essay that renders Gertrude an insufficient cause to explain Hamlet's actions, and, in doing so, reconfigures Eliot's insight in such a way as to suggest that what aesthetic form cannot represent is femininity. If, for Eliot, the enigma of femininity is coterminous with the enigma of interpretation itself, this is because femininity troubles the symbolic economy so as to figure as at once deficient and excessive, and, in this uncontainable doubleness, operate a series of displacements within aesthetic representations that opens them onto their own sexual outside. This problematic also troubles the psychoanalytic accounts of Freud and Ernest Jones, which cannot, despite their explicit focus on sexuality, manage the feminine disruption. The affect of anxiety accompanies these symptomatic failures and, in doing so, paradoxically also unveils the fantasies that both aesthetic and sexual discourses unexpectedly share.

Unsurprisingly, the psychology of mourning and melancholia operates in such aesthetic and sexual fantasies, which are also attempts to work through primordial experiences of loss. In "Virginia Woolf and the Death of Modernism" (1998), Rose shows how Freud's theorization of mourning itself arises as a reaction against the "cultural dismay" precipitated by the First World War, and thus takes on some of the tones of the incalculable (with tropes such as "interminable," "fluid," and so on). For Rose, the writings of Virginia Woolf are especially redolent with the dramas of lost belief which—in ways that function as an implicit critique of Freud's own attempts to retrieve his belief in Western culture and defend against loss—"have no truck with his fine psychic and face-saving discriminations" (247–48 herein). Focusing on Woolf's first novel, *The Voyage Out*, Rose wants to suggest how the unbearable "absent presence" of death insists and shapes that novel, putting into question the economic motifs of work that pervade not only Freudian accounts of mourning, but other major discourses of profit and loss.

Reflecting Rose's facility for bravura close-reading no less is "Daddy," which originally appeared as chapter 6 of *The Haunting of Sylvia Plath* (1991)—Rose's groundbreaking monograph on the eponymous poet. As the book's ambiguous title suggests, Plath was not only haunted by traumas from the past— which she herself put to use and reflected upon in her poetry—but her legacy itself continues to haunt. It is also a haunting legacy in the sense of being a lingering, distressing sadness. It is, moreover, an extremely complex and disturbing legacy, at once biographical and literary, and is so in such a way as to put into question the very distinction between biography and literature. Specters, psychoanalytically speaking at least, always bear testimony to unpaid symbolic debts—debts whose provenance and import is at once obscure and oppressive, whose limits seem, in principle, to be impossible to locate, and whose demands may well be insatiable. In this extract, Rose considers perhaps Plath's most famous poem, "Daddy"—the poem whose "I" seems to betray dangerous, unjustifiable identifications, even usurpations of traumas belonging to others, indeed the Holocaust: the ur-trauma of our time. In the course of this reading, Rose picks up on the literally impossible temporality projected by the poem, its peculiar relationship to the dead-present father and the suffering body, to its most flagrantly and famously outrageous identifications (with "the Jew" and "the fascist," for example). As Rose says, "even at the most personal level of this poem, there is something more general at stake." The concluding formulations are particularly striking, as Rose suggests that women may have a special relationship to the power of fantasy.

One cannot become a woman, however, without having first been a child— and it is upon this fact that Rose's classic monograph *The Case of Peter Pan, or, The Impossibility of Children's Fiction* (1984) is elaborated. Freud recognized that the apparent meaninglessness of adult memories of childhood had at least a double sense. On the one hand, it meant that childhood is always with us: that we can never absolutely rupture with our own infantile inheritance. Freud acknowledged the priority of the great romantic writers of the late-eighteenth and early-nineteenth centuries in this regard, feeling that he had merely given their insights a firmer "scientific" basis. On the other hand, Freud also realized that adult memories of childhood were often not, strictly speaking, memories at all, but themselves fantasies, "screen memories," which, in their apparent arbitrariness, ciphered ongoing conflicts within the psyche. "Childhood" for the adult thus functions paradoxically: it at once secretly persists, pressing forward as it were, in unknown ways, while a dissimulating image of childhood is rammed back into the past. To take Freud seriously means, among other things, not desperately trying to squash the child into a fortifying frame of coherent motivations, nor, for that matter, a human life into a self-securing developmental narrative. Yet attempts to do just this recur in all manner of places, evincing the ubiquitous drive to make childhood a "sanction" of "a concept of pure origin." What clearly interests Rose in J. M. Barrie's classic *Peter Pan* (or, rather, in the multifarious texts that this rather peculiar proper name has come to designate) is the way it so intriguingly betrays the mechanisms by which such adult ideals of childhood come to be sold back to children as if those ideals were the children's desire all along. Part of being a child is having to pretend to accept that the stuff that is allegedly addressed to you is actually addressed to you; to be seen to be saying "Yes!" to adults' desires that their disavowed desires are really yours.

We have also included here several extracts from Rose's novel *Albertine* (2001), which is based on the character in Marcel Proust's *In Search of Lost Time*. *Albertine* picks up one of the major characters in Proust, and rewrites a number of key scenes from the perspective of Proust's women. No longer simply the enigmatic, double-dealing, pain-inflicting love interest of Proust's narrator, the orphan Albertine Simonet and her friend Andrée take on a different life in Rose's rewriting, providing a substantial feminist answer to the question: what happens when the narrated narrate the narrator in their turn? Both here and throughout Rose's writings on literature, one discerns an extreme attentiveness to the lability and "shiftiness" of the "I"—surely the most uttered and the most treacherous of all English words.

This volatile "I" is central to Rose's uniqueness as a scholar. From the late 1970s, many of the most influential Anglophone literary critics, such as Fredric Jameson, Edward Said, Stephen Greenblatt, Gayatri Spivak, and Homi Bhabha have also used literary texts as exemplary forms of analysis of postcolonial and nationalist struggles; many others, such as Shoshana Felman, Judith Butler, Jane Gallop, Avital Ronell, and the late Eve Kosofsky Sedgwick, repurposed psychoanalysis in the service of heterogeneous forms of feminism. Undoubtedly, Rose is part of this heterodox constellation of scholarship, but there's a personal quality to her work that sets it apart. As she puts it in the interview that concludes this reader,

> "Criticism has always been a place where I could transmute into some kind of form things that were preoccupying me at the most profound personal and often unconscious level. This brings literary criticism closer to the world of the dream in the sense that Christopher Bollas writes about people dreaming their lives through the objects they encounter and which they transform and which transform them—so literary criticism would be my transformative object.

For Rose, criticism is not just a tool of a profession, in the analysis of socio-cultural phenomena, or a mode of intellectual transmission. It is also a mode of transformative self-othering.

—*Justin Clemens and Ben Naparstek*

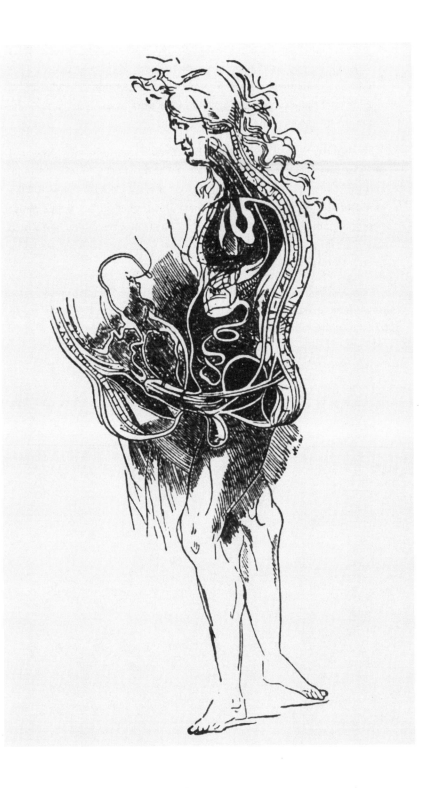

Sexuality in the Field of Vision

In an untypical moment Freud accuses Leonardo of being unable to draw.[1] A drawing done in anatomical section of the sexual act is inaccurate. What is more it is lacking in pleasure: the man's expression is one of disgust, the position is uncomfortable, the woman's breast is unbeautiful (she does not have a head). The depiction is inaccurate, uncomfortable, undesirable, and without desire. It is also inverted: the man's head looks like that of a woman, and the feet are the wrong way around according to the plane of the picture— the man's foot pointing outwards where the woman's foot should be, and her foot in his place. In fact, most of Freud's monograph on Leonardo is addressed to the artist's *failure*, that is, to the restrictions and limitations which Leonardo himself apparently experienced in relation to his potential achievement. Freud takes failure very seriously, even when it refers to someone who, to the gaze of the outside world, represents the supreme form of artistic success. But in this footnote on the sexual drawing, Freud goes beyond the brief of the largely psychobiographical forms of interpretation that he brings to Leonardo's case. He relates—quite explicitly—a failure to depict the sexual act to bisexuality and to a problem of representational space. The uncertain sexual identity muddles the plane of the image so that the spectator does not know where she or he stands in relationship to the picture. A confusion at the level of sexuality brings with it a disturbance of the visual field.

An artistic practice which sets itself the dual task of disrupting visual form and questioning the sexual certainties and stereotypes of our culture can fairly return to this historical moment (historical analytically as well as artistically, since the reference to Leonardo is now overlaid with the reference to the beginnings of psychoanalysis itself). Not for authority (authority is one of the things being questioned here), but for its suggestiveness in pointing up a possible relation between sexuality and the image. We know that Freud's writing runs parallel to the emergence of "modern" art; he himself used such art as a comparison for the blurred fields of the unconscious psychic processes which were the object of his analytic work.[2] But in this footnote on Leonardo's failure in the visual act, we can already see traced out a specific movement or logic: that there can be no work on the image, no challenge to its powers of illusion and address, which does not simultaneously challenge the fact of sexual difference, whose self-evidence Leonardo's drawing had momentarily allowed to crumble.[3]

The rest of Freud's writing shows that sexual difference is indeed such a hesitant and imperfect construction. Men and women take up positions of symbolic and polarized opposition against the grain of a multifarious and bisexual disposition, which Freud first identified in the symptom (and genius . . .) before recognizing its continuing and barely concealed presence across the range of normal adult sexual life. The lines of that division are fragile in exact proportion to the rigid insistence with which our culture lays them down; they constantly converge and threaten to coalesce. Psychoanalysis itself can therefore explain the absence of that clear and accomplished form of sexuality that Freud himself had unsuccessfully searched for in the picture.

Freud often related the question of sexuality to that of visual representation. Describing the child's difficult journey into adult sexual life, he would take as his model little scenarios, or the staging of events, which demonstrated the complexity of an essentially visual space, moments in which perception *founders* (the boy child refuses to believe the anatomical difference that he sees) or in which pleasure in looking tips over into the register of *excess* (witness to a sexual act in which he reads his own destiny, the child tries to interrupt by calling attention to his presence).[4, 5] Each time the stress falls on a problem of seeing. The sexuality lies less in the content of what is seen than in the subjectivity of the viewer, in the relationship between what is looked at and the developing sexual knowledge of the child. The relationship between viewer and scene is always one of fracture, partial identification, pleasure, and distrust. As if Freud found the aptest analogy for the problem of our identity as human subjects in failures of vision or in the violence which can be done to an image as it offers itself to view. For Freud, with an emphasis that has been picked up and placed at the centre of the work of Jacques Lacan, our sexual identities as male or female, our confidence in language as true or false, and our security in the image we judge as perfect or flawed are fantasies. And these archaic moments of disturbed visual representation, these troubled scenes, which expressed and unsettled our groping knowledge in the past, can now be used as theoretical prototypes to unsettle our certainties once again. Hence one of the chief drives of an art which today addresses the presence of the sexual in representation—to expose the fixed nature of sexual identity as a fantasy and, in the same gesture, to trouble, break up, or rupture the visual field before our eyes.

The encounter between psychoanalysis and artistic practice is therefore *staged*, but only insofar as that staging has *already taken place*. It is an encounter which draws its strength from that repetition, working like a memory trace of something we have been through before. It gives back to repetition its proper meaning and status: not lack of originality or something merely derived (the commonest reproach to the work of art), nor the more recent practice of appropriating artistic and photographic images in order to undermine their previous status; but repetition as insistence, that is, as the constant pressure of something hidden but not forgotten—something that can only come into focus now by blurring the field of representation where our normal forms of self-recognition take place.

The affinity between representation and sexuality is not confined to the visual image. In fact, in relation to other areas of theoretical analysis and activity, recognition of this affinity in the domain of the artistic image could be said to manifest something of a lag.[6] In one of his most important self-criticisms, Barthes underlined the importance of psychoanalysis in pushing his earlier exposé of ideological meanings into a critique of the possibility of meaning itself.[7] In his case studies Freud had increasingly demonstrated that the history of the patient did not consist of some truth to be deciphered behind the chain of associations which emerged in the analytic setting; it resided within that chain and in the process of emergence which the analysis brought into effect. Lacan immediately read in this the chain of language which slides from unit to unit, producing meaning out of the relationship between terms; its truth belongs to that movement and not to some prior reference existing outside its domain. The divisions of language are in themselves arbitrary and shifting: language rests on a continuum which gets locked into discrete units of which sexual difference is only the most strongly marked. The fixing of language and the fixing of sexual identity go hand in hand; they rely on each other and share the same forms of instability and risk. Lacan read Freud through language, but he also brought out, by implication, the sexuality at work in all practices of the sign. Modernist literary writing could certainly demonstrate, alongside the syntactic and narrative shifts for which it is best known, oscillations in the domain of sexuality, a type of murking of the sexual proprieties on which the politer world of nineteenth-century realist fiction had been based. Although the opposition between the two forms of writing has often been overstated, it is no coincidence that, in order to illustrate this tension between "readerly" and "writerly" fiction, Barthes chose a story in which the narrative enigma turns on a castrato (Balzac's *Sarrasine*).[8] The indecipherable sexuality of the character makes for the trouble and the joy of the text.

It is worth pausing over the implications of this for a modernist and postmodernist artistic practice which is increasingly understood in terms of a problematic of reading and a theory of the sign. Again, the historical links are important. Freud takes modern painting as the image of the unconscious. But the modernist suspension of the referent, with its stress on the purity of the visual signifier, belongs equally with Saussure who, at the same time, was criticizing the conception of language as reference and underlining the arbitrary nature of the sign (primacy to the signifier instead of language as a nomenclature of the world). Lacan's move then simply completes the circuit by linking Saussure back to Freud. The unconscious reveals that the normal divisions of language and sexuality obey the dictates of an arbitrary law undermining the very possibility of reference for the subject since the "I" can no longer be seen to correspond to some pre-given and permanent identity of psychosexual life. The problem of psychic identity is therefore immanent to the problem of the sign.

The same link (of language and the unconscious) can be made to that transition to postmodernism which has been read as a return of the referent, but the referent as a problem, not as a given.[9] Piles of cultural artefacts bring back something we recognise but in a form which refuses any logic of the same. The objects before the spectator's eyes cannot be ordered: in their disjunctive relation, they produce an acuter problem of vision than the one which had resulted when reference was simply dropped from the frame. Above all—to return to the analogy with the analytic scene—these images require a reading which neither coheres them into a unity, nor struggles to get behind them into a realm of truth. The only possible reading is one which repeats their fragmentation of a cultural world they both echo and refuse.

At each point of these transitions—artistic and theoretical—something is called into question at the most fundamental level of the way we recognise and respond to our own subjectivity and to a world with which we are assumed to be familiar, a world we both do and do not know. Yet in each of these instances, it is precisely the psychoanalytic concepts of the unconscious and sexuality, specifically in their relationship to language, which seem to be lost.

Thus the modernist stress on the purity of the visual signifier easily dis-solves into an almost mystic contemplation. Language can be used to rupture the smoothness of the visual image but it is language as pure mark unin-formed by the psychoanalytic apprehension of the sign. Cultural artefacts are presented as images within images to rob them of the values they seem naturally to embody, but the fundamental sexual polarity of that culture is not called into account. Finally, meaning is seen to reside in these images as supplement, allegory, or fragment, but with no sexual residue or trace—the concept of textuality is lifted out of psychoanalytic and literary theory but without the sexual definition that was its chief impetus and support.

Across a range of instances, language, sexuality, and the unconscious *in their mutual relation* appear as a present-absence which all these moments seem to brush against, or elicit, before falling away. The elisions can be summarised schematically.

— purity of the visual signifier and the unconscious as mystique (no lan-guage);
— language as rupture of the iconicity of the visual sign (no unconscious);
— cultural artefacts as indictment of the stereotype (no sexual difference);
— reading as supplement, process, or fragment (no sexual determinacy of the signifier or of visual space).

Artists engaged in sexual representation (representation *as* sexual) come in at precisely this point, calling up the sexual component of the image, drawing out an emphasis that exists *in potentia* in the various instances they inherit and of which they form a part.[10] Their move is not therefore one of (moral) corrective. They draw on the tendencies they also seek to displace, and clearly belong, for example, within the context of that postmodernism which demands that reference, in its problematised form, re-enter the frame. But the emphasis on sexuality produces specific effects. First, it adds to the concept of cultural artefact or stereotype the political imperative of feminism which holds the image accountable for the reproduction of norms. Second, to this feminist demand for scrutiny of the image, it adds the idea of a sexuality which goes beyond the issue of content to take in the parameters of visual form (not just what we see but how we see—visual space as more than the domain of simple recognition). The image therefore submits to the sexual reference, but only insofar as reference itself is questioned by the work of the image. And the aesthetics of pure form are implicated in the less pure plea-sures of looking, but these in turn are part of an aesthetically extraneous political space. The arena is simultaneously that of aesthetics and sexuality, and art and sexual politics. The link between sexuality and the image produces a particular dialogue which cannot be covered adequately by the familiar opposition between the formal operations of the image and a politics exerted from outside.

The engagement with the image therefore belongs to a political intention. It is an intention which has also inflected the psychoanalytic and literary theories on which such artists draw. The model is not one of applying psychoanalysis to the work of art (what application could there finally be which does not reduce one field to the other or inhibit by interpretation the potential meaning of both?). Psychoanalysis offers a specific account of sexual difference but its value (and also its difficulty) for feminism lies in the place assigned to the woman in that differentiation. In his essay on Leonardo, Freud himself says that once the boy child sees what it is to be a woman, he will "tremble for his masculinity" henceforth.[11] If meaning oscillates when a castrato comes onto the scene, our sense must be that it is in the normal image of the man that our certainties are invested and, by implication, in that of the woman that they constantly threaten collapse.

A feminism concerned with the question of looking can therefore turn this theory around and stress the particular and limiting opposition of male and female which any image seen to be flawless is serving to hold in place. More simply, we know that women are meant to *look* perfect, presenting a seamless image to the world so that the man, in that confrontation with difference, can avoid any apprehension of lack. The position of woman as fantasy therefore depends on a particular economy of vision (the importance of "images of women" might take on its fullest meaning from this).[12] Perhaps this is also why only a project which comes via feminism can demand so unequivocally of the image that it renounce all pretensions to a narcissistic perfection of form.

At the extreme edge of this investigation, we might argue that the fantasy of absolute sexual difference, in its present guise, could be upheld only from the point when painting restricted the human body to the eye.[13] That would be to give the history of the image in Western culture a particularly heavy weight to bear. For, even if the visual image has indeed been one of the chief vehicles through which such a restriction has been enforced, it could only operate like a law which always produces the terms of its own violation. It is often forgotten that psychoanalysis describes the psychic law to which we are subject, but only in terms of its *failing*. This is important for a feminist (or any radical) practice which has often felt it necessary to claim for itself a wholly other psychic and representational domain. Therefore, if the visual image in its aesthetically acclaimed form serves to maintain a particular and oppressive mode of sexual recognition, it does so only partially and at a cost. Our previous history is not the petrified block of a singular visual space since, looked at obliquely, it can always be seen to contain its moments of unease.[14] We can surely relinquish the monolithic view of that history, if doing so allows us a form of resistance which can be articulated *on this side of* (rather than beyond) the world against which it protests.

Among Leonardo's early sketches, Freud discovers the heads of laughing women, images of exuberance which then fall out of the great canon of his art. Like Leonardo's picture of the sexual act, these images appear to unsettle Freud as if their pleasure somehow correlated with the discomfort of the sexual drawing (the sexual drawing through its failure, the heads of laughing women for their excess). These images, not well known in Leonardo's canon, now have the status of fragments, but they indicate a truth about the tradition which excludes them, revealing the presence of something strangely insistent to which these artists return. *"Teste di femmine, che ridono"*—laughter is not the emphasis here, but the urgent engagement with the question of sexuality persists now, as it did then.[15] It can no more be seen as the beginning, than it should be the end, of the matter.

Hamlet: The "Mona Lisa" of Literature

It does not seem to have been pointed out that T. S. Eliot's famous concept of the "objective correlative," which has been so influential in the assessment of literature and its values, was originally put forward in 1919 in the form of a reproach against the character of a woman.[1] The woman in question is Gertrude in Shakespeare's Hamlet, and the reproach Eliot makes is that she is not good enough aesthetically, that is, *bad* enough psychologically, which means that in relationship to the affect which she generates by her behaviour in the chief character of the drama—Hamlet himself—Gertrude is not deemed a sufficient *cause*.

The question of femininity clearly underpins this central, if not indeed the central, concept of Eliot's aesthetic theory, and this is confirmed by the fact that Eliot again uses an image of femininity—and by no means one of the most straightforward in its own representation or in the responses it has produced—to give us the measure of the consequent failure of the play. *Hamlet* the play, Eliot writes, is "the Mona Lisa of literature," offering up in its essentially enigmatic and indecipherable nature something of that maimed or imperfect quality of appeal which characterises Leonardo's famous painting.[2] The aesthetic inadequacy of the play is caused by the figure of a woman, and the image of a woman most aptly embodies the consequences of that failure. Femininity thus becomes the stake, not only of the internal, but also of the critical drama generated by the play.

Equally important, however, is the fact that femininity has been at the heart of the psychoanalytic approach to *Hamlet*, from Ernest Jones onwards—a fact which has again been overlooked by those who have arrested their attention at the famous oedipal saga for which his reading of the play is best known. "Hamlet was a woman" is just one of the statements about *Hamlet* which Jones quotes as indicating the place of the "feminine" in a drama which has paradoxically been celebrated as the birth of the modern, post-

Renaissance, conception of man.³ In this essay, I will try to focus what I see as the centrality of this question of femininity to an aesthetic theory which has crucially influenced a whole tradition of how we conceptualise literary writing, and to the psychoanalytic theory which was being elaborated at exactly the same time, at the point where they converge on the same object— Shakespeare's *Hamlet*—described by Freud as an emblem of "the secular advance of repression in the emotional life of mankind."⁴

I

To start with T. S. Eliot's critique of *Hamlet*. T. S. Eliot in fact sees his reading of the play as a move away from psychological approaches to Hamlet which concentrate too much on the characters to the exclusion of the play itself: "*Hamlet* the play is the primary problem, and Hamlet the character only secondary."⁵ Eliot therefore makes it clear that what he has to say exceeds the fact of the dramatis personae and strikes at the heart of aesthetic form itself. The problem with *Hamlet* is that there is something in the play which is formally or aesthetically unmanageable: "like the *Sonnets*" (another work by Shakespeare in which a question of sexual ambivalence has always been recognised) "*Hamlet* is full of some stuff that the writer could not drag to light, contemplate, or manipulate into art."⁶ Eliot then describes the conditions, as he sees it, of that in which *Hamlet* fails—the successful manipulation of matter into artistic form. It is here that he produces the concept of the "objective correlative" for the first time: "The only way of expressing emotion in the form of art is by finding an 'objective correlative'; in other words, a set of objects, a situation, a chain of events which shall be the formula of that particular emotion; such that when the external facts . . . are given, the emotion is immediately evoked. . . . The artistic 'inevitability' lies in this complete adequacy of the external to the emotion."⁷

Emotion, or affect, is therefore only admissible in art if it is given an external object to which it can be seen, clearly and automatically, to correspond. There must be nothing in that emotion which spills over or exceeds the objective, visible (one could say conscious) facts, no residue or trace of the primitive "stuff" which may have been the original stimulus for the work of art. This is where *Hamlet* fails: Hamlet the man is dominated by an emotion which is inexpressible, because it is in *excess* of the facts as they appear. And that excess is occasioned by Gertrude, who precipitates Hamlet into despondency by her "o'er hasty" marriage to his dead father's brother and successor, who turns out also to have been the agent of the former king's death. For Eliot, Gertrude is not an adequate equivalent for the disgust which she evokes in Hamlet, which "envelops and exceeds her" and which, because she cannot adequately contain it, runs right across the fabric of the play.[8] Gertrude is therefore disgusting, but not quite disgusting *enough*. Eliot is, however, clear that he is not asking for a stronger woman character on the stage, since he recognises that it is in the nature of the problem dealt with in this play—a son's feelings towards a guilty mother—that they should be in excess of their objective cause. On this count, Gertrude's inadequacy turns around and becomes wholly appropriate: "It is just *because* her character is so negative and insignificant that she arouses in Hamlet the feeling which she is incapable of representing."[9]

What is at stake behind this failing of the woman, what she fails to represent, therefore, is precisely unrepresentable—a set of unconscious emotions which, *by definition*, can have no objective outlet and which are therefore incapable of submitting to the formal constraints of art. What we get in *Hamlet* instead is "buffoonery"—in Hamlet himself the "buffoonery of an emotion which can find no outlet in action," for the dramatist the "buffoonery of an emotion which he cannot express in art."[10] Such "intense," "ecstatic" (Gertrude uses the word "ecstasy" to describe Hamlet's madness in the bed-chamber scene of the play), and "terrible" feeling is for Eliot "doubtless a subject of study for the pathologist," and why Shakespeare attempted to express the "inexpressibly horrible" we cannot ever know, since we should have finally "to know something which is by hypothesis unknowable and to understand things which Shakespeare did not understand himself."[11]

Today we can only be struck by the extraordinary resonance of the terms which figure so negatively in Eliot's critique—buffoonery, ecstasy, the excessive and unknowable—all terms in which we have learnt to recognise (since Freud at least) something necessarily present in any act of writing (*Hamlet* included) which only suppresses them—orders them precisely into form—at a cost. Eliot's criticism of *Hamlet* can therefore be turned around. What he sees as the play's weakness becomes its source of fascination or even strength.

In this context, the fact that it is a woman who is seen as cause of the excess and deficiency in the play and again a woman who symbolises its aesthetic failure starts to look like a repetition. Firstly, of the play itself—Hamlet and his dead father united in the reproach they make of Gertrude for her sexual failing ("O Hamlet what a falling off was there"), and *horror* as the exact response to the crime which precedes the play and precipitates its drama ("O horrible! O horrible! most horrible!").[12] Secondly, a repetition of a more fundamental drama of psychic experience itself as described by Freud, the drama of sexual difference in which the woman is seen as the cause of just such a failure in representation, as something deficient, lacking, or threatening to the system and identities which are the precondition not only of integrated artistic form but also of so-called normal adult psychic and sexual life. Located by Freud at the point where the woman is first seen to be different, this moment can then have its effects in that familiar mystification or fetishisation of femininity which makes of the woman something both perfect and dangerous or obscene (obscene if *not* perfect).[13] And perhaps no image has evoked this process more clearly than that of the "Mona Lisa" itself, which at almost exactly this historical moment (the time of Freud and Eliot alike) started to be taken as the emblem of an inscrutable femininity, cause and destination of the whole of human mystery and its desires: "The lady smiled in regal calm: her instincts of conquest, of ferocity, all the heredity of the species, the will to seduce and to ensnare, the charm of deceit, the kindness that conceals a cruel purpose— all this appeared and disappeared by turns behind the laughing veil and buried itself in the poem of her smile. Good and wicked, cruel and compassionate, graceful and feline she laughed."[14]

By choosing an image of a woman to embody the inexpressible and inscrutable context which he identified in Shakespeare's play, Eliot ties the enigma of femininity to the problem of interpretation itself: "No one has solved the riddle of her smile, no one has read the meaning of her thoughts," "a presence . . . expressive of what in the way of a thousand years men had come to desire."[15] Freud himself picks up the tone in one of his more problematic observations about femininity when he allows that critics have recognised in the picture "the most perfect representation of the contrasts which dominate the erotic life of women; the contrast between reserve and seduction, and between the most devoted tenderness and a sensuality that is ruthlessly demanding—consuming men as if they were alien beings."[16]

What other representation, we might ask, has so clearly produced a set of emotions without "objective correlative," that is in excess of the facts as they appear? T. S. Eliot's reading of *Hamlet* would therefore seem to suggest that what is in fact felt as inscrutable, unmanageable, or even horrible (ecstatic in both senses of the term) for an aesthetic theory which will only allow into its definition what can be controlled or managed by art is nothing other than femininity itself.

At the end of Eliot's essay, he refers to Montaigne's "Apologie of Raymond

Sebond" as a possible source for the malaise of the play. Its discourse on the contradictory, unstable, and ephemeral nature of man has often been seen as the origin of Hamlet's suicide soliloquy; it also contains an extraordinary passage anticipating Freud where Montaigne asks whether we do not live in dreaming, dream when we think and work, and whether our waking merely be a form of sleep.[17] In relation to the woman, however, another smaller essay by Montaigne—"Of Three Good Women"—is equally striking for the exact reversal which these three women, models of female virtue, represent vis-à-vis Gertrude herself in Shakespeare's play, each one choosing self-imposed death at the point where her husband is to die.[18] The image is close to the protestations of the Player Queen in the Mousetrap scene of Hamlet, who vows her undying love to her husband; whereupon Gertrude, recognising perhaps in the Player Queen's claims a rebuke or foil to her own sexual laxness, comments, "The lady doth protest too much" (a familiar cliché now for the sexual "inconstancy" of females).[19] So what happens, indeed, to the sexuality of the woman, when the husband dies, who is there to hold its potentially dangerous excess within the bounds of a fully social constraint? This could be seen as one of the questions asked by Hamlet the play and generative of its terrible effect.

Before going on to discuss psychoanalytic interpretations of Hamlet, it is worth stressing the extent to which Eliot's theory is shot through with sexuality in this way and its implications for recent literary debate. Taking their cue from psychoanalysis, writers like Roland Barthes and Julia Kristeva have seen the very stability of the sign as index and pre-condition for that myth of linguistic cohesion and sexual identity which we must live by but under whose regimen we suffer.[20] Literature then becomes one of the chief arenas in which this struggle is played out. Literary writing which proclaims its integrity, and literary theory which demands that integrity (objectivity/correlation) of writing, merely repeat that moment of repression when language and sexuality were first ordered into place, putting down the unconscious processes which threaten the resolution of the oedipal drama and of narrative form alike. In this context, Eliot's critical writing, with its stress on the ethical task of writer and critic, becomes nothing less than the most accomplished (and influential) case for the interdependency and centrality of language and sexuality to the proper ordering of literary form. Much recent literary theory can be seen as an attempt to undo the ferocious effects of this particularly harsh type of literary superego—one whose political repressiveness in the case of Eliot became more and more explicit in his later allegiance to Empire, Church, and State.

Eliot himself was aware of the areas of psychic danger against which he constantly brushed. He was clear that he was touching on "perilous" issues which risk "violating the frontier of consciousness," and when he talks of writing as something "pleasurable," "exhausting," "agitating," as a sudden "breakdown of strong habitual barriers," the sexuality of the writing process which he seeks to order spills over into the text.[21] And Eliot's conception of that order, what he sees as proper literary form, is finally an oedipal drama in itself. In his other famous essay "Tradition and the Individual Talent," which was written in the same year as the "Hamlet" essay, Eliot states that the way the artist can avoid his own disordered subjectivity and transmute it into form is by giving himself up to something outside himself and surrendering to the tradition that precedes and surrounds him. Only by capitulating to the world of dead poets can the artist escape his oppressive individuality and enter into historical time: "Set [the artist] for contrast and comparison among the dead" for "the most individual parts of his work are those in which the dead poets, his ancestors, assert their immortality most vigourously."[22] Thus, just as in the psychoanalytic account, the son pays his debt to the dead father, symbol of the law, in order fully to enter his history, so in Eliot's reading the artist pays his debt to the dead poets and can only become a poet by that fact. Eliot's conception of literary tradition and form could therefore be described as a plea for appropriate mourning and for the respecting of literary rites—that mourning whose shameful inadequacy, as Jacques Lacan points out in his essay on *Hamlet*, is the trigger and then constant refrain of the play: the old Hamlet cut off in the "blossom" of his sin; Polonius interred "hugger mugger"; Ophelia buried wrongly—because of her suicide—in consecrated ground.[23]

In Eliot's reading of *Hamlet*, therefore, the sexuality of the woman seems to become the scapegoat and cause of the dearth or breakdown of oedipal resolution which the play ceaselessly enacts, not only at the level of its theme, but also in the disjunctions and difficulties of its aesthetic form. Much has been made of course of the aesthetic problem of *Hamlet* by critics other than Eliot, who have pondered on its lack of integration or single-purposiveness, its apparent inability to resolve itself or come to term (it is the longest of Shakespeare's plays), much as they have pondered on all these factors in the character of Hamlet himself.

Hamlet poses a problem for Eliot, therefore, at the level of both matter and form. Femininity is the image of that problem; it seems in fact to be the only image through which the problem can be conceptualised or thought. The principal danger, femininity thus becomes the focus for a partly theorised recognition of the psychic and literary disintegration which can erupt at any moment into literary form.

One more example, and perhaps the most graphic, can serve to illustrate how far femininity is implicated in this aesthetic theory—the lines which Eliot uses from Tourneur's *The Revenger's Tragedy* to describe the artist surrendering to his inspiration before ordering it into form.

> And now methinks I could e'en chide myself
> For doating on her beauty, though her death
> Shall be revenged after no common action.
> Does the silkworm expend her yellow labours
> For thee? For thee does she undo herself?
> Are lordships sold to maintain ladyships
> For the poor benefit of a bewildering minute?
> Why doth yon fellow falsify highways,
> And put his life between the judge's lips,
> To refine such a thing—keeps horse and men
> To beat their valours for her?[24]

For a play that has also been discussed as excessive and perhaps even more than *Hamlet*, this moment gives the strongest measure of that excess. The speech is made by Vindice, the Revenger, to the skull of his former mistress who was poisoned by the Duke for resisting his advances. His revenge takes the form of wrapping this skull in the full bodied attire of the woman and dowsing its mouth with poison so that the Duke will first be seduced and then poisoned in its embrace. In this crazed image, the woman appears at once as purity and lust, victim and destroyer, but the split representation shows how the feminine can serve as a receptacle for a more fundamental horror of sexuality and death. Femininity becomes the place in which man reads his destiny, just as the woman becomes a symptom for the man.[25]

Likewise in *Hamlet*, these two themes—of death and sexuality—run their course through the play, both as something which can be assimilated to social constraint and as a threat to constraint and to the social altogether. For *Hamlet* can be seen as a play which turns on mourning and marriage—the former the means whereby death is given its symbolic form and enters back into social life, the latter the means whereby sexuality is brought into the orbit of the law. When *Hamlet* opens, however, what we are given is *too much* of each (perhaps this is the excess)—too much mourning (Hamlet wears black, stands apart, and mourns beyond the natural term) and too much marriage

(Gertrude passes from one husband to another too fast). As if these two regulators of the furthest edges of social and civil life if they become overstated, if there is too much of them, tip over into their opposite and start to look like what they are designed to hold off. Eliot's essay on *Hamlet*, and his writing on literature in general, gives us a sense of how these matters, which he recognises in the play, underpin the space of aesthetic representation itself and how femininity figures crucially in that conceptualisation.

II

If Eliot's aesthetic theories move across into the arena of sexuality, Ernest Jones's psychoanalytic interpretation of *Hamlet* turns out also to be part of an aesthetic concern. His intention is to use psychoanalysis to establish the integrity of the literary text, that is, to uncover factors, hidden motives and desires, which will give back to rational understanding what would otherwise pass the limits of literary understanding and appreciation itself: "The perfect work of art is one where the traits and reactions of the character prove to be harmonious, consistent and intelligible when examined in the different layers of the mind."[26] Jones's reading, therefore, belongs to that psychoanalytic project which restores to rationality or brings to light, placing what was formerly unconscious or unmanageable under the ego's mastery or control. It is a project which has been read directly out of Freud's much contested statement "*Wo Es war, soll Ich werden*," translated by Strachey "Where id was, there ego shall be."[27] Lacan, for whom the notion of such conscious mastery is only ever a fantasy (the fantasy of the ego itself) retranslates or reverses the statement: "There where it was, so I must come to be."[28]

For Jones, as for Eliot, therefore, there must be no aesthetic excess, nothing which goes beyond the reaches of what can ultimately be deciphered and known. In this context, psychoanalysis acts as a key which can solve the enigma of the text, take away its surplus by offering us as readers that fully rational understanding which Shakespeare's play—Jones recognises like Eliot—places at risk. The chapter of Jones's book which gives the oedipal reading of *Hamlet*, the one which tends to be included in the anthologies of Shakespeare criticism, is accordingly entitled "The Psychoanalytic Solution."[29] Taking his reference from Freud's comments in *The Interpretation of Dreams*, Jones sees Hamlet as a little Oedipus who cannot bring himself to kill Claudius because he stands in the place of his own desire, having murdered Hamlet's father and married his mother.[30] The difference between Oedipus and Hamlet is that

Oedipus unknowingly acts out this fantasy, whereas for Hamlet it is repressed into the unconscious revealing itself in the form of that inhibition or inability to act which has baffled so many critics of the play. It is this repression of the oedipal drama beneath the surface of the text which leads Freud to say of *Hamlet*, comparing it with Sophocles's drama, that it demonstrates the "secular advance of repression in the emotional life of mankind."[31]

But Jones's book and the psychoanalytic engagement with *Hamlet* does not stop there and it is finally more interesting than this oedipal reading which, along with Jones's speculations on Hamlet's childhood and Shakespeare's own life, has most often been used to discredit them. For while it is the case that Jones's account seems to fulfill the dream of any explanatory hypothesis by providing an account of factors which would otherwise remain unaccountable, a closer look shows how this same reading infringes the interpretative and sexual boundaries which, like Eliot, it seems to be putting into place.

The relationship of psychoanalysis to *Hamlet* has in fact always been a strange and repetitive one in which Hamlet the character is constantly given the status of a truth, and becomes a pivot for psychoanalysis and its project, just as for Eliot *Hamlet* is the focal point through which he arrives at a more general problem of aesthetic form. For Freud, for instance, Hamlet is not just Oedipus, but also melancholic and hysteric, and both these readings, problematic as they are as diagnoses of literary characters, become interesting because of the way they bring us up against the limits of interpretation and sexual identity alike. The interpretative distinction between rationality and excess, between normality and abnormality, for example, starts to crumble when the melancholic is defined as a madman who also speaks the truth. Freud uses *Hamlet* with this meaning in "Mourning and Melancholia," written in 1915: "We only wonder why a man has to be ill before he can be accessible to a truth of this kind. For there can be no doubt that if anyone holds an opinion of himself such as this (an opinion which Hamlet holds of himself and of everyone else) he is ill, whether or not he is speaking the truth or whether he is being more or less unfair to himself."[32]

Taken in this direction, *Hamlet* illustrates not so much a failure of identity as the precarious distinction on which this notion of identity rests. In "Psychopathic Characters on the Stage," Freud includes *Hamlet* in that group of plays which rely for their effect on the neurotic in the spectator, inducing in her or him the neurosis watched on stage, crossing over the boundaries between onstage and offstage and breaking down the habitual barriers of the mind.[33] A particular *type* of drama, this form is nonetheless effective only through its capacity to implicate us *all*: "A person who does not lose his reason under certain conditions can have no reason to lose."[34] Jones makes a similar point and underscores its fullest social import when he attributes the power of *Hamlet* to the very edge of sanity on which it moves, the way that it confuses the division which "until our generation (and even now in the juristic sphere) separated the sane and the responsible from the irresponsible insane."[35] T. S. Eliot also gave a version of this, but from the other side, when he described poetry in "Tradition and the Individual Talent" as an escape from emotion and personality, and then added, "But, of course, only those who have personality and emotion can know what it means to want to escape from these things."[36] So instead of safely diagnosing Hamlet, his oedipal drama, his disturbance, and subjecting them to its mastery and control, the psychoanalytic interpretation turns back onto spectator and critic, implicating the observer in those forms of irrationality and excess which Jones and Eliot in their different ways seek to order into place.

Calling Hamlet a hysteric, which both Freud and Jones also do, has the same effect in terms of the question of sexual difference, since it immediately raises the question of femininity and upsets the too tidy oedipal reading of the play.[37] Freud had originally seen the boy's oedipal drama as a straightforward desire for the mother and rivalry with the father, just as he first considered the little girl's oedipal trajectory to be its simple reverse. The discovery of the girl's pre-oedipal attachment to the mother led him to modify this too easy picture in which unconscious sexual desires in infancy are simply the precursors in miniature of the boy's and the girl's later appropriate sexual and social place.[38] We could say that psychoanalysis can become of interest to feminism at the point where the little girl's desire for the father can no longer be safely assumed. But equally important is the effect that this upset of the original schema has on how we consider the psychic life of the boy. In a section called "Matricide" normally omitted from the anthologies, Jones talks of Hamlet's desire to kill, not the father, but the mother.[39] He takes this from Hamlet's soliloquy before he goes to his mother's bedchamber in Act III, scene ii of the play:

> Let not ever
> The soul of Nero enter this firm bosom;
> Let me be cruel, not unnatural.
> I will speak daggers to her, but use none.[40]

and also from Gertrude's own lines "What wilt thou do? Thou wilt not murder me? Help! Ho!"⁴¹ (the murder of Polonius is the immediate consequence of this). Thus desire spills over into its opposite and the woman becomes guilty for the affect which she provokes.

This is still an oedipal reading of the play since the violence towards the mother is the effect of the desire for her (a simple passage between the two forms of excess). But the problem of desire starts to trouble the category of identification, involving Jones in a discussion of the femininity in man (not just desire *for* the woman but identification *with* her), a femininity which has been recognised by more than one critic of the play.⁴² Thus on either side of the psychoanalytic "solution," we find something which makes of it no solution at all. And Hamlet, "as patient as the female dove," becomes Renaissance man only to the extent that he reveals a femininity which undermines that fiction.⁴³ Femininity turns out to be lying behind the oedipal drama, indicating its impasse or impossibility of resolution, even though Freud did himself talk of its dissolution, as if it suddenly went out of existence altogether. But this observation contradicts the basic analytic premise of the persistence of unconscious desire.

The point being not whether Hamlet suffers from an excess *of* femininity, but the way that femininity itself functions *as* excess—the excess of this particular interpretative schema (hence presumably its exclusion from the summaries and extracts from Jones), and as the vanishing point of the difficulties of the play. And in this, Ernest Jones outbids T. S. Eliot vis-à-vis the woman: "The central mystery [of Hamlet] has well been called the Sphinx of modern literature."⁴⁴ The femininity of Hamlet is perhaps finally less important than this image of the feminine which Jones blithely projects onto the troubled and troubling aesthetic boundaries of the play.

III

If the bad or dangerous woman is aesthetic trouble, then it should come as no surprise that the opposite of this disturbance—an achieved aesthetic or even creativity itself—then finds its most appropriate image again in femininity, but this time its reverse: the good enough mother herself. As if completing the circuit, André Green turns to D. W. Winnicott's concept of the maternal function as the basis for his recent book on *Hamlet*.⁴⁵ Femininity now appears as the very principle of the aesthetic process. Shakespeare's Hamlet forecloses the femininity in himself, but by projecting onto the stage the degraded and

violent image of a femininity repudiated by his character, Shakespeare man-
ages to preserve in himself that other femininity which is the source of his
creative art: "Writing *Hamlet* had been an act of exorcism which enabled its
author to give his hero's femininity—cause of his anxieties, self-reproaches
and accusations—an acceptable form through the process of aesthetic creation. . . . By creating *Hamlet*, by giving it representation, Shakespeare, unlike
his hero, managed to lift the dissociation between his masculine and feminine
elements and to reconcile himself with the femininity in himself."[46]

The reading comes from Winnicott's paper "Creativity and Its Origins,"
which ends with a discussion of Shakespeare's play.[47] It is a fully psychological
reading of the author, but its interest once again lies in the way that femininity moves and slips across the different levels of the text and the analytic
process—the enigma and source of the analysis as of the play. More clearly
and explicitly for Winnicott than for the other writers discussed so far, it is
aesthetic space itself that is conceptualised in terms of sexual difference and
the place of femininity within that. Creativity per se (the creativity in all of
us—so this is not just the creativity of the artist) arises for Winnicott out of a
femininity which is that primordial space of being which is created by the
mother alone. It is a state of being which is not yet a relationship to the object
because there is as yet no self, and it is, as Green defines it, "*au-dela le la
représentation*," the other side of representation, before the coming of the sign
(this comes very close to French feminists such as Luce Irigaray on femininity
and language).[48] But it is worth noting how the woman appears at the point
either where language and aesthetic form start to crumble or else where they
have not yet come to be. "Masculinity does, femininity is" is Winnicott's
definition. It took a sceptical analyst in the audience when Winnicott first
presented the paper to point to its fully literary and mythical origin; it transpires that Winnicott had been reading Robert Graves's "Man Does, Woman
Is," but the observation from the floor was not included when Winnicott's
famous paper was subsequently published in his book.[49]

Winnicott's definition, like Green's, and like that of Eliot before them, once
again starts to look like a repetition (one might ask what other form of
analysis can there be?) which reproduces or repeats the fundamental drama of
Hamlet, cleaving the image of femininity in two, splitting it between a degradation and an idealisation which, far from keeping each other under control
(as Green suggests), set each other off, being the reverse sides of one and the
same mystification. And like Eliot, Green also gets caught in the other face of
the idealization, the inevitable accusation of Gertrude: "Is the marriage of

Gertrude consequence or cause of the murder of Hamlet's father? I incline towards the cause [*Je pencherai pour la cause*]."[50] And at the end of his book he takes off on a truly wild speculation which makes Gertrude the stake in the battle between the old Fortinbras and the old Hamlet before the start of the play.

But the fact that *Hamlet* constantly unleashes an anxiety which returns to the question of femininity tells us above all something about the relationship of aesthetic form and sexual difference, about the fantasies they share—fantasies of coherence and identity in which the woman appears repeatedly as both wager and threat. "Fantasy in its very perversity" is the object of psychoanalytic interpretation, but this does not mean that psychoanalysis might not also repeat within its own discourse the fantasies, or even perversions, which it uncovers in other forms of speech.[51]

In Lacan's own essay on *Hamlet*, he puts himself resolutely on the side of the symbolic, reading the play in terms of its dearth of proper mourning and the impossibility for Hamlet of responding to the too literal summons of the dead father who would otherwise represent for the hero the point of entry into his appropriate symbolic place (the proximity between this essay and Eliot's "Tradition and the Individual Talent" is truly striking). Lacan therefore places the problem of the play in the symbolic, on the side of the father we might say; Green in the "before" of representation where the mother simply *is*. The difference between them is also another repetition, for it is the difference between the law of the father and the body of the mother, between symbol and affect (one of Green's best known books in France was an account of the concept of "affect" in Freud and a critique of Lacan's central premise that psychic life is regulated by the exigencies of representation and the linguistic sign).[52] But it is a difference with more far-reaching implications, which reconnect with the question of the fantasy of the woman and her guilt with which this essay began. For the concentration on the mother, on her adequacies and inadequacies, was the development in psychoanalytic theory itself which Lacan wanted to redress, precisely because, like *Hamlet*, it makes the mother cause of all good and evil, and her failings responsible for a malaise in all human subjects, that is in men *and* in women, which stems from their position in the symbolic order of culture itself. The problem of the regulation of subjectivity, of the oedipal drama and the ordering of language and literary form—the necessity of that regulation and its constant difficulty or failing—is not, to put it at its most simple, the woman's fault.

Finally, therefore, a question remains, one which can be put to André

Green when he says that Shakespeare saved his sanity by projecting this crazed repudiation of the feminine onto the stage, using his art to give it "an acceptable form."[53] To whom is this acceptable? Or rather what does it mean to us that one of the most elevated and generally esteemed works of our Western literary tradition should enact such a negative representation of femininity, or even such a violent repudiation of the femininity in man? I say "esteemed" because it is of course the case that Eliot's critique has inflated rather than reduced *Hamlet*'s status. In "Tradition and the Individual Talent," Eliot says the poet must "know" the mind of Europe; *Hamlet* has more than once been taken as the model for that mind.[54] Western tradition, the mind of Europe, Hamlet himself—each one the symbol of a cultural order in which the woman is given too much and too little of a place. But it is perhaps not finally inappropriate that those who celebrate or seek to uphold that order, with no regard to the image of the woman it encodes, constantly find themselves up against a problem which they call femininity—a reminder of the precarious nature of the certainties on which that order rests.

Virginia Woolf and the Death of Modernism

When grief ceases to be speculative, sleep sees her opportunity.
—Samuel Beckett: "Yellow," *More Pricks than Kicks* (1934)

By taking flight into the ego love escapes extinction.
—Sigmund Freud, "Mourning and Melancholia" (1915)

"To enjoy your perfection—"

"I take your point. One must exclude."

"The greater part of everything."
—Virginia Woolf, "The Evening Party" (1918)

There is a strange moment on the first page of "Mourning and Melancholia" when Freud mentions, almost in passing, that mourning can be sparked, not only by the loss of a loved one, but equally by some abstraction: "such as one's country, liberty, an ideal." Since Freud is writing in 1915, it seems clear, as the papers on war from the same year will confirm, that what he is alluding to is the loss of belief in the redeeming power of Western civilisation precipitated by the carnage of the war. So when Freud goes on to insist that mourning is something to be worked at, completed, got over—already strange for a psychoanalysis which maintains that nothing ever goes away—I think it is fair to assume that a drive for political, or cultural, as much as psychic self-protection is at stake. Once the losses of the war have been mourned, Freud goes on to write, in his 1917 paper on "Transience," "it will be found that our high opinion of the riches of civilisation has lost nothing from the discovery of their fragility." To put it simply, mourning must come to an end so that we can believe in ourselves once more. Seen in these terms, Freud's famous paper can be read as an attempt to drive mourning away (or at least to provide a narrative for mourning with a beginning, middle, and an end). I want to use this essay to suggest that this view of mourning bears all the signs of its genesis in a moment of cultural dismay; that if you are not seeking to preserve the abstraction of civilisation—or rather this particular abstraction of that civilisation—then mourning shifts her colours and her terms. No longer something to be dispatched, mourning becomes more amorphous and fluid, more interminable as one might say. Taking on the incalculable nature of mourning could then be seen as one of the defining features of modernism. And nowhere so intensely, I will also be suggesting here, than in the writing of Virginia Woolf.

The first publication of the Hogarth Press in 1917 was *Two Stories*, "The Mark on the Wall" by Virginia Woolf, often reprinted, and "Three Jews" by Leonard Woolf, more or less unheard of since—"a signpost," as Hermione Lee, Virginia Woolf's most recent biographer, puts it, "pointing down a road he would not take" (in fact, the success of this first publication played a key part in allowing the press to expand). Two Jews meet on a park bench and discuss their loss of belief. They only go to synagogue ritually and out of "pure habit" at Yom Kippur: "I don't believe in it, of course; I believe in nothing—you believe in nothing—we're all sceptics." The third Jew is a cemetery-keeper even more sceptical and disbelieving than the first two.

> We can't believe everything in the Bible. There's the Almighty of course, well, who can say? He may exist, he may not—I say I don't know. But a life hereafter, I don't believe in it. One don't have to believe everything now: it was different when I was young. You had to believe everything then.

"I thought," responds the first, who is telling the story of this graveside encounter, "of our race, its traditions, its faith, how they are vanishing in the life that surrounds us . . . vanishing in the universal disbelief": "Even he doesn't believe, the keeper of Jewish graves!"

If that was all there was to it, this would be a story of the modern Jew stranded between two forms of non-belonging: no assimilation, no faith; no fervour of ritual and spiritual belonging to set against the felt repudiation of the English countryside: "How it comes out! under the apple-blossom and blue sky." And yet, in this year of the Balfour Declaration, these Jews do belong; they "belong to Palestine still." And this belonging is the sign not, as for so many, of nationalist or religious commitment, but of a Jewishness reduced to nothing but the external marks of itself: "We're Jews only externally now" (which is why these Jews so instantly recognise each other against the English sky). It is not hard to imagine the likely response if these portraits, clearly intended to clinch the point, had been penned or spoken by a non-Jew.

His dark fat face and the sensual mouth, the great curve of the upper lip and the hanging lower one. A clever face dark and inscrutable, with its large mysterious eyes and the heavy lids; and a nose, by Jove, Sir, one of the best, one of those noses, white and shiny, which, when you look at it full face, seems almost flat on the face, but immensely broad, curving down, like a broad high-road from between the bushy eyebrows down over the lips. And side-face it was colossal; it stood out like an elephant's trunk with its florid curves and scrolls.

I start with this story because it focuses so sharply on a drama of lost belief which has nowhere, except Palestine, to run. It offers, if you like, a modern Jewish version of the scepticism which Freud, at almost exactly the same time, will give as one of the grounds to grieve (the year of Balfour, one might say, is the year that the Jews had to steel themselves to belief). It seems more than coincidental that the story comes to centre on a cemetery, and that it finally transpires that Jewishness is something which comes out, not only against the apple-blossoms, but "among the tombs." By the end of the story, the cemetery-keeper turns out to have the true spirit after all because of the ruthlessness with which he repudiates a son who marries out of the faith (Leonard had married Virginia in 1912). Belief never turns so ugly, you might say, than when it thinks it has done with itself.

What Leonard Woolf seems to me to be saying is that the lost spirit of the sceptic is in the custody of the keeper of tombs. That even if you lose all belief, the spirit of identity will pass through the generations almost despite itself. These Jews are in mourning, one might say, but there is something they cannot give up, even if they think they have, something which, even if they are sure they have lost it, will not go away. You may think you've stopped believing, but something—call it the unconscious—knows better than you think. To put it another way, for faith to continue despite one's best scepticism, it requires, even if only unconsciously, a form of involuntary, blind, identification with the dead.

Leonard Woolf writes this story in the same year as Freud's paper on "Transience." Given that the *Standard Edition of the Complete Psychological Works* of Freud gathered in the basement of the Woolfs' Hogarth House, it is not perhaps too much to suggest that these two different, somewhat disparate, Jewish cautionary tales of discontinuity shadowed Virginia Woolf's writing life (in fact, she did not start reading Freud until just before the Second World War). Today we know the historical outcome of that passing gesture—at once embraced and refused—towards Palestine (by 1928, when he writes *Imperialism and Civilisation*, Woolf will acknowledge the "Arab national movement in Palestine"). We know, that is, how anxiety about continuity can transmute itself into demonic repetition. But Leonard Woolf's story is per-haps all the more remarkable for offering us a glimpse into one version of the kind of refuge that Palestine would become. Not externally (as would become more and more urgent in ways neither Leonard Woolf nor Freud could have predicted in 1917), but internally: Palestine as a place to run, or rather as something which almost slips out between the features of the Jewish dis-believer, to atone and redeem a threatened internal collapse. Loss of belief may represent a new freedom, but Woolf shares with Freud the conviction that it is also a danger and a threat. As a caution against pure scepticism, the cemetery-keeper warns his interlocutor that too much thinking can drive you mad: "Now you may think for yourself. And *mind you*, it don't *do* to think too much; if you think too much about these things, you go mad, raving mad."

Leonard Woolf's despairing sceptics bear a more than passing resemblance to the melancholic which, in "Mourning and Melancholia," Freud sets against the one who successfully grieves (he offers us Hamlet who also thought too much). Famously in this paper, Freud opposes mourning as work to the pathology of melancholia which fails to detach itself from the lost object because it identifies with the object instead. "The shadow of the object," writes Freud, "falls across the ego"; or to take the second epigraph of this article: "By taking flight into the ego love escapes extinction." A number of questions immediately raise themselves (or rather they did when I reread this paper after a long gap in the course of the past year). Not just what was Freud trying to hang on to by way of cultural belief, but also—as the accompaniment and extension of that first anxiety—what psychic agenda is this? Just how much, in letting go of mourning, was he willing to let go? What does it mean, for example, to say that in mourning, in contradistinction to melancholia, "there is nothing about the loss that was unconscious"? Couldn't one instead say, paraphrasing Freud on the hysteric, that the one who grieves knows and does not know at the same time? Or, we might ask, what is this love that, in mourning as opposed to melancholia, steadfastly, dedicatedly, works to ex-tinguish itself? Again, we could turn back on to Freud his famous observation that no subject can envisage her or his own death. Love would not be love if it were able to contemplate, let alone work to bring about, its own end.

And what is Freud doing when he makes ambivalence a peculiarity of the melancholic: "The conflict due to ambivalence," he writes, "must not be overlooked among the preconditions of melancholia"—a distinction which later in the same paper he has to retract. We might ask, then, not so much what distinguishes mourning from melancholia, but what is it about mourning that Freud is using melancholia to offload? It starts to look as if melancholia is being asked, among other things, to carry off the most violent part of identification. Mourning can be mollified, pacified, if melancholia bears the brunt of an ambivalence which Freud describes as nothing less than a struggle to the death: "Each struggle of ambivalence [loosens] the fixation of the libido to the object by disparaging it, denigrating it and even as it were killing it."

We should remember, however, that Freud himself was the one who most convincingly argued that the object which has been murdered is precisely the one which is most mourned, that murdering an object is the start of identification and not the end (in "Thoughts for the Time on War and Death," written in the same year as "Mourning and Melancholia," he placed the ambivalence that arises through mourning at the foundation of our ethical life). What limits is Freud packing around the idea of mourning? What on earth does it mean, we might ask, to suggest that the living do not, should not, identify with the dead? Isn't it in fact Freud who teaches us—it is the opening premise of Diana Fuss's *Identification Papers*—that identification is by definition a ghostly affair? Something very strange is going on here. One by one or, to use Freud's own words, "bit by bit, at great expense of time and cathectic energy," the cornerstones of psychoanalysis—the unconscious, identification, ambivalence, and love—are purged from the mind. All this—in 1917 at least, as the relentless toll of the dead brings belief crashing to the ground—for sanity's sake. There is only so much, we might say, that even psychoanalysis can bear.

Recently reviewing Hermione Lee's new biography of Virginia Woolf, I found myself brought up short by this sentence, with which the chapter entitled "Madness" begins: "Virginia Woolf was a sane woman with an illness." It struck me that for anyone working on Woolf's life and writing, there is an almost insoluble problem. To defend Woolf's sanity is to save her from one kind of dismissal; it is one way of giving her her due. But to side with her reason is to sidestep the thread of her writing which unwinds, unbearably and at the risk of what she herself more than once called her own "madness," from the place of the dead. It is hard not to read the cemetery-keeper's warning as Leonard's coded warning to Virginia Woolf.

Now you may think for yourself. And *mind you*, it don't *do* to think too much; if you think too much about these things, you go mad, raving mad.

Hard, that is, not to see it as his way of acknowledging that loss of belief in a viable culture, Bloomsbury scepticism as we might call it, coupled with too much personal loss, might bring her, or her reason, to grief. Freud's comment in the paper on "Transience" slides from one to the other, from the personal to the public, with strange and discomforting ease: "Once the mourning is over, it will be found that our high opinion of the riches of our civilisation has lost nothing from the discovery of their fragility." But Leonard, Virginia, and their famous group did not believe in "civilisation" (any more indeed than in his better moments, many commentators would insist, did Freud). The patriotic fervour of the war was one of the things which drove Virginia Woolf, arms outstretched, over the edge.

> Honour, patriotism, chastity, wealth, success, importance, position, pa-
> tronage, power—their cries rang and echoed from all quarters, "Anywhere,
> anywhere, out of this world!" was the only exclamation with which one
> could stave off the brazen din.

This is how John Maynard Keynes, one of the first generation of Blooms-bury, opens *The Economic Consequence of the Peace*, which he wrote in 1919 after recovering from a nervous breakdown following the war.

> The power to become habituated to his surroundings is a marked charac-
> teristic of mankind. Very few of us realise with conviction the intensely
> unusual, unstable, complicated, unreliable nature of the economic organi-
> sation by which Western Europe has lived for the last half century. We
> assume some of the most peculiar and temporary advantages as natural,
> permanent, and to be depended on and we lay our plans accordingly. On
> this sandy and false foundation we scheme for social improvement and
> dress our political platforms, pursue our animosities and particular ambi-
> tions, and feel ourselves with enough margin in hand to foster, not assuage,
> civil conflict in Europe.

In March 1915, in the middle of the war, Virginia and Leonard Woolf had moved into Hogarth House. Ill, with four nurses in attendance, by her own later account she lay in her room: "mad, and seeing the sunlight quivering like gold water, on the wall . . . listening to the voices of the dead."

For the rest of this essay I want to suggest that Virginia Woolf's life and writing can be read as the creative response to Freud's anxious imperative— only insofar as there can be an end to it, only if the end is pre-given, let mourning begin. That she would have no truck with his fine psychic and face-saving discriminations. More simply, that she knew (although "knew" isn't quite the right word here) better, or knew more. We know that grieving started very early in Woolf's life. Which might be one reason why her writing offers us such a forceful riposte to the idea that it should, or could, be brought to an end. Lee's biography graphically conveys the extent to which Woolf's life was shadowed by death. First private—the deaths of her mother, half-sister, father in the ten years between 1895 and 1904 (for Woolf death rings in the new century, as it were). Then public—the whole of her writing life passes across the two world wars. When, as Virginia Stephen, she moves with Vanessa and Thoby from Hyde Park Gate to Bloomsbury after her father's death in 1904, one of the most striking, and freeing things about the new residence was, as Lee puts it, that "no one was dying in this house" (two years later her brother Thoby would die).

You can read Woolf's life as her attempt to move out of those early deaths (literally from Kensington to Bloomsbury), and then artistically transmute them into form. Or you can see her writing going back the other way and death as giving a unique form of authority to her fiction. In the words of Walter Benjamin, the storyteller used to "borrow his authority from death" ("There used to be no house, hardly a room, in which someone had not once died"). But, in the course of modern times, dying has been pushed more and more out of the perceptual world of the living. "Though almost all her novels are dominated by a death," writes Lee, "in almost all the death is not written in." This makes death the absent-presence which stalks Virginia Woolf's writing, turning it Janus-like back as well as forwards through literary and historical time. Private and public trauma, death for Virginia Woolf is, one could say, more than elegy, more than mourning, more than a fear or pull to which she finally succumbs. Rather it is something through the eyes of which—literally in the case of her first novel, as I will go on to discuss—she *sees*. More than once, she herself places death at the source, as the life-pulse, of her own artistic vision: "examine feelings with the intense microscope that sorrow lends, it is amazing how they stretch, like the finest goldbeater's skin, over immense tracks of substance"; "my mother's death veiled and intensified, as if a burning glass had been laid over what was shaded and dormant . . . as if something were becoming visible without any effort." We might then ask, contra Freud, not how mourning can be completed, but what is it that death, or remaining with death, might permit. As the narrator of *The Voyage Out* puts it: "A barrier which usually stands fast had fallen, and it was possible to speak of motives which are generally only alluded to between men and women when doctors are present, or the shadow of death." Seen in this context, Virginia Woolf's suicide, oddly, has detracted from death, acted as a screen. By acquiring something in the nature of a monopoly, it has crowded out the voices of all the rest.

Virginia Woolf's first novel, *The Voyage Out*, published in 1915, is normally considered as a piece of literary apprenticeship or literary-cum-sexual initiation. The heroine, Rachel Vinrace, travels on a ship to South America, a voyage of "self-discovery" as the Penguin blurb puts it, except that the price of this discovery, which includes her own engagement, is that she contracts typhoid and dies. The novel is often read biographically, as a sign—it was written during her engagement to Leonard Woolf—of the lengths Virginia Woolf would go to to avoid intimacy. Since it includes moments of psychic devastation—one graphic passage of nightmare persecution by a blubbering and monstrous male presence—it is taken as a coded narrative: Woolf telling her readers of the early sexual invasions which would lead her body to part definitively from her mind. According to this reading, when Rachel Vinrace finally goes under, we are being given a premonitory version of Woolf in 1941 sinking beneath the waves.

I don't want to disparage this reading (although I know it sounds as if I have). It is true, for example, that the thoughts of the surviving fiancé, "No two people have ever been as happy as we have been," bear an uncanny resemblance to the famous note that, more than a quarter of a century later, Virginia Woolf will leave for Leonard on the day she dies. But it does seem to me that to read the book in this way is to overlook what Virginia Woolf uses the death of her female character *for*. It overlooks, that is, the extent to which this inverse initiation—you go into, rather than emerge, from the depths—precisely because it is writing (this is not Virginia Woolf dying), is identification. In this first novel by Woolf, the first flickers of that fragmentary vision most famously associated with her writing weave their way—against Freud's warning one might say—into a dying mind.

This is the main passage:

> For six days indeed she had been oblivious of the world outside, because it needed all her attention to follow the hot, red, quick sights which passed incessantly before her eyes. She knew that it was of enormous importance that she should attend to these sights and grasp their meaning, but she was always being just too late to hear or see something which would explain it all. For this reason, the faces,—Helen's face, the nurse's, Terence's, the

doctor's,—which occasionally forced themselves very close to her, were worrying because they distracted her attention and she might miss the clue. However, on the fourth afternoon she was suddenly unable to keep Helen's face distinct from the sights themselves; her lips widened as she bent down over the bed, and she began to gabble unintelligibly like the rest. The sights were all concerned in some plot, some adventure, some escape. The nature of what they were doing changed incessantly, although there was always a reason behind it which she must endeavour to grasp. Now they were among trees and savages, now they were on the sea, now they were on the tops of high towers; now they jumped; now they flew. But just as the crisis was about to happen, something invariably slipped in her brain, so that the whole effort had to begin over again. The heat was suffocating. At last the faces went further away; she fell into a deep pool of sticky water, which eventually closed over her head. She was nothing and heard nothing but a faint booming sound, which was the sound of the sea rolling over her head. While all her tormentors thought that she was dead, she was not, but curled up at the bottom of the sea. There she lay, sometimes seeing darkness, sometimes light, while every now and then someone turned her over at the bottom of the sea.

I suggest we read this passage as one of the inaugural moments of modernist fiction. It is because Rachel Vinrace is literally passing away that she receives her impressions in that peculiar mix of oversharp and disintegrating relief. Like a caricature of one of Woolf's own readers, she panics at her failed attempt—hopeless although never relinquished—to read the clues. The decoder of modernism determined to wrench meaning from the world will always be too soon or too late: "She knew it was of enormous importance that she should attend to those sights and grasp their meaning, but she was always being just too late to hear or see something which would explain it all." There is a narrative here: "some plot, some adventure, some escape"; but it is narrative as false promise which slides into repetition and sends you back to the beginning again: "Just as the crisis was about to happen, something invariably slipped in her brain, so that the whole effort had to begin over again." For a mind in fever ("hot, red, quick"), reason falls out of the world at exactly the same moment as the faces of others—held by more seemly forms of fiction at a comfortable distance—move in suffocatingly close.

It is perhaps almost too easy to recognise here the defining features of modernism. But we might ask, under what conditions, other than what goes by the term of madness, does reason so dramatically, so literally, so physically, slip away? Much has been written about the body in relation to Virginia Woolf—it is the defining trope of what has come to be defined as *écriture feminine*; although to call it a trope is already to settle a question, since it is the body as sheer physicality which is meant to rise to the surface of the text. But in what circumstances does a body so decisively usurp or dismantle the organising capacities of the mind? This is from a few pages on in the text:

> For long spaces of time she would merely lie conscious of her body floating on the top of the bed and her mind driven to some remote corner of her body, or escaped and gone flitting round the room.

In the endless debates about Virginia Woolf's sanity, madness might then be the unacknowledged codeword for death. The dying mind gropes for reason. The irony is perhaps that it should be death, more conventionally taken for the ultimate ending, which brings the possibility of narrative, closure, meaning, and reason to an end. There is, we might say, no rhyme or reason to death. Why, as the surviving characters repeatedly ask in the penultimate chapter of *The Voyage Out*, did Rachel Vinrace have to die? "It seems so inexplicable," Evelyn continued. "Death, I mean. Why should she be dead, and not you or I."

We might then go back and look again at the feminist argument which opposes femininity as body to the false telos of masculine logic, and consider recasting these terms. "It seems clear," writes Barthes in his essay on Poe's "Valdemar," "that what is taboo in death, what is essentially taboo, is the passage, the threshold, the dying." In Woolf's novel at least, the body that forces itself to the surface of consciousness, the body most acutely a body, is the body about to die. What stands against reason is not femininity, but death. That penultimate chapter of *The Voyage Out* takes the form of a set of dialogues in most of which it feels as if the characters are talking to themselves. Reason/unreason—what it is reasonable to feel, to believe, or to expect—is all that the death of Rachel Vinrace leaves them with.

> "You have heard, of course. My wife feels that she was in some way responsible. She urged poor Miss Vinrace to come on the expedition. I'm sure you will agree with me that it is most *unreasonable* to feel that. . . ."
> There must be some reason why such things happen, she thought to herself, as she closed the door.
> Have I any *reason* to hope . . . ? I do not ask for a date . . . that would be most *unreasonable* [my emphasis].

It is like a refrain. But once you place death on the far side of reason, then the line that runs from mourning to scepticism (Freud's and Leonard Woolf's) becomes clear.

> "It seems so inexplicable," Evelyn continued. "Death, I mean. Why should she be dead, and not you or I? It was only a fortnight ago that she was here with the rest of us. What d'you believe?" she demanded of Mr Perrot. "D'you believe that things go on, that she's still somewhere—or d'you think it's simply a game—we crumble up to nothing when we die? I'm positive Rachel's not dead."

Evelyn is the character who is left with the question. She carries forward into the rest of Virginia Woolf's fiction, as a matter of principle, the open-ended uncertainty we have come to associate with Woolf's later texts: "She had a natural dislike of anything final and done with; she liked to go on and on—always on and on." But running alongside that familiar refusal is a more radical uncertainty which turns the whole world into a blur. Modernism—we might say—as a way of refusing the appropriate relations of presence and absence which should hold between the living and the dead.

> Suddenly the keen feeling of someone's personality, which things that they have owned or handled sometimes preserves, overcame her; she felt Rachel in the room with her; it was as if she were on a ship at sea, and the life of the day were as unreal as the life in the distance.

To say that this first strain of Woolf's modernism—in a novel which is otherwise conventional and mainly realist in form—emerges from the place of death might seem far-fetched or at least peculiar to her own history. But Woolf is not alone in allowing death to determine the contours of her writing, even if hers is a particularly intense and proximate relation. We need, before passing back into Woolf's own vision, to stretch things out a little. Michael Levenson, in *A Genealogy of Modernism*, gives this reading of the first stanza of *The Waste Land*:

> Has there been sufficient emphasis (I think not) upon the peculiar angle of vision that governs the first line of *The Waste Land*? Spring comes not to men and women, nor to trees and birds, but to lilacs, which do not flower as one might expect, but are bred out of the north. The view, that is, settled toward the ground. To be more precise, it looks at spring from beneath the ground, a fact that becomes more clear in the next few lines, which specify

that there are "roots" that are stirred and "tubers" that nourish. The eye here sees from the point of view of someone (or something) that is buried. In what other circumstances would snow act as a cover? How else could tubers feed a "little life"? Grover Smith has traced this latter image to James Thomson's "To Our Ladies of Death," in which there appears a line, "Our Mother feedeth thus our little life," and, more pertinent still, the line that follows: "That we in turn may feed her with our death." Thomson goes on to imagine his body after death, mingling with the soil: "One part of me shalt feed a little worm. . . . One thrill sweet grass, one pulse in bitter weed." Given these considerations, may I be permitted my speculation that the opening of *The Waste Land* looks at spring from the point of view of a corpse?

As Levenson goes on to discuss, this is a corpse that sprouts. Life is breathed back into the body through a redemption which Eliot struggled towards and eventually reached, but which was not a viable option for most of the Bloomsbury group. But what links the two writers (apart from a literary life in common, the fact that Hogarth Press published Eliot's poem after it had first appeared in *The Dial* in 1922) is their shared genesis in the historic crisis of the war. It is public as much as private catastrophe that sends these two writers underground (death was at once her and her whole generation's "special knowledge," to use the phrase of Gillian Beer). The carnage of the war robs death of contingency, turning it into an experience which, regardless of who is actually hit, regardless that is of whether you live or die, everyone has to share. This is Freud writing again in 1915: "Death is no longer a chance event. To be sure, it still seems a matter of chance whether a bullet hits this man or that; but a second bullet may well hit the survivor; and the accumulation of death puts an end to the impression of chance" ("Our Attitude Towards Death"). To say that Freud's remark precludes women, which at one level is obviously true, is precisely to limit what the power of identification can do. Claiming allegiance with the dead in fantasy, living death on the other's behalf, might be one way a woman writer could lay claim to a historically refused form of belonging. Behind Freud's remark lies what might be seen as a crushing banality (which his strictures on melancholia might be seen at least partly to defer). It just might—it could—it will, one day, be you.

Virginia Woolf had a very clear sense of the tragedy of her generation: "It's life itself, I think sometimes, for us in our generation so tragic," she wrote in 1921. Or more brutally: "This generation must break its neck in order that the next may have smooth going." In 1927, she would proclaim: "Can't you see that nationality is over? All divisions are rubbed out, or about to be." "They would all," as Hermione Lee comments in parentheses after giving this quote, "spend the next fourteen years seeing the flaws of this argument." By the time she met the dying Freud in January 1939, she knew of course that both her optimistic convictions were a myth, that there was to be no smooth going for the next generation, that European civilisation would not so easily redeem itself. Perhaps, she suggested, if they had failed, Hitler would not have been (it was precisely to avert such triumphant catastrophe that Maynard Keynes had written *The Economic Consequences of the Peace*). But Freud insisted "with great emphasis" that, had they failed, Hitler would have been "infinitely worse." On this occasion the idea of a horror working itself out through one generation for the sake of the next has passed from Woolf, who doesn't believe it any more, to Freud. On Sunday 29 January 1939, she records in her diary: "Dr Freud gave me a narcissus. On Hitler. Generation before the poison will be worked out." As in 1915, writing in the middle of the First World War, Freud hung a great deal—against the psychic and historical odds one could say—on this idea of work. Compare Keynes: "The spokesmen of the French and British peoples have run the risk of completing the ruin which Germany began."

Freud, we could say, sends work back through the generations and forward through time. You work to grieve; you work to disperse the poison from the fabric of social, civilised, life. Things, as the saying has it, will work out. When he writes like this, Freud is using work as a synonym for telos; the belief that, given the right type of effort and exertion, matters can be brought to a satisfactory or appropriate end (that the best end of the world was foretold in how the world began). Freud was, as has often been noted, attached to the language of economies: "Transience value," as he puts it—to give just one example of the economic saturation of his language—"is scarcity valor in time." Although he was in fact aware that, on the subject of mourning, the economic metaphor upholding his concept of work was weak: "We do not even know the economic means by which mourning overcomes its task." He knew, that is, that there was something immeasurable involved: "Mourning is a great riddle, one of those phenomena which cannot be explained but to which other obscurities can be traced back."

It has often been pointed out that Freud's economic theories, his belief in an organism driven towards its own stasis, carries the relics of a biologism which the rest of psychoanalysis went some, if not all the way, to discard. But today, given the resurgence of interest in Keynesian economics, it might seem something of an irony that Freud, despite moments such as those just cited, sought to invest the idea of work with the measure of the calculable, to make work economically viable at the very same time that Maynard Keynes was mounting his critique of classical *Homo economicus*, rational economic man. "The first step in Keynes's thought," writes Will Hutton in *The Revolution that Never Was*, "is to interpret *Homo economicus* as a creature who while driven by self-interests is not always certain how he should go about it and is subject to all kinds of hopes and fears." Keynes's view of the economy is one of radical instability—"a permanent process of uncertain experimentation" (against the idea of a market which naturally achieves its own stability, he proposed a market in constant tension: "between the financial system's desire for liquidity —and the need for illiquidity in order for the real economy to finance the acquisition of physical capital assets"). True to his principles, one might say— or to what one commentator refers to as his "combination of generosity and gambler's instincts"—in 1920 Keynes ruined "not only himself but much of Bloomsbury, and even their distant relations by speculation in currencies."

Above all, what classical economics ignores, according to Keynes, is the problem of time. In his 1937 article on "The General Theory of Unemployment," he wrote,

> We have, as a rule, only the vaguest ideas of any but the most direct consequences of our acts. . . . [O]ur knowledge of the future is fluctuating, vague and uncertain. . . . [T]he sense in which I am using the term (uncertain) is that in which the prospect of a European war is uncertain, or the price of copper and the rate of interest twenty years hence, or the obsolescence of a new invention, or the position of private wealth-owners in the social system in 1970. About these matters there is no scientific basis on which to form any calculable probability whatever. We simply do not know.

Knowledge with a foretaste of its own ignorance, or knowledge brushing at its limits, would be one way of defining the unconscious. But once you introduce the unconscious into the frame—or even Keynes's radical uncertainty— then it becomes impossible, even perhaps beyond Freud's own account, to regulate the forms of traffic between present, future, and past, between the living and the dead. To be a subject, as Nicolas Abraham has best formulated it, is to be haunted. How could identity free itself—would it still be an identity?—of the traces of those who went before? Haunting, or being haunted, might indeed be another word for writing. This is Virginia Woolf:

> Is it not possible—I often wonder—that things we have felt with great intensity have an existence independent of our minds; are in fact still in existence? and if so, will it not be possible, in time, that some device will be invented by which we can tap that? . . . Instead of remembering here a scene and there a sound, I shall fit a plug into the wall; and listen in to the past. I shall turn up August 1890. I feel that strong emotion must leave its trace; and it is only a question of discovering how we can get ourselves attached to it, so that we shall be able to live our lives through from the start.

Mourning, in conclusion, no more comes to an end than history (the end of history contained more than a casual allusion to the triumph of free market economies against which Maynard Keynes's voice has had to be raised again today). But Freud's paper and Leonard Woolf's story, which is where I started, do indeed present us with a problem. And that is the problem of how best to think about the relationship of our psychic and political futures to our past. The idea that, "bit by bit, at great expense of time and cathectic energy," we sever our links with the dead does not seem to me an idea on which any kind of viable psychic or political future can be built. Even if Leonard Woolf's story with its reference to Palestine is there to remind us that identity hanging on to its ancestry because it is frightened at the prospect of its own demise is capable of no end of historic injustice. Virginia Woolf played out her own particular version of this dilemma. In a way, the circumstances of her own personal life meant that she had no choice. But through the lines of her writing—and not only in the novel I have chosen to focus on here—can be glimpsed a way of negotiating these brutal alternatives. A way, that is, of refusing to let go of the dead while also refusing to identify with what Freud, still in 1915, was able to refer to without self-consciousness as the "riches" of Western civilisation.

"Daddy"

For a writer who has so consistently produced outrage in her critics, nothing has produced the outrage generated by Sylvia Plath's allusions to the Holocaust in her poetry, and nothing the outrage occasioned by "Daddy," which is just one of the poems in which those allusions appear. Here is one such critic, important only for the clarity with which he lays out the terms of such a critique. Leon Wieseltier is reviewing Dorothy Rabinowicz's *New Lives: Survivors of the Holocaust* in an article entitled "In a Universe of Ghosts," published in the *New York Review of Books*.

> Auschwitz bequeathed to all subsequent art perhaps the most arresting of all possible metaphors for extremity, but its availability has been abused. For many it was Sylvia Plath who broke the ice. . . . In perhaps her most famous poem, "Daddy," she was explicit. . . . There can be no disputing the genuineness of the pain here. But the Jews with whom she identifies were victims of something worse than "weird luck." Whatever her father did to her, it could not have been what the Germans did to the Jews. The metaphor is inappropriate. . . . I do not mean to lift the Holocaust out of the reach of art. Adorno was wrong—poetry can be made after Auschwitz and out of it. . . . But it cannot be done without hard work and rare resources of the spirit. Familiarity with the hellish subject must be earned, not presupposed. My own feeling is that Sylvia Plath did not earn it, that she did not respect the real incommensurability to her own experience of what took place.[1]

It is worth looking at the central terms on which this passage turns—the objection to Plath's identification with the Jew: "the Jews with whom she identifies"; to the terms of that identification for introducing chance into Jewish history (into history): "victims of something worse than 'weird luck' "; above all, to Plath's failure to recognise the "incommensurability to her experience of what took place." Wieseltier is not alone in this criticism. Similarly,

Joyce Carol Oates objects to Plath "snatching [her word] metaphors for her predicament from newspaper headlines"; Seamus Heaney argues that in poems like "Lady Lazarus," Plath harnesses the wider cultural reference to a "vehemently self-justifying purpose"; Irving Howe describes the link as "monstrous, utterly disproportionate"; and Marjorie Perloff describes Plath's references to the Nazis as "empty" and "histrionic," "cheap shots," "topical trappings," "devices" which "camouflage" the true personal meaning of the poems in which they appear.[2] On a separate occasion, Perloff compares Plath unfavourably to Lowell for the absence of any sense of personal or social history in her work.[3] The two objections seem to cancel and mirror each other—history is either dearth or surplus, either something missing from Plath's writing or something which shouldn't be there.

In all these criticisms, the key concept appears to be metaphor—either Plath trivialises the Holocaust through that essentially personal (it is argued) reference, or she aggrandises her experience by stealing the historical event. The Wieseltier passage makes it clear, however, that if the issue is that of metaphor ("Auschwitz bequeathed to all subsequent art perhaps the most arresting of all possible metaphors for extremity") what is at stake finally is a repudiation of metaphor itself—that is, of the necessary difference or distance between its two terms: "Whatever her father did to her it cannot be what the Germans did to the Jews." Plath's abuse (his word) of the Holocaust as metaphor (allowing for a moment that this is what it is) rests on the demand for commensurability, not to say identity, between image and experience, between language and event. In aesthetic terms, what Plath is being criticised for is a lack of "objective correlative" (Perloff specifically uses the term).[4] But behind Wieseltier's objection, there is another demand—that only those who directly experienced the Holocaust have the right to speak of it—speak of it in what must be, by implication, non-metaphorical speech. The allusion to Plath in his article is there finally only to make this distinction—between the testimony of the survivors represented in Rabinowicz's book and the poetic metaphorisation (unearned, indirect, incommensurate) of Plath.

Turn the opening proposition of this quotation around, therefore, and we can read in it, not that "Auschwitz bequeathed the most *arresting* of all possible metaphors for extremity," but that in relation to literary representation— or at least this conception of it—Auschwitz is the place where metaphor is *arrested*, where metaphor is brought to a halt. In this context, the critique of Plath merely underlines the fact that the Holocaust is the historical event which puts under greatest pressure—or is most readily available to put under such pressure—the concept of linguistic figuration. For it can be argued (it has recently been argued in relation to the critic Paul de Man) that, faced with the reality of the Holocaust, the idea that there is an irreducibly figurative dimension to all language is an evasion, or denial, of the reality of history itself.[5] But we should immediately add here that in the case of Plath, the question of metaphor brings with it—is inextricable from—that of fantasy and identification insofar as the image most fiercely objected to is the one which projects the speaker of the poem into the place of a Jew. The problem would seem to be, therefore, not the *slippage* of meaning, but its *fixing*—not just the idea of an inherent instability, or metaphoricity, of language, but the very specific fantasy positions which language can be used to move into place. Criticism of "Daddy" shows the question of fantasy, which has appeared repeatedly as a difficulty in the responses to Plath's writing, in its fullest historical and political dimension. . . .

Reviewing the American publication of *Ariel* in 1966, *Time* magazine wrote,

> Within a week of her death, intellectual London was hunched over copies of a strange and terrible poem she had written during her last sick slide toward suicide. "Daddy" was its title; its subject was her morbid love-hatred of her father; its style was as brutal as a truncheon. What is more, "Daddy" was merely the first jet of flame from a literary dragon who in the last months of her life breathed a burning river of bale across the literary landscape.[6]

Writing on the Holocaust, Jean-François Lyotard suggests that two motifs tend to operate in tension, or to the mutual exclusion of each other—the preservation of memory against forgetfulness and the accomplishment of vengeance.[7] Does "Daddy" take up the two motifs one after the other, or does it present something of their mutual relation, the psychic economy that ties them even as it forces them apart? There is a clear narrative in "Daddy"—from victimisation to revenge. It is the form of that sequence which has allowed the poem to be read purely personally as Plath's vindictive assault on Otto Plath and Ted Hughes (the transition from the first to the second mirroring the biographical pattern of her life). It is however only a preliminary privileging of the personal which allows the reproach for her evocation of history because Plath identifies with the Jew.

The first thing to notice is the trouble in the time sequence of this poem in relation to the father, the technically impossible temporality which lies at the center of the story it tells.

DADDY

You do not do, you do not do
Any more, black shoe
In which I have lived like a foot
For thirty years, poor and white,
Barely daring to breathe, or Achoo.

Daddy, I have had to kill you.
You died before I had time—
Marble-heavy, a bag full of God,
Ghastly statue with one gray toe
Big as a Frisco seal

And a head in the freakish Atlantic
Where it pours bean green over blue
In the waters off beautiful Nauset.
I used to pray to recover you.
Ach, du.

What is the time sequence of these verses? On the one hand, a time of unequivocal resolution, the end of the line, a story that once and for all will be brought to a close: "You do not do, you do not do / Any more." This story is legendary. It is the great emancipatory narrative of liberation which brings, some would argue, all history to an end. In this case, it assimilates, combines into one entity, more than one form of oppression—daughter and father, poor and rich—licensing a reading which makes of the first the metanarrative of all forms of inequality (patriarchy the cause of all other types of oppression, which it then subordinates to itself). The poem thus presents itself as protest and emancipation from a condition which reduces the one oppressed to the barest minimum of human, but inarticulate, life: "Barely daring to breathe or Achoo" (it is hard not to read here a reference to Plath's sinusitis). Blocked, hardly daring to breathe or to sneeze, this body suffers because the father has for too long oppressed.

If the poem stopped here then it could fairly be read, as it has often been read, in triumphalist terms—instead of which it suggests that such an ending is only a beginning, or repetition, which immediately finds itself up against a wholly other order of time: "Daddy, I have had to kill you. / You died before I had time." In Freudian terms, this is the time of "*Nachtraglichkeit*" or after-effect: a murder which has taken place, but after the fact, because the father who is killed is already dead; a father who was once mourned ("I used to pray to recover you") but whose recovery has already been signalled, by what precedes it in the poem, as the precondition for his death to be repeated. Narrative as repetition—it is a familiar drama in which the father must be killed insofar as he is already dead. This at the very least suggests that, if this is the personal father, it is also what psychoanalysis terms the father of individual prehistory, the father who establishes the very possibility (or impossibility) of history as such.[8] It is through this father that the subject discovers—or fails to discover—her own history, as at once personal and part of a wider symbolic place. The time of historical emancipation immediately finds itself up against the problem of a no less historical, but less certain, psychic time.

This is the father as godhead, as origin of the nation and the word—graphically figured in the image of the paternal body in bits and pieces spreading across the American nation-state: bag full of God, head in the Atlantic, big as a Frisco seal. Julia Kristeva terms this father "*Père imaginaire*," which she then abbreviates "PI."[9] Say those initials out loud in French and what you get is "pays" (country or nation)—the concept of the exile. Much has been made of Plath as an exile, as she goes back and forth between England and the United States. But there is another history of migration, another prehistory, which this one overlays—of her father, born in Grabow, the Polish Corridor, and her mother's Austrian descent: "You are talking to me as a general American. In particular, my background is, may I say, German and Austrian."[10]

If this poem is in some sense about the death of the father, a death both willed and premature, it is no less about the death of language. Returning to the roots of language, it discovers a personal and political history (the one as indistinguishable from the other) which once again fails to enter into words.

In the German tongue, in the Polish town
Scraped flat by the roller
Of wars, wars, wars.
But the name of the town is common.
My Polack friend

Says there are a dozen or two.
So I never could tell where you
Put your foot, your root,
I never could talk to you.
The tongue stuck in my jaw.

> It stuck in a barb wire snare.
> Ich, ich, ich, ich,
> I could hardly speak.
> I thought every German was you.
> And the language obscene

Twice over, the origins of the father, physically and in language, are lost—through the wars which scrape flat German tongue and Polish town, and then through the name of the town itself, which is so common that it fails in its function to identify, fails in fact to name. Compare Claude Lanzmann, the filmmaker of *Shoah*, on the Holocaust as "a crime to forget the name," or Lyotard: "the destruction of whole worlds of names."[11] Wars wipe out names, the father cannot be spoken to, and the child cannot talk, except to repeat endlessly, in a destroyed obscene language, the most basic or minimal unit of self-identity in speech: "ich, ich, ich, ich" (the first draft has "incestuous" for "obscene"). The notorious difficulty of the first-person pronoun in relation to identity—its status as shifter, the division or splitting of the subject which it both carries and denies—is merely compounded by its repetition here. In a passage taken out of her journals, Plath comments on this "I."

> I wouldn't be I. But I am I now; and so many other millions are so irretrievably their own special variety of "I" that I can hardly bear to think of it. I: how firm a letter; how reassuring the three strokes: one vertical, proud and assertive, and then the two short horizontal lines in quick, smug, succession. The pen scratches on the paper I . . . I . . . I . . . I . . . I . . . I.[12]

The effect, of course, if you read it aloud, is not one of assertion but, as with "ich, ich, ich, ich," of the word sticking in the throat. Pass from that trauma of the "I" back to the father as a "bag full of God," and "Daddy" becomes strikingly resonant of the case of a woman patient described at Hamburg, suspended between two utterances: "I am God's daughter" and "I do not know what I am" (she was the daughter of a member of Himmler's ss).[13]

In the poem, the "I" moves backwards and forwards between German and English, as does the "you" ("Ach, du"). The dispersal of identity in language follows the lines of a division or confusion between nations and tongues. In fact language in this part of the poem moves in two directions at once. It appears in the form of translation, and as a series of repetitions and overlappings—"ich," "Ach," "Achoo"—which dissolve the pronoun back into infantile patterns of sound. Note too how the rhyming pattern of the poem sends us back to the first line. "You do not do, you do not do," and allows us to read it as both English and German: "You du not du," "You you not you"—"you" as "not you" because "you" do not exist inside a space where linguistic address would be possible.

I am not suggesting, however, that we apply to Plath's poem the idea of poetry as *écriture* (women's writing as essentially multiple, the other side of normal discourse, fragmented by the passage of the unconscious and the body into words). Instead the poem seems to be outlining the conditions under which that celebrated loss of the symbolic function takes place. Identity and language lose themselves in the place of the father whose absence gives him unlimited powers. Far from presenting this as a form of liberation—language into pure body and play—Plath's poem lays out the high price, at the level of fantasy, that such a psychic process entails. Irruption of the semiotic (Kristeva's term for that other side of normal language), which immediately transposes itself into an alien, paternal tongue.

Plath's passionate desire to learn German and her constant failure to do so is one of the refrains of both her journals and her letters home: "Wickedly didn't do German for the last two days, in a spell of perversity and paralysis" . . . "do German (that I *can* do)" . . . "German and French would give me self-respect, why don't I act on this?" . . . "Am very painstakingly studying German two hours a day" . . . "At least I have begun my German. Painful, as if 'part were cut out of my brain'" . . . "Worked on German for two days, then let up" . . . "Take hold. Study German today."[14] In *The Bell Jar*, Esther Greenwood says: "Every time I picked up a German dictionary or a German book, the very sight of those dense, black, barbed wire letters made my mind shut like a clam."[15]

If we go back to the poem, then I think it becomes clear that it is this crisis of representation in the place of the father which is presented by Plath as engendering—forcing, even—her identification with the Jew. Looking for the father, failing to find him anywhere, the speaker finds him everywhere instead. Above all, she finds him everywhere in the language which she can neither address to him nor barely speak. It is this hallucinatory transference which turns every German into the image of the father, makes for the obscenity of the German tongue, and leads directly to the first reference to the Holocaust.

And the language obscene

An engine, an engine
Chuffing me off like a Jew.
A Jew to Dachau, Auschwitz, Belsen.
I began to talk like a Jew.
I think I may well be a Jew.

The snows of the Tyrol, the clear beer of Vienna
Are not very pure or true.
With my gypsy ancestress and my weird luck
And my Taroc pack and my Taroc pack
I may be a bit of a Jew.

The only metaphor here is that first one that cuts across the stanza break—
"the language obscene // An engine, an engine"—one of whose halves is
language. The metaphor therefore turns on itself, becomes a comment on the
(obscene) language which generates the metaphor as such. More important
still, metaphor is by no means the dominant trope when the speaker starts to
allude to herself as a Jew.

Chuffing me off *like* a Jew.
I began to talk *like* a Jew.
I *think* I may well be a Jew.
I may be a *bit* of a Jew.

Plath's use of simile and metonymy keeps her at a distance, opening up the
space of what is clearly presented as a partial, hesitant, and speculative identification between herself and the Jew. The trope of identification is not substitution but displacement, with all that it implies by way of instability in any
identity thereby produced. Only in metaphor proper does the second, sub-
stituting term wholly oust the first; in simile, the two terms are co-present,
with something more like a slide from one to the next; while metonymy is, in
its very definition, only ever partial (the part stands in for the whole).

   If the speaker claims to be a Jew, then, this is clearly not a simple claim
("claim" is probably wrong here). For this speaker, Jewishness is the position
of the one without history or roots: "So I never could tell where you / Put
your foot, your root." Above all, it is for her a question, each time suspended
or tentatively put, of her participation and implication in the event. What the
poem presents us with, therefore, is precisely the problem of trying to claim a

relationship to an event in which—the poem makes it quite clear—the speaker did not participate. Given the way Plath stages this as a problem in the poem, presenting it as part of a crisis of language and identity, the argument that she simply uses the Holocaust to aggrandise her personal difficulties seems completely beside the point. Who can say that these were not difficulties which she experienced in her very person?[16]

If this claim is not metaphorical, then, we should perhaps also add that neither is it literal. The point is surely not to try and establish whether Plath was part Jewish or not. The fact of her being Jewish could not *legitimate* the identification—it is, after all, precisely offered as an identification—any more than the image of her father as a Nazi which now follows can be *invalidated* by reference to Otto Plath. One old friend wrote to Plath's mother on publication of the poem in the review of *Ariel* in *Time* in 1966 to insist that Plath's father had been nothing like the image in the poem (the famous accusation of distortion constantly brought to bear on Plath).[17]

Once again these forms of identification are not exclusive to Plath. Something of the same structure appears at the heart of Jean Stafford's most famous novel, *A Boston Adventure*, published in 1946.[18] The novel's heroine, Sonie Marburg, is the daughter of immigrants, a Russian mother and a German father who eventually abandons his wife and child. As a young woman, Sonie finds herself adopted by Boston society in the 1930s. Standing in a drawing-room, listening to the expressions of anti-Semitism, she speculates,

> I did not share Miss Pride's prejudice and while neither did I feel strongly partisan towards Jews, the subject always embarrassed me because, not being able to detect Hebraic blood at once except in a most obvious face, I was afraid that someone's toes were being trod on.[19]

It is only one step from this uncertainty, this ubiquity and invisibility of the Jew, to the idea that she too might be Jewish: "And even here in Miss Pride's sitting-room where there was no one to be offended (unless I myself were partly Jewish, a not unlikely possibility). . . . "[20] Parenthetically and partially, therefore, Sonie Marburg sees herself as a Jew. Like Plath, the obverse of this is to see the lost father as a Nazi: "What occurred to me as [Mrs. Hornblower] was swallowed up by a crowd of people in the doorway was that perhaps my father, if he had gone back to Würzburg, had become a Nazi"—a more concrete possibility in Stafford's novel, but one which turns on the same binary, father/daughter, Nazi/Jew, that we see in Plath.[21]

In Plath's poem, it is clear that these identities are fantasies, not for the banal and obvious reason that they occur inside a text, but because the poem addresses the production of fantasy as such. In this sense, I read "Daddy" as a poem about its own conditions of linguistic and phantasmic production. Rather than casually produce an identification, it asks a question about identification, laying out one set of intolerable psychic conditions under which such an identification with the Jew might take place.

Furthermore—and this is crucial to the next stage of the poem—these intolerable psychic conditions are also somewhere the condition, or grounding, of paternal law. For there is a trauma or paradox internal to identification in relation to the father, one which is particularly focused by the Holocaust itself. At the 1985 Hamburg Congress of the International Association of Psychoanalysis, David Rosenfeld described the "logical-pragmatic paradox" facing the children of survivors: "To be like me you must go away and not be like me; to be like your father, you must not be like your father."[22] Lyotard puts the dilemma of the witness in very similar terms: "If death is there [at Auschwitz], you are not there; if you are there, death is not there. Either way it is impossible to prove that death is there" (compare Levi on the failure of witness).[23] For Freud, such a paradox is structural, oedipal, an inseparable part of that identification with the father of individual prehistory which is required of the child: "[The relation of the superego] to the ego is not exhausted by the precept: 'You *ought to be* like this (like your father).' It also comprises the prohibition: 'You *may not be* like this (like your father).' "[24] Paternal law is therefore grounded on an injunction which it is impossible to obey. Its cruelty, and its force, reside in the form of the enunciation itself.

"You stand at the blackboard, Daddy / In the picture I have of you"—it is not the character of Otto Plath, but his symbolic position which is at stake. In her story "Among the Bumblebees," Plath writes of the father: "Alice's father feared nothing. Power was good because it was power."[25] Commenting on what he calls the "*père-version*" of the father, the French psychoanalyst Jacques Lacan writes: "Nothing worse than a father who proffers the law on everything. Above all, spare us any father educators, rather let them be in retreat on any position as master."[26] The reference is to the father of Schreber, eminent educationalist in pre-Nazi Germany, whose gymnasia have been seen as part of the institutional and ideological prehistory of what was to come.[27] It might then be worth quoting the following lines from Otto Plath's "Insect Societies" (he was a professor of entomology, famous for his work *Bumblebees and Their Ways*).[28] Whether or not they tell us anything about what he was like as a person, they can be cited as one version of such paternal "perversion," of such an impossible paternal ideal: "When we see these intelligent insects dwelling together in orderly communities of many thousands of individuals, their social instincts developed to a high degree of perfection, making their marches with the regularity of disciplined troops . . . ," or this citation from another professor, with which he concludes,

> Social instincts need no machinery of control over antisocial instincts. They simply have no antisocial tendencies. These were thoroughly eliminated many millions of years ago and the insects have progressed along a path of perfect social coordination. They have no need for policemen, lawyers, government officials, preachers or teachers because they are innately social. They have no need of learning the correct social responses. These are predetermined by their social constitution at the time of birth.[29]

Loss or absence of the father, but equally symbolic overpresence of the father (only the first is normally emphasised in relation to Plath)—it is the father as master who encapsulates the paradox at the heart of the paternal function, who most forcefully demands an identification which he also has to withhold or refuse. On more than one occasion, Plath relates the celebrated violence of her writing to the violence of that function. In "Among the Bumblebees," the father sits marking scripts: "The vicious little red marks he made on the papers were the color of the blood that oozed out in a thin line the day she cut her finger with the bread knife."[30] For those who would insist that what mattered most for Plath was the loss of her father, we might add that the only other father who can stand in for this overmastery of the paternal function is the father who is dead.

One could then argue that it is this paradox of paternal identification that Nazism most visibly inflates and exploits. For doesn't Nazism itself also turn on the image of the father, a father enshrined in the place of the symbolic, all-powerful to the extent that he is so utterly out of reach? (and not only Nazism—Ceauşescu preferred orphans to make up his secret police). By rooting the speaker's identification with the Jew in the issue of paternity, Plath's poem enters into one of the key phantasmic scenarios of Nazism itself. As the poem progresses, the father becomes more and more of a Nazi (note precisely that this identity is not given, but is something which emerges). Instead of being found in every German, what is most frighteningly German is discovered retrospectively in him.

I have always been scared of *you*,
With your Luftwaffe, your gobbledygoo.
And your neat moustache
And your Aryan eye, bright blue.
Panzer-man, panzer-man, O You—

Not God but a swastika
So black no sky could squeak through.

The father turns into the image of the Nazi, a string of clichés and childish nonsense ("your gobbledygoo"), of attributes and symbols (again the dominant trope is metonymy) which accumulate and cover the sky. This is of course a parody—the Nazi as a set of empty signs. The image could be compared with Virginia Woolf's account of the trappings of fascism in *Three Guineas*.[31]

Not that this makes him any the less effective, any the less frightening, any the less desired. In its most notorious statement, the poem suggests that victimisation by this feared and desired father is one of the fantasies at the heart of fascism, one of the universal attractions for women of fascism itself. As much as predicament, victimisation is also *pull*:

Every woman adores a Fascist,
The boot in the face, the brute
Brute heart of a brute like you.

For feminism, these are the most problematic lines of the poem—the mark of a desire that should not speak its name, or the shameful insignia of a new licence for women in the field of sexuality which has precisely gone too far: "In acknowledging that the politically correct positions of the Seventies were oversimplified, we are in danger of simply saying once more that sex is a dark mystery, over which we have no control. 'Take me—I'm yours,' or 'Every woman adores a fascist.'"[32] The problem is only compounded by the ambiguity of the lines which follow that general declaration. Who is putting the boot in the face? The fascist certainly (woman as the recipient of a sexual violence she desires). But, since the agency of these lines is not specified, don't they also allow that it might be the woman herself (identification *with* the fascist being what every woman desires)?

There is no question, therefore, of denying the problem of these lines. Indeed, if you allow that second reading, they pose the question of women's implication in the ideology of Nazism more fundamentally than has normally been supposed.[33] But notice how easy it is to start dividing up and sharing out the psychic space of the text. Either Plath's identification with the Jew is the problem, or her desire for/identification with the fascist. Either her total innocence or her total guilt. But if we put these two objections or difficulties together? Then what we can read in the poem is a set of reversals which have meaning only in relation to each other: reversals not unlike those discovered in the fantasies of the patients described at Hamburg, survivors, children of survivors, children of Nazis—disjunct and sacrilegious parallelism which Plath's poem anticipates and repeats.

If the rest of the poem then appears to give a narrative of resolution to this drama, it does so in terms which are no less ambiguous than what has gone before. The more obviously personal narrative of the next stanzas—death of the father, attempted suicide at twenty, recovery of the father in the image of the husband—is represented as return or repetition: "At twenty I tried to die / And get back, back, back to you" . . . "I made a model of you," followed by emancipation: "So daddy, I'm finally through," and finally "Daddy, daddy, you bastard, I'm through." They thus seem to turn into a final, triumphant sequence the two forms of temporality which were offered at the beginning of the poem. Plath only added the last stanza—"There's a stake in your fat black heart," etc.—in the second draft to drive the point home, as it were (although even "stake" can be read as signaling a continuing investment).

But for all that triumphalism, the end of the poem is ambiguous. For that "through" on which the poem ends is given only two stanzas previously as meaning both ending: "So daddy, I'm finally through" and the condition, even if failed in this instance, for communication to be possible: "The voices just can't worm through." How then should we read that last line—"Daddy, daddy, you bastard, I'm through"? Communication *as* ending, or dialogue *without* end? Note too how the final vengeance in itself turns on an identification—"you bastard"—that is, "you father without father," "you, whose father, like my own, is in the wrong place."[34]

A point about the more personal narrative offered in these last stanzas, for it is the reference to the death of the father, the attempted suicide, and the marriage which calls up the more straightforward biographical reading of this text. Note, however, that the general does not conceal—"camouflage"—the particular or personal meaning. It is, again, the relationship of the two levels which is important (it is that relationship, part sequence, part overdetermination, which the poem transcribes). But even at the most personal level of this poem, there is something more general at stake. For the link that "Daddy" represents between suicide and a paternity, at once personal and symbolic, is again not exclusive to Plath. If "Daddy" is a suicide poem, it is so only to the extent that it locates a historically actualised vacancy, and excess, at the heart of symbolic, paternal law.

I have said relatively little about the sexual politics of the poem. Although there is nothing to mark its gender identity until fairly late, the poem can nonetheless be read as offering—after Sherry Ortner—the equation "as father to daughter" so "Nazi to Jew" (Ortner's formula was "as nature to culture" so "woman to man").[35] According to this interpretation, the representation of the father as Nazi would reveal something about the violence of patriarchy (patriarchy as violence). The speaker's own violence would then be a legitimate and triumphant retaliation—one feminist reading of the text. Clearly this is one way in which the poem can be read, but, taken on its own, the celebration of this narrative seems as problematic as that other feminist celebration of the breakdown or fragmentation of language to which I have already referred.

Assertion of the ego versus a body and language without identity or form— these are two positions on the poetic language of women which correspond respectively to the political demand for equality and to the demand for difference in the most fundamental psychic sense of the term. But perhaps more than any other poem by Plath, "Daddy" seems to offer a type of corrective in advance to them both. It demonstrates the psychic and political cost of that desire for fragmentation (both in terms of origin and effects); but it also insists on the speaker's (and reader's) full participation in the most awkward of fantasies, fantasies which the feminist assertion of selfhood can read only as a type of psychic false consciousness, as the internalisation of patriarchy and mimicry of the eternal behaviour of men. It is particularly awkward for this second reading that the father oppresses to the precise extent that he is not there. Once again it is the category of fantasy that these readings have to play down—which also means, perhaps paradoxically, that they have to play down the concrete history in which the poem is set. For fascism must surely be distinguished from patriarchy, even if in some sense it can be seen as its effect. Fantasy and history are both lost in these two readings—in the eternal sameness of patriarchy and of women's singular relationship to it, in the eternal sameness of the femininity which erupts against its law.

Writing on Nazism in their famous book *The Inability to Mourn*, Alexander and Margarete Mitscherlich describe how vengeance as an alternative to failed mourning constitutes one of the unconscious subtexts of what they call "a particular German way of loving."[36] If we add the mourning to the vengeance, then we cannot read "Daddy" simply in terms of revenge against the oppressor. If we take the revenge and the mourning together, as the poem seems to do, we can reintroduce the concept of fantasy as that which links the motifs of memory and revenge, whose separation in responses to the Holocaust is discussed by Lyotard. More important, if we take their co-presence as a counternarrative or caution against any straightforward narrative reading of the poem as a whole, then "Daddy" appears as a poem that represents a set of fantasies which, at a precise historical moment and with devastating consequences, found themselves at the heart of our collective political life. In this context, there seems no point in trying to establish a one-way relation between the personal and the wider political history the poem evokes. The poem offers the implication of the one in the other—implication, rather than determination, precisely because one cannot establish a single, one-track relation between the two.

Whether the poem reproduces these fantasies or exposes them, whether it offers them to the reader for a further identification or critique, is not a question which I think can be answered. Saul Friedlander makes the difficulty of this distinction central to his book *Reflections of Nazism*, which describes the preoccupation with Nazi fantasies in our contemporary cultural life.[37] But the question is not yet historically settled as to whether knowledge of our implication in these fantasies, or the idea that we can and should separate ourselves from them completely, is most likely to prevent their repetition in the world today. In this context, what is most striking about "Daddy" is its mobility of fantasy, the extent to which it takes up psychic positions which, it is often argued, if they cannot be clearly distinguished, lead to the collapse of morality itself. Plath, on the other hand, moves from one position to the other, implicating them in each other, forcing the reader to enter into something which she or he is often willing to consider only on condition of seeing it as something in which, psychically no less than historically, she or he plays absolutely no part.

Plath was a pacifist. The question then arises of the relation between her politics and these fantasies—between her pacifism and the psychic violence she represents in this poem, and of course not only here. In a much earlier psychoanalytic conference on the psychology of peace and war, held in London in 1934, two years after Wiesbaden, Edward Glover discusses the different relationships between violence in the inner and outer worlds.[38] Pacifism, he suggests, can be as much a repetition of, as a solution to, the problem of inner war. The militarist, on the other hand, is too desperately in search of inner peace to forgo war. But normality, or equilibrium, far from being the ideal scenario, is in many ways the most risky state of all.

> The drawbacks to this state of equilibrium are threefold. First, having no urgent inner problem to solve, the man in the street is likely to ignore the real external urgency of war problems; secondly, the equilibrium will not withstand the panic and excitement of a war crisis; thirdly, it prevents the man in the street ever realising that the problem of war is his own unconscious problem.[39]

I offer Glover's remarks not as an analysis of Plath, nor indeed of pacifism, but in order to suggest something of the reversibility that might hold between pacifism and the commitment to (inner) war. (As Plath puts it in the *Journals*: "I know it is too simple to wish for war, for open battle.")[40] In order to suggest too—although Glover does not say it—something of the possible link between knowing the war is in fact one's own unconscious war, and working for peace. More simply, to note how little concepts such as antagonism, illegitimate appropriation, or theft (the terms of that critique of Plath with which this chapter began) can help us to understand the relation of these two concerns, the coexistence of external and inner urgency, in Plath's work.

Finally, I would suggest that "Daddy" does allow us to ask whether the woman might not have a special relationship to fantasy—the only generalisation in the poem regarding women is, after all, that most awkward of lines: "Every woman adores a fascist." It is invariably taken out of context, taken out of the ghastly drama which shows where such a proposition might come from—what, for the woman who makes it, and in the worse sense, it might *mean*. Turning the criticism of Plath around once more, could we not read in that line a suggestion, or even a demonstration, that it is a woman who is most likely to articulate the power—perverse, recalcitrant, persistent—of fantasy as such? Nor would such an insight be in any way incompatible with women's legitimate protest against a patriarchal world. This is for me, finally, the wager of Plath's work.

Marguerite Duras's *La douleur* is her wartime diary. It describes the time when she was waiting for her husband to return from the camps, and her resistance during the war. At the end of this narrative, she introduces two stories.

Therese is me. The person who tortures the informer is me. So also is the one who feels like making love to Ter, the member of the Militia. Me. I give you the torturer along with the rest of the texts. Learn to read them properly: they are sacred.[41]

The psychic terrain that Duras is covering here seems to be not unconnected to that represented in "Daddy" by Plath—as if the story of the victim (concretely and historically in this instance) had to be followed by the story of herself as torturer, as well as by the story of desire. The last word, however, goes to Sylvia Plath. It is her first outline for the story "The Shadow," a passage from the unedited journals at Smith, not included in the published text.

My present theme seems to be the awareness of a complicated guilt system whereby Germans in a Jewish and Catholic community are made to feel, in scapegoat fashion, the pain, psychically, the Jews are made to feel in Germany by the Germans without religion. The child can't understand the wider framework. How does her father come into this? How is she guilty for her father's deportation to a detention camp? [As (sic)] this is how I think the story will end. Joanna will come in on her own with the trapeze, Uncle Frank and the fiction of perfect goodness.[42]

14

Peter Pan and Freud: Who Is Talking and to Whom?

We have been reading the wrong Freud to children.

We do not realise that Freud was first brought up against the unconscious when asking how we remember ourselves as a child. The unconscious is not an object, something to be laid hold of and retrieved. It is the term which Freud used to describe the complex ways in which our very idea of ourselves as children is produced. In 1897, two French psychologists, V. and C. Henri, published a monograph of adult recollections of childhood and were baffled by a number of apparently meaningless memories. Freud found their very "innocence . . . mysterious."[1] Setting himself to analyse one of his earliest recollections, he found that the event he remembered had never taken place. The importance of the memory was not, however, any the less for that. For what it revealed was the unresolved conflicts affecting the way in which he was thinking about himself *now*. The most crucial aspect of psychoanalysis for discussing children's fiction is its insistence that childhood is something in which we continue to be implicated and which is never simply left behind. Childhood persists—this is the opposite, note, from the reductive idea of a regression to childhood most often associated with Freud. It persists as something which we endlessly rework in our attempt to build an image of our own history. When we think about childhood, it is above all our investment in doing so which counts. The very ambiguity of the term "children's fiction"—fiction the child produces or fiction given to the child?—is striking for the way in which it leaves the adult completely out of the picture.

Childhood is not an object, any more than the unconscious, although this is often how they are both understood. The idea that childhood is something separate which can be scrutinised and assessed is the other side of the illusion which makes of childhood something which we have simply ceased to be. In most discussions of children's fiction which make their appeal to Freud, childhood is part of a strict developmental sequence at the end of which stands the cohered and rational consciousness of the adult mind. Children may, on occasions, be disturbed, but they do not disturb us as long as that sequence (and that development) can be ensured. Children are no threat to our identity because they are, so to speak, "on their way" (the journey metaphor is a recurrent one). Their difference stands purely as the sign of just how far we have progressed.

We have been reading the wrong Freud to children, because this is the most reductive, even if it is the most prevalent, reading of Freud. It is reductive to the extent that it holds off the challenge, which is present in Freud's own work, to the very notions of identity, development, and subjective cohesion which this conception of childhood is so often used to sustain.

When Freud analysed that first memory and laid out—not so much what it might mean as the processes of transformation which lay between the original event and what he chose to recall—he was demonstrating the divisions and distortions which are characteristic of our psychic life. Later he would formulate these processes more precisely in relation to dreams, jokes, and slips of the tongue—phenomena which could not be dismissed as neurotic, but which revealed an essential continuity between the disturbances of Freud's patients and the psychic mechanisms of normal adult life. What Freud had discovered in that first recollection was that there are aspects of our psychic life which *escape* our conscious control. Childhood amnesia or partial recollection of childhood has nothing to do with a gradual cohering of the mind as we get older and our ability to remember improves. Instead it reveals that there are aspects of our childhood which one part of our mind, a part over which we precisely do not have control, would rather forget.

That moment was the starting point for two sets of questions which would be closely related throughout Freud's work, and which are crucial to any consideration of fiction for the child: the question of the unconscious—its constant pull against our seeming identity (the unconscious is not the site of some irrational truth, its truth is merely this repeated slippage); the question of childhood—its threat to the idea that we have neatly picked up and resolved everything that came before on the way to where we are now. The issue of childhood sexuality is subordinate to these two questions. For it is relatively easy to acknowledge in the child a sexuality different from our own, if we can see this sexuality as something which is simply grown out of (rather like a set of clothes). In fact, Freud uncovered in the sexual life of children the same perverse sexuality that analysis revealed in the symptoms of his patients and which was expressed indirectly in their dreams. By stating that this perverse sexuality was in fact quite normal to the extent that it could be located in the sexual life of the child, and by insisting, furthermore, that it was only spoken in the form of a symptom because it was a form of sexuality which had to be so totally repressed elsewhere, Freud effected a break in our conception of both sexuality and childhood from which we do not seem to have recovered. The neurotic simply bears witness to the effects of what is always at some level an impossible task—the task of cohering the fragmented, component, and perverse sexuality of the child. The fact that Freud used a myth to describe how this ordering is meant to take place (the myth of Oedipus) should alert us to the fictional nature of this process, which is at best precarious, and never complete.

In discussions of fantasy in children's writing, it is, however, always this notion of an ultimate identity which is involved. Bettelheim, in the book which has become the model for this type of analysis, discusses the fairy tale in terms of the function it can serve in "fortifying" (the word is his) the child's personality and resolving its oedipal drama (this is the *use* of enchantment).[2] Bettelheim's work is distinguished by its attention to the complexity of unconscious process for both adult and child; but the concept of mastery—with its associated meaning of coherence in psychic and sexual life—is nonetheless the central term through which this complexity is conceived and by means of which it is finally resolved. The unconscious does not therefore challenge the human ego, its seeming coherence and identity; the unconscious "enriches" the ego, and, much as a quantity of energy or a current, it can be transferred into the ego where it becomes neutralised and safe. "The human personality," writes Bettelheim, "is indivisible."[3] The purpose of the fairy tale is to allow the child that early instability or instance of disruption in order to ensure that any such instability will, in the last analysis, be more effectively removed. Thus, although this account fully recognises in the fairy tale the difficulty of the unconscious fantasies of the child, it does so only to the extent that the form of their appearance is also the mode of their resolution (the ordering of the narrative and the end of the story).

The issue is not, therefore, just that of the sexuality of the child; it is, more crucially, that of how our subjectivity is divided in relation to itself. In his book *Philosophy and the Young Child*, Gareth Matthews criticises Jean Piaget, the educational psychologist, for being unable to grasp that, in relation to its dream, the child is in two places at once.[4] Piaget wants to transform this division into two stages of a sequence—at first the child thinks that he is both in the bed and actually on the other side of the room, but eventually he will realise that the dream, and that other part of himself, are both safely inside his head. The child becomes a unified subject, and the idea that the dream might suggest otherwise is dismissed as an error of logic. It is, however, the very meaning of the unconscious to undermine exactly this unity, and it is not by chance that Freud first formulated how it does so in relation to the interpretation of dreams.

In the preface to the fourth edition of his major work on sexuality, Freud stated that the concept of the unconscious had been easily assimilated into common knowledge, as compared with the total resistance that he had met with in relation to the sexual life of the child.[5] He was wrong. For it can be argued that the concept of the unconscious has been refused at exactly that point where it throws into question the idea of our subjectivity as something which we can fully know, or that ultimately can be cohered. Childhood sexuality was in this sense *easier* to acknowledge. It could, eventually, become an object of curiosity and investigation, something to be mastered—the very meaning of sexual development as it is commonly understood.

Freud, it must be recognised, was at least partly responsible for this. His own investigation of childhood was in many ways inconsistent and contradictory. But there is one movement in his discussion of childhood sexuality which makes it clear that the issue of sexuality cannot be separated from that of the unconscious without losing sight of what is central to the importance of each. In 1915, he added to the second of the *Three Essays on the Theory of Sexuality* on infantile sexuality, a section entitled "The Sexual Researches of Childhood."[6] In this section he described how infantile sexuality starts to turn on a number of questions which the child sets itself, questions about its own origin (the birth of children) and its sexual identity (the difference between the sexes) which the child will eventually have to resolve. By describing the child's development in terms of a *query*, Freud moves it out of the realm of an almost biological sequence, and into that of fantasy and representation where things are not so clear. In one sense both these questions can be answered—children are born of parents, and the difference between the sexes is there for all to see. But equally they cannot be answered—behind the question about origins is the idea of a moment when the child did not exist, and behind the question about difference is the recognition that the child's sexual identity rests solely in its differentiation from something (or someone) which it is not. There is a level, therefore, at which both these questions undermine the very identity which they simultaneously put in place. We answer them for the child at the cost of deceiving ourselves.

Deception is, however, for Freud, in the very order of language. When we speak, we take up a position of identity and certainty in language, a position whose largely fictional nature only the occasional slip, and at times the joke, is allowed to reveal. Deception is what characterises human utterances since language can be used to say the opposite of what is true (this is no doubt why, for Locke, the lie is the ultimate monstrosity in the child).[7] Language is not something which we simply use to communicate, as everything in psychoana-. lytic practice makes clear. Psychoanalysis directs its attention to what cannot be spoken in what is actually being said. It starts from the assumption that there is a difficulty in language, that in speaking to others we might be speaking against ourselves, or at least against that part of ourselves which would rather remain unspoken. This includes, necessarily, speaking *to* children, answering their questions and telling them tales. But the problem of language—the idea that language might *be* a problem—is the dimension of psychoanalysis which has been most rigorously avoided in discussions of fiction for the child.

How we think about children—what it might mean to address them, to speak to them and write them down—is, therefore, directly implicated in this question of language. Our relationship to language is no more fixed and stable than our relationship to childhood itself. We use language to identify ourselves and objects in the world. But the pronoun "I," which apparently gives us that identity, only has as its meaning whoever happens to be using it at the time; and it is no simple term of unity or cohesion, as the processes of the dream, our ability to lie, or merely to deceive ourselves, all too clearly demonstrate. Objects are defined in language, but the relation between the linguistic term and its referent is arbitrary (this was for Locke the "imperfection" of words); and the meaning of one word can only be fixed with reference to another, in a process which finally has us going round in circles (the chase through the dictionary from one entry to the next to find out what a word *really* means).[8] Freud located all these difficulties in his attempt to negotiate the complex, overdetermined and contradictory meanings of symptoms, dreams, and jokes. But they came up first, and most forcefully, in response to the question he started by asking—the question of how we produce our image of the child.

In one of Freud's most famous case histories—the case of "The Wolf Man"—he attempted to identify the exact meaning of a childhood event, as if it were a single point of significance which could resolve the patient's past and remove his present symptoms together.[9] As in the case of those earlier memories—which was where it had all started—he discovered that there was no single event, that possibly nothing had ever happened, but that the multiple associations and images uncovered in the course of the analysis belonged to the still continuing history of his patient.[10] Freud thought that the "Wolf Man" had *seen* something—his parents engaged in a sexual act which would answer for him the question of generations. But what flashed up in the analysis over and over again was more like a piece of staging, a theatrical performance which represented for the patient the question of sexual difference and origins which he was still attempting to answer for himself. What Freud uncovered in that analysis is that there is no straightforward answer to the question, no single meaning to an event, and no childhood which is simply over and done with. For Freud, neither childhood nor meaning can be pinned down—they shift, and our own identity with them.

The discussion of children's fiction often takes the form of a re-run of the debate between Freud and Jung. Alan Garner, for example, is a Jungian, and he builds Jung's philosophy quite openly into his writing for children. Jung has in fact been much better received than Freud in relation to children's fiction, which might seem surprising given Jung's self-confessed lack of interest in individual childhood.[11] Jung's interest was in the history of the *race*, and he saw the unconscious as the repository of a set of myths and symbols which our culture has destroyed.[12] The appeal to Jung, in relation to children's writing, is therefore in direct line with that mystification which places the child at the origin of all human history. But there is more to it than this. The dispute between Freud and Jung is not just about childhood. It is, more crucially, about this question of language, about whether meaning is something stable which can be directly interpreted and fixed.

For Freud, the often contradictory and inconsistent ways that childhood appears in analysis undermines any notion of a straightforward sequence and throws into crisis our relationship to meaning itself. Meaning is not simply there—it is built up, it can be determined by totally contradictory associations, and can emerge long after the event which apparently gives it form. For Jung, on the other hand, if childhood appears after the fact, then it is a fantasy which indicates that the patient is going backwards and running away from the tasks of real life. For Jung, distortion, overdetermination, repetition (the terms which Freud uses to characterise our relationship to the unconscious) are the signs of an almost moral evasion. Meaning is no more divided than subjectivity itself (hence his central term "individuation"). Jung's main concern is to restore the original meaning of the symbol or archetype, a meaning which is fixed for all time. Interpreting it serves to establish both our psychic and our historical continuity. Meaning is something which can be grasped according to a strict chronology which leads from the infancy of the race directly to the apotheosis of mankind.

The idea that symbols simply *speak* is one with which Freud is most often associated. For Freud, it is thought, what they speak is sexual, for Jung mythical, but in terms of the concept of language and meaning which is involved, there is not much to choose between them. In both cases, the symbol contains a hidden meaning to which we possess the key. Although Freud did at times use this method, he introduces his own method for interpreting dreams by castigating this type of symbolic reading as useless, and it is a concept of meaning which everything else in his work undercuts.[13] But it remains the form of interpretation—where one thing straightforwardly *equals* another—which seems to predominate in the analysis of children's writing. We see this frequently in symbolic interpretations of fairy tales (the wolf in *Little Red Riding Hood is* the oedipal father), and, in another guise, in biographical readings of children's books (behind *Peter Pan* is Barrie and nothing else).[14] What is striking about this type of interpretation is the way that it bypasses any problem of language, any question of how meaning is constructed, of how it builds up and shifts. Instead it presupposes a type of original innocence of meaning which the act of criticism can retrieve—the very notion of how meaning (and childhood) operate which Freud himself had had to discard.

It seems to me that it is no coincidence that symbolism and biography are the two forms of "Freudian" analysis which are most commonly associated with children's fiction (which is why someone like Matthews, in his discussion of fantasy, dismisses Freud more or less out of hand).[15] I consider these forms of analysis to be the "worst" of Freud, not least because of the other, more difficult, aspects of Freud's work on childhood and language which they avoid. Both presuppose a pure point of origin lurking behind the text which we, as adults and critics, can trace. This is, of course, the ultimate fantasy of much literary criticism which tries to uncover the true and primary meaning of a work. But in the analysis of children's fiction, the child seems to become implicated in the process. It is as if the child serves to sanction that concept of a pure origin because the child is seen as just such an origin in itself. The child is there, and the original meaning is there—they *reinforce* each other. Thus a strange complicity can be seen between the archaic status of the fairy tale, for example, and the idea of the child as the true, unconscious recipient of its meaning ("the child understands this intuitively, though he does not 'know' it explicitly");[16] or in the case of biographical criticism, the idea of the child behind the writer (Barrie as eternal child) supports a form of analysis which allows us to take the work back to its beginning and to stop it there.[17]

We need to ask why interpreting children's fiction—reading it *for* the child—seems to be untouched by the idea that language itself might be unstable, and that our relationship to it is never safe. We need to ask why we appear to straddle our present division in language across the present of the book and its past—that original meaning which we can uncover by so totally *knowing* the child.

In the discussion of children's fiction, I repeatedly come across the most emphatic of refusals or demands: that there should be no disturbance at the level of language, no challenge to our own sexuality, no threat to our status as critics, and no question of our relation to the child. These demands are all impossible; they carry a weight that no individual child could be expected to support. The fact that they are impossible is nowhere clearer than in the case of *Peter Pan*.

> If a book exists which contains more knowledge and more love of children, we
> do not know it.
> —Review of J. M. Barrie's *The Little White Bird, Times Literary Supplement,*
> 14 November 1902

Writing for children is an act of love. It is a way of "knowing" the child. Loving the child and knowing the child—the idea is one of an innocent attachment, all the more effective for the casual ease with which it binds the child to its purpose. Love and knowledge can both be used with reference to the child—in 1902 at least—with no hint of the sexuality at play. Today we might recognise the sexuality contained in the first, but we are perhaps still no more likely to notice the disturbance conveyed by the very certainty of the second.

The Little White Bird, to which this quotation from the *Times Literary Supplement* refers, was not written for children. It was written by J. M. Barrie as a novel for adults and published in 1902. Most of the book, however, is told by the narrator as a story to a little boy who is addressed inside the book; and one of the stories which the narrator tells to this child is the story of *Peter Pan. The Little White Bird* is not often discussed in relation to *Peter Pan,* and when it is, it is mainly in terms of the biographical information which it provides about J. M. Barrie.[18] *The Little White Bird,* it is said, reveals Barrie's longing for and adoration of a child who is identified as George Llewellyn Davies, one of the five Llewellyn Davies boys whom Barrie finally adopted. Placing the child thus firmly outside the limits of the text, however, absolves us of the need to ask what might be happening to the child who is contained, equally firmly, within it.

"Telling tales to children"—the formulation jars, since telling tales is something which children are meant to do *to*, or *against*, each other. It also carries the idea of deception and dishonesty, as if something is told as a tale to the extent that it is not true. Adults do not tell *tales* to children, they tell *stories*. Even if the story is a fantasy, its truth is nonetheless guaranteed by the simple and unquestioned communication which passes between the adult and child.

The idea that there could be a problem at just that level of communication, a troubling of intention and address, is not one which is often entertained in discussion of children's fiction. In fact one effect of the increasing attention being paid to the content and meanings of children's books seems to be that this issue is hardly ever raised. The history of *Peter Pan*, however, has so visibly hung on a set of repeated (and largely failed) attempts to remove this problem of address from the area of what properly constitutes children's fiction, that it starts to look like a case of censorship. The history of *Peter Pan* suggests, if anything, that children's fiction relies, for its continuity and untroubled existence, on the fact that this issue is normally ruled out of bounds.

Linguistics has a term for this whole area of potential trouble and confusion. It is the term "enunciation" which does not refer to what is being said, but asks who speaks and to whom, and why, by implication, they are speaking.[19] "Enunciation" exists as a term in linguistics solely to differentiate this question from the content of any individual utterance. When we speak, there is an "I" behind the statement, who is never the same as the person or thing to which we refer, even when (or especially when) we are speaking about ourselves (that "about" in itself reveals the distance between these two moments of an apparent identity). "Enunciation" is the term for that division in language which speaking to anyone (including children) necessarily reveals. It marks a potential dislocation at the heart of any utterance (that same dislocation which Freud identified at its most insistent in the gap between the dreamer and the message of his or her dream). Above all, it undermines the idea of language as a simple tool of communication by allowing us to ask what might be the relationship—of procurement or desire—which holds between the one who speaks and what he or she offers as the innocence of their statement.

We cannot think about *Peter Pan*—its endless rewritings, its confusion of address, and the adoration which it has received as if it were itself a child—

without thinking about this problem of what lies behind or produces the very act of speech. It has emerged constantly in the history of *Peter Pan* only to be ignored, forgotten or repressed. *The Little White Bird*, for example, speaks of this problem and of virtually nothing else. What matters in this book is the way that the child is placed in the story, and why (although the question may seem gratuitous) he is there at all.

The Little White Bird tells the story of a bachelor clubman who anonymously befriends a courting couple, and then, after their marriage, becomes friend and storyteller to their child. One of these stories is the story of Peter Pan, who lives in Kensington Gardens—where the narrator and the little boy, David, take their walks—and of his encounter with a little girl, Maimie Mannering, who meets him when she breaks the rules and stays in the gardens overnight. Around this story is wrapped that of the narrator's relationship to the little boy to whom he tells it, which is in turn interspersed with his own memories and fantasies, and which ends when David leaves for school. This structure of stories within stories (*"en abîme"*) makes *The Little White Bird* a story about storytelling itself, and of the child's vital place in that process.

This is a fuller extract from the *Times Literary Supplement*'s review of 1902:

> The book is all Barrie-ness; whimsical, sentimental, profound, ridiculous Barrie-ness; utterly impossible, yet absolutely real, a fairy tower built on the eternal truth. To say what happens in it is to stultify one's praise for one of the most charming books ever written. A middle-aged and bachelor clubman, who becomes so enamoured of someone else's baby that he kidnaps him, perambulator and all, into Kensington-gardens, and there wheels him about, dexterously dodging the anxious mother, for half a day—who squabbles openly and unashamedly in public places with Irene the nurse (the daughter of his own club-waiter) about her cap and his own moral influence—such a man is as impossible as his St. Bernard dog, who turns a while into a human being, or as Peter Pan, half baby, half bird, who dwells on the island in the Serpentine and plays his pipe at the fairies' ball in the gardens. The clubman, it is true, is careful to warn us that he is whimsical; but we heed him not. The most whimsical of bachelors would never do such things; but it does not matter . . . the smallest details of his adored David, his braces and behaviour in the bath, are not too trivial to dwell on; and all the while it is clear that the details are but symbols, that the man's whole mind is given to developing and revealing the best that is in himself, lest any speck of contamination should fall on the boy who was

not his son. . . . In fine, here is an exquisite piece of work. To analyse its merits and defects—its fun, its pathos, its character-drawing, or its sentimentality, its improbability, its lack of cohesion—would be to vivisect a fairy.[20]

In *The Little White Bird*, talking to the child is, therefore, an act of love, but it is also a claim on the child, a demand made on the child as a means of holding it fast. The child, David, does not belong to the narrator, but to another couple with whom the narrator is vicariously involved (he spends most of his time following them and watching them). The narrator is trying to steal the child, to get at the mother and replace the father. His involvement with the child is, therefore, anything but innocent. In fact it can be traced back to an unconsummated sexual desire for which David is the substitute and replacement. This is not, it should be stressed, an "analysis" of the book—the motives and the past history are all given by the narrator himself. It is no doubt the easy slippage between description and diagnosis which has, more recently, made this book such a biographical landmine in relation to Barrie himself. But the effect of locating this disturbance in Barrie is, paradoxically, that his communication with the child is seen as all the more unproblematic and complete: Barrie wrote *Peter Pan* as part of his interaction with the Llewellyn Davies boys, but about the work itself very little needs to be said. This is to ignore, however, the disturbance, the difficulty, and above all the impossible questions—about origins and sexual difference—which circulate between the narrator and child in *The Little White Bird*, and which lead straight into (one could almost say *engender*) the story of Peter Pan.

The Little White Bird starts with the narrator telling David the story of the child's own origins. The time of the narrative spans the courtship of David's parents, and David's birth, up to the present relationship between David and the narrator whose end brings the book to a close. David is, therefore, implicated in the story at a number of different levels, each with their own form of ambiguity. The story is told *to* him, but since it goes back to before his beginning, he has to disappear in order for it to be told: "As I enter the club room you are to conceive of David vanishing into nothingness."[21] This child is produced inside the story and the story stands in for him when he leaves. He is, therefore, multiply caught up in, possessed and owned by the story. This is an impossible position which effectively sets David up as a total object of desire (the "be-all and end-all" of the story). Like any other object of such an absolute investment, there is a sense in which David does not exist.

"It doesn't make me littler does it?" he asked anxiously, and then, with a terrible misgiving: "It doesn't make me too little, does it father?" by which he hoped that it would not do for him altogether.[22]

The child's place in the story which is told to him, and about him, is therefore highly equivocal. At one point in the narrative, when the narrator is about to reconcile David's parents during their courtship (an event which is after all crucial if David is to be born), David reappears, interrupts the story, and hesitates before he allows it to take its course. Being a witness at your own birth is, it would seem, rather like being present at your own funeral.

In *The Little White Bird*, the question of origins, of sexuality and of death are all presented as inherent to the very process of writing. Writing the book in itself seems to be nothing more than a constant return to these points of difficulty around which it gravitates and stalls. In the end, the book is presented as a substitute, not only for David who leaves to go to school (this in itself is described as an act of abduction by the schoolmaster, Pilkington), but also for a dead child, Timothy. This child was already a fantasy of the narrator's, invented by him in a dialogue with David's real father on the night when David was born. Later in the story, the narrator pretends that Timothy has died in order to pass on his clothes to David, when he follows David's mother to a pawnshop and realises that she is in financial need. The child, Timothy, is therefore a pure fantasy who dies. This may seem to be a contradiction in terms, but it touches on the nerve of what it might mean to talk of a child who could last for ever. As *The Little White Bird* so clearly demonstrates, there are only two ways of making sure of this—having the child die early or, alternatively, writing the child down. The narrator of *The Little White Bird*, in his total worship (love? knowledge?) of the child, does both—worship of course always carries with it this ambiguity that what is being worshipped is never really there. The narrator produces the book when David is about to leave him and his mother gives birth to a second child: "When in the fullness of time, she held her baby on high implying that she had done a big thing, I was to hold up the book."[23]

The sexuality of *The Little White Bird* operates in a similar mode of difficulty and confusion. What is important at this level is not what, sexually, the narrator can or cannot do (I consider this to be of no interest), but what it is, in the very process of writing, that cannot be *conceived*, in both senses of the term. Much of the early part of the story is taken up with David's life as a bird before he was born (this is told as David's own recollection). In *The Little*

White Bird, all children are birds before they are born, which means first that they can be produced out of thin air (the title of the book refers to the fantasied child, Timothy), and secondly that the narrator can claim true ownership of David on the grounds that he saw him before anyone else: "The first time I ever saw David was on a Sword behind the Baby's walk. He was then a misselthrush."[24]

Together with this disavowal of origins, or conception, goes a corresponding refusal of sexual difference. *The Little White Bird* starts with the narrator rejecting all communication with David's mother (his voyeurism is the obverse of this rejection), and it ends when, despite the narrator's insisting to David that the new child will be a boy, she gives birth to a girl. At the few points in the book when the narrator seems to be talking to a child who is outside the text, this child is clearly a boy: "Girls can't really play cricket, and when you are watching their futile efforts, you make funny sounds at them. You are a solitary boy while all this is taking place."[25] This over-insistence on the presence and value of the male child also appears in the way that children's literature, in the more familiar sense of the term, is used in *The Little White Bird*. Towards the end of the book, the narrator tells David and his friend, Oliver, a shipwreck story (he calls them "wrecked island" stories), drawing quite explicitly on that branch of children's literature which had, in the previous fifty years, specifically been designated as literature for boys (the story is presented as a parody of its genre). In this book, however, landing the children on the island is used by the narrator to abrogate the threat of their departure when they are about to leave for school. Literature for children is, therefore, a way of colonising (or wrecking) the child; and it is emphatically literature for boys only.

The story of *Peter Pan* is told in the middle of *The Little White Bird* as part of this interaction, its refusals and its demands. This is no doubt what makes for its unquestioning (and largely unquestioned) innocence.

What, therefore, do we mean by talking to, or addressing, the child—what are we asking *of* the child in doing just that? The very strangeness of *The Little White Bird*—its present absence behind the classic which we know—suggests that the only story we can ever tell the child is the story of the child's (and our) coming-to-be. "Coming-to-be" is a story which we repeat continually to ourselves. It is there, not just in *The Little White Bird* but in the form of most narratives which we expect to set up a problem and then bring it to a successful resolution. It is present in the sexual query—where do babies come from?—which the adult is asked by the child; and, in another form, in the philosophical puzzle of what happened "before the beginning," to which there is no satisfactory reply.[26] What is most significant about *The Little White Bird* is the way in which this same query is expressed as a question which the adult sends *back* to the child. Put at its crudest, the narrator of *The Little White Bird* cannot answer the question of sexuality, of origins and difference, so he turns to a little boy instead: where did he come from and what was the sexuality in that? Or could it have happened in some other way which would remove the problem altogether? Peter Pan is a little boy who flies away because he does not want to grow up (this remains in the play and in most of the versions which we know today), but the island to which he flies is the place from which unborn babies are dispatched by birds (that bit has been dropped). The sexual query which lies behind the telling of the story to the child surfaces right in the middle of it.

The sexuality of *The Little White Bird* is not, therefore, just that of a man and a little boy, although the possessiveness, the "adoration" (the word is that of the *Times Literary Supplement* in 1902), or even "teasing" of the child (*Observer*, 1979), all suggest that too in their way.[27] The sexuality which matters is both more and less explicit than this. It is sexuality in the form of its repeated disavowal, a relentless return to the question of origins and sexual difference which is focused time and again on the child. The child is there, purely and simply, to bear the weight of that impossible question.

The story of *Peter Pan* which is given in *The Little White Bird* has never, strictly speaking, been distributed as a book for children, even with the surrounding narrative cut out. *Peter Pan in Kensington Gardens*, with illustrations by Arthur Rackham, has always hovered on the edge of the children's book market as something of an art book—a collector's item destined less and less to be read and more and more to be cherished and preserved.[28] This ambiguity merely reproduces at another level the confusions of intention and address which we have seen internally to *The Little White Bird* in the chapters which have been removed. Thus the question of the distribution of *Peter Pan* (the child outside the text) and the question of how it symbolises its relationship to the child inside the text can be seen as related.

It could also be, however, that this Peter Pan story is not so well known because of the residual forms of disturbance which are present in the narrative itself. Peter Pan is a "Betwixt-and-Between" who hovers between the island of birds and the nursery—the two places which offer the two different versions of where babies come from (the "stork" and the "true-life" version of the same story). When he hesitates too long, he is locked out of the nursery, which is why he endlessly returns to the same place—the play *starts* here. But what this story indicates far more explicitly than any of the versions to follow is the difficulty of Peter Pan's relationship to the child, and the anxiety and disturbance in that.

Peter Pan's task in Kensington Gardens is to bury the dead children who break the rules by staying in the gardens over night. His own favorite birds are the house-swallows, which, unlike all the other birds, are not unborn children, but children who were born and then died. One child, Maimie Mannering—forerunner of Wendy—gains access to Peter by transgressing the rules and staying in the gardens after "Lock-Out" time. As will be the case with Wendy, their interaction partly takes the form of a courtship which cannot finally be fulfilled (Maimie leaves, as Wendy will leave the Never Land, when she hears how Peter Pan was barred from the nursery). But unlike Wendy, who becomes the very model of normality, Maimie is a "strange" girl—an "ordinary" girl in the daytime when she looks up to, and imitates, her brother (like little girls should), but "terrible at night" when she charges him with an imaginary goat and terrifies him out of his wits (like little girls should not).[29] The encounter with Peter starts with this, because Maimie only stays in the gardens when her brother, Tony, backs down in fear from his original pledge to do so himself. Peter therefore meets Maimie instead of Tony, the little girl instead of the little boy, but things could (indeed, *should*) have been different. The encounter between Peter and Maimie also ends with this. When Maimie goes home, she sends back to Peter, in a magic incantation, her night-time goat, which he turns into a real goat and rides. Thus Peter Pan touches, or belongs, on the edge of the difference between boys and girls, and of their fears, just as he does on the death of the child. His story, which makes up the central chapters of *The Little White Bird*, ends with these lines:

> But how strange for parents, when they hurry into the Gardens looking for their lost one, to find the sweetest little tombstone instead. I do hope that Peter is not too ready with his spade. It is all rather sad.[30]

In subsequent versions of *Peter Pan* all these elements are rearranged in ways which I will go on to discuss now. But there is a sense in which their very openness here already makes them innocent. For as a set of themes and references in a narrative about children, the whole problem of address, out of which they were produced, starts to fade. They become, more simply, a story which is told, as opposed to something whose difficulty, and challenge to us, lies in the process of its telling.

Turning the story of Peter Pan into a play—the form in which it was first a success and is perhaps still best known today—carries out this transformation before it does anything else. There is no one who tells the story in a play since everyone speaks their own lines. A play is performed before one's eyes, and the immediacy and visibility of the performance gives it a ring of authenticity which is even harder to challenge than that of a story being told. Staging something always relies for its effect on the impression that it is happening then and there. As a play, *Peter Pan* is above all famous for the moment when Peter Pan turns to the audience and asks it if it believes in fairies. This is merely an extreme version of the demand of any play that, at least for the duration of its performance, the audience should believe that it is true.

And yet the term "staging" carries its own ambiguity, which is why Freud used it to describe the unconscious, whose truth lies solely in its challenge to what we conventionally recognise as real. The dreaming child in Piaget's example saw himself on the other side of the room, taking part in a scenario in which he both did, and did not, recognise himself. Once again it is the process of dreaming, and not just its content, which poses the real threat to the idea that there is a straightforward continuity to our psychic life. For Freud, the very immediacy of the visual image forces us to think again.

Setting the child up as a spectacle, shining a light on it and giving it up to our gaze—there is something in this which also needs to be questioned. It reenacts in another form that strange and over-insistent focus on the child which we saw in *The Little White Bird*. It also links up with a history of the visual image in relation to the child, in which *Peter Pan* has its part. Barrie, like Lewis Carroll, took photographs of children. In Barrie's case they were little boys, in Carroll's they were for the most part, but not exclusively, little girls.[31] Barrie's collection, *The Boy Castaways of Black Lake Island*, consists of thirty-six photographs of the Llewellyn Davies boys, and the rudiments of an adventure narrative.[32] Together with *The Little White Bird*, it almost constitutes a second source book for *Peter Pan*. Only two copies of it were ever produced, one of which Arthur Llewellyn Davies, the boys' father, promptly mislaid on a train. The rarity, the exclusive and precious nature of this work has contributed to its status as one of the ultimate records of Barrie's personal history. It is as if it has been moved sideways into the fetishism of the document so we do not need to think about the fetishism in the gaze.

A photograph offers itself as something innocent and authentic which speaks for itself—merely capturing the moment it records. Its immediacy belies the technique, the framing, the pose, all of which make the photograph possible (terms of artifice and calculation which are cancelled out by the natural and effortless feel of the best pictures). The innocence of the photograph as a record or document seems to vouch for the innocence of our pleasure in looking, and no more so perhaps than when what we are looking at is a child. This might explain why it was such a scandal when a number of Graham Ovenden's photographs of Victorian street urchins were discovered to be fakes; for it exposed too sharply that what was represented by the photograph was not the desire to recapture a moment of history, but rather that same history at the service of the desire to look at the child (in this case little girls).[33]

The Boy Castaways of Black Lake Island is made up almost exclusively of photographs of little boys. The book comprises thirty-six captioned photographs, a preface, and a series of chapter headings with no text. The book is dedicated to "our mother in cordial recognition of her efforts to elevate us above the brutes." The preface is the only extended piece of writing in the book.

I have been requested by my brothers to write a few words of introduction to this little volume, and I comply with pleasure, though well aware that others may be better acquitted for the task. The strange happenings here set forth with a *currente calamo* are expansions of a note-book kept by me while we were on the island, but I have thought fit, in exercise of my prerogative as general editor, to omit certain observations with regard to *flaura, fauna,* etc., which, however valuable to myself and to others of scientific bent, would probably have but a limited interest to the lay mind. I have also in this edition excluded a chapter on *strata* as caviare to the general.

The date on which we were wrecked was this year on August 1, 1901, and I have still therefore a vivid recollection of that strange and terrible summer, when we suffered experiences such as have probably never before been experienced by three brothers. At this time, the eldest, George, was eight and a month, Jack was approaching his seventh *lustrum*, and I was a good bit past four. Perhaps a few words about my companions will not be deemed out of place.

George was a fine, fearless youth, and had now been a term at Wilkinson's. He was modest withal. His chief fault was wanting to do all the shooting, and carrying the arrows inside his shirt with that selfish object. Jack is also as brave as a lion, but he also has many faults (see pp. 25–29), and he has a weakness, perhaps pardonable, for a pretty face (bless them!). Of Peter, I prefer to say nothing, hoping that the tale, as it is unwound, will show that he was a boy of deeds rather than words, which was another of Jack's blemishes (see p. 41, also pp. 93 and 117). In conclusion, I should say that the work was in the first instance compiled as a record simply, at which we could whet our memories, and that it is now published for Michael's benefit. If it teaches him by example lessons in fortitude and manly endurance we shall consider that we were not wrecked in vain.[34]

The voice of this is unmistakably the voice of the narrator of *The Little White Bird* when he was both recreating the boys' adventure story and parodying the didacticism of its tone. It is also clearly the voice of an adult who offers the document as instruction for the boy, Michael, as well as a record of his childhood (proof, indeed, that he once was a child). But this question of voice is not restricted to the preface—it is evoked by the photographs themselves. For, in exactly the same way as the adult reveals himself here in the writing, the innocence of the photographs (the idyllic romping, the adventure) calls up the question of who—that is, which adult is taking them? Where, we ask, is the creator of these pictures, the very transparency of the image (boys presented to us so unequivocally at play, that is, *their* play and *their* story) uneasily evoking the necessary presence of the one who is watching (in this case, as we know, Barrie himself). Capturing a moment has, therefore, two meanings—the record of a past history which is lost (reconstituted so fully by Andrew Birkin in *J. M. Barrie and the Lost Boys*), and the seizing of the child by an image which, as the very condition of its effectivity, leaves outside its frame the look of the adult who creates it.[35]

What are we doing, therefore, when we put the child on the stage? This is not as uncalled for a question as it might seem. Barrie was a highly successful playwright when *Peter Pan* was first performed as a play in 1904, and it had been billed as his new theatrical extravaganza. The audience was made up of London's theatregoing elite, and there was hardly a child among them.[36] Calling *Peter Pan* a play for children, we have to ask not only what we think we are doing when we put the child on the stage, but also what we are doing when we assume, as we have for more than three-quarters of a century, that the child belongs in the audience.

The 1904–5 production script *of Peter Pan* and the 1905 script for Act I are prefaced with "A Note. On the Acting of a Fairy Play."[37] This note emphatically places the child on the stage, but it never once refers to any children in the audience. What distinguishes a fairy play from a realistic drama is the fact that all its characters are children: "This applies to the so-called adults of the story as well as to the young people."[38] I think that this has to mean by implication that children are not real. But they are the authors of the play which was "written by a child in *deadly* earnestness," and they are also behind the scenes: "The scenic artist is another child in league with them."[39] The whole performance and its staging is, therefore, given up to the child; but what about the child in the audience?

Barrie's note in fact indicates that stage space, in and of itself, redistributes in another form the divisions which lie behind any act of representation. There is an off-stage to the play, where Barrie's note puts the child as "scenic artist," but where the child in the audience cannot go, and which it is not allowed to see without risking the collapse of the whole stage illusion. And there is a barrier in the theatre between the stage and the audience, which the audience, for much the same reason, is not allowed to cross. The distinction between a pantomime and a real children's play (a distinction sometimes used mistakenly in relation to *Peter Pan*) is often made on this basis—what distinguishes a real play for children is that the child does not go on the stage and join in. The child is there precisely to watch what is happening, to query only up to the point of the limits on either side of the stage, and to recognise itself in the scenario which unfolds before its eyes. But that recognition also has its limits. The actors are mostly adults, and, as likely as not, there will be an adult with the child in the audience, watching the child at least as much as what is going on on-stage. If we want to call *Peter Pan* a play for children, therefore, we should start by recognising our place in its history and performance, and the complexity of the relations which once again lie behind the transparency of the term.[40]

Spectacle of childhood for *us*, or play for *children*? The question goes beyond the issue of trying to determine how many children might have seen *Peter Pan* (millions by now), or whether or not they said they liked it (for that you will find evidence either way).

When *Peter Pan* becomes a play, the first thing to notice is the way that this question of how a space of representation is being constituted for the child has been forced to the outer limits of its performance. *Peter Pan* takes the difficulties of *The Little White Bird*—of the adult-child relationship, and of how and why a story is told to the child—and either cuts them out completely, or reduces them to mere child's-play. From this point on in *Peter Pan*'s history we will see all these difficulties surfacing constantly in different forms, and just as constantly being suppressed. It is, however, the very definition of suppression—according to Freud at least—that it never really works, especially perhaps when what is being got rid of are all the queries, at the level of sexuality and language, which Freudian psychoanalysis was uncovering at exactly the same time that *Peter Pan* was being promoted and reproduced. As Freud himself puts it in another context: "The distortion of a text resembles a murder: the difficulty is not in perpetrating the deed, but in getting rid of its traces."[41]

Roger Lancelyn Green has pointed out that *Peter Pan* is the perfect adventure story.[42] A little boy breaks into a nursery and takes the children away to an island of redskins and pirates, where they act out the adventures which they normally read in books, before safely returning home. In *Peter Pan*, these adventures, with all their risk and danger, come true, but their threat is contained, first by Peter Pan himself who comes from the island to which he takes the children, and who has already been through the whole thing several times before, and secondly by the nursery which is the start and the finishing point of the whole story. This structure—of an exploration which is finally held in place by the world which we recognise and know as real—is one which is frequently used in children's fiction to this day. It is central to the early works of Alan Garner, and it forms the basis of Maurice Sendak's most famous book.[43]

Bringing the children home is one of the most striking things which happens in *Peter Pan* as a play. The child is put back in the nursery (the central battle was about this in *The Little White Bird*), and the act of telling stories is given to the little girl, Wendy. It is because of the stories which Wendy knows that she is invited to the island to tell stories to the lost boys. Mothers tell stories to their children, and nothing could be safer than that. As a play, therefore, *Peter Pan* assigns the act of telling stories to its socially recognisable context. The difficult relationship between the narrator and the boy child of *The Little White Bird* is turned into a relationship between a mother and her child. Hook is the male villain, but he so recognisably belongs to literary and theatrical convention that the sexual problem is dissolved. The success of *Peter Pan*, then, would stem from the way in which it brings together adventure fantasy and the recognisable domestic scene.

None of this, however, really works. Staging always carries with it something of the question of how things are done, as well as for whom, and by whom, they are produced, the question which the child first asks when confronted with the family drama. No nursery is ever *just* safe, and in *Peter Pan* it is the repository of much of the disturbance which was present in *The Little White Bird*. The play opens with the Darling children (the name of the family) playing at mothers and fathers, acting out the history of their own birth and stopping the game when there is one of them whom they do not wish to be born: "Michael. Am I not to be born at all?"[44] Peter Pan, like the child in the audience, watches from outside. This is the one performance in which he cannot play a part. The play therefore opens with the question of the child's place in the most familiar, and primary, of family scenes. It is a question which is repeatedly posed in the play, and it shows up in the most unlikely of places. On the island, Wendy tells the story of growing up and of life back in the nursery (this is unheard of in the adventure stories of Marryat, Kingston, and Henty, and in any case she had been invited to tell *Cinderella*). It is when Peter Pan challenges her story as untrue, and tells her that, like him, she will not be able to go home, that the whole island sequence breaks up and the children rush to depart. This leads to the final confrontation between Peter Pan and Hook, and then between Peter and Wendy after he has taken her back to the nursery. Barrie did not know how to end the play and the difficulty appears to have revolved around the two relationships—between Peter and Hook and between Peter and Wendy—in which the sexual difficulty had only seemingly been neutered.

There are in fact two conflicts in *Peter Pan*, that between the nursery and the Never Land (originally the Never Never Never Land), and that waged by Peter Pan against both. Thus Peter Pan attacks the family scene in the home underground and precipitates its break-up, but this is in turn attacked by Hook and the pirates who are waging war on Peter. Peter Pan, having differentiated himself from the children, is left behind and it is the children who are captured. Putting it crudely, we can say that this was not what Hook was after since his object was Peter himself. This produces a series of structural confusions and panics which spread across the different arenas of the spectacle—thus Hook tries to get at Peter and fails, Tinkerbell swallows the poison in order to save Peter, Peter comes *off*-stage in order to get the children in the audience to save Tinkerbell (the famous episode), and then goes off to save the children which leads to the battle with Hook. The fight between Peter and Hook has a clear logic in relation to the family drama—part of a retaliation fantasy, the completion of the oedipal circuit for John and Michael with Peter Pan exactly the "avenger" (Mr Darling and Hook almost invariably double in performance)—but it has the secondary effect of bringing Peter, who had been left behind, back up against the maternal nursery. Peter's battle with

Hook, therefore, leads to his accidentally siding with the nursery, and the difficulties of the final act can then be read in terms of the need to re-differentiate him.

In point of fact it is too easy to give an oedipal reading *of Peter Pan*. The father, Mr Darling, is humiliated—he plays a joke on Nana the nurse (the Newfoundland dog) which falls flat and then challenges the family: "Am I master in this house or is she?"[45] The children fly off and he crawls into the kennel out of shame. On the island, the children meet their father in another form, symbolically murder him through Peter Pan, and return home. Where-upon Mr Darling crawls out of the kennel and the children can grow up.

It is equally easy to describe the difficulties which Barrie had in writing, and especially in ending *Peter Pan*, in terms of the magic elusiveness of the play and the mystery of the eternal boy child: "no real beginning and no real end . . . obviously a little piece of immortality";[46] "there was behind this willingness to change a feeling that [this finale] was rather out of keeping with the character of Peter himself who, as is the case with creations of genius, was beginning to develop an independent personality of his own."[47] The drama of the performance—the fact that the actors were all sworn to secrecy and that no one knew how the play was going to end—can then be seen as appropriate to something which defies description, understanding, and even representa-tion, an intangible factor which can only add to the essential mystique of the play.[48]

I see these responses as related, because of their shared resistance to the idea of any trouble or disturbance in the play: whether that of the diffi-culty which always persists from any oedipal "resolution," or whether that of Barrie's own confusion which seems to have manifested itself in an almost physical inability to write the play down.[49] The problem of the ending can easily be exaggerated (for instance, revisions and major editing, right up to and even after the first performance, were a regular feature of pantomime production). On the other hand, looking through the different production scripts, programmes, reviews, and the various endings which they offer of the play, it is clear that the particular forms of hesitancy, at the level of writing and performance, belong in different ways to those questions about origins, sex-uality, and death which the play tries, unsuccessfully, to bring to a resolution.

The main problem is Peter Pan himself. How can he be got rid of or "resolved" given that it is the very definition of the child who does not grow up that he will always remain and constantly returns to the same place? Peter Pan is *stuck*, and the play with him. In all versions, Peter fails to answer the sexual query which Wendy puts to him when he invites her back to the island: "But what as, Peter, what as?," she asks, to which he replies "Your son" (not the reply she wanted); and his failure merely underlines the fact that the play cannot assimilate him to the "normality" which it has constructed all around him. But in the earliest versions *of Peter Pan*, this sexuality is far more explicit. There is a seduction attempt on the part of Tiger-Lily which is subsequently cut out. Furthermore, Peter recognises that Tinkerbell, Wendy, and Tiger-Lily all want the same thing which he cannot understand.

> *Peter.* Now then, what is it you *want*?
> *Tiger-Lily.* Want to be your squaw.
> *Peter.* Is that what you want, Wendy?
> *Wendy.* I suppose it is, Peter.
> *Peter.* Is that what you want, Tink?
> Bells answer.
> *Peter.* You all three want that. Very well—that's really wishing to be my mother.[50]

There is also the other side of this sexual refusal, Hook's desire for Peter, which in the earliest versions brings him hot on Peter Pan's tail and right into Kensington Gardens.[51]

The effect of all of this is that *Peter Pan* constantly slides into moments of excess (disavowal always has something of the overstatement about it), as the insistence on motherhood (Wendy as a mother to Peter as opposed to anything else) starts to go over the top. The best example is "The Beautiful Mothers Scene" which was performed for part of the first run of the play, in which the assorted mothers of London rush onto the stage to lay claim to the lost boys and are subjected to various tests of true maternity (the scene was mercifully cut during the first run).[52] But the same insistence can be seen in scenes which are still performed today, such as the front-scene of the final act in which the pirate, Starkey, has been taken prisoner by the Redskins and is left to watch over their babies (an unlikely combination, but one which has its logic here).

As was the case with *The Little White Bird*, there is an anxiety about sexuality and birth which goes hand in hand with this all-too-cloying innocence, sweetness, and light (the last act is called "Home Sweet Home"). In one of the earliest versions of the play's ending, Peter reacts with distress when Wendy claims as her own a baby who appears under a pile of leaves in Kensington Gardens where they are living together.[53] That distress is most

obvious in Barrie's *Afterthought*, the ending of the play which was only performed once in 1908.[54] Peter Pan returns to the nursery after many years and
finds Wendy a grown woman with a child. Faced with the "living proof" of the
irreducible difference between them (the fact of growing up and of passing
time), Peter goes to Wendy's daughter, Jane, with a dagger (the resistance is
already there in the title of the piece—conception as something which can
only be *thought* of, if indeed it *can* be thought of *after*). This version copes
with the crisis by having the child wake up and address Peter Pan with exactly
the same words that Wendy had used in the opening scene of the play which
then sets off the cycle again. This in itself shows how repetition, in the sense of
doing the same thing over and over again, serves above all to ward off something with which it is impossible to deal.

Between the lines of *Peter Pan*, we can see not only the question of origins
(mothers and fathers), and of sexuality (boys and girls), but also the reference
to death which is latent to the other two. An autographed addition to the
second draft of the 1908 ending gives us the term around which *Peter Pan*
endlessly circulates.

> Don't be anxious, Nana. This is how I planned it; if he ever came back.
> (You see—I think now—that Peter is only a sort of dead baby—he is the
> baby of all the people who never had one.)[55]

There is no way of talking about sexuality and origins without raising this as
an issue; but in a play for children it can, finally, have no place. The end of
Peter Pan, as it is best known, removes most of this. Peter Pan takes the
children home and then returns to the island, where Wendy visits him once a
year to do the annual spring-clean. The island is domesticated, Wendy will
grow up, and Peter Pan is sent back to where he came from (the ultimate
clean-up job we could say).

Peter Pan has, therefore, come into its own by the successive repudiation of
those questions which every child has the right to ask despite the fact—or
perhaps precisely because—they are virtually impossible to answer; questions
out of which *Peter Pan* was itself produced and without which Peter Pan's
innocence becomes not only lost as we know it, but also without meaning.
They are there, however, in the various trouble spots which remain in the play,
but perhaps even more in the demand that we continue to make on the child
that it should recognise itself in that scenario—both in the place of the child
spectator (which is also that of Peter Pan at the window), and in the happy
family scene which is so miraculously reconstituted before its eyes. *Peter Pan*

plays itself out with all the innocence of the symptom—which speaks what it intends, and exactly the opposite, at one and the same time.

In 1926, J. M. Barrie published a short story in an anthology for children, *The Treasure Ship*, called "The Blot on Peter Pan" (he originally called it "The Truth about Peter Pan" but changed the title for publication).[56] In this story, the narrator tells a group of children about how he based *Peter Pan* on his relationship with a little boy, Neil. Although written specifically with reference to the play, it has not been heard of since that first publication in 1926 (Roger Lancelyn Green refers to it as a "scrap of ephemera").[57] The story is a type of child's version of *The Little White Bird* which reintroduces the relationship between the writer and child which was cut out of *Peter Pan*, and gives back something of its difficulty. In this story, writing for the child is an act of rivalry *with* the child—the "truth" about, or "blot" on Peter Pan is his cockiness for vying with the narrator and trying to outdo him as a writer. On the opening night of *Peter Pan*, Neil produces his own play, in his own special language, and has it performed as an opening piece when the playwright is out of the theatre.

MACCD

MNO

OSAR

EMMA SEES DE GOLDFISH

This was a problem in three lines and a glass bowl that I had given to some youthful onlookers at that luckless Monday's rehearsal and it stumped them as it had stumped me when propounded to me once by a friend. I see it also stumps you, but debase yourselves sufficiently and you will find it reads:

> Emma sees de Goldfish
> 'Em no goldfish,
> Oh ess A are Goldfish.

You follow? I agree with you that 'tis but a tiny joke, and at once it passed out of all our minds save one. That mind was the awful mind of Neil. Though none was in the secret but his Nannie it was suddenly revealed to him how plays are written; quick as a lucky one may jump through a paper hoop and come out on the other side a clown, he had gained access through that friend of mine to a language which he could read, write and spell.[58]

The child's own play and its own language—not in the sense of some spontaneous and unspoilt form of expression which speaks for itself (another mystification), but a language which cannot simply be read, and which challenges our own. Neil's play is a rebus or puzzle (Freud, perhaps not coincidentally, used the model of the rebus for his method of interpreting dreams).[59] It breaks up the page and demands a special type of attention, inserting its difficulty into the otherwise perfect communication between the adult and child.

Playing with language—in this sense of undercutting its transparency and ease—is something else which has, for the most part, been pushed to the outer limits of children's writing. Edward Lear and Lewis Carroll are the best-known nineteenth-century exceptions, but Lear is covered by the fact that he wrote poetry (specifically designated as nonsense);[60] and Carroll's multiple use of the pun in *Alice* is generally recognised as something unique which tends to be related more to the eccentricity, or even madness, of the author than it is to the linguistic jests and verbal play of the child.[61] But this other side of language, as it appears here in this mostly forgotten story as an explicit challenge or threat to adult forms of speech, has largely been kept out of children's fiction in much the same way as the adult-child relationship implicit in telling stories has been dropped from *Peter Pan*. The two problems are in fact different forms of the question with which I started—that of our relationship to childhood and to language, and the way in which we constantly gloss over what is most uncomfortable, and yet insistent, in both.

It should be clear by now that what is important about *Peter Pan* is the very partial nature of the success with which it removes this problem from our view. But, if none of this is normally allowed into children's fiction, then what—we can legitimately ask—have children been given in its place?

15

Excerpts from *Albertine: A Novel*

It was a Friday afternoon late in August, damp and sultry, the air heavy. The sea breeze came halfway towards us and then seemed to be towed away. We were left, the three of us in the thickness of the day—Andrée and him and me. I don't think he was that ill, not then, so our sense of being dragged through something against our best will and purpose must have come from somewhere else. In any case I know I felt it fully as much as he did. And I know that we were already sharing something, passing it round between us, not quite frantically but with a fierce determination that no one of us should be landed with it, so that whatever was going on, however discomfiting, must never be allowed to stop. Our physical gestures were as they had come to be, fleet and playful. He was caressing the back of my neck, while I was running my fingers and letting them catch in her hair.

He wanted to know when we were leaving. The season was drifting to a close. Since he so dreaded the slightest change in his circumstances, he was trying to find something he could hold on to to the last. At the time, although I was still as it seemed his prime object, the terms of his courtship meant that he had also turned his attention to her. So it wasn't immediately clear to whom the question was addressed. We pulled away and looked at each other to see which of us would answer first. Since we gained no guidance from each other's confusion, we replied in one voice. And then muffled our amazement —although it is not clear who would have been betrayed had we revealed it. We had contradicted each other, and even worse—it was the first thin crack between us—had each spurted out exactly the opposite of what the other had guessed. "At least another month." "No longer than two weeks." "Then I will see you every other day," he said to me. "And you daily. To be fair to you both." So the one who had offered more was to be portioned. And the one who had hurried forward her departure would not, for as long as she was still within reach, be allowed to get away. But how he read us! For I had indeed hoped, by making myself more present, to reduce the heat of his expectation. Just as she had wanted to fan the flames by bringing the finale close. Effortlessly he had shut us inside our unspoken gambits and today I can only admire his talent. It set the pattern to come. Like a hidden alternator, he would break and reconnect the circuit, bringing one pair together, then, closing the shutter, block the one in front of him and open the conduit to the third. When it finally surfaced, his jealousy would be the product of his own craft. But in these early days what he knew best was how to make us restless, embarrassed by our eagerness, whether for less or for more.

I think it was that day, or perhaps the day after, that I invited him to my room. My aunt drifted in and out of the season, mainly leaving me to my own devices. But on this day she summoned me on one of her ventures. Before the evening was upon us, she had swept into the villa and gathered up everything she thought we both required. Not for the first time I had the impression that I belonged inside her suitcase. A former lady-in-waiting to a noblewoman from southern France whom she had encountered on one of her journeys with my uncle, had just married into the solid upper ranks of the Parisian bourgeoisie. The kind of progress my aunt most admired and an example for me. In the past she had always dismissed her as frivolous—insufficiently obsequious in her attendance on her mistress and far too flighty with everybody else. But now things had turned around and we were to return to the city without delay. As though she feared—thereby defeating her own purpose—that her friend's new-found status might at any moment disappear.

I had to be up at the crack of dawn and didn't want to disturb my friends so early. We had been basking in her absence, Gisèle, Rosamonde, Andrée, and I. Taking our nights slowly and never making our appearance until well into the following afternoon. We would blow on the embers of the evening to keep them alive until long after the dawn. Rushing for a train in the morning would have spoilt the luxury of a rhythm which relied on all of us keeping time. So I asked my aunt to book me into the hotel for a night. It was one of those things she could easily afford, and was indeed happy to grant me, since it gave her a grandiose sense of her own powers. Not for one moment did she suspect. I was determined to seduce him. Soiling my future was to be my avenue out of her absurdities. It would have the twin advantage of satisfying my curiosity and of ruining her carefully nursed plans.

I made my entrance into the hotel thrilled at no longer being confined to its public space. As for those who now had to serve me, I wanted them to remember me acutely while having to feign complete ignorance of my previous role. I loved the height of it. Our games had been all length and breadth. I think we felt that if we played things that way, spread ourselves horizontally, we could ignore the finely graded elevations which were the hotel's foundation and reason for being, the grounds on which it stood. I don't think I had ever looked up before. All around the lobby rose vast pillars of alabaster and marble crowned with gold-encrusted foliage, riches out of reach and hoarded uselessly at the top. The main staircase poured its carpet of roses from floor to floor before, halfway between the lower landing and the ground level, swelling out on either side like a pregnant frog. Even I could see that no one was quite meant to walk up this staircase. Like the three ladies in white crinolines, skirts swishing from step to step as I entered the lobby, three black-suited monocled gentlemen bending one step behind them in attendance, you had to be grand enough and high enough to make your descent. As I traveled up in the lift I felt the awe of someone suddenly elevated, who once, in another life, had been confined below stairs. I had never been level with the lights—all drooping crystal, scattering the currents which pulsed mechanically into the fragments of the glass. I wanted to stroke all the surfaces. Shamelessly they seemed to be reaching out to me for a response. I was so enraptured by the plushness that it took a while before I started to feel it closing in.

But, I thought, if my little band had been with me, we would swing out from the landing, wrap our legs around the white torsos of the pillars, and—to gasps of amazement or even applause, it would not be us who broke the silence—slide to the floor. It was a circus, after all.

My room was at the end of a corridor which went on so long it was as if, politely but firmly, I was being led back out on to the beach. When I finally arrived the room was dimmed with a grey-blue light, broken only by the sway of the curtains casting their shadow across the reflection of the sea. Everything looked as if it was moving. Red velvet, damask, mahogany gripped fast on to the walls and furnishings, but however much they boasted their solidity, they were powerless against the currents lifted into the room from the outside air. I knew that the proper response was not to be awed by the history on display but rather to run it back, without effort, into your own past. For as long as I stayed in this room, regardless of who I was before I entered, its lineage became mine. I couldn't be an interloper even if I tried. It was as if someone, without consulting you, had opened up a piece of costly litigation on your behalf. Only the sounds and the movement of the light, flickering at the far end of the room, stopped me from turning right around and walking back out through the door.

I laid out my few possessions and started to prepare for his visit, threw my pink satin dressing gown, with the fringe of its belt dangling, over the screen at the end of the bed, a half-undone corset, a silk stocking, my white-laced bodice, here and there, like confetti scattered incongruously by the bride. I had told him exactly at what time he should come. And also that he should tell absolutely nobody else. I was aware that this would mean some subterfuge on his part, since he had already been resident so long at this hotel that his every move and preference, in order to be properly catered for, had to be known in advance. I wanted the secrecy, but it was also my way of increasing our excitement before he so much as walked through the door.

I had suggested that he come at a time when I had already retired to bed. Resting and at his disposal—although I had used the excuse of a cold to explain why I had to have dinner, for which I had invited him to join me, in recline. I had often imagined such a scenario and gone to extraordinary lengths to produce reasons beyond my willpower as to why, against my upbringing and better judgment, I was so deliciously about to lapse. Something had to have happened which compelled me towards some small violation of the rules, making possible everything to come. I could happily avert any sense of transgression by turning it into a pressure I had to grapple with and of which I was innocent because it came from outside. As a child I had often pictured myself being captured and carried off. But not, as you might too readily assume, because I wanted to be ravished. Far from it. What looked like submission was camouflage. It was my way of concealing the true nature of an experience to be brought on at my bidding alone.

I loosened my hair in the way he had told me he liked it. When I played around on the beach or in the grounds it often became unclasped and I had always enjoyed its touch on my shoulders and neck. So far his delight concurred with my freedom. Even if the others mocked my display. Even if they already felt that my flagrancy was being too generously shared. As I sat waiting in my bed, I turned its dark curls in my fingers, letting them slip through the crevices, then wound them tighter and let go. I liked the contrast. I liked the softness as they slipped between the joints and then the tautness of my own pull. I was practising—unaware that the one thing that you cannot rehearse is a pleasure. Not, that is, if you have in mind to share it with somebody else. There was a whole world to cross, as I was to discover, between my indolent, self-caressing gesture and the games that were about to begin.

He came into the room holding an ebony stick I had never seen before, and stopped, one hand to his moustache, with his chin a fraction in the air. This was his territory and his home. He belonged. His awareness of the fact that I didn't gave him a certain arrogance, but it was slight and immediately tempered by his concern. He would protect me, not from himself, but from everything oppressive about the social charade you became part of once you officially or properly entered this hotel. He always had the finest sense of our social inequality, hoping to find a way of redeeming my relative poverty without rubbing it in. But if he looked confident he also looked almost aghast. Something extra had drained from the customary pallor of his face. His black hair, normally boyish, was pressed hard against his temple, small beads of moisture were barely visible at the top of his brow. Everything else—his mouth, his cheeks—had gone dry and white at their own heat. It was as though his daring—and up to that point it had never occurred to me that he too might have something to dare—excited but also appalled him. He seemed to be asking, "What on earth are we doing here? Is this the only way for us to endanger what we both hate most?" All at once, our setting started to feel like an insult. It made a mockery of what was finest about our ambitions, of the best plans that we had unconsciously formed for each other: to use the other as a means of pulling ourselves away—for me from a social, and for him from a no less constant, physical distress.

You might want to say that ours was just about as conventional an arrangement between a man and woman as could be. She hands over her favours in return for his prestige. But ours was no ordinary situation. It was in the nature of his body and my status dramatically to raise the stakes. Even in the normal course of events, when such accommodations are expected although largely unspoken, there is a risk. In every encounter—however fumbling, however graced—the woman must sweep away the phantom of failure; while the more he hastens to raise her standing and deflects her from her class, the more he shows his revulsion at what she is struggling to leave behind. What infinite potential for humiliation! In our case it was made richer by his frailty and by my history, which disappeared beyond any strata into the unknown. I was so much the bolder only because I was already so demeaned. Not that it is easy for a woman to wrap herself around the body of a man as he stoops.

How could anyone ever succeed at such a task? Is that why they say that lovers are reborn? And why passion is so urgent and so brief? Because it has to gamble everything against the relics of its own past. Not just allaying, but pretending that there was never anything to fear. What kind of conjuring act is this? It was to be our peculiar magic to chart the agonies of such spurious arrangements. In my stronger moments I like to think it was a mark of our quality. We were to be granted our desires, but inside out. What we sought to leave behind would drive us so hard that it would never disappear. Instead it would show up as our unwelcome but devoted companion. He would raise me to the stars and then shut out the lights, like a master of ceremonies who suddenly decides to stop his own show, or turn his players and audience blind. And I would please him beyond his wildest dreams. But the more I did so the more I became his tormentor, body and soul.

All this is clear to me now, but even had I seen it then I am not sure that things would have turned out any differently. It was a delusion of his—it fuelled his intensity—to believe that understanding is the same as changing or redeeming yourself. So even though I can see it now, I still wish I could go back to the beginning, to those first moments in the room when what over-powered me, alongside the fraught nature of his attention, was the joy he took from being so intimately and unexpectedly in my presence. I could see the relish in his eyes, the way he noted my negligent hair, his reluctant excitement at the fall of my nightclothes, all creases and openings, over my skin. His response played beautifully to my tune. There could be no danger, not now, not ever, because his delight felt beckoned and prepared.

We hardly talked. In fact I cannot remember a word that we said, since what followed came so unremitting and so fast. He moved towards me and sat on the edge of the bed, looking at us as if our lives depended on it. I had never been that close, never been alone with him before. I had never felt him breathing. I had never had the occasion—there had always been too much noise and mental clutter—to watch the rise and fall of his chest. You are not alive unless you are moving, even if imperceptibly to yourself and others, all the time. You are not alive unless your heart is pumping the air through your lungs without fail. Increase the pace and it is not always obvious if someone is more alive or less. Why do we talk of bodies being transported? Do we ever ask ourselves how or where they are supposed to stop? As he caught his breath, I had no way of telling whether I was to be the occasion for his utmost fulfillment or distress. Just for a second, the danger and the passion circled round me before returning to their own place. I knew they had been for me, but it was unclear what he had wanted me to do with them, whether I was meant to excite him or haul him back. Such a question was not one I was expecting to have to put to myself. I was not expecting to have to think at all. As his face came towards me I could barely see it, except to register a look as ecstatic as it was remote. The closer he got to me the further he appeared to be travelling from himself. It crossed my mind with the speed of light that I was being summoned to an embrace in which at least one of us was to be lost. I was frightened not because I was vulnerable or in his power, although in one sense both these were of course true. The terror came from what he was letting me see. Later I would discover that, in his eyes, it was the risk which empowered him. It made him feel that, with nothing more to play for, the universe was in his hands. But for me at that moment, it was like looking into a crystal ball and watching yourself die.

As he flung himself towards me, I moved my head to one side of the pillow. If he landed it would not be on the softness of my face. You cannot, I am told, smother yourself. Almost falling, he reached out, so as to steady himself, for the arm which I had started to raise above my head. And then—recognising my purpose—he watched disbelieving while I pulled as hard on the bell cord as I could. We both froze. First shrill, and then duller and duller, the sound travelled—carrying me with it—through the thickness of the walls and out into the big wide world of the hotel.

We had had the unlikely experience of breath mingling without the accompanying embrace. Against all the evidence of the senses—since I am not sure we even touched—all I wanted was to pull us apart. As soon as I rang the bell he made to leave the room. But he did not believe it. He knew, as I did, that there could be no such conclusion except according to a set of rules which we had already irrevocably broken even if, to an innocent eye, it might appear that nothing had taken place. I had tried to fall back on etiquette, but neither of us was fooled. It would make no difference at our next meeting when I told him, flaunting my best outrage, that he was never to try again. It was my futile attempt to pretend that nothing, bar a misunderstood flirtation, a boy who tried to go too far, had happened. But I was sure there would be a sequel. I knew that we now belonged together. Never before had I felt so solicitous— both for myself and another—and so aroused. What had passed unstated between us gave new meaning to the idea of seeing something through to the end. It was to be my subsequent misfortune that I would never manage to communicate to any of the parties involved that none of my preferences had changed. If all my former pleasures were affected, it is because from that day onwards I couldn't help but take my sexual bearings from him. But if they radiated out from his centre, it didn't follow that their orbit would be any less wide. And, as we were all to discover, it wasn't obvious—not to me or to anyone else—whether I wanted to hand myself over to him completely or flee.

From this day on, a man's and a woman's body, the delight they gave me, would set off on endlessly separating lines. But although they were never to meet, I could never enjoy one without it provoking my need for the other. To this day I do not fully understand why my desire to take things further became so intense. I would go in pursuit of him with a grim but enchanted sense of prophecy. Dreadful as it was, that first evening seemed to hold the secret to something else. He had made me believe he was the one who, for better or worse, would teach me what it felt like to be out of this world.

As I think back on it today, I date the beginning of our disaster to one day that summer at the dance. I felt so sure, so confident, that all the different pieces of my life were safe. I should have been more suspicious. Mostly the fragments felt in danger of collision and I would put them at arm's reach, whereas on this day for some reason they seemed to be endlessly moving but each one gyrating perfectly in its own place. I think I believed that I could keep everything and everyone alive by nurturing my private knowledge. It was all locked away blindly inside my own head. For the first time for a very long time, there we were, all three of us—Andrée, he, and I—somewhere in the same room.

In the hotel the grandest space of all was the ballroom. It was solid like an ocean liner but, since no one ever stopped there, provisional like the sea. Whichever way you looked, it was declaring its mastery of space. This is harmony, this is proportion. Magnificence which will never perish because each line and detail offers to every other such unhesitant, unwavering support. Everything in the room always seemed to me to be smiling at everything else. Wall to wall of wooden floors polished so hard that you looked down at faces plunged beneath a lake. Mirrors to the ceiling framed by pure white mould-ings in the shape of ribbons and bows, so the whole room appeared to be moving under the skirts of an ivory satin ball dress. And the biggest, brightest chandelier I had ever seen, scattering its rays, bathing us all in glory, a chorus of tiny glistening gems raising their voices to the heights. As I danced I could feel its shadow hovering over me like a giant moth, wings in perpetual move-ment, while we slid and trod, bodies gliding across the floor, oblivious to its pale, barely discernible reflection breaking and closing beneath our feet.

On the dance floor we were all equal. There was so much light and space around us that, whatever happened, however distressing, you could be sure that something in the atmosphere would make it evaporate. Whisk it off. Or drown it—the waves would close over again, not a ripple to be seen. Without registering the slightest tremor. I am sure that it was the emptiness which made this room feel so welcoming to me. Vast enough and gracious enough to

308 THE JACQUELINE ROSE READER

absorb any slight without a blush. We have seen it all. Everything nodded benignly in agreement. You will not be able to shock us. Nothing could ever go wrong here.

He would never dance with me. There he would sit, in his dark suit and buttoned black patent shoes, legs crossed, face supported in the palm of his hand, watching while he chatted to one of his friends. His thin black eyebrows, almost meeting in the centre, ran a stark line across the white of his brow. But he didn't look as if he were frowning, rather concentrated and haughty, if somewhat mystified by his own distaste. His cupped chin, as always, was slightly raised. His moustache, thicker now than when I first met him and curling up a fraction at the ends, concealed an upper lip with the fullness of a girl's. A perfect white orchid, pale but crisp, like an ivory carving of itself, was pinned to his lapel.

I marvelled at the way his eyes followed us round the room while engaging his companion with the perfect dose of intensity. Just enough for the other not to feel insulted or neglected. At least, if it crossed their minds for a moment, they never let it show. I couldn't even be sure that they had noticed the obsessive concentration he managed, throughout their dialogue, to bestow on me. For some reason, I was quite confident that I was not the object of their joint attention. Oh, I know that men love to boast, but they weren't, I assure you, talking about me. I could bear his eyes all over me, even in public, so long as it was strictly between us. Our affair. Wasn't that our arrangement? He was not going to share me with anyone. He would simply divide himself in half. With you I will be debonair. To you, a fox. I put any trust in his possessiveness. Wrongly as it turned out. His lids looked heavier and more drooping from a distance. He only ever looked to me like a dandy in this room.

On this particular high-season summer evening all three of us, plus several of my little band, were there together amid the grandest company of the hotel. It was unusually warm. None of us was used to the heat, which rarely crept this far up the coast. I could feel the droplets gathering on my skin. It was as if a plague had hit the town and we were all waiting. On whose body would the dreaded signs first break? It made dancing an act of cruelty. Gingerly, gingerly, we all went. Back and forwards, back and forwards. Arms lilting and outstretched, hardly touching, tips of fingers to tips of fingers. Hands brushing the small of your back. No whirring around. Not even a hint. Today we all had a secret. We passed it round the ballroom from one to the other without anyone having to speak. I felt I was listening to the ever-repeating overture of a concerto which none of the musicians had intended to play.

Andrée was busy at her own game. Like—but then again quite unlike—his. She was flirting with a tall blond boy to whom she always granted just enough attention to keep him both on the ready and at bay. But she would look across at me whenever the chance arose. I could feel it even without looking back. Of course I would be lying if I didn't admit that being so intimately linked to him and to her without either of them suspecting gave me an exhilarating feeling of power. Not the kind of excitement which would lead me to drop my caution. Not in that room, not on that night. I am always careful. I have long known that if you want to maximise your pleasure, you should always start by being circumspect. Tonight all my instincts in that direction were buoyed by the general mood. Who was meant to know? Who was meant to see? Are you surprised that I started to get confused? That I made what I now see as my first serious mistake? I believed—wrongly—their ignorance would be my cover. How foolish to think that just because you are in the know, you won't be the one groping in the dark.

It all started when the two Jew girls wafted into the room. There they went, all free and easy—he called them slatterns—meandering up and down through the tables along the side, their white muslin slipping off their shoulders, like two beautiful silver snakes. Only one of them had dark hair. You could feel the thickness fit to pull on piled up against all the laws of gravity on her head. Her face was too long, but not wan. Not a flicker of pathos. Such a large, lush face was the backdrop for features more extravagant and handsome, I thought, than I had ever seen. They swelled and pushed, against all posturing, into everyone else's carefully nurtured poise. Next to her her sister looked dressed. She was giving far less away. Everything about her was curled under and folded inside. But you got glimpses. Her eyes swept up to the corners of her brow, where they seemed to be about to slide happily off the edge of her face. Because she was so much smaller, she had to reach up to the arm of her sister, who seemed to be half lifting, half dragging her along. It made the taller one look as if she had chosen to go out walking accompanied by her marionette.

These girls were notorious. Shameless in a way I would never have dared to be. They weren't trying to shock anyone. Not like my little band in our youth, as I liked to call it, stretching years behind me like gauze. They really didn't care what anybody thought. They existed on their own terms. I knew that, in this world, we were meant to look down on them. But from where I was standing to be so flagrant was luxury untold. They may have been outsiders, but to my mind they embodied the proud spirit of the ballroom more than anybody else. Nobody could touch them. They could be sure they would go on for ever simply because they already had. Back to the beginning, they trailed their strength, flying in the face of a world that hated them. Would this be what it meant to belong? Really belong? A class. Why mock them for that? I would rather—a million times over—have been lost and lost and lost to the world, and then left to create my own with creatures like myself, than lost and, as the final insult, picked up as I had been, dusted over, found.

I looked round the room for Andrée. She could be my partner. We had danced together here many many times before without the faintest hint of scandal. There always seemed to be more girls and women than men in the ballroom. Or perhaps it was just that so many of the men held themselves back against the walls, moulding themselves into the pillars. Atlas holding up the universe. We are the loadbearers of this great hall. Immovable. Of course he was never like that, even if just by sitting there he took on some of the stubborn superciliousness of their line. But as I scanned the room to all its corners, he looked diminished. He faded back into the glow of the white. Perhaps I thought that, because he seemed almost invisible, he could no longer see me?

I wanted to find Andrée because I was starting to panic. Those girls. I could see they had spotted me. Were they watching? Could we, just by a glance, eyes barely brushing, all tell what we liked? It is one of the strangest things about love between women—between men perhaps, for all I know—that it leaves you, in the early stages at least and as the necessary prelude to plunging beyond them, so utterly dependent on a world of codes and signs. If I took Andrée on to the dance floor, we could swirl around as we always did until they took notice. While pretending not to see. Why didn't I think of the risk? Why didn't I reckon with the possibility that everything would turn the other way round? I would use Andrée to send my silent message invisibly to them across the room. Why did it never occur to me that their greatest delight—their generosity—would lie in their frankness, that they would respond, metaphorically speaking at least, with open arms? They were so splendidly unabashed. In their eyes precautions were a joke. One, two, three, they started to sidle across to us on the floor. Mimicking us, showing they had got the message, and then leading us on, and then on and on. We were two duos on the way to being a quadrille. As I held Andrée to me a little too close for the weather, their wonderfully outspoken gestures started to work their magic. Let's face it, we were pushing our luck. Cheek to cheek, breast to breast. A touch such as no man on earth will ever enjoy. All the pressure above the waist, and a slow slow moistness collecting between our legs with nothing—girls can be confident, it is our little privilege—to show. But something had broken. When I glanced in his direction, I could see another man in his group, a real killjoy and spoilsport whom we had crossed in the hotel more than once, turn and point, flushed and angry, across the room. The effect was instantaneous. His audacity—his crude, plump, thrusting finger making tracks through the dance floor—swept the cover from ours. Before I had time to register, all my care, the whole beautifully constructed edifice which had hidden me to date, started crumbling. By the time we had finished dancing, it lay there in shards beneath me, vanishing into nowhere at my feet.

PART IV Interventions

Interventions

Newspaper opinion pieces and speeches might not typically find a home inside an academic reader. Such public interventions are generally tied to current events and written for a particular historical moment, rather than intended to make a lasting contribution to a research field. Yet any neat segregation between Rose as a "public intellectual" and as an academic theorist would be disingenuous given how deeply her political commitments inspire and pervade her scholarly work. Presenting Rose's academic writings alone would mean overlooking her dedication to placing ideas in the public arena in the service of social and political change. Particularly in recent years, her elegant and forceful contributions to the *London Review of Books* and the *Guardian*, among other influential print and broadcast media outlets, have formed a crucial strand of her career.

Although Rose had engaged with questions of Jewish history and anti-Semitism in her work on Plath and Dorothy Richardson and with Israel in *States of Fantasy* of 1996, her career reached a new level of public engagement in 2005 with the publication of *The Question of Zion*, her first book-length treatment of the vexed psychopolitical questions surrounding Israel-Palestine; the urgency of finding a way out of the political deadlock made reaching an audience beyond academe not merely desirable but also essential. She describes that book as an extended footnote to Edward Said's *The Question of Palestine*, and the late Palestinian-born intellectual—who sought desperately to redress the historic injustices perpetrated against his people—remains an evident lodestar for Rose, as a Jewish woman protesting against the Israeli state brutalities waged in the name of the Jewish people. Rose's increasingly vocal opposition to the policies of the Israeli state led her to co-found the high-profile protest organization Independent Jewish Voices (ijv) in 2007, and, the following year, to publish *A Time to Speak Out*, a collection of essays by dissident Jewish voices edited by Rose and three other ijv signatories.

If Rose's participation in the media dissemination of ideas is somewhat unusual for an Anglophone academic, it certainly aligns with the more common Continental view of the public role of academics—reflecting perhaps the influence of Rose's French academic training. The pieces we've included in this short section show Rose as a thinker responding to the political exigencies of her time. "Infinite Justice" was part of a symposium of short responses by regular *London Review of Books* contributors to the terrorist attacks of 11 September 2001; Rose calls for a more complex and provisional conception of justice than the absolutist notions promulgated by the George W. Bush administration. Such is Rose's agility as a writer that she can here treat in 350 words the topic which she'd earlier explored at length in "Just, Lasting, and Comprehensive." In "We Are All Afraid, but of What, Exactly?"—a newspaper piece published at the outbreak of the Iraq War—Rose demonstrates how psychoanalytic ideas can be brought to bear in mainstream political debate. We should, she writes, "be asking what fantasy we are being required to sustain. America's aim of 'full spectrum dominance' is like the rage of a child when he hits the limits of his powers."

Most of these occasional pieces emerge out of Rose's preoccupation with Israel-Palestine, which forms the nucleus of her public persona. We include the speech Rose delivered in a public debate in London in 2005, when, along with the prominent Israeli "new historian" Avi Shlaim and the award-winning *Ha'aretz* correspondent Amira Hass, Rose argued in favor of the motion that "Zionism Today Is the Real Enemy of the Jews." Against all predictions, and despite huge pressure on the organizers to cancel the event, the motion was carried against an opposition comprising the right-wing columnist Melanie Phillips, the former Israel foreign minister Shlomo Ben-Ami, and the Hebrew University academic Raphael Israeli. Here, too, is Rose's contribution to the "Responses to the War in Gaza," published by the *London Review of Books*, in January 2009, alongside short pieces by intellectuals and writers such as Tariq Ali, Eric Hobsbawm, Rashid Khalidi, Ilan Pappe, John Mearsheimer, and Eliot Weinberger. Once again, Rose joins a community of public intellectuals, but her contribution to this symposium sits alongside the voice of Israeli dissidence, as a Diaspora Jew—a position which invariably attracts the charge of anti-Semitism or Jewish self-hatred.

Rose's comment on Caryl Churchill's play *Seven Jewish Children* mounts a defense of a play that had been denounced as anti-Semitic by writers such as novelist Howard Jacobson. In "Holocaust Premises: Political Implications of the Traumatic Frame," originally written for an exchange with Judith Butler held at Royal Holloway in Senate House, University of London, Rose discusses the continuing centrality of the Holocaust to the psychic life of the Israeli state and how the Jewish people's most traumatic collective memories remain acted out in state policy today. Far from sitting oddly with the rest of the reader, the pieces in this section form a fitting conclusion to a book that set out to showcase the work of a scholar whose formidable learning and originality takes her well beyond the call of an academic's duty to raise the tenor of public debate on some of the most urgent political questions of our time.

—*Justin Clemens and Ben Naparstek*

16

"Infinite Justice"

"Infinite Justice"—the provisional, perhaps already discarded name for the coming U.S. military operation—could have meant recognising that justice is not the property of any one man, nation, or even religion. Knowing that the just course in dangerous times requires slowing down historical time, making "time for time" to cite a Jewish proverb; pausing, not as a gesture before the real action begins, but pausing for thought. Acknowledging that those who behave unjustly, you could say "inexcusably," may even so, in terms of the distribution of the globe's resources, also have justice on their side. The victims of injustice—last week, unequivocally, the U.S.—are not always, automatically, just. The state of Israel, for example, was founded on the back of a horror perpetrated against the Jewish people which was for some the worst, for others the culmination of the injustices carried out against the Jewish people over centuries. This has not made the state of Israel just towards the Palestinians. We should be wary, above all, of the language of righteousness. As we watch our Prime Minister binding us once again to the United States, not as bellicose in his rhetoric as Bush, but unswerving in his belief, we might choose to remember that less than a week before September 11, in Durban, Britain was involved in blocking an attempt by the world's 300 million indigenous peoples—Maoris, Aboriginals, and Native Americans—to have their rights protected under international law.

Infinite justice could involve recognising these complexities. We talk of infinite compassion or mercy. But if, instead, infinity has been claimed for our hold over justice, then we are in danger of believing—like the Islam now held accountable for all the ills in the world—that our justice, and our justice alone, is divinely sanctioned and follows the path of God. Then infinite justice is most likely to mean—with dreadful and unpredictable consequences for some of the poorest, most deprived, peoples of the world—being struck ad infinitum (the struggle, we are told, will be long), being pounded over and over again.

17

We Are All Afraid, But of What, Exactly?

Fear is in the air. It is being manipulated to ratchet up the fever of war. More than once, Tony Blair has insisted that if there is one word which explains his passionate conviction, it is "fear." And yet it is not clear exactly where or to whom the fear belongs. This alone, together with all the other reasons for opposing this war, should make us suspicious.

We were told we should be very frightened indeed of Saddam Hussein, although the threat from his regime to Britain and the U.S. is negligible. So we were told we should be frightened of him at some unspecified future date when terrorists will access the weapons he will develop if not disarmed. It is in fact far more likely that such weapons are being accessed in Russia right now. It is also far more likely that we will become the object of such attacks as a consequence of this war.

The government has told us we should start laying in supplies for an unknown, unpredictable assault. A group of children interviewed about the war spoke of their fear of an attack on England by Iraq as if this were a war rather than an invasion. Fear is all over the place, endlessly exploitable, impossible to pin down. In his preface to last September's National Security Strategy of the U.S.A., George Bush states: "The war against terrorists of global reach is a global enterprise of uncertain duration." The task is interminable. We are being asked to enter into a state of infinite war.

It would be naïve not to recognise that since September 11, many of us are indeed living in a new era of fear. I find myself envying my mother for having brought up her daughters in what might well come to look like a bubble of relative safety, for the citizens of central Europe at least, stretching from 1945 to 2001. One of the most disturbing things about September 11 was that the attack was so visible in the skies, the agents a multiplicity of proliferating invisible cells. This is the exact reverse of Kosovo, where it was not the agent—the strutting boastful Milosevic—but his crimes, the mass graves, that had to be found. So let us take out a villain who all the world knows to be a villain and who all the world can see. It is meant to make "us" feel better.

Reporting recently from Washington on Channel 4 News, David Smith described the U.S. rhetoric of war as "low on specifics, high on fear." High on fear is right, although he may well not have intended this second meaning. If fear is so manipulable, it is because it is also exciting. "Shock and awe" sounds less like a threat than a rallying cry.

Fear of the unknown is, of course, the most powerful fear of all, because it tells us that we are vulnerable in ways we cannot control. Writing in the middle of the First World War, Freud remarked that wars encourage us to see death as drama and catastrophe, rather than as something natural which we will all get round to doing in good time. As if in response to September 11, which gave us such a breathtaking image of death as disaster, the U.S. seems intent on creating a world in which death—or rather our deaths—can be averted (even if maintaining this delusion requires that a lot of other people will have to die). In the days following September 11, the same news networks which endlessly recycled the image of the collapsing towers pulled the footage of bodies falling to the ground. This was out of respect for the dead, but as one American film professor suggested, it also stems from the Western attitude that bodies must not be seen to die.

Invoking fear in politics is a dangerous game. As he rallies us to war, Blair seems to be saying simultaneously: we have never been so vulnerable, we have never been so sure. Perhaps the rhetoric is unconvincing, not just because we were never given the evidence, but because he has been unintentionally more effective than he realises. We are left, not with the strength of his conviction, but of his fear. War is no solution to fear.

Behind the argument for war, we can therefore glimpse another fear—fear of impotence—which no one is talking about. In government circles you only name a fear if you can blast it. When Bush talks of securing a new world order, when supporters of the war speak of liberating the people of Iraq, we should not just be questioning whether this, rather than oil or control of the Middle East, is the true motive. We should also be asking what fantasy we are being required to sustain. America's aim of "full spectral dominance" is like the rage of a child when he hits the limits of his powers. Except that unlike the raging child, the U.S., as the strongest military might in the globe, has the capacity to unleash forces a child can only dream about. Against the official credo, it is this, I believe, that we— not to speak of the thousands of Iraqis whose possible deaths we are meant to be able to contemplate with impunity—should be most frightened of.

18

Why Zionism Today Is the Real Enemy of the Jews

We meet two days before the anniversary of the liberation of Auschwitz, and in a week when there have been a series of vicious attacks on young Jewish men in North London. How—I know many of you will be thinking—can the statement of this motion be true? How can Zionism today, rather than Jew-hatred, be the real enemy of the Jews?

Let me say straight away that in supporting this motion you are not being asked to deny the momentousness of the Holocaust, nor indeed the increase in anti-Semitism today. Nor, perhaps even more crucially, although it should not need stating, Israel's right to exist. What you will be supporting—if you support this motion—is a very simple idea. That the nation of Israel, and the Zionism on which it was founded, are in urgent need of the most profound reckoning with themselves.

What then is Zionism? Zionism is not one thing—it is and always has been crucially contested from within. We can define Zionism as the movement for the national self-determination of the Jewish people. But you can interpret this in different ways. Way back in the 1930s and 40s, Ahad Ha'am, founder of spiritual Zionism, argued that the Balfour Declaration gave the right to estab-lish a homeland *for* the Jewish people in Palestine, but not the right to remake Palestine as the exclusive national home *of* the Jewish people. "What nation," asked Martin Buber two weeks after the declaration of the state of Israel in 1948, "will allow itself to be demoted from that of majority to that of minority without a fight?" "Where do truth and justice determine our deeds?"

Recently I came across these words of Gudi Gofberg, a young Jewish soldier serving in an occupied village in the Golan Heights in 1973, words he wrote after spending the night in a bombed-out school, warming himself by a fire made out of pupils' desks.

Every front has a back . . . and if in the front the desert was blooming, in the back Palestinian olive trees were being uprooted, and if in the front Israeli culture was flourishing, in the back Palestinian culture was withering, and if in the front Israelis had dignity, in the back Palestinians were humiliated. The Israelis have made their pleasure contingent on Palestinian suffering.

We are often told that the Jewish state is peace-loving and that every act of aggression it undertakes purely in legitimate self-defense. But Israel was created on the back of the dispossession of 800,000 Palestinians. 413,000 inhabitants of 213 villages had been displaced from their homes before a single shot was fired in the war of 1948. That the Jews felt the need, desperately, for a homeland after the horrors of the Second World War, and indeed the pogroms before, is not in dispute. But I ask you—how can the creation of a Jewish nation on the back of the suffering—or, in the words of our soldier on the Golan Heights, the humiliation—of another people, how can this not be dangerous for the Jews?

Now you might argue instead, not that Zionism was innocent, but that this is how nations have to be founded and that no nation can do otherwise and that the Jews had a unique historical case. So let me make another point. Up to very recently the dispossession of the Palestinians was never mentioned in the histories of the nation. Even today those who argue, as I would, that Israel was created on the back of an historic injustice towards the Palestinians still awaiting redress, are accused of betrayal. But the truth cannot betray you. Only lies can. If Zionism requires the Jewish people to deny, or gloss, what is now a central, defining, part of their own history, then is that not surely dangerous for the Jews?

We are often told that to critique Zionism is to fuel rising anti-Semitism in the world. We need to pause here. If this is true, then why is it that the two countries in Europe with the lowest rate of anti-Semitic incidents—Denmark and Holland—are the same countries where the general population is most critical of the actions of the Israeli state? To those who argue that to critique Zionism is to fuel anti-Semitism, I would say that the opposite is the case. It seems to me to be sheer folly, another form of self-blinding, not to recognise that Ariel Sharon's policies—targeted assassination, curfew, collective punishment, house demolition—are playing their part in the rise of anti-Semitism today. They are not the sole cause of anti-Semitism. But it is Sharon who claims that in enacting these policies he acts for the Jewish community/worldwide. It is Sharon who insists that what Israel does, it does in the name of all Jews. These policies are not making the Jewish people safe, not in Israel, not across the world. Last year I was at a meeting of Israelis and European Jews. "An unjust Israel," a retired Israeli army colonel said to the Europeans among us, "harms you."

And how can Jewish people possibly hope to defeat anti-Semitism, on the grounds of the universal rights of all human subjects, if they do not speak out against the abuse of those rights by the state purporting to represent them? If you support this motion you will be sending out a clear message that the Jewish people stand for the universal rights of citizens regardless of race, colour, religion, or creed. When I read next to each other on the same page of the newspaper that attacks on Jews in London are increasing and that the government's children bill dispenses asylum and immigration authorities of the obligation to protect the welfare of children, I fear for the asylum seeker and the immigrant, as we Jews in Europe once were, as much as for myself. Unless we make such common cause, we are all in danger.

I speak here tonight as a Jewish woman who is proud to be Jewish. But the Jewishness of which I am proud is not the one embodied by the form of Zionism in the ascendant today, which makes me tremble. It is not the Jewishness of Esther pleading with Ahasueras or Ahashverosh for another day of slaughter against the enemies of the Jews: "Thus the Jews smote all their enemies with the stroke of the sword, and slaughter and destruction, and did what they would unto those that hated them."

But there is another Jewish ethic, captured by the spirit of the jubilee called for in Leviticus; that every fifty years all those who became slaves as a result of debt should be freed, and all family lands sold out of need any time over the past fifty years should be returned to their owners. I am not, just in case you were starting to wonder, suggesting that is what Israel should do. It's an ideal of course but it's a better one, and it's light years from what is happening in Israel today, where in secret session, and with the stroke of a pen, the Israeli cabinet decided on July 8 this summer to declare all property in East Jerusalem owned by residents of the West Bank absentee property that can therefore be seized by the state without compensation or appeal.

Let me stress again. We are not talking about turning back history. Israel has a right to exist. Nor are we denying the resurgence of anti-Semitism in Europe and across the Arab world. We are talking about recognition, about the capacity to transform oneself. You all know the expression: "He is his own worst enemy." It is in this sense that we can say that Zionism today has become the enemy of the Jews.

I urge you to support us. If you do, you will be sending out a message all around the world—I believe the interest in this evening has been, how shall I put it, far-reaching and intense—that the Jewish people did not survive attempted genocide to become the brutal oppressors of another people. Enough. No more. There is a better ethic and there can be a better, safer, future for the Jews.

19

Reflections on Israel's 2008 Incursion into Gaza

The only abiding law for Israel in this onslaught seems to be the ethics of self-defence, and yet Israel's defence cannot be secured by such a path and there are, it would seem, no ethics. How can such unrestrained and indiscriminate violence—a hundred, and more, dead for every Israeli, including hundreds of children—be justified? "We are very violent," the commander of the Yahalom unit observed, according to *Ha'aretz*. "We do not balk at any means to protect the lives of our soldiers." Another senior IDF officer was reported as commenting on the offensive so far, "It's not the movie, it's only the coming attractions," with a knowing smile.

If it sometimes seems as if a new limit has been breached, we need to trace this language back to the creation of Israel and before, to the founding belief that Israel would be the redemption for the historic suffering, and passivity, of the Jews, a belief given new urgency by the genocide in Europe and which would lay the grounds for the ruthless dispossession of the Palestinians. At a rally in support of Israel's war in Gaza in Trafalgar Square, one banner read: "We will not be victims again." As the rally dispersed, those of us protesting as Jews against Israel's actions were spat at and met with cries of "Kapos." The Holocaust is still the felt justification, in the midst of this new war. Israel is the fourth most powerful military nation in the world, yet it lives in a permanent state of fear, always fighting the last war.

So while everyone is asking "Who is the aggressor?," another equally important question is going unasked. Who claims the monopoly of suffering? Whose suffering is felt to warrant a form of state power that is above the law? Already we are being told that there will be no legal reckoning. Faced with war crimes allegations in the past, Israel has blocked all attempts by the UN to investigate its conduct and it is not a signatory to the International Criminal Court.

To say this is in no way to diminish the traumatic impact of the Holocaust but to register it all the more powerfully. The effect of trauma is precisely to freeze people in time. There is a psychological dimension to this conflict that seems almost impossibly difficult to shift. In its own eyes, Israel is never the originator and agent of its own violence, and to that extent its violence is always justified. The Palestinians do not count. Even when the worst of what has been done to them is registered inside Israel, it is still the Israeli who suffers more.

We are all waiting to see what Barack Obama will do. My hope is that he is ring-fencing his new appointees (Rahm Emanuel and Hillary Clinton) so he can intervene more forcefully to change the U.S.'s unconditional support for Israel. But even if he were to do so early on, a single breach of any agreement by Hamas—even if, as most likely, provoked by Israel—might be enough for him to adopt Israel's language of state security as the justification of all means. "As soon as anyone mentions security," Miri Weingarten of Physicians for Human Rights commented on a visit last year to Britain, "everyone stands up straight and stops thinking."

20

Why Howard Jacobson Is Wrong

In his critique of Caryl Churchill's *Seven Jewish Children: A Play for Gaza* in *The Independent* last week, the novelist Howard Jacobson laments what he describes as the "unreasoning," "deranged," "hysteria," and "virulence" he sees as currently directed against Israel. It is indeed a time to be sober, but his piece offers no such antidote to unreason. In fact, quite the opposite.

First of all, Jacobson and other critics of the play seem to me to have misread its fundamental nature. *Seven Jewish Children* is not a diatribe. Instead, it offers a set of voices in pained dialogue with each other about how to tell a child an unbearable history. Its central refrain is "Tell her," "Don't tell her." It therefore stages for its audience the vexed question of how adults, in the very words they use, can best fulfill their responsibilities towards the next generation at a time of historical crisis. What story should be told? War hardens language as well as hearts. In this context, to allow the speakers such anguished uncertainty is a gift. In its final scene—which is shocking, as Churchill herself describes it—the crude rhetoric of war has won. This is a tragedy.

The question then becomes: how did a people who can fairly claim to be among the most persecuted, if not the most persecuted, in history come to be the violent oppressors of another people? Hence the journey of the play from the Holocaust to Gaza—three of its seven scenes are set in Europe—as well as the title, *Seven Jewish*, as opposed to *Seven Israeli*, *Children*, to which critics have also objected. The point is to make us think about how trauma transmutes itself into ruthless self-defence. To suggest that this is what has happened to the Israeli people is not anti-Semitic. It was Primo Levi who, in a 1982 interview, remarked, "Everybody is somebody's Jew, and today the Palestinians are the Jews of the Israelis."

Jacobson is out of tune with some of Israel's most revered writers who do not hesitate to make the link between the founding of Israel and past persecution of the Jews. Thus S. Yizhar, in his famous 1948 short story, *Khirbet Khizeh*, depicts an Israeli soldier in the process of evacuating an Arab village, suddenly struck with the analogy between the Palestinian predicament and the exile of his forefathers: "Our nation's protest to the world: exile! . . . What had we perpetrated here today?" Yizhar is hardly, to use Jacobson's words, "punishing Jews with their own grief," or "cancelling out all debts of guilt and sorrow." He is warning the new nation of the perils of what it is doing to the Palestinians, a reality of which Gaza is merely the most recent, devastating instance.

Repeatedly, Jacobson selects lines from the play as if they self-evidently supported his case. But how can a line like this one—"Tell her it's the land God gave us"—be anti-Semitic, when David Ben-Gurion, Israel's first prime minister, stated more than once, "The Bible is our Mandate"? Or, to take another example: "Tell her we're the iron fist now," when it was the early Zionist Vladimir Jabotinsky who coined the concept of the "Iron Wall" to convey the idea that the new Jewish nation should be invincible in order to force the Arabs into submission. Unusual for acknowledging the inherent violence of Zionism, Jabotinsky has been the inspiration for the prime ministers Menachem Begin, Benjamin Netanyahu, Ariel Sharon, and Ehud Olmert. Even some of the most provocative statements in the last scene: "Tell her they don't understand anything but violence," or "Tell her you can't believe what you see on television" are routinely made by Israeli politicians—the last by Mark Regev, Olmert's spokesman, during the Gaza offensive when questioned about Palestinian casualties by Jon Snow.

Jacobson asks for balance. First of all, despite his insistence to the contrary, critics of Israel's actions in Gaza, among whom I count myself, have clearly condemned the Hamas rocket attacks on the civilian population of Israel. Nor have critics of Israel, Jewish and non-Jewish, hesitated to criticise Palestinian politics, as he also implies they have, or indeed hesitated to call for understanding between the two peoples. The late Edward Said would be the most obvious example. Nevertheless, Jacobson seems to be living in an unreal political world. How balanced, for example, is this comment: "Was not the original withdrawal from Gaza and the dismantling of the rightly despised settlements a sufficient signal of peaceful intent, and a sufficient opportunity for it to be reciprocated?" The answer to this rhetorical question must surely be, "No." Here, a few facts might be in order. In the year following the pull-out of 8,000 settlers from Gaza, 12,000 new settlers were moved into the West

Bank. In August 2004, Sharon's senior adviser, Dov Weisglass, stated unequivocally that the objective was to "freeze the political process" and "prevent the
establishment of a Palestinian state."

At moments, it is hard to know what Jacobson knows and what he doesn't
know (to rephrase one of his objections to Churchill). He cites Ben-Gurion's
declaration that Arab rights "must be guarded and honoured punctiliously"
with no allusion whatsoever to the discrimination towards its own Arab citizens that has characterised Israel since its birth. Nor when he refers to the
expulsion of Jews from East Jerusalem, does he mention the expulsion of
750,000 Palestinians in 1948 (half of whom had left before a single shot was
fired in the 1948 war), not to speak of the occupation, which has now lasted
more than twice as long as the period between 1967 and the founding of the
state. In his speech to the Knesset on receipt of the Wolf Prize in 2004, Daniel
Barenboim did not hesitate to draw attention to the vast gulf between the
principles enshrined in the Declaration of Independence and the reality in
Israel today. But then, Israelis have always been happier to criticise their
nation—in their case, the charge of anti-Semitism would be absurd—than
those who claim to be supporters of Israel in the West.

In fact, *Seven Jewish Children* is precise and focused in its criticisms of
Israeli policies: control of water, house demolitions, checkpoints, and the
destruction of olive trees. If it builds to a crescendo, it is because of the drastic
deterioration of the situation, and the sense, shared by many, that an injustice
is being perpetrated while the rest of the world more or less stands idly by—
or, indeed, actively supports Israel's war on Gaza. (An Amnesty report this
week has claimed that most of the weapons used by Israel were provided by
the U.S.) Churchill's play is outraged. As it should be. Israel has just voted in
the most right-wing government of its history, with an avowed racist, Avigdor
Lieberman, as kingmaker. In a poll conducted by *Ha'aretz* in ten schools
across the country, Lieberman won with an outright majority. A recent survey
conducted by one of the world's leading political psychologists, Daniel Bar-
Tal, reported that Israel is characterised by a remarkable proximity between
official state rhetoric and popular opinion, and that the consciousness of the
majority of Israeli Jews is characterised by "a sense of victimisation, a siege
mentality, blind patriotism, belligerence, self-righteousness, dehumanisation
of the Palestinians and insensitivity to their sufferings."

This is not, of course, true of all Israelis: there has always been a powerful,
if today politically impotent, tradition of dissent. It is neither the whole of
Israel, nor what Israel has to, or will inevitably, be. But in the context of these

political realities (unmentioned by Jacobson), the graffiti left by Israeli soldiers on the excrement-smeared walls of destroyed houses in Gaza, as reported by the *Ha'aretz* journalist Amira Hass—"The Zionist conqueror was
here," "We are here to annihilate you"—testify to a nation that is in danger of
losing its soul. "We turn our backsides to what we do not want to know about
and bury it in distaste, like our own ordure," writes Jacobson. What language
of reason is this? Who, we might ask, is he talking about?

As early as 1948, Martin Buber lamented a situation "in which we as
individuals live humanely but as members of a nation we live lives that are less
than human." For many Jews today, appalled by Gaza, it is impossible not to
ask what has happened to the Jewish ethic of justice and righteousness, an
ethic that many hoped would be the new nation's gift to the world. In 2006,
Olmert said of the Lebanese war of that year: "This is a war fought for all the
Jews." For those of us who reject this claim, it is imperative for Jews to speak
out against Israel's actions towards the Palestinians. Not to do so is to allow
the belief to go unchallenged that Israel's worst actions are being conducted
in the name of all Jews. It is this belief, rather than criticism of Israel, that fuels
anti-Semitism today and, in fact, weakens the fight against it.

Jacobson has got things the wrong way round. Anti-Semitism is an affront
to the inalienable, and so often destroyed, rights of the Jewish people. How on
earth are we meant to challenge it, if we do not object when the rights of
another people are being so flagrantly violated by the nation that claims to
represent us?

Holocaust Premises: Political Implications of the Traumatic Frame

Our title is "Holocaust Premises." I have spent some time musing on this title, which is, I assume, like our subject, deliberately ambiguous and fraught. That the Holocaust could have become a premise—that is, a proposition which produces its own logical conclusions—is striking, or rather strikingly different from seeing it, for example, as unrepresentable atrocity, as unassimilable or barely assimilable trauma in the way Judith Butler, citing Primo Levi, has so powerfully described: "Many survivors of war or other complex and traumatic experiences tend unconsciously to filter their memory. . . . [T]hey dwell on moments of respite. . . . [T]he most painful episodes . . . lose their contours." Suffering "crystallises" as a story. Telling the story is crucial testimony to the event, but it can also lead—sometimes as a condition of survival she suggests —to the memory being lost.

The idea of "Holocaust Premises" has a far more controlling ring to it than this, suggesting that the Holocaust casts its shadow over the future, not just as recurrent pain but as something that can dictate the logical or thinkable possibilities of what the future will be allowed to be. I think that this is what we mean by instrumentalisation of the Holocaust, the sense which I share with Judith Butler and others that the Holocaust is used by one strand of dominant discourse inside Israel, although not only inside Israel, as justification for the violence of state power. "We must remember," Ariel Sharon said at the Jerusalem ceremony to commemorate the liberation of Auschwitz in January 2005, "that this is the only place in the world in which we, the Jews, have the right and the power to defend ourselves with our own strength." And, forgetting the liberators, forgetting we might say the occasion: "We know that we can trust no one but ourselves." Countering this way of thought, the Israeli writer Shulamith Hareven writes in her 1986 article "Identity: Victim": "During the Second World War, not only did the world not remain silent, it lost more than sixty million men fighting Hitler. True they were not fighting because of us, and certainly they would not have offered aid for our sakes only. They were fighting against fascism in general. . . . But the loss of more than sixty million men in a war does not exactly mean that the world sat by with its arms crossed. . . . Sixty million families suffered losses, and those of us who survived, including the small numbers of us then inhabiting Israel, survived because of them."

As I thought about it, it seemed to me that the idea of "premises" as diktat over the future might also do as a working definition of trauma. When I was studying Sylvia Plath a long time ago, and trying to understand the appearance of the Holocaust motif in her writing as something other than the opportunism of which she was accused, I read an article by the German psychoanalyst Ilse Grubrich-Simitis on working with second-generation Holocaust survivors that has stayed with me ever since. She described how the language of these patients was characterised by a dull, thudding referentiality, with no mobility or play, as if they were saying—in a way only made clear after the most difficult and patient analytic listening—"this *happened*," "*happened*" "*happened*" over and over again, to compensate for the silence, the psychic refusal to acknowledge the reality of the Holocaust, in the generation before. And in one of his most evocative articles, "The Trauma of Incest" of 1989, the psychoanalyst Christopher Bollas describes how trauma shuts down the mind of the patient. The problem is not believing what they say, but the fact that that is *all* they have to say, so that there is nowhere else left for them to go inside their minds.

We are talking then, not about the inability of the trauma to pass into speech, and its loss at the moment of articulation, but an endless appeal—as in court of appeal—to its reality, which then clouds the horizon to infinity, and brutally cuts down everything else that might be possibly thought or seen. "The question is," Judith Butler asks, "whether [the trauma] is mobilised for political purposes with the consequence of displacing the pain and losing the referent itself." Perhaps, paradoxically, loss of the referent and its endless invocation can be one and the same thing. Perhaps invocation of the Holocaust in the public domain is a way of settling accounts with its psychic intractability, of trying to lay it to rest. To the further question she poses— does trauma act upon those who invoke it for political purposes, or is it pursued and orchestrated for its traumatising effect?—we would then indeed have to reply: both.

In November 2004, something in the nature of a national crisis was provoked inside Israel by the photograph of an Arab man being forced to play the violin at a roadblock. "If we allow Jewish soldiers to put an Arab violinist at a roadblock and laugh at him," wrote Yoram Kaniuk, author of a book about a Jewish violinist forced to play for a concentration camp commander, "we have succeeded at arriving at the lowest moral point possible. Our entire existence in this Arab region was justified, and is still justified, by our suffering; by Jewish violinists in the camps." The soldiers, he stated, should be put on trial not for abusing Arabs but for disgracing the Holocaust. As commentators were swift to point out, this episode caused far greater concern than the news in the same week of an army officer repeatedly shooting Iman al-Hams, a thirteen-year-old Palestinian girl, and then saying that he would have shot her even if she had been three. Or the report, also about the same time, of Chief of Staff Dan Halutz, who in 2002 had dropped a one-ton bomb on the house of Hamas leader Saleh Shehadeh, killing Shehadeh and fifteen civilians including eleven children, and who, asked how he felt about such moments, replied that he felt "a light bump in the plane." In discussion after the play *My Name Is Rachel Corrie*, performed in London in 2005, Corrie's father stated that his greatest anxiety was aroused when she told him not to worry because the army always aimed their bullets inside the houses low—he said that he knew, from his experience in Vietnam, that the bullet would ricochet to cause maximum damage and that the army was therefore out of control (Corrie was killed by an Israeli bulldozer as she was protesting the demolition of a Palestinian home).

The point is not to demonise the army. Occupying armies the world over inevitably corrupt and brutalise themselves. It is far more a question of seeing how—alongside this reality and often in strenuous denial of it—the Holocaust takes up its place inside the collective imagination as something which purifies—or must purify—the Jewish soul. The Holocaust, not just, as Kaniuk states, the reason *for* the state; nor, as Sharon implies, the *reason of state*, but as redemption of the people. This is sacralisation of the Holocaust (which can lead, as Judith Butler points out, to a no less violent desacralisation, or downplaying of the Holocaust aimed to discredit what is felt to be its misuse). Commentators have also pointed out that to see the Holocaust in this way comes dangerously close to giving the worst catastrophe of Jewish history a type of divine sanction—implicit indeed in the term "Holocaust," which endows the disaster with the status of an act of God. "To name the Nazi genocide 'the Holocaust,' " writes Gillian Rose in "Athens and Jerusalem: A Tale of Three Cities," "is already to over-unify it and to sacralise it, to see it as providential purpose—for in the Hebrew scriptures, a *holocaust* refers to a burnt sacrifice which is offered in its entirety to God without any part of it being consumed."

During the summer of 2005, as part of the preparation for a new course I was about to start teaching at Queen Mary, "Palestine—Israel, Israel—Palestine: Politics and the Literary Imagination," I read about the Holocaust as it impacts on the new nation of Israel. For me, David Grossman provides the most brilliant exploration in fiction in his 1989 novel, *See Under: Love*, of how the Holocaust appeared as an object of shame for the founders of the nation after the war. Grossman's child hero, the boy Momik, has to dig deep into the cellar of his home to find the traces of the Nazi beast that his family will not talk about. He is the only one to rejoice at the arrival of his long-lost grandfather who had been presumed to have disappeared in the camps. But it was only reading around that novel, notably Idith Zertal's 1998 book, *From Catastrophe to Power: Holocaust Survivors and the Emergence of Israel*, and now more recently, her *Israel's Holocaust and the Politics of Nationhood* of 2005, that I realised that Grossman's story was in fact the tip of the iceberg. He was not only writing to bring the beast of Nazism out of the closet. He was also writing a literary exposé of the shameful treatment of survivors, a shame which Zertal persuasively argues was in many ways constitutive of the state.

The entry of the Holocaust into the national imagination was conditional. The annual day of commemoration, Yom Hashoah v'haGevurah, or Day of Destruction and Heroism, was declared in 1952 on the twenty-seventh day of the Hebrew month of Nisan, as close to the date of the Warsaw Uprising as religious laws relating to Passover would permit. "The decade-and-a-half that preceded the capture and trial of Eichmann," writes Zertal, "were marked, in Israel and in other countries such as France and the United States, by public silence and some sort of statist denial regarding the Holocaust" (a 220-page textbook of Jewish history published in 1948 contained one page on the Holocaust, but ten on the Napoleonic wars). Eichmann's trial ushered in a new phase because his arrest and the staging of the trial on Israeli soil could be seen in itself as a sign of the triumph of the nation over history. It was also intended to incorporate Israelis of non-European origin into a singular, narrative collective. "I can testify for myself," writes Zertal, "a high school student at the time, and for my friends: the trial was an event of major influence for us. Although my father served as a soldier in Europe in World War II, worked with Jewish survivors after the war, and published a book about his war experiences; and although his entire family perished in the Holocaust, *he never talked about it at home. The trial was thus my first encounter with the horrors*, brought to us by the trial witnesses' testimonies that were broadcast live" (my emphasis).

There is of course no question of passing judgment on Israel for the slow, pained, process with which the horror came to be spoken, nor indeed for the need of the new nation to qualify the horror with the image of the resisting Jew. But part of the problem in Israel's relationship to the Holocaust is that the very gesture that welcomed the survivors to the shores of the fledgling nation, and used them—and "used" is not too strong a word—as rationale for the state, also entailed a kind of hatred—and "hatred" is also not too strong a word—of who and what they were. In his recent book on the tension between Diaspora and Israeli Jewry, *The Divided Self: Israel and the Jewish Psyche Today*, David Goldberg cites the early youth leader Moshe Tabenkin on hearing of the fate of the European Jews: "Rejection of the Diaspora . . . now turned into personal hatred of the Diaspora. I hate it as a man hates a deformity he is ashamed of." "It will be hell if all the [DP] camps come [to Palestine]," Ben-Gurion was told by rescue operatives in Europe in early 1946, "All this filth, just as it is, you [the Jewish Agency/Ben-Gurion] plan to move to Palestine?" Ben-Gurion never queried the use of the word "filth," even as, as Zertal demonstrates, he expresses in his diary the deepest anguish at the plight of the survivors. But he silences the anguish. And in the meantime, although he himself on one occasion describes the camp survivors as "holy," the rhetoric takes hold in public that *only the bad* could have survived. "Had they not been what they were," he stated to the central committee of his party four years after the war, "bad, harsh, egotistic—they would never have survived." (All quotes from Ben-Gurion taken from Idith Zertal, *Israel's Holocaust.*)

Somewhere inside the nation's self-image, the survivors—the shame of the Holocaust that they represent—are interred. When, therefore, Ariel Sharon states: "We must remember that this is the only place in the world in which we, the Jews, have the right and the power to defend ourselves with our own strength," it seems to me that such statements, their unswerving conviction, bear the traces of that repudiated past. Not to speak of the guilt of the new nation towards the Jews of Europe. "If they [the survivors] arrive and perceive us as the prosecuted and they the prosecutors," Ben-Gurion stated in a lecture to the farmers' youth movement after the war, "we will have to bear it . . . even if it arouses anger and revulsion within us." I read Ben-Gurion as offering a kind of self-diagnosis which opens up the link between anger, or even revulsion, and guilt. "Us as the prosecuted"—could the *Yishuv*, and the new nation, be prosecuted—placed on trial—for its failure to save the European Jews? For Hareven, guilt is unavoidably part of the picture. A generation without grandparents transposed their loneliness and insecurity into the strongest, often self-denying, resolve. "When the families who had remained abroad perished in the Holocaust, all these feelings became overlaid with a sense of guilt," she writes in her 1988 essay "Israel: The First Forty Years," "the Guilt of Noah, it can be called, for Noah, too, according to the Scriptures, did not take his parents on the Ark."

In his 2005 book, *The Suppression of Guilt*, the Israeli former journalist and media analyst Daniel Dor shows how the Israeli media, of Left and Right, have equally produced a narrative of the conflict between Israel and the Palestinians in which Israel is never guilty and must not be blamed. Reading that statement of Ben-Gurion's, I am wondering if behind the suppression of guilt towards the Palestinians, as Dor describes it, there might not be another layer, which is the guilt of the Jewish people towards themselves. Redemption, therefore, might carry another meaning—not just redemption from catastrophe, but redemption from blame.

In our exchanges Judith Butler asked me if I would address the relationship between messianism and how catastrophe repeats itself over time. Following Gershom Scholem, I believe messianism, in its apocalyptic strain, to have been one of the defining instances of Jewish self-definition, and that it played its part in the language of the emergent Israeli state. Not exclusively—Zionism was crucially the movement of self-determination of the Jewish people driven by the urgencies of their history—but as its often-present shadow and only partially acknowledged accompaniment. Again reading for the new course at Queen Mary, I have understood from writers such as Sidra Ezrahi, Saul Friedlander, and Adam Seligman the extent to which the Holocaust became part of a messianic vision. "During the early statist period [up until the late 1950s] a commemoration day and commemoration sites were established," write Friedlander and Seligman in their 1994 article "The Israeli Memory of the Shoah," "but it was only during the later phase that the Shoah became a central myth of the civil religion of Israel." If the Eichmann trial and the 1967 war were a turning point, nonetheless the path had been laid long before, in the causal link established from the beginning between the destruction of European Jewry and the birth of Israel, combining both events in a new symbolic unity of catastrophe and redemption. The 1967 war opened a "new phase" in which Arab hostility became equated with Nazism, and the Holocaust was mobilized for the first time to justify the policies of the state, but this move was "inherent in the very symbolic logic which identified the Israeli state with the redemptive moment in history." In his famous exhortation to Polish Jews on the eve of the Shoah, Ze'ev Jabotinsky proclaimed, "What else I would like to say to you on this day of Tisha B'Av [the day of the destruction of the Temple] is whoever of you will escape from the catastrophe, he or she will live to see a great Jewish wedding—the rebirth and rise of a Jewish state." "The notion that we can use our enemies for our own salvation," Hannah Arendt wrote in a set of notes she prepared for a *Look* magazine interview in 1963, "has always been the 'original sin' of Zionism."

The worst disaster becomes Israel's saving grace. In fact the link from the Shoah to state policy was laid down by Moshe Dayan at the time of Eichmann's trial: "What is becoming clear at the Eichmann trial is the active passivity of the world in the face of the murder of the six million. There can be no doubt that only this country and only this people can protect the Jews against a second Holocaust. And hence every inch of Israeli soil is intended only for Jews" (cited in *Davar*, 1 July 1961, and reproduced by Zertal).

When Menachem Begin came to power, he suggested that the Shoah be commemorated on the day of the destruction of the Temple, instead of on the date which, binding the link between disaster and heroism, had been chosen to commemorate the Warsaw Uprising. His proposal was rejected by the Knesset. The redemptive link between the Holocaust and the resurgence of the Jewish people would remain, and still does. Pursuing this link, I discovered a document issued by the Cambridge University Centre for Modern Hebrew Studies in 1992 which consists of a translation of poems by Uri Zvi Greenberg, prophetic Zionist poet, to commemorate the centenary of his birth. Attached to two of the poems is a note from the translators explaining that although the poems were written in the early 1930s, they "fittingly commemorate" the anniversary of both the Palestine Disturbances of 1936 and the Warsaw Uprising of 1943, which occurred on the same day. One of the poems, "Beyond the Veil," contains these lines:

> And the brows of a people shamed shall grow horns of iron
> Wherewith they shall gore their foes.
> Their heels shall be brass and their foes a pile of olives
> For treading into a kingdom

The other poem, "The Tower of Corpses," ends by speaking of "the tower of corpses which my Jewish race will erect in the world." The reprinting of these poems, and especially their attachment both to the Palestinian riots of the thirties and the Warsaw Uprising, both of which happened *after* the poems were written, seems a striking illustration of the way disaster turns into a hallowed identity which then knows no bounds. To defend itself the nation will gore its foes and litter the world with corpses.

To end, however, on a more positive note, I offer two counter-instances from within the same narrative, one from outside Israel, the other from inside. First from inside. Before the disengagement from Gaza in the summer of 2005, one group of messianic settlers insisted that they would resist removal on the grounds that their allegiance was to the land, as divinely sanctioned, over the state. "When the state behaves like a state of all its residents," says one, "and not as the Jewish state, the attitude towards it changes. I respect it as I do any other government, but it is no longer 'the beginning of our redemption.'" For one rabbi, however, Rabbi Fruman of Tekoa in Gush Etzion, he too would choose the land over the state, but for diametrically opposite reasons— in order to retain the links with the Palestinians amongst whom he has lived for so many years. There could, he speculates, be a new type of settlement as model for the future, no longer the dawn of redemption, but "the dawn of peace." Messianism is not singular. It can take unexpected paths and even undo itself.

The second is from Marcel Liebman, the Belgian socialist historian. I was privileged to write the introduction to his memoir of life in Nazi-occupied Belgium—*Born Jewish*—when it was translated for the first time into English, in 2005. His brother was deported to Auschwitz at the age of fifteen, while the rest of the family survived. He went on to become an outspoken critic of Zionism. Liebman could hardly forget the Holocaust. His adult life was wholly determined by the tragedy he witnessed as a young boy. But becoming an historian, he saw his role as a form of remembering that would not involve "cultivating the harm." Disaster must not be turned into an identity. In this he is very close to Shulamith Hareven who has written so eloquently on the danger for the Jews in Israel in defining themselves in perpetuity as victims. For Hareven, the lesson of the Holocaust should be: "Even if often in history, I have been the victim of others, I will never oppress those weaker than myself and never abuse my power to exile them." The mistake is to "define my uniqueness in terms of the past alone." Unlike Hareven, Liebman did not go to Israel, was no Zionist, not even one with the humane and universalising qualifications which she brought to her place as an Israeli woman in the modern world. But reading him in this context, it seems that he may have been unable to identify with the new nation partly because he knew it would hold no place for grief.

For critiquing Israel and Zionism, Liebman was often accused of betraying the memory of his brother. But for him, the best tribute he could pay him was to refuse any redemption—national or otherwise—for his loss. Some disasters cannot be made good. In Liebman's story, memory of the Holocaust and its unassimilable trauma moves towards psychic pain and away from collective belonging. I share with Judith Butler a fear that, to date, these two have seemed to be incompatible. "Has the discourse now taken on a life of its own," she asks, "one that grows at the expense of memory?" From the 1950s in Israel, personal memorials were slowly replaced by collective inheritance, public anniversaries supplanting the commemoration of the death of loved ones. In the redemptive, national, narrative, this one brother has no place. Idith Zertal ends her study of Israel's response to the Holocaust survivors with these words: "Zionism's work of mourning (Freud's *Trauerarbeit*) for the Jewish catastrophe still remains to be done."

An Interview with Jacqueline Rose

Justin Clemens and Ben Naparstek: In your afterword to a posthumously pub-
lished collection of critic Allon White's writings, you discuss his essay "Why Am I a
Literary Critic?," where he describes criticism as a way of distancing himself from
the most painful recesses of his interior world.[1] "I am a critic," you quote White as
saying, "because there in the writing out of the other the distance is perfect and I
am safe." Jacqueline, why are you a critic? Is criticism a safe vocation?

Jacqueline Rose: Well, I think Allon White made that statement at least partly
out of the fear of his own unconscious childhood memories, which came
flooding back when he had leukaemia, and also *because* he had leukaemia as
he describes so beautifully in his memoir, *Too Close to the Bone*. Therefore, it
doesn't seem generalisable beyond his story. I don't think for me criticism has
ever been to do with making myself safe, except insofar as I found that I could
do it. And when you find you can do something, it becomes somewhere you
can go to that has a certain safety to it. But in terms of the content of what I
have written about—from *Peter Pan* to Sylvia Plath and notably my passion for
psychoanalysis—criticism has always been a place where I could transmute
into some kind of form things that were preoccupying me at the most profound personal and often unconscious level. This brings literary criticism
closer to the world of the dream in the sense that Christopher Bollas writes
about people dreaming their lives through the objects they encounter and
which they transform and which transform them—so literary criticism would
be my transformative object.

My criticism has also always been profoundly fuelled by my feminism, and
my belief that feminism needed to take on board the psychoanalytic project—
that the historic injustices which the political movement of feminism seek to
redress need to be backed by an understanding of our own psychic investment
as women in everything we engage in, including our own oppression. This is

more unsettling than safe. It was why Juliet Mitchell's intervention in 1973 with *Psychoanalysis and Feminism* was so important to me.

How did your collaboration with Juliet Mitchell as joint editors of Lacan's Feminine Sexuality *build on that 1973 intervention?*

As an undergraduate, I'd been involved in feminism and campaigning for child-care for the women in the Cowley industrial estate on the outskirts of Oxford. It was a very important piece of political self-education, but I felt there was something missing from the vocabulary of that kind of polemical engagement—something about the need to explore oneself, I suppose. Oddly perhaps, the class difference was probably crucial in setting me on that path. We were a bunch of middle-class undergraduate girls going into working-class families to talk about child-care and equality. There was a limit to what we could say—for example we could talk about child-care, but made the mistake of thinking we could raise the question of abortion rights to a predominantly Catholic community. We needed to listen in a different way, which forced us to think more self-consciously about who we were, our own histories, and where we were coming from.

When I went to Paris as a graduate student, I then started reading Freud, really for the very first time. In fact I'd come at psychoanalysis through Jung, which had been life-transformative. I thought, "I need this way of thinking to understand my family history. I need this way of thinking to *be*." Reading *Psychoanalysis and Feminism* in 1973 was a huge relief: "Oh, thank God, you can be a feminist *and* be interested in Freud." Up to that point, my Freudianism was a closet activity and feminism was being out on the street, quite literally. I had no idea that it was possible to try to bring them together.

I met Sally Alexander, the very distinguished feminist historian, and she told me that there had been a bust-up in the Red Rag collective about Juliet's book, because some of the feminists were sympathetic to it and some were very hostile. Sally Alexander said, "You must meet Juliet Mitchell." We hit it off in this extraordinary way, and rapidly conceived the project of doing the Lacan book together. Lacan comes in at the end of *Psychoanalysis and Feminism*, and I had my own developing interest in his writing, so it followed logically from where we both were.

It's surprising to hear that you came to psychoanalysis through Jung.

Yes, it surprises everybody who hears it. I have a very close relationship with my cousin, Braham Murray, who is the artistic director of the Manchester Royal Exchange Theatre. He was very important to me when my family went into crisis in my late teens and early twenties. He basically said, "To get through this, you need to read Jung." I read Jung's autobiography, *Memories, Dreams, Reflections*, and it was an absolute inspiration. But another very important person in my life was the critic Colin MacCabe who took the opposite line, and said, "I think Jung sold out on Freud." I was very defensive on Jung's behalf, but then an inner voice said, "Oh, wait a minute, perhaps you should read Freud." So I read a bit of Freud and I was won over immediately. To this day, I have arguments with my cousin, who has remained a Jungian, whereas I now think that Jung was frightened of what Freud was uncovering and tried to sublimate it.

Colin MacCabe was the literature academic who was denied tenure at Cambridge in 1981 due to his embrace of "post-structuralism"?

Yes, he was.

And Frank Kermode, who supervised your Ph.D. at the University College London, resigned from his post at Cambridge in protest?

He and Raymond Williams saw it as a very retrograde move not to give Colin tenure at Cambridge.

How did you find working with Frank Kermode?

I'd been an M.A. student in Paris on a French government grant. When I got back from Paris, I wanted to carry on studying and do a Ph.D. It was Colin who said, "The only person in England who is really interested in French critical theory is Frank Kermode." So I submitted a proposal on children's literature in the nineteenth century, based on Gillian Avery's work. It was very conservative and I was accepted. But in the meantime, I had started to read Freud and came up with the idea of working on *Peter Pan* and fantasy. So I walked into Frank Kermode's office and I had in my hand a new proposal on *Peter Pan*, and he had in his hand the Gillian Avery proposal. I said, "Look, I know this is what you accepted me for, but since then I've become passionately involved in psychoanalysis and I think this is a much more interesting topic." He sat there looking from one to the other lighting his pipe and then he said in his wonderfully understated manner, "You know, the one we accepted you for is very boring." I owe him a huge debt for immediately seeing that this slightly peculiar thesis on *Peter Pan* and psychoanalysis might, just might, be viable. And he never wavered in that belief in me. He also introduced me to Masud Khan, through whom I met and translated articles by J. B. Pontalis and Victor Smirnoff for the *International Journal of Psychoanalysis*, an exceptional opportunity for a woman in her early twenties.

The other way in which he had an enormous influence on me is in relationship to writing. At that stage, my ego-ideal was *Screen* magazine and I believed, like many of the people on *Screen*—and many Althusserians, which I never was, and Lacanians, which I sort of was—that the test of an intellectual vocabulary is its resistance to commonsense and the facility of meaning. The argument was that ideology and consciousness—ideology for Marx and consciousness for Freud—were deceptive, and that therefore the vocabularies through which we recognise ourselves are illusory so you have to create something artificial to break them. It also, in relationship to Freud, related very specifically to his own feeling, and certainly Lacan's feeling, that by going to America and giving the *Five Lectures on Psycho-Analysis*, he allowed the vulgarisation of his own thinking, which lead to its subsequent incorporation by ego psychology in America.

Well, Frank Kermode was having none of it. He just said, "You can't write like this!" We really fought it out. I partly won, and he partly won. I never ended up writing like him. He was *the* person who introduced theory into British literary critical discourse, but he never took on the Marxist component of theory and increasingly he didn't like the way things were going, felt—to cite one of his books—that the *appetite* for poetry was being lost. I would occasionally sit in lectures hearing him let rip on certain branches of new historicism, for example, and, while not a new historicist, I'd think, "Why am I escaping these attacks?" For some reason, I slipped through, and I think it's because he has a profound respect and feel for psychoanalysis and therefore went on supporting me.

The British Academy, to which you were elected in 2006, calls you a writer who "works always at points of difficulty, whether conceptual, political, or aesthetic." Is "difficulty" a criterion for the topics you choose and the arguments you attempt to mount?

Well, Juliet Mitchell once told me that she never writes unless she needs to understand something and doesn't. That's true for me as well, but I'd want to add something else, which is that writing is about going to a place of difficulty, feeling one's way around in it, and seeing whether one can survive by creating some kind of order out of it. If you think about Sylvia Plath and psycho-analysis and the Middle East, they do all have a certain pitch of tension and anxiety which is completely inseparable from the intellectual problems that they pose. In each case something had been troubling me. In Plath's case, it was the power of the writing and the tragedy of the story, but also my dismay at the way she had been pathologised by a whole generation of male criticism, and how that had in turn been matched by the idealising of her by another generation of feminist criticism. In both cases, it was an evacuation of diffi-culty. If you pathologise Sylvia Plath, then you don't have to talk about her anymore except as a case. And, in the second case, to make that into a virtue meant that the psychic pain of Plath was being lost.

The same thing went on in analysing Dora, which was one of my first interventions into psychoanalytic feminist criticism. After the pathologising of hysteria, there was a feminist reappropriation of Dora as a kind of heroine, whose story could be read as a female writing of the body, which I thought avoided the psychic distress of what it means to be a hysteric. In the case of *Peter Pan*, there was an idealisation of this image of the child as this object in which we all—because it's an adult problem, not a child problem—recognise ourselves, which gave this text iconic status. The more I looked into the sexual and psychological history of this story, the more troubled and disturbing I felt it to be. The demand on the child—that it be innocent—is, psychoanalytically speaking, a psychosis-inducing demand. But just to say that seemed to me to be very evasive, as the culture had turned this troubled text into an icon, so we are all implicated. In relation to all these concerns, I am always appealing to the basic ethos of psychoanalysis which is that we grow more through con-fronting what is difficult than not.

Can you offer an example of a crucial point of difficulty from your own life?

My mother's eldest sister was born in Poland, but my mother was born in England; so that makes her second-generation and me third-generation, al-though the terms are ambiguous. It was a traumatised family. The whole of my grandmother's family were sent to Chelmno concentration camp, whereas she got out because she came to join her husband—she had to leave because there was a problem with their being from different religious groupings. So, she escaped, but the rest of her family were lost in the Holocaust.

Our family was then one type of North London Jewish survivor family who, to survive internally, entrenched itself in Jewish ritual. I have no criticism of that, I think it was in some ways inevitable in view of what had happened. But it was a very rigid, defensive form of Jewishness closed in on itself, with no sense of Jewishness as culture, knowledge, or history. There was no sense of joy. I think much of my work and Gillian's work became a journey around that story, to reconnect with the form of Jewishness that we couldn't possibly have handed to us because there wasn't the psychological space for it. What also accompanied that was an over-idealisation of family life, always central to Jewishness as something to be held onto against the perils of the world, but especially I think then.

Not being able to talk about the Holocaust, because that was silenced, and then gradually realising the impact it had on the family meant that there were corridors of silence and fervently wished perfection, which I needed to undo to get to anything that felt like a psychologically true condition. When I went to Paris and started reading Freud, I thought, "This is giving me an understanding of what's been going on and how I can think with it creatively and come through it." I think that is one reason why I see idealisation, whether self-idealisation, or idealisation of nation, race, or creed, as a mistake.

Do you see the scholarly ambition that you and your sister shared as in any way traceable to your family history? For your body of work remains remarkable for its ambition—the difficulty of your topics and their range.

There is an important point to be made here in relation to the critics of my work on Zionism, who hate my use of psychoanalysis to talk about Zionist history and ideology, see it as a form of insult. Instead I have always seen psychoanalysis as a form of freedom and creativity. Psychic conflict and difficulty are not shameful for Freud, for whom such difficulty was part of human entitlement and whose aim was to restore the dignity of the psyche, of the unconscious mind. Be that as it may, I think that those components of my history played a huge part in launching me on an academic path. The mind was the place where I could go. That is not to say that it made me feel safe, but that it was a place to go where I could negotiate my own history, and then renegotiate my path to political and historical reality, in my own way.

Given how deeply your work is concerned with the subjective origins of critical reason, one could imagine memoir-writing as a genre you're keen to explore, like so many writers with whom you share a close affinity—Allon White, Gillian Rose, and Edward Said, and also Derrida and Cixous?

No, it's not, at least not for now. My literary agent wants me to write a book about Gillian. And I've told him I won't do that because it's still too close and too many people are alive. But I did have a plan—and still do, in a way—to write a book about Edith Stein, this incredible German-Jewish woman who became Husserl's philosophical assistant and then converted to Christianity and became a Carmelite nun and ended by being deported to Auschwitz. The resonances with my sister's life are very profound: her deep engagement with German philosophy, in her case predominantly through Hegel, her involvement with Auschwitz—she was one of the symposium on the future of Auschwitz organised by the Polish government—the Jewishness, and the conversion. Even though the differences are also key—Gillian's final turn to Christianity was for her a continuation, not a repudiation, of Judaism, to which her relationship was profound to the last. But I do somewhere still have a project to write something which will be an interweaving of those two lives.

But you did start a memoir—about the adoption of your daughter—which you then abandoned to write Albertine. *Was this turn to fiction a deflection from the personal? Or a sign that the novel is very personal?*

Well, it was very personal in two ways. Apart from "Virginia Woolf and the Death of Modernism," it was the first thing I wrote after the death of my sister. I could only write the Virginia Woolf piece because it was about mourning. It is one of the few places in my writing where I am very critical of Freud. "Mourning and Melancholia" is the most cited of his papers, but I feel it has a fault line running through it. I don't accept the idea of a mourning that completes itself any more than I accept the idea of an Oedipus complex that completes itself, as he suggests in "The Dissolution of the Oedipus Complex," as if he wants to definitively shatter any chance of the boy lurking in that psychic space. But in psychoanalysis, it is crucial that everything, somewhere, is preserved—Freud's famous model was of the city preserved under the lava of Pompeii—so it seems to me that when Freud talks about completion he's being very non-Freudian. My mourning for Gillian will never be complete, nor would I want it to be.

I also felt after her death that I couldn't write anything academic, because that way of writing was too close to her life and work. Suddenly I got this idea for a novel. It started when I read the sleep sequence in Proust where Albertine is lying in her bed asleep and Marcel comes in and he masturbates against her. I thought, "Wait a minute, she's not asleep, this is ridiculous, no woman would sleep through that!" I thought it would be interesting to write that scene from the point of view of the woman, awake unknown to the man.

The other project I had was indeed to write about the adoption of my daughter. After a couple of pages, I thought, "No, this is her story, she does not need me to write it for her." So I started writing *Albertine* and, about a quarter of the way through, it came into consciousness that—of course, I should have known from the beginning—Albertine is an orphan, and therefore they were deeply connected. Somehow I had worked my way back to the story I said I wouldn't write, not through my daughter, whose privacy I felt I should respect, but through Proust.

Elsewhere you've characterised that feminist response to the sleep sequence as "untypical" for you. How exactly would you describe your relationship to feminism today?

I'd come to feminism through a generation that, after the first affirmation of equality and rights, was more suspicious of just giving to women the strength and presence denied to them historically without at least raising the question of what in doing that we are encouraging women to become and identify with. We were therefore wary of the self-assertiveness of women out of fear that it could lead, as it did in the seventies and eighties in Britain, to Margaret Thatcher—that's to say, a woman who, by asserting herself in the ways that men have asserted themselves, wreaked havoc. This is really Virginia Woolf's argument in *Three Guineas*—that if women join the procession (she meant the pomp and paraphernalia of fascism) they will go to war. But it is also a form of feminism taken further by writers like Julia Kristeva who propose that the presence of the feminine leads, or should lead, to a disruption or disaggregation of symbolic forms. So my feminism was very much: of course women should have equal pay, equal rights, free abortion on demand, educational equality, domestic equality, police protection in relation to domestic violence—all of that—but the demand for equality must never lose track of, not so much difference (i.e., men and women are just different), but the fact that women might be differently positioned in relationship to symbolic identification, which gives them a different edge, an oblique take on the world—they are less taken in—and we mustn't lose that. So we don't just wake up "the woman," à la Albertine, and assert, "Excuse me, I—the woman—is here!" and "I matter as much as you (the man)!"—in this case, at least as much we could say given the circumstances of this extraordinary moment in the novel. But that was exactly the reaction I found myself having in response to that scene.

So is Albertine *a feminist text?*

It's a feminist text insofar as it's a reply to Proust's lines which form its epigraph—"The pages I would write Albertine would certainly not have understood. . . . Had she been capable of understanding them, she would, for that very reason, not have inspired them." So the novel gives back to the woman a form of knowledge. But it's not a feminist text in the sense that I save Albertine, literally save her—I don't—from the complexities, and at moments the perverse complexities, of her own psychic agenda. I'm not interested in rendering her innocent, even though she is the victim of his psychic violence without question. So it's feminist as a protest at one level, but then I hope it has a dimension that makes that a question rather than an answer.

Especially given your unflinching treatment of race in your critical work, why did you erase the anti-Semitism of Proust's Albertine?

I could not make the imaginative leap. I had to enter into her skin and to enter into the skin of an anti-Semite would have been very, very difficult for me. It would have just felt like an act of self-brutalisation.

In the introduction to On Not Being Able to Sleep, *you note that the essays of literary criticism focus on women whereas the psychoanalytic essays concern men; elsewhere, you quarrelled with your close friend Edward Said about the absence of women in his work. What's the importance to you of writing about women writers?*

Nearly all the women writers I talk about—Christina Rossetti, Sylvia Plath, Mary Butts, Elizabeth Bowen, Melanie Klein, Julia Kristeva, and so on—describe inequality and injustice and oppression, but not one of them does that without implicating herself in a pained psychic dynamic of who and what a woman's identity is. I'm interested in how all of these writers take a risk of trying to say two things which historically have almost been incompatible— one, there is injustice and men tend to embody it for the most part; two, I am a complex psychic subject with various levels of pain, anxiety, unconscious fantasy. We need a world in which those two things are not seen as mutually exclusive. Women's protest must not be at the cost of their psychic life.

What would you say you've inherited or learned from Julia Kristeva's work?

Ah, Julia Kristeva was crucial for me because she was a Marxist, a feminist, a psychoanalytic critic, and she wore lipstick! She was completely my ego-ideal. I just thought, "Oh my goodness, you can wear nice clothes and get your hair done and still be a feminist and a serious intellectual!" To supplement a French government scholarship for my *maîtrise* in Paris, I'd worked at Yves Saint Laurent, and I have a passion for fashion. I would get my Yves Saint Laurent clothes dirt cheap because I was a salesgirl, and there was one par- ticular silk scarf which I had to tie over my customers' bosoms so that the letters Y.S.L. would fall visibly over their chest. When I got back to Oxford and people asked what it was, I would guiltily pass it off as "Young Socialist League." It was the first generation of early seventies second-wave feminism, which had a puritanical streak. I remember at least one person saying to me, "I can't take you seriously, Jacqueline, because of how you dress."

Julia Kristeva was political *and* psychoanalytic, and I cannot overstate what a profound release that was for me. I just didn't think there was any way to get the sort of agitational feminist politics I had started with and the psycho- analytic insight on the same page. Juliet helped, obviously, but Kristeva took it one stage further because her form of psychoanalysis was not just Freudian, it was also Lacanian, and therefore she went further in terms of psychoanalysis as a dislocating discourse. For Juliet, psychoanalysis could explain the inter- nalisation of norms, whereas for Kristeva the stress was far more on the impossibility of all identities. I think you need both.

Did you ever consider becoming a clinical psychoanalyst?

Yes, of course! When I got back to England in '73, my ambition was to be Ben Brewster, who was the editor of *Screen* magazine. He'd been the translator of Althusser, he had a huge influence on a lot of the articles that made *New Left Review* famous in its most influential period in the sixties. I just thought, "This is the life I want, as a sort of free-floating Parisian intellectual hanging out in Soho at the café Madame Berthoud and translating." And indeed the first thing I did was to translate Lacan. But then Ben told me that this was an absolutely impossible life, your life as a translator is too precarious, and he took an academic job. The moment he did that, I saw the writing on the wall and thought, "Obviously you have to have an academic job to survive." But my aim was to be a psychoanalyst.

As soon as I got my appointment at the University of Sussex, I went to a training analyst in London four times a week. Within practically minutes of starting, I realised the idea that I was having an analysis to become an analyst was a supreme kind of defenciveness against having any kind of analysis whatsoever. So the question mainly got suspended, and then became superseded by my commitment to writing and teaching. But part of me was, and remains at times, sorrowful about that decision simply because I will see a student with a problem or a difficulty and have to utterly respect the boundaries, which make it inappropriate for me to do anything other than listen to what they might say to me and refer them on. But that is hard, especially when you're teaching Freud. There's something quite painful about being aware that there is a whole other experience to which teaching Freud is alluding, which you can't go to in the seminar.

Did you have a Lacanian analysis?

No. I did not want a Lacanian analysis because there was too much buzz around him as an iconic figure and too many questions about his therapeutic practise. Also, I felt if I was going to have an analysis, I had to have it in English because I had to negotiate my mother tongue.

How important has translating been to you?

For me, translating is to do with my passionate affiliation for the French language. Whenever I arrive in France, within twenty seconds I find myself thinking in French. The French language, along with psychoanalysis, really allowed me to become who I am. It was leaving England, going and living in Paris at the age of twenty-one, and living in French that gave me a sense of creative possibility. Translating is a chance to go back and continue the dialogue between my English self and my French self.

Lacan has clearly been a pivotal influence on your work and yet you hesitate to say you were ever a "Lacanian."

What interested me about Lacan was the instability to which every human subject becomes radically entitled in his thinking. When he spoke, he thought he was putting himself in the place of the symptom and free-associating, and the audience was meant to be the analyst. He was attempting to redistribute power through the utterance in a way that did and didn't work. If you do that once, it's a radical gesture. If you do it twice, it's a stylistic tic. Do it three times, and you've founded a school. The radical moment can't last, by definition; it becomes a fashion, a style. There's no question that Lacan was a kind of autocrat, at the same time as he produced, in my view, the best analysis of the perversion of paternal power of any analyst to date. I was very attracted to a writing that could display the destitution of subjectivity against ideologies of completion, plenitude, and normalcy, and push that right to the limit. This also has the most profound ethicosocial implications, as Lacan's *Ethics* seminar I think makes clear. I therefore don't agree, at the same time as I admire her enormously, with Judith Butler's critique of Lacan in *Antigone's Claim*, which makes him above all a theorist of kinship networks and of symbolic normalcy. But I like even less the proselytising of the Lacanian followers and the extent to which his work has become a kind of "teaching." I find that sense of a purity of thought very unsettling—it turns Lacan's speech into a type of gospel.

Let's turn to your style. Your approach to punctuation is a trademark of your writing, with its often-winding sentences studded with parentheses, dashes, colons, semi-colons, and rhetorical questions; and your prose, though sometimes conversational and colloquial, can also be elusive. Is there a sense in which you don't want to be in control of—to master—your language (a suggestion that most writers, though perhaps not you, would take as an indictment)?

You're right, for me that's a compliment. You're also right that most of my sentences take several paths at once. It's because there are very few moments in my thinking where the possibility of alternative avenues to thought don't present themselves in the process of writing them down. What I'm trying to do all the time is produce a form of writing which throws up possibilities, in the course of a single sentence, that give you pause. I know I hesitate all the time I write and I think that's what comes out in the form. Perhaps I am striving for an academic version of the literary female sentence in which you do not carve your way through, but are halting all the time as you go.

Are you talking about anxiety manifesting itself at a textual level?

Maybe you're right, that I'm trying to produce a syntactic equivalent of a kind of inner hesitancy or even fear of certain directions or pathways which I nonetheless feel myself obliged to take. But I would also want to say that in all this discussion of me as someone who is going for difficult subjects and who is committed to psychoanalysis, there is a risk of aestheticising that process. It becomes a form of play, or stylistic nuance, or a false self-display of something which is actually very disturbing. So there is a pull in two directions—a forward movement, but also a sense of digressive qualification, which might be seen as anxiety. Certainly it is intended to give me and the reader pause.

One of the reasons why I wrote the novel is because I was very aware that more and more of my scholarly writing was being determined by the rhythms of sentences as much as by their content. I wanted to work in the space in which that would be absolutely fine. The simile became crucial since similes are the point where you make an unlikely correspondence or a connection, and all similes are therefore a form of free-association. You cannot do that in academic or political writing in the same way. You cannot drift.

The unforeseeable is I think what was also liberating about it, because it was so unknown both in terms of process—compared with academic writing it was like writing in the dark—and in terms of destination or audience.

Are the insights of your early critical-theoretical background implicit in your later work as an essayist and high-end journalist, or do you think that your writing has undergone a radical transformation over the decades?

A transformation in my style, I'm sure. The generation of the seventies around *Screen* magazine and the feminist journals *m/f* and *Camera Obscura*, all of which I was involved in, really believed in theory. I think that was an absolutely necessary moment and I would not want to knock it—as some people knock it—as apolitical. On the contrary, it was part of a political engagement with the norms of the recuperative, normative—what Althusser would call *interpellated*—language of commonsense. The figures of thought that entered into my vocabulary through that process—figures that come from Freud and from Lacan, in particular, and also Roland Barthes and Julia Kristeva—are there all the time when I write now. These writers are still my unconscious interlocutors but they've been assimilated into another level of reference. More recently my work has been based on the conviction that psychoanalytic thought has something crucial to say about public political identities, groups, and forms of collective belonging. That too goes back to my work on feminism where psychoanalysis was part of a political project, as a way of understanding how women were, and were not, formed as women. The links I am proposing today between psychoanalysis and our public lives is to that extent continuous with the very beginning.

So, would you still call yourself a "theorist"?

I will never forget Jean-Louis Schefer, the French analyst and historian of art and cinema saying to me in a conversation when I was a graduate student in Paris that it is crucial to distinguish between theory and method. He said something along the lines of, "Theory is another word for thought; it's thought which is self-reflexive. Whereas method is when you apply something because you think you have a program which will automatically yield up knowledge in relationship to its object." If theory is a form of self-scrutinising and self-critical thinking, then I like to think that I'm still a theorist.

Where do you see the current standing of psychoanalytic theory in the academy?

Psychoanalysis presents the academy with a set of very specific difficulties. A colleague at Sussex University suggested about twenty years ago that the only reason why I had been able to teach it was because there was no professional psychoanalytic establishment inside the universities who were controlling what psychoanalysis could be. So, peculiarly, its non-academic status produced total freedom in the academy to teach it. You then have the problem, however, that psychoanalysis becomes assimilated to literary criticism or the humanities more generally, which certainly happened in the early stages of psychoanalysis's presence in the academy, which means it gets cut off from its institutional bases and bases of practice. It's a real price that's been paid for the acceptance of psychoanalysis in humanities departments. At graduate level that is less so, with the plethora of psychoanalytic M.A.s in Great Britain, many of which have precisely set themselves to address this problem. I think psychoanalysis will continue to be taught, but will always be in an ambiguous and complicated position in relation to other branches of knowledge.

When you were writing a Ph.D. on children's fiction, would you have predicted that your work would eventually become so preoccupied with questions of geopolitics?

Well, the *Peter Pan* project was political in the Barthesian sense, which was to take a mythology and undo it. This is also the politics of deconstruction, you might say, that comes from Derrida. But was also part of a Marxist analysis of the capacity of state power and dominant cultural forms to coerce identities. Remember that the key image in Barthes's *Mythologies* was a photo on the cover of *Paris Match* of a "Negro" saluting the French flag. Barthes used the image to expose the myth proper to Western imperialist fantasy that everybody, regardless of racial difference and the history of imperial exploitation, belonged to a single harmoniously unified family. There was therefore a geopolitical dimension to semiotics at that moment. So there was always something political going on, but the precise form it would take I couldn't have predicted.

The question of my own identity as a Jewish woman was not central to my writing in the seventies, although I think it is latent to the preoccupation with Freud, and may well have been there in my finally siding with him as Jew against Jung (the irony of course was that he needed Jung before they split to counter the charge that psychoanalysis was a "Jewish" science). But the question becomes important far earlier than the work on Israel and Zionism, contrary to what some critics have said—it is there in my discussions of Plath's allusions to the Holocaust, of Lionel Trilling and anti-Semitism, and of Dorothy Richardson and the Jew. I do, however, remember a very important conversation with Laura Mulvey, the famous feminist film critic, where I was talking about the disturbance in Plath's writing, and she made the link for me, by saying, "Given what your family went through, given that history, how could you not get into such troubled waters." That helped me articulate that a subtext of my interest in what is disturbing about identity was my particular legacy and relationship to Jewish history. So I would say that it's been pressing more and more on my consciousness, and I've eventually been able to come to meet it. Today I see it as an ongoing project.

What part did your relationship with the Palestinian literary theorist Edward Said play in this increasing dialogue with your Jewish heritage?

It turned into a friendship, but started off with a major disagreement. When I met him, I'd just been asked to give the Clarendon lectures at Oxford, and when I was introduced to him I very naïvely announced, thinking to impress him, "I'm giving the first Clarendon lecture on Amos Oz." To which he replied: "You can't do that! Amos Oz is a *sabra*" [first-generation native-born Israeli who carried much of the weight of the pioneering ideal]. He was also angry because Oz had described the recently signed Oslo Accords as "the second victory of Zionism." This started off a long discussion about Amos Oz and about how you deal with writers who you might find politically suspect, as Oz was in Said's view, whereas I thought that Amos Oz was the most brilliant exposer of the fantasmatic underside of right-wing revisionist Zionism. So even though I shared some of the criticisms of Oz's political position, I thought there was something very important going on in that writing. In fact, I felt, and still feel, that one of the most important things to be learned from Said is his own understanding of the equivocation of writing, as in his discussions of Conrad for example. I think we need to take from him his remarkable ability to combine the clearest condemnation of what is being done to his people, and at the same time a plea for a form of identity for the Palestinians as a people which will be a different kind of national identity—more "contrapuntal" to use his favourite expression from music—which will not fossilise into a rigid form of ethnic nationalism. He then lived this ideal at the end of his life through the West-Eastern Divan Orchestra of young Arab and Israeli musicians, still playing worldwide today, which he founded with Daniel Barenboim.

What do you imagine Said would have thought about The Question of Zion, *had he lived to read it?*

Well, when we talked about it, he asked me if I was writing an apology for Zionism and I replied, "No, but I am trying to understand it." He wanted to read the lectures as I was writing them, and offered to help, but I thought that while his writing has been of huge importance to me, I really needed to do this on my own. I assumed of course that he would read the lectures and that we would have ample opportunities to talk about it, but tragically that did not happen, by a matter of days. I'll regret that for the rest of my life. I think he would have thought that to enter into the spirit of Zionism, to understand its deepest psychic impulses, was slightly high risk. Having said that, I see the whole book as a footnote to one strand of his famous article "Zionism from the Standpoint of Its Victims," from *The Question of Palestine*, which is that the Arab people need to understand the terror and exaltation out of which Zionism was born—

they need to understand what Zionism means for the Jews, without modifying for a minute their legitimate demands. My feeling was that the critics of Israeli policy also need to understand the same thing. I wanted a position where you could be critical but also enter into the force of the identification.

The reception to The Question of Zion *has, it's probably not unfair to say, been largely hostile.*

By no means exclusively. I have had amazingly positive responses as well. But I do find it quite extraordinary the level of vitriol that you receive when you go into this field. Nothing can prepare you for the extent to which you're misrepresented, willfully it seems and by definition. It makes working on Plath when I had to deal with the Plath Estate, Olwyn, and Ted Hughes, which was not easy to say the least, feel like a Sunday school picnic. For example, recently I've been accused of saying that the Holocaust is the reason why Israel attacked Gaza. Or that Israelis indoctrinate their children to be insensitive to Palestinian suffering, or that Israel is demonic. Repeatedly I get the sense that what offends most in the book is the use of psychoanalysis, because the feeling is that if you use psychoanalysis to talk about the unconscious dimension of a political identity, you are denigrating that identity. As if to talk about psychoanalysis in relation to Israel is to deny there was a rational component to the Zionist project. I believe that Zionism was the legitimate response to the legitimate need for a homeland for a persecuted people, and I say this on the second page of the book. But while there can be very serious historical reasons why something goes into place, other reasons to do with fantasy and desire and self-identification and longing can be just as important. The early Zionists themselves were very happy to diagnose the fantasmatic dimension of their project.

Was it difficult to balance scholarly rigor with polemic drive in writing The Question of Zion?

Well, I hope not, would have to be my answer. I decided that I wanted to understand Zionism better after writing *States of Fantasy*. It was a real question. At the same time I started from two premises: that the conflict seems to be intractable, and that Israel is the one with the power who therefore has the greater responsibility to struggle for a settlement in relationship to the Palestinian people. So there were two polemical starting points, if you like, but then it was all research, reading the earliest Zionist voices and trying to understand what they were saying. When I discovered early-twentieth-century statements about the project of Zionism, from Chaim Weizmann, for example, saying, "It [Palestine] will be as Jewish as England is English," it seemed to me there was a line that could be run from that kind of unequivocal ruthlessness at the heart of early Zionism—historically driven by persecution which has also to be understood—through to things which are happening on the ground as we speak. To that extent the book shares with the historian Avi Shlaim in his crucial book, *The Iron Wall*, the belief that there has been a predominant line of thought politically in Israel, certainly ascendant today, which has to date made negotiations with the Palestinians, or even recognition of them as equal human beings, well-nigh impossible. So I think the politics and the polemic and the scholarship are deeply intertwined.

But your theoretical writings mostly stress doubt, ambiguity, and the disavowal of blame. Does this project of disrupting stable meaning and confident assertions of right and wrong never conflict with the necessarily adversarial and combative character of your political interventions?

Well, yes and no. Part of the point of my exploration of Zionism was to unearth the profound ambiguities of the project in terms of those thinkers, of whom Martin Buber, Hans Kohn, Ahad Ha'am, and Hannah Arendt are the most important, who saw the fissures, the writing on the wall, from as early as 1930, and provided a sustained critique of the dangers of one version of Zionism. You scrape away the surface and there's a whole other story being told underneath; that's where the ambiguity is. If I thought Zionism was only intractable, there would have been no point writing the book. But it's central to the book that Zionism has within it the knowledge of what's wrong with it, or with the version that has repeatedly triumphed over other possible paths. So I would say the polemic, which is, "Look at the worse aspects of this journey," and the ambiguity, which is, "Somewhere deep down Zionism knows this," are again inseparable.

In The Haunting of Sylvia Plath *you assert that "there is no history outside its subjective realisation" and that "the division between history and subjectivity, between external and internal reality, between the trials of the world and the trials of the mind, is a false one." How do you see the concrete facts of historic persecution and injustice, with which your political analysis is concerned, interacting with the "facts" of psychic fantasy?*

Well, for me, psychic subjectivity is a concrete fact. Not in the sense that it would be amenable to positivist interpretation because the meaning of a dream is available for infinite ramification and reinscription, but nonetheless our psychic reality has the same order, the same thickness or consistency, as our political and historical reality, and in fact they're inseparable. Central to the project on Plath was to show that she was engaging in political arguments about what men and medical institutions and sexual power were, but she did it by going into the deep recesses of her own mind. So you can see that as a dry run for the later project on Zionism, which is to say, "Okay, there is a political situation here which is intractable. What are the deeply felt dimensions of that intractability?" I don't think facts are incompatible with that. It is a fact, for example, that about 400,000 Palestinians had been expelled from British-mandated Palestine before a single shot was fired in the 1948 war. I've never believed that establishing facts is not an essential part of what a political argument is, especially in the context of Israel where denial of the facts of 1948 has formed such a crucial role in the nation's over-benign image of itself. But the key is to show the uncertain moments of the history, the alternative possible paths, the still open moments of anxiety out of which a new way of thinking can still emerge.

One last question: in a tribute to Hannah Arendt published on the hundredth anniversary of her birth, you noted the ironic tone of Eichmann in Jerusalem *and remarked upon "her playfulness, the slight oddity of her style—as if the modern curse of nations, their militant conviction, resided at least partly in a failure to observe the proper tone."[2] Can you talk about the importance of tone in your writing about politics and nationalism?*

What I think Arendt was talking about is what Edward Said describes in relationship to Joseph Conrad—it is the reason why he won't dismiss him just as an imperialist or racist as Chinua Achebe does—which is that the language is so precarious. There is something so uncertain and so virtual about meaning in the novel that the very fact of empire, the historical reality, is put under a vacillating instability. As if the language is refusing to buy into the myth of a fixed eternal reality which empire attests to and through which it justifies itself. So I would say a hesitancy of tone—and in Arendt's case, it's an often biting irony—about our identity, that reflects itself in the language you use, is a key part of not conceding to solidified myths of ethnic or religious or racial purity, or of any concept of a fixed immutable identity.

Notes

Introduction: Reading Jacqueline Rose

1. Jacques Lacan, *Ecrits*, trans. Bruce Fink with Héloïse Fink and Russel Grigg (New York: Norton, 2006), 413.

2. Jacqueline Rose, *Sexuality in the Field of Vision* (London: Verso, 1986), 87.

3. Jacqueline Rose, "Translator's Note," *Feminine Sexuality: Jacques Lacan and the école freudienne*, ed. Juliet Mitchell and Jacqueline Rose, trans. Jacqueline Rose (New York: Norton, 1982), 59.

4. Jacqueline Rose, *Sexuality in the Field of Vision* (London: Verso, 1986).

5. Jacqueline Rose, "Feminism and the Psychic," in *Sexuality in the Field of Vision* (London: Verso, 1986), 7.

6. Sigmund Freud, "Analysis Terminable and Interminable," Standard Edition 23, 248.

7. Jacqueline Rose, *The Case of Peter Pan, or, The Impossibility of Children's Fiction* (Philadelphia, Pa.: University of Pennsylvania Press, 1993), xii.

8. Jean Laplanche and J. B. Pontalis, "Fantasy and the Origins of Sexuality," *International Journal of Psycho-analysis*, no. 49 (1968): 2–3, emphasis added. Note that certain psychoanalytical orientations, such as those influenced by Melanie Klein, often insist on a distinction between "fantasy" and "phantasy," the latter designating a strictly unconscious status.

9. Jacqueline Rose, *Sexuality in the Field of Vision* (London: Verso, 1986), 13.

10. Ibid., 168.

11. Republished as "Sylvia Plath—Again," in Jacqueline Rose, *On Not Being Able to Sleep: Psychoanalysis and the Modern World* (London: Chatto and Windus; Princeton, N.J.: Princeton University Press).

12. This transgenerational tragedy has now been extended by another act: the suicide of Nicholas Hughes, the son of Ted and Sylvia, on 16 March 2009.

13. Jacqueline Rose, *The Haunting of Sylvia Plath* (Cambridge, Mass.: Harvard University Press, 1992), 8.

14. Jacqueline Rose, *Why War? Psychoanalysis, Politics, and the Return to Melanie Klein*, Bucknell Lectures in Literary Theory (Oxford: Blackwell, 1993), 170.

15. Jacqueline Rose, *States of Fantasy*, 1994 Clarendon Lectures (Oxford: Oxford University Press, 1996), 51–52.

16. Jacqueline Rose, "Dorothy Richardson and the Jew," in *Between "Race" and Culture: Representations of "the Jew" in English and American Literature*, ed. Bryan Cheyette (Stanford, Calif.: Stanford University Press), 118.

17. Moustapha Safouan, *Jacques Lacan and the Question of Psychoanalytic Training*, trans. and intro. Jacqueline Rose (Houndmills, U.K.: Macmillan, 2000), 8.

18. Jacqueline Rose, *On Not Being Able to Sleep: Psychoanalysis and the Modern World* (London: Chatto and Windus; Princeton, N.J.: Princeton University Press), 8.

19. Jacqueline Rose, "On the Myth of Self-Hatred," in *A Time to Speak Out: Independent Jewish Voices on Israel, Zionism and Jewish Identity*, ed. Anne Karpf, Brian Klug, Jacqueline Rose, and Barbara Rosenbaum (Verso: London, 2008), 84–96.

20. Amnon Rubenstein, "A World without Israel," *Jerusalem Post*, 15 November 2005.

21. Avner Falk, *Anti-Semitism: A History and Psychoanalysis of Contemporary Hatred* (Westport, Conn.: Praeger, 2008), 119.

22. Melanie Phillips, "Intelligence Squelched," *Melanie Phillips' Diary*, 28 January 2005, http://www.melaniephillips.com/ (accessed 26 April 2009).

23. Jacqueline Rose, *The Haunting of Sylvia Plath* (Cambridge, Mass.: Harvard University Press, 1992), 129.

24. Gillian Rose, *Love's Work* (London: Chatto and Windus, 1995), 44–45.

25. Jacqueline Rose, *On Not Being Able to Sleep: Psychoanalysis and the Modern World* (London: Chatto and Windus; Princeton, N.J.: Princeton University Press), 218.

26. Compare with Rose's description in her novel *Albertine* of the heroine's "elegance of purpose" ([London: Chatto and Windus, 2001], 110).

27. Janet Malcolm, *The Silent Woman: Sylvia Plath and Ted Hughes* (New York: Knopf, 1994), 173, emphasis added.

28. Suzie Mackenzie, "Out of the Ivory Tower," *The Guardian*, 4 January 2003.

29. Jacqueline Rose, "The Height of the Matter," in *Bad Character* (A Festschrift for Mary-Kay Wilmers on the occasion of her seventieth birthday), ed. Andrew O'Hagan (London: privately printed, 2008), 82.

30. Jacqueline Rose, *The Haunting of Sylvia Plath* (Cambridge, Mass.: Harvard University Press, 1992), 70.

31. A short note on editorial considerations. Due to its range, Rose's work has had recourse to a variety of referencing systems that we have tried to rationalize as much as possible. However, although Rose usually relies on the *Standard Edition* for her quotations of Freud, this is not the case for the essay on *Mass Psychology*, which originally appeared as the preface to the new Penguin translation of that work. Moreover, to secure continuity within and between some of the articles that appear here, small emendations have sometimes been made to the text.

Chapter 1: Femininity and Its Discontents

1. Chapter 3 from *Sexuality in the Field of Vision* (London: Verso, 1986), 83–104. First published in *Feminist Review* 14 (summer 1983): 5–21, this essay was originally requested by the editors of *Feminist Review* to counter the largely negative representation of psychoanalysis which had appeared in the journal, and as a specific response to Elizabeth Wilson's "Psychoanalysis: Psychic Law and Order," *Feminist Review* 8 (summer 1981). (See also Janet Sayers, "Psychoanalysis and Personal Politics: A Response to Elizabeth Wilson," *Feminist Review* 10 [1982].) As I was writing the piece, however, it soon became clear that Elizabeth Wilson's article and the question of *Feminist Review*'s own relationship to psychoanalysis could not be understood independently of what has been—outside the work of Juliet Mitchell for feminism—a fairly consistent repudiation of Freud within the British Left. In this context, the feminist debate over Freud becomes part of a larger question about the importance of subjectivity to our understanding of political and social life. That this was in fact the issue became even clearer when Elizabeth Wilson and Angie Weir published an article, "The British Women's Movement," in *New Left Review* 148 (November–December 1984), which dismissed the whole area of subjectivity and psychoanalysis from feminist politics together with any work by feminists (historians and writers on contemporary politics) who, while defining themselves as socialist feminists, nonetheless query the traditional terms of an exclusively class-based analysis of power.

2. Wilson, "Psychoanalysis," 63.

3. Juliet Mitchell, *Psychoanalysis and Feminism: A Radical Reassessment of Freudian Psychoanalysis* (1974; New York: Basic, 2000).

4. Perry Anderson, "Components of the National Culture," *New Left Review* 50 (July–August 1968).

5. Rose, *Sexuality in the Field of Vision*, 81; David Cooper, "Freud Revisited" and "Two Types of Rationality," *New Left Review* 20 (May–June 1963) and 29 (January–February 1965); R. D. Laing, "Series and Nexus in the Family" and "What Is Schizophrenia?," *New Left Review* 15 (May–June 1962) and 28 (November–December 1964).

6. Perry Anderson, "Origins of the Present Crisis," *New Left Review* 23 (January–February 1964); see also E. P. Thompson, "The Peculiarities of the English," *Socialist Register 1965*.

7. Louis Althusser, "Freud and Lacan," trans. Ben Brewster, *New Left Review* 55 (March–April 1969); Jacques Lacan, "The Mirror Phase," trans. Jan Meil, *New Left Review* 51 (September–October 1968).

8. Juliet Mitchell, "Why Freud?," *Shrew* (November–December 1970), and *Psychoanalysis and Feminism*.

9. Michael Rustin, "A Socialist Consideration of Kleinian Psychoanalysis," *New Left Review* 131 (January–February 1982).

10. Michèle Barrett, *Women's Oppression Today* (London: New Left Books, 1980), chap. 2, 80–83.

11. See Gayle Rubin, "The Traffic in Women: Notes on the 'Political Economy' of Sex," *Toward an Anthropology of Women*, ed. Rayna R. Reiter (New York: Monthly Review Press, 1975), 157–210; and for a critique of the use of Levi-Strauss on which this reading is based, Elizabeth Cowie, "Woman as Sign" (1978), *Feminism and Film*, ed. E. Ann Kaplan (New York: Oxford University Press, 2000), 48–49.

12. Nancy Chodorow, *The Reproduction of Mothering* (Berkeley: University of California Press, 1978).

13. Ibid., 3.

14. Sayers, "Psychoanalysis and Personal Politics," 92.

15. Sigmund Freud, "The Dissolution of the Oedipus Complex" (1924); "Some Psychical Consequences of the Anatomical Distinction between the Sexes" (1925), Standard Edition 19, Pelican Freud 7; "Female Sexuality" (1931), Standard Edition 21, Pelican Freud 7.

16. Ernest Jones, "The Phallic Phase," *International Journal of Psychoanalysis* 14, part 1 (1933): 265; Karen Horney, "On the Genesis of the Castration Complex in Women" (1924), *Feminine Psychology* (London: Norton and Norton, 1967), 53.

17. Elizabeth Wilson, "Reopening the Case: Feminism and Psychoanalysis," opening seminar presentation in discussion with Jacqueline Rose, London, 1982. This was the first of a series of seminars on the subject of feminism and psychoanalysis which ran into 1983; see articles by Parveen Adams, Nancy Wood, and Claire Buck, *m/f* 8 (1983).

18. Althusser, "Freud and Lacan," see publisher's note in *Lenin and Philosophy and Other Essays* (London: New Left Books, 1971), 189–90.

19. For a more detailed discussion of the relative assimilation of Kleinianism through social work in relation to children in this country, especially through the Tavistock Clinic in London, see Rustin, "A Socialist Consideration of Kleinian Psychoanalysis," 85 and note. As Rustin points out, the state is willing to fund psychoanalysis when it is a question of helping children to adapt, but less so when it is a case of helping adults to remember.

20. Judith Walkowitz, *Prostitution and Victorian Society: Women, Class and the State* (London: Basic Books, 1980).

21. Carol Dyhouse, *Girls Growing Up in Late Victorian and Edwardian England* (London: Routledge and Kegan Paul, 1981).

22. Angus McLaren, *Birth Control in Nineteenth Century England* (London: Taylor and Francis, 1978).

23. Walkowitz, *Prostitution and Victorian Society*, 69.

24. Ibid., 59.

25. Ilza Veith, *Hysteria: The History of a Disease* (Chicago: University of Chicago Press, 1975), 229.

26. Breuer and Freud, *Studies on Hysteria*, Standard Edition 2:122; Pelican Freud 3:187.

27. Freud, "Preface and Footnotes to Charcot's Tuesday Lectures" (1892–94), Standard Edition 1:137.

28. Freud, *Studies on Hysteria*, Standard Edition 2:117; Pelican Freud 3:181.

29. Freud, *Three Essays on the Theory of Sexuality*, part 1, Standard Edition 7; Pelican Freud 7.

30. Ferdinand de Saussure, *Cours de linguistique générale* (1915) (Paris, 1972); trans. Roy Harris, *Course in General Linguistics* (London: Duckworth, 1983), 65–70.

31. Jones, "The Phallic Phase," 15.

32. Horney, "The Flight from Womanhood" (1926), *Feminine Psychology* (London: Norton and Norton, 1967), 68.

33. Freud, *Three Essays on the Theory of Sexuality*, Standard Edition 7:146n., Pelican Freud 7:57n.

34. Shulamith Firestone, *The Dialectic of Sex* (London: Cape, 1970).

35. See Juliet Mitchell, "Shulamith Firestone: Freud Feminised," in Mitchell, *Psychoanalysis and Feminism*, part 2, sec. 2, chap. 5.

36. Firestone, *The Dialectic of Sex*, 170.

37. Ibid., introduction by Rosalind Delmar.

38. Sayers, quoted by Wilson in "Reopening the Case."

39. Michèle Barrett and Mary McIntosh, "Narcissism and the Family: A Critique of Lasch," *New Left Review* 135 (September–October 1982).

40. Sheila Rowbotham, Lynne Segal, and Hilary Wainwright, *Beyond the Fragments: Femininism and the Making of Socialism* (London: Alyson, 1979).

41. Sayers, "Psychoanalysis and Personal Politics," 92–93.

Chapter 2: Feminine Sexuality

This excerpt is from an essay that was originally published as the second part of the introduction to Jacques Lacan, *Feminine Sexuality: Jacques Lacan and the école freudienne*, ed. Juliet Mitchell and Jacqueline Rose, trans. Jacqueline Rose (New York: Norton, 1982).

1. Lacan, *The Four Fundamental Concepts of Psychoanalysis* (London: Hogarth, 1977), 146.

2. Lacan, "Le stade du miroir comme formateur de la fonction du Je" (1936), *Ecrits* (Paris: Seuil, 1966) ("The Mirror Stage as Formative of the Function of the I," *Ecrits: A Selection* [London: Tavistock, 1977]).

3. D. W. Winnicott, "Mirror-Role of Mother and Family in Child Development" (1967), *Playing and Reality* (London: Tavistock, 1971).

4. Lacan, "Cure psychanalytique à l'aide de la poupée fleur," *Revue française de psychanalyse* 4 (October–December 1949): 567.

5. Emile Benveniste, "La nature des pronoms," *Problèmes de linguistique générale*; trans. "The Nature of Pronouns," *Problems in General Linguistics*.

6. Sigmund Freud, *Project for a Scientific Psychology* (1895), Standard Edition 1:319; *Beyond the Pleasure Principle*, 18:14–17, 11:283–87.

7. This can be compared with, for example, Melanie Klein's account of symbol formation (Melanie Klein, "The Importance of Symbol Formation in the Development of the Ego," *International Journal of Psychoanalysis* 11 [1930]) and also with Hannah Segal's ("Notes on Symbol Formation," *International Journal of Psychoanalysis* 38 [1957]), where symbolisation is an effect of anxiety and a means of transcending it on the path to reality, a path which is increasingly assured by the strengthening of the ego itself. Consult also Lacan's specific critique of Ernest Jones's famous article on symbolism (Ernest Jones, "The Theory of Symbolisation," *British Journal of Psychoanalysis* 11.2 [1916], and Jacques Lacan, "A la mémoire d'Ernest Jones: Sur la théorie du symbolisme" [1959], *Ecrits*), which he criticised for its definition of language in terms of an increasing mastery or appropriation of reality, and for failing to see, therefore, the structure of metaphor (or substitution) which lies at the root of, and is endlessly repeated within, subjectivity in its relation to the unconscious. It is in this sense also that Lacan's emphasis on language should be differentiated from what he defined as "culturalism," that is, from any conception of language as a social phenomenon which does not take into account its fundamental instability (language as constantly placing, and *displacing*, the subject).

8. Lacan, "La signification du phallus" (1958), *Ecrits*; trans. "The Meaning of the Phallus," *Feminine Sexuality*, 80.

9. Freud, "On the Universal Tendency to Debasement in the Sphere of Love" (1912), Standard Edition 11:188–89, Pelican Freud 7:258.

10. Lacan, "The Meaning of the Phallus," 81.

11. Juliet Mitchell, "Introduction 1," in Lacan, *Feminine Sexuality*, 1–26.

12. Freud, *Three Essays on the Theory of Sexuality* (1905), Standard Edition 7:144–46n., Pelican Freud 7:57n.

13. Lacan, *The Four Fundamental Concepts*, trans. Alan Sheridan (New York: Norton, 1998), 189.

14. *Ornicar?* 20–21 (summer 1980): 16. *Ornicar?* is the periodical of the department of psychoanalysis, under Lacan's direction up to 1981, at the University of Paris VIII (Vincennes).

15. Lacan, *The Four Fundamental Concepts*, 205.

16. Ibid., 181.

17. Lacan, *Le séminaire 2: Le moi dans la théorie de Freud et dans la technique de la psychanalyse* (1954–55) (Paris: Seuil, 1978), 267.

18. Ibid., 296.

19. Lacan, "Propos directifs pour un congrès sur la sexualité féminine" (1958), *Ecrits*, "Guiding Remarks for a Congress on Feminine Sexuality," *Feminine Sexuality*, 725.

20. Nancy Chodorow's reading of psychoanalysis for feminism (*The Reproduction of Mothering* [Berkeley: University of California Press, 1979]) paradoxically also

belongs here, and it touches on all the problems raised so far. The book attempts to use psychoanalysis to account for the acquisition and reproduction of mothering, but it can only do so by displacing the concepts of the unconscious and bisexuality in favor of a notion of gender imprinting ("the establishment of an unambiguous and unquestioned gender identity" [158]—the concept comes from Robert Stoller, "A Contribution to the Study of Gender Identity," *International Journal of Psychoanalysis* 45 [1965]) which is compatible with a sociological conception of role. Thus the problem needing to be addressed—the acquisition of sexual identity and its difficulty—is sidestepped in the account. The book sets itself to question sexual *roles*, but only within the limits of an assumed sexual *identity*.

21. Lacan, "La phase phallique et la portée subjective du complexe de castration," *Scilicet* 1 (1968) ("The Phallic Phase and the Subjective Import of the Castration Complex," *Feminine Sexuality*, 117). *Scilicet* was the review published in Lacan's series, *Le champ freudien*, at Editions du Seuil in Paris; apart from those by Lacan, the articles in the first issues were unsigned.

22. Lacan, "Les formations de l'inconscient," *Bulletin de Psychologie* 2 (1957–58): 13.

23. Lacan, "The Meaning of the Phallus," 80.

24. Lacan, "Les formations de l'inconscient," 14.

25. Ibid., 8.

26. Moustapha Safouan, "Is the Oedipus Complex Universal?" (trans. Ben Brewster from chap. 7 of *Etudes sur l'oedipe* [Paris: Seuil, 1974]), *m/f* 5–6 (1981): 9.

27. Lacan, "Intervention sur le transfert" (1966), *Ecrits*, 223, "Intervention on Transference," 69.

28. Lacan, *Le séminaire 17: L'envers de la psychoanalyse* (1969–70), 6, 10 (unpublished seminar, references to week and page of the transcript).

29. Safouan, "Is the Oedipus Complex Universal?," 127.

30. Lacan, "D'une question preliminaire à tout traitement possible de la psychose" (1955–56), *Ecrits* ("On a Question Preliminary to Any Possible Treatment of Psychosis," *Ecrits: A Selection*, 198).

31. For a fuller discussion of both of these points, see Lacan's "The Phallic Phase" and "Feminine Sexuality in Psychoanalytic Doctrine," *Feminine Sexuality*.

32. Lacan, "L'Instance de la lettre dans l'inconscient ou la raison depuis Freud" (1957), *Ecrits* ("The Agency of the Letter in the Unconscious or Reason since Freud," *Ecrits: A Selection*, 151).

33. Lacan, "Une lettre d'amour," *Le séminaire 20: Encore* (1972–73) (Paris, 1975) ("A Love Letter," *Feminine Sexuality*, 150).

34. Lacan, "The Phallic Phase," 113.

35. Lacan, "The Meaning of the Phallus," 82.

36. Ibid., 82.

37. Lacan, "Guiding Remarks for a Congress on Feminine Sexuality," 90.

38. Joan Rivière, "Womanliness as Masquerade," *International Journal of Psychoanalysis* 10 (1929); reprinted in *Formations of Fantasy* (London: Routledge, 1986).

39. Lacan, "Guiding Remarks for a Congress on Feminine Sexuality," 90.

40. Ibid., 95.

41. Safouan, *La sexualité féminine dans la doctrine freudienne* (Paris: Seuil, 1976), 110. The difficulty of these terms is recognised by Safouan, but the problem remains; compare also Eugénie Lemoine-Luccioni, *Partage des femmes* (Paris: Seuil, 1976) where there is the same collapse between the Other to be recognised by the woman in her advent to desire, and the real man whom, ideally, she comes to accept ("the Other, the man," 83; "the Other, the man as subject," 87). There seems to be a constant tendency to literalise the terms of Lacan's account and it is when this happens that the definitions most easily recognised as reactionary tend to appear. We can see this in such apparently different areas as Maud Mannoni's translation of the Name of the Father into a therapeutic practise which seeks to establish the paternal genealogy of the psychotic child (Maud Mannoni, *L'enfant, sa "maladie" et les autres* [Paris, 1967]; trans. *The Child, Its "Illness" and the Others* [New York: Pantheon, 1970]) and in Lemoine-Luccioni's account of the real Other who ensures castration to the woman otherwise condemned to pure narcissism. Lemoine-Luccioni's account is in many ways reminiscent of that of Helene Deutsch ("The Significance of Masochism in the Mental Life of Women," *International Journal of Psychoanalysis* 11 [1930]), who described the transition to femininity in terms of a desire for castration which is produced across the woman's body by the man.

Chapter 3: Negativity in the Work of Melanie Klein

First published as chapter 5 from Jacqueline Rose, *Why War?: Psychoanalysis, Politics, and the Return to Melanie Klein* (Oxford: Blackwell, 1993).

1. Leo Bersani gives a largely critical appraisal of Klein in "Death and Literary Authority: Marcel Proust and Melanie Klein," *The Culture of Redemption* (Cambridge, Mass.: Harvard University Press, 1990), chap. 1; *Women: A Cultural Review* devoted a large section of its second issue, *Positioning Klein*, to Melanie Klein (November 1990). These appear, however, to be exceptions. There is no full discussion of Klein, e.g., in the influential collection *The Trial(s) of Psychoanalysis*, ed. Françoise Meltzer (Chicago: University of Chicago Press, 1988). For discussion of feminism and Klein, see nn. 3 and 4 below.

2. Elizabeth Bott-Spillius, ed., *Melanie Klein Today: Developments in Theory and Practice*, vol. 1, *Mainly Theory*; vol. 2, *Mainly Practice*, New Library of Psychoanalysis, vols. 7 and 8 (London: Routledge in association with the Institute of Psycho-Analysis, 1988).

3. The clearest statement of these criticisms, focusing more directly on Ernest Jones but also addressing Klein, is given in Lacan, "The Phallic Phase and the Subjective Import of the Castration Complex," *Feminine Sexuality: Jacques Lacan and the école freudienne*, ed. Juliet Mitchell and Jacqueline Rose, trans. Jacqueline

Rose (London: Macmillan; New York: Norton, 1982), 99–122; also Juliet Mitchell, introduction to *Feminine Sexuality*, 1–26; and Jacqueline Rose, "The Cinematic Apparatus: Problems in Current Theory," *Sexuality in the Field of Vision* (London: Verso, 1986), 211n. Bersani, "Death and Literary Authority"; Noreen O'Connor, "Is Melanie Klein the One Who Knows Who You Really Are?," *Women: A Cultural Review* 1.2: 180–88. For a suggestive discussion of Lacan and Klein, see Malcolm Bowie, *Lacan* (London: Fontana Modern Master; Cambridge, Mass.: Harvard University Press, 1991), 144–48.

4. See, e.g., Madeleine Sprengnether, "(M)other Eve: Some Revisions of the Fall in Fiction by Contemporary Women Writers," *Feminism and Psychoanalysis*, ed. Richard Feldstein and Judith Roof (Ithaca, N.Y.: Cornell University Press, 1989), 298–322. The absence of Klein, both in this article and in Sprengnether's more recent book, *The Spectral Mother: Freud, Feminism, and Psychoanalysis* (Ithaca, N.Y.: Cornell University Press, 1990), which describes the absence of/haunting by the mother in Freud's work and the place of the pre-oedipal mother in subsequent analytic theory, seems striking. In discussion following the original presentation of "(M)other Eve" as a paper at "Feminisms and Psychoanalysis," a conference held at the University of Illinois, Normal, in 1986, Sprengnether explained the absence of Klein in terms of the negative component of Klein's work. See also *The (M)other Tongue: Essays in Feminist Psychoanalytic Interpretation*, ed. Shirley Nelson Garner, Claire Kahane, and Madeleine Sprengnether (Ithaca, N.Y.: Cornell University Press, 1985) and Jane Gallop's critique in terms of what she calls "the dream of the mother without otherness" ("Reading the Mother Tongue: Psychoanalytic Feminist Criticism," in Meltzer, *Trial[s] of Psychoanalysis*, 136).

5. Pearl King and Riccardo Steiner, eds., *The Freud-Klein Controversies 1941–45*, New Library of Psychoanalysis, vol. 11 (London: Routledge in association with the Institute of Psycho-Analysis, 1991); and Melanie Klein, Paula Heimann, Susan Isaacs, and Joan Rivière, *Developments in Psycho-Analysis*, ed. Joan Rivière, preface by Ernest Jones, International Psycho-Analytic Library, vol. 43 (London: Hogarth, 1952; Maresfield, 1989).

6. The fullest and most informative account is given by Riccardo Steiner, "Some Thoughts about Tradition and Change Arising from an Examination of the British Psychoanalytical Society's Controversial Discussions (1943–44)," *International Review of Psycho-Analysis* 12.27 (1985): 27–71; see also Pearl King, "Early Divergences between the Psycho-Analytical Societies in London and Vienna," and Teresa Brennan, "Controversial Discussions and Feminist Debate," both in *Freud in Exile*, ed. Edward Timms and Naomi Segal (New Haven, Conn.: Yale University Press, 1988), 124–33, 254–74; and Gregorio Kohon, "Notes on the History of the Psychoanalytic Movement in Great Britain," introduction to *The British School of Psychoanalysis: The Independent Tradition*, ed. Gregorio Kohon (London: Free Association Books, 1986), 24–50. For a discussion of the controversy, specifically in relation to the

concept of phantasy, see Anne Hayman, "What Do We Mean by 'Phantasy'?," *International Journal of Psycho-Analysis* 70 (1989): 105–14.

7. Janet Sayers, *Mothering Psychoanalysis: Helene Deutsch, Karen Horney, Anna Freud, Melanie Klein* (London: Hamish Hamilton, 1991); *Women: A Cultural Review* 1.2. The first reappraisal of Klein in this context, although not explicitly addressed to feminism, is Juliet Mitchell's introduction to *The Selected Melanie Klein*, ed. Juliet Mitchell (Harmondsworth, U.K.: Penguin, 1986). Nancy Chodorow discusses Klein in *The Reproduction of Mothering* (Berkeley: University of California Press, 1978), criticizing her for instinctual determinism, but praising her recognition, contra Freud, of the girl's early heterosexuality.

8. Nicholas Wright, *Mrs Klein* (London: Nick Hem Books, 1988); and review by Elaine Showalter, "Mrs Klein: The Mother, the Daughter, the Thief and Their Critics," *Women: A Cultural Review* 1.2: 144–48. Paul Roazen, *Freud and His Followers* (New York: Knopf, 1974; London: Allen Lane, 1975).

9. François Roustang, *Un destin si funeste* (Paris: Minuit, 1976) (trans. Ned Lukacher, *Dire Mastery* [Baltimore: Johns Hopkins University Press, 1982]); Jacques Derrida, "Du tout," *La carte postale: De Socrate à Freud et au-delà* (Paris: Flammarion, 1980), 525–49 (trans. Alan Bass, in *The Post Card: From Socrates to Freud and Beyond* [Chicago: University of Chicago Press, 1987], 497–521); Phyllis Grosskurth, *Freud's Secret Ring: Freud's Inner Circle and the Politics of Psychoanalysis* (London: Cape, 1991).

10. Derrida, "Du tout," 548; trans. *The Post Card*, 520.

11. Julia Kristeva, "The True-Real," *The Kristeva Reader*, ed. Toril Moi (Oxford: Blackwell, 1986), 214–37. Kristeva is undoubtedly the French psychoanalytic theorist who draws most consistently on the work of Melanie Klein.

12. None of the papers published in the 1952 *Developments in Psycho-Analysis* correspond exactly to the versions delivered to the scientific meetings of the British Society. I therefore use the different versions where appropriate, always indicating the source in the notes.

13. Donald Meltzer comments: "Any systematic attempt to teach Melanie Klein's work runs almost immediately into difficulties that are the exact opposite of the problems facing one in teaching Freud. Where the theoretical tail wags the clinical dog with him, hardly any theoretical tail exists to be wagged with her" (*The Kleinian Development*, part 2, *Richard Week by Week* [Perthshire: Clunie Press for the Roland Harris Educational Trust, 1978], 1).

14. R. Andrew Paskauskas, ed., *The Complete Correspondence of Sigmund Freud and Ernest Jones 1908–1939* (Cambridge, Mass.: Harvard University Press, 1993); compare also Steiner, "Some Thoughts about Tradition and Change."

15. Ernest Jones, preface to Rivière, *Developments in Psycho-Analysis*, v.

16. Rivière, *Developments in Psycho-Analysis*, 1.

17. Ibid., 2.

18. Ibid.

19. Susan Isaacs, opening statement, "Fifth Series of Scientific Discussions" (19 May 1943), in King and Steiner, *The Freud-Klein Controversies*, 444.

20. Marjorie Brierly, opening comments on Paula Heimann's paper "Some Aspects of the Role of Introjection and Projection in Early Development," in "Sixth Discussion of Scientific Controversies" (20 October 1943), in King and Steiner, *The Freud-Klein Controversies*, 538–39.

21. Paula Heimann, "Seventh Discussion of Scientific Controversies" (17 November 1943), in King and Steiner, *The Freud-Klein Controversies*, 569–70.

22. Rivière, introduction to *Developments in Psycho-Analysis*, 23–24.

23. Meltzer sees this as *the* central problem of Kleinian thought: "It requires an immense shift in one's view of the world to think that the outside world is essentially meaningless and unknowable, that one perceives the form but must attribute the meaning. Philosophically, this is the great problem in coming to grips with Kleinian thought and its implications" (*The Kleinian Development*, 86).

24. Rivière, introduction to *Developments in Psycho-Analysis*, 2–3.

25. Heimann, "Some Aspects of the Role of Introjection and Projection," 511.

26. For a critique of Klein's "instinctual reductionism," see Lacan, "The Phallic Phase," and Chodorow, *The Reproduction of Mothering*; Jean Laplanche and Jean-Bertrand Pontalis, "Fantasme originaire, fantasme des origines, origine du fantasme," *Les Temps modernes* 215 (1964)(trans. "Fantasy and Origins of Sexuality," *Formations of Fantasy*, ed. Victor Burgin, James Donald, and Cora Kaplan [London: Methuen, 1986], 5–34; first published in English in *International Journal of Psycho-Analysis* 49.1 [1969]) (their criticisms are directed more at Susan Isaacs than Klein); also Nicolas Abraham and Maria Torok, who refer to Kleinian "panfantastic instinctualism," in "Deuil ou melancolie, introjecter incorporer," *L'Écorce et le noyau* (Paris: Flammarion, 1987), 259–74 (trans. "Introjection-Incorporation: Mourning or Melancholia," *Psychoanalysis in France*, ed. Serge Lebovici and D. Widlocher [New York: International Universities Press, 1980], 3–16).

27. Isaacs, Balint, Lantos, in King and Steiner, *The Freud-Klein Controversies*, 272, 347, 349; Edward Glover, "Examination of the Klein System of Child Psychology," *Psycho-Analytic Study of the Child* 1 (1945): 103.

28. Rivière, "On the Genesis of Psychical Conflict in Earliest Infancy," in *Developments in Psycho-Analysis*, 43; paper published in *International Journal of Psycho-Analysis* (1936): 395–422.

29. Isaacs, replying to discussion of her paper "The Nature and Function of Phantasy," in "Second Discussion of Scientific Controversies" (17 February 1943), in King and Steiner, *The Freud-Klein Controversies*, 373.

30. Anna Freud, *The Ego and the Mechanisms of Defense* (London: Hogarth Press and the Institute of Psycho-Analysis, 1937), 57; passage cited by Susan Isaacs, "The Nature and Function of Phantasy," in King and Steiner, *The Freud-Klein Controversies*, 295. See also Anna Freud, "Notes on Aggression," 1949 (1948): "The presence of mental conflicts and of the guilt feelings consequent on them presupposes that a

specific, comparatively advanced stage in ego development has been reached" (*Indications for Child Analysis and Other Papers 1945–1956*, vol. 4 of *The Writings of Anna Freud* [New York: International Universities Press, 1968], 70).

31. Glover, "Examination of the Klein System," 88n., citing his own paper "Grades of Ego-Differentiation," *International Journal of Psycho-Analysis* (1930): 1–11.

32. Barbara Lantos, continuation of discussion of Isaacs's "The Nature and Function of Phantasy," in "Third Discussion of Scientific Controversies" (17 March 1943), in King and Steiner, *The Freud-Klein Controversies*, 413.

33. Isaacs, concluding discussion on "The Nature and Function of Phantasy," in "Fifth Discussion of Scientific Controversies," 460.

34. Rivière, "On the Genesis of Psychical Conflict in Earliest Infancy," 45.

35. Rivière, introduction to *Developments in Psycho-Analysis*, 29.

36. Rivière, "On the Genesis of Psychical Conflict in Earliest Infancy," 45.

37. Melanie Klein, "The Emotional Life and Ego-Development of the Infant with Special Reference to the Depressive Position," in King and Steiner, *The Freud-Klein Controversies*, 781.

38. Rivière, "On the Genesis of Psychical Conflict in Early Infancy," 45n.; introduction to *Developments in Psycho-Analysis*, 15.

39. Rivière, "On the Genesis of Psychical Conflict in Earliest Infancy," 54–55; Isaacs, "The Nature and Function of Phantasy," in Rivière, *Developments in Psycho-Analysis*, 302; Heimann, "Some Aspects of the Role of Introjection and Projection," 518.

40. Klein, *Narrative of a Child Analysis: The Conduct of the Psychoanalysis of Children as Seen in the Treatment of a Ten-year-old Boy*, vol. 4 of *The Writings of Melanie Klein* (London: Hogarth, 1975; Virago, 1988), 339.

41. Rivière, "On the Genesis of Psychical Conflict in Earliest Infancy," 47, 49.

42. Klein, "On Observing the Behaviour of Young Infants," also cited by Rivière, introduction to *Developments in Psycho-Analysis*, 270n., 30; compare Heimann: "Freud did not enter into the question of what happens in the infant's mind when he abandons the object" ("Certain Functions of Introjection and Projection," in Rivière, *Developments in Psycho-Analysis*, 145).

43. Klein, "The Emotional Life and Ego-Development of the Infant," 763–64.

44. See Phyllis Grosskurth, *Melanie Klein: Her World and Her Work* (New York: Knopf; London: Maresfield, 1986), 376–77.

45. Isaacs, "The Nature and Function of Phantasy," 103–7; Isaacs, "Fifth Discussion of Scientific Controversies" and "Sixth Discussion of Scientific Controversies," 466–67, 554, respectively; Heimann, "Some Aspects of the Role of Introjection and Projection," 505–6.

46. Rivière, introduction to *Developments in Psycho-Analysis*, 10.

47. Heimann, "Certain Functions of Introjection and Projection," 128.

48. Jacques Lacan, "Introduction au commentaire de Jean Hyppolite sur la 'Ver-

neinung' de Freud"; "Réponse au commentaire de Jean Hyppolite sur la 'Vernein-ung' de Freud"; "Appendice 1: Commentaire parlé sur la 'Verneinung' de Freud, par Jean Hyppolite," *Écrits* (Paris: Seuil, 1966), 369–80, 381–400, 879–88. Throughout this section, where I cite these articles in English, I am making use of Anthony Wilden's unpublished translations of the texts kindly made available to me by Richard Macksey.

49. Lacan, *Le Séminaire, Livre 1: Les écrits techniques de Freud* (Paris: Seuil, 1975), 63–73; trans. John Forrester, *Freud's Papers on Technique* (New York: Norton; Cambridge: Cambridge University Press, 1988), 52–61.

50. Freud, "Negation" (1925), Standard Edition 19:239, Pelican Freud 11:441.

51. Rivière, "On the Genesis of Psychical Conflict in Earliest Infancy," 52.

52. Hyppolite, "Commentaire parlé sur la 'Verneinung' de Freud," 886.

53. Ibid., 880. Hyppolite's reading, and Lacan's through Hyppolite, derives strongly from Hegel: "The dissimilarity which obtains in consciousness between the ego and the substance constituting its object, is their inner distinction, the factor of negativity in general. We may regard it as the defect of both opposites, but it is their very soul, their moving spirit" (*The Phenomenology of Spirit*, trans. J. B. Baillie, rev. ed. [London: Allen and Unwin; New York: Humanities Press, 1949], 96–97); compare too Alexandre Kojève's commentary: "In contrast to the knowledge that keeps man in a passive quietude, Desire dis-quiets him and moves him to action. Born of Desire, action tends to satisfy it, and can do so only by the 'negation,' the destruction, or at least the transformation of the desired object: to satisfy hunger, for example, the food must be destroyed or, in any case, transformed. Thus, all action is 'negating'" (*Introduction à la lecture de Hegel* [Paris: Gallimard, 1947], 11; trans. James H. Nichols Jr., *Introduction to the Reading of Hegel* [Ithaca, N.Y.: Cornell University Press, 1969], 3–4). For a discussion of negativity in relation to Hegel and psychoanalysis, see Kristeva, "La negativité, le rejet," *La révolution du language poétique* (Paris: Seuil, 1974), 101–50; trans. Margaret Waller, *Revolution in Poetic Language* (New York: Columbia University Press, 1984), 107–64.

54. Lacan, "Introduction au commentaire de Jean Hyppolite," 379–80.

55. Ella Sharpe, discussion of Melanie Klein's paper "The Emotional Life and Ego-Development of the Infant," in "Ninth Discussion of Scientific Differences" (1 March 1944), in King and Steiner, *The Freud-Klein Controversies*, 811.

56. Hyppolite, "Commentaire parlé sur la 'Verneinung' de Freud," 883.

57. Klein, "The Importance of Symbol-Formation in the Development of the Ego" (1930), *Love, Guilt and Reparation and Other Works, 1921–1945*, vol. 1 of *The Writings of Melanie Klein* (London: Hogarth, 1975; Virago, 1988); Lacan, *Le Séminaire*, 81–83, 95–103, 83 (trans. Forrester, *Freud's Papers on Technique*, 68–70, 78–88, 70). For a discussion of Lacan's reading of Klein's paper, see Shoshana Felman, "Beyond Oedipus: The Specimen Story of Psychoanalysis," *Jacques Lacan and the Adventure of Insight: Psychoanalysis in Contemporary Culture* (Cambridge, Mass.:

Harvard University Press, 1987), 105–28. For a discussion in relation to Lacan and Kristeva, see Mary Jacobus, " 'Tea Daddy': Poor Mrs Klein and the Pencil Shavings," *Women: A Cultural Review* 1.2: 160–79.

58. Melitta Schmideberg, "Intellektuelle Hemmung and Ess-Störung" (Intellectual inhibition and eating disorders), *Zeitschrift für psychoanalytische Pädagogie* 8 (1934): 110–16; Lacan, "Réponse au commentaire de Jean Hyppolite," 396–98.

59. Lacan, "Réponse au commentaire de Jean Hyppolite," 396.

60. Sharpe, "Ninth Discussion of Scientific Differences," 804–5.

61. Freud, "Negation," Standard Edition 19:236–37, Pelican Freud 11:439; cited by Heimann, "Some Aspects of the Role of Introjection and Projection," 505–6; by Isaacs, "Sixth Discussion of Scientific Controversies," 554–55; by Klein, formal reply to discussion of "The Emotional Life and Ego-Development of the Infant," in "Tenth Discussion of Scientific Differences" (3 May 1944), in King and Steiner, *The Freud-Klein Controversies*, 838 and 843n. (Klein offers a different translation from the version cited here; see editor's note, 843.)

62. See n. 26 above.

63. Isaacs, "The Nature and Function of Phantasy," 104.

64. Ibid.

65. Isaacs, "Sixth Discussion of Scientific Controversies," 555.

66. Isaacs, "The Nature and Function of Phantasy," 106.

67. P. Heimann and S. Isaacs, "Regression," paper presented 17 December 1943, in King and Steiner, *The Freud-Klein Controversies*, 706. See also Ella Sharpe's 1940 paper on metaphor in which she describes all speech as metaphor—"an avenue of outer-ance" (in itself a play on words)—through which the child, gradually controlling its bodily orifices, makes speech the outlet for tensions no longer relieved by physical discharge: "So that we may say that speech in itself is metaphor, that metaphor is as ultimate as speech" ("Psycho-Physical Problems Revealed in Language: An Examination of Metaphor," *Collected Papers on Psycho-Analysis*, International Psycho-Analytical Library, vol. 36 [London: Hogarth, 1950], 155–69).

68. See n. 26 above.

69. Rivière, introduction to *Developments in Psycho-Analysis*, 16, citing Isaacs, "The Nature and Function of Phantasy," 83. Note that in a footnote to this remark Rivière insists that, contrary to responses to Isaacs's paper at the time, this is central to Klein's conceptualization and not an innovation by Isaacs.

70. Isaacs, "The Nature and Function of Phantasy," in King and Steiner, *The Freud-Klein Controversies*, 313.

71. Rivière, "On the Genesis of Psychical Conflict in Earliest Infancy," 40.

72. Isaacs citing Freud, "The Nature and Function of Phantasy," in King and Steiner, *The Freud-Klein Controversies*, 280.

73. Ibid., 96, 94.

74. Rivière, "On the Genesis of Psychical Conflict in Earliest Infancy," 50.

75. Heimann, "Some Aspects of the Role of Introjection and Projection," 518;

Klein, discussion of Heimann's and Isaacs's paper on "Regression," in "Eighth Discussion of Scientific Differences" (16 February 1944), in King and Steiner, *The Freud-Klein Controversies,* 747.

76. See n. 23 above. Compare too Steiner: "The term phantasy . . . after being bounced back and forth throughout these lengthy discussions, seems to have assumed an enigmatic, evocative power. For one side it came to be synonymous with new discoveries—the more the term was analysed, the more it was enriched with new meanings. For the others it seemed to mean something not unlike belief in a new and hazily-defined mysticism. Some of the latter even saw it as something to be exorcised by the expulsion of the entire group led by Klein" ("Some Thoughts about Tradition and Change," 49–50).

77. Kate Friedlander, Marjorie Brierly, Friedlander, Brierly, in King and Steiner, *The Freud-Klein Controversies,* 409, 536, 539, 536.

78. Isaacs, "Fifth Discussion of Scientific Controversies," 19 May 1943, in King and Steiner, *The Freud-Klein Controversies,* 467; Heimann, "Seventh Discussion of Scientific Controversies," 17 November 1943, ibid., 580, 572, 570; original emphasis.

79. Anna Freud, "Indications for Child Analysis," *The Psycho-Analytic Treatment of Children* (London: Imago, 1946), 86, my emphasis.

80. Brierly, "Sixth Discussion of Scientific Controversies," 537. For a discussion of the possibility of distinguishing between incorporation and introjection in terms of metaphor, see Abraham and Torok, "Introjection-Incorporation."

81. Heimann, "Seventh Discussion of Scientific Controversies," 571.

82. Sharpe, "Seventh Discussion of Scientific Controversies," 582. For a discussion of these problems in relation to Freud's writing, see Mikkel Borch-Jacobsen, *Le sujet freudien* (Paris: Flammarion, 1982); trans. Catherine Porter, *The Freudian Subject* (London: Macmillan; Stanford, Calif.: Stanford University Press, 1982). Also Abraham and Torok, "Introjection-Incorporation."

83. Brierly, "Sixth Discussion of Scientific Controversies," 562.

84. Glover, "Sixth Discussion of Scientific Controversies," 56.

85. See, e.g., Samuel Weber, *The Legend of Freud* (Minneapolis: University of Minnesota Press, 1982); Derrida, "Speculer sur Freud," *La carte postale,* 257–409; Borch-Jacobsen, *Le sujet freudien.*

86. Walter Schmideberg, "The Second Extraordinary Business Meeting"; Karin Stephen, "Resolutions and the First Extraordinary Business Meeting," in King and Steiner, *The Freud-Klein Controversies,* 86, 50.

87. Brierly, "Sixth Discussion of Scientific Controversies," 536–47.

88. Glover, "Seventh Discussion of Scientific Controversies," 586.

89. Friedlander, "Discussion on 'Regression' " (discussion circulated only) (December 1943), in King and Steiner, *The Freud-Klein Controversies,* 728; Glover, ibid., 715.

90. Rivière, "On the Genesis of Psychical Conflict in Earliest Infancy," 47.

91. Heimann, "Certain Functions of Introjection and Projection," 161.

92. Rivière, "On the Genesis of Psychical Conflict in Earliest Infancy," 53.

93. Heimann and Isaacs, "Regression," 703.

94. Klein, "The Emotional Life and Ego-Development of the Infant," 201.

95. Ibid.

96. Klein, "Tenth Discussion of Scientific Differences," 836.

97. Klein, "The Oedipus Complex in the Light of Early Anxieties" (1945), *Love, Guilt and Reparation*, 408.

98. Heimann, "Some Aspects of the Role of Introjection and Projection," 523.

99. Klein, "The Emotional Life and Ego-Development of the Infant," 777–78; Lacan, *Le Séminaire*, 97 (trans. Forrester, *Freud's Papers on Technique*, 83).

100. Klein, "Tenth Discussion of Scientific Differences," 834.

101. Isaacs in reply to Glover, "Fifth Discussion of Scientific Controversies," 456–57; Klein, "A Contribution to the Psychogenesis of Manic-Depressive States" (1935), *Love, Guilt and Reparation*, 265.

102. Rivière, "On the Genesis of Psychical Conflict in Earliest Infancy," 60, 62.

103. Ibid.

104. Meltzer, *The Kleinian Development*, 46–47. Meltzer relates this issue to Klein's uncertainty about the conceptual status of the depressive position: "She had never absolutely crystallised this in her mind, for sometimes she speaks of 'penetrating' the depressive position, 'overcoming,' 'surpassing,' all of which have different implications regarding the meaning of the 'depressive position' " (114).

105. Heimann and Isaacs, "Regression," 183; compare also: "[Klein] has shown too that specific anxieties not only contribute in both sexes to fixations and regressions, but also play an essential part in stimulating the libido to move forward from pre-genital positions to the genital one" (175); and Meltzer: "The badness must be sufficiently split off . . . [but] it must not be so widely split off as to diminish the anxiety below the level that is sufficient for development" (*The Kleinian Development*, 64).

106. Heimann, "Certain Functions of Introjection and Projection," 162.

107. Heimann and Isaacs, "Regression," 703.

108. Isaacs, "The Nature and Function of Phantasy," 75; original emphasis.

109. See esp. Klein, "Early Stages of the Oedipus Conflict" (1928), *Love, Guilt and Reparation*, 186–98.

110. Klein, "The Emotional Life and Ego-Development of the Infant," 223, 209.

111. Klein, "The Importance of Symbol-Formation," 227; Lacan, *Le Séminaire*, 102 (trans. Forrester, *Freud's Papers on Technique*, 87).

112. Anna Freud, *Ego and the Mechanism of Defence*, 57, cited by Isaacs, "The Nature and Function of Phantasy," in King and Steiner, *The Freud-Klein Controversies*, 295.

113. Despite the stress on development in Anna Freud's writing, one could equally argue that it is a simplification to read her work exclusively in such terms. Her famous paper "Studies in Passivity" gives an extraordinary account of the possible

vicissitudes of sexual identification and desire in relation to masculinity and of the resurgence in adulthood of the most primary forms of identification, at the same time as recognizing the limits of its own model of explanation: "These interpretations are not satisfying. . . . What is left unexplained," etc.—i.e., the text can be read aporetically as much as developmentally ("Studies in Passivity" [1952] [1949–51], *Indications for Child Analysis*, 245–59).

114. Glover, "Examination of the Klein System," 112.

115. Ibid., 110.

116. Ibid., 116.

117. Hedwig Hoffer, continuation of discussion of Isaacs's paper "The Nature and Function of Phantasy," in "Fourth Discussion of Scientific Controversies" (7 April 1943), in King and Steiner, *The Freud-Klein Controversies*, 428, my emphasis.

118. Glover, "Examination of the Klein System," 99.

119. Rivière, introduction to *Developments in Psycho-Analysis*, 18–19.

120. Ibid., 36.

121. As Grosskurth comments: "The Discussions were dominated by women— and what women they were!" (*Melanie Klein*, 316). This quote from the manuscript of Virginia Woolf's *To the Lighthouse*, however, relates interestingly to Rivière's remark: "Don't we communicate more expressive better silently? Aren't we (women at any rate) more expressive silently gliding high together, side by side, in the curious dumbness which is so much [more] to our taste than speech" (cited by Lyndall Gordon, *Virginia Woolf: A Writer's Life* [Oxford: Oxford University Press, 1984], 195). A whole history of women's relationship to language and of psychoanalysis's relation to modernism is implicit in Rivière's extraordinary comment.

122. Sharpe, "Some Comments on Mrs. Klein's Theory of a 'Depressive Position,'" in "First Discussion of Scientific Controversies," in King and Steiner, *The Freud-Klein Controversies*, 340, 805.

Chapter 4: Mass Psychology

First published as the introduction to Sigmund Freud, *Mass Psychology and Other Writings* (London: Penguin Modern Classics, 2004); reprinted in *The Last Resistance* (London: Verso, 2007).

1. Sigmund Freud, *Mass Psychology and Other Writings*, trans. Jim Underwood (London: Penguin Modern Classics 2004), 17; all quotations, unless otherwise stated, are taken from this edition.

2. See Dennis B. Klein, *Jewish Origins of the Psychoanalytic Movement* (Chicago: University of Chicago Press, 1981); Carl E. Schorske, *Fin-de-siècle Vienna: Politics and Culture* (Cambridge: Cambridge University Press, 1981); Steven Beller, *Vienna and the Jews 1867–1938* (Cambridge: Cambridge University Press, 1989).

3. Freud, *Mass Psychology*, 54.

4. Ibid., 57–58.

5. Freud, *The Letters of Sigmund Freud*, selected and edited Ernst L. Freud (New York: Basic Books, 1960), cited in Marthe Robert, *From Oedipus to Moses: Freud's Jewish Identity*, trans. Ralph Manheim, Littman Library of Jewish Civilisation (London: Routledge and Kegan Paul, 1974), 46–47.

6. Freud, *Mass Psychology*, 36, 26.

7. Ibid., 26.

8. Ibid., 22.

9. Ibid., 117.

10. Ibid., 68.

11. Ibid., 69, original emphasis.

12. For a discussion of some of these internal paradoxes see Mikkel Borch-Jacobsen, *The Freudian Subject*, trans. Catherine Porter (Basingstoke: Macmillan, 1988), chap. 3, "The Primal Band"; also "The Freudian Subject: From Politics to Ethics," trans. Richard Miller and X. P. Callahan, *The Emotional Tie: Psychoanalysis, Mimesis and Affect* (Stanford, Calif.: Stanford University Press, 1992).

13. Freud, *Mass Psychology*, 43, 45, 47, 73.

14. Ibid., 47.

15. Ibid., 43.

16. Ibid., 41.

17. Ibid., 42.

18. Ibid., 43.

19. Ibid., 84.

20. Ibid., 45.

21. Ibid., 36.

22. Ibid.

23. Ibid., 5.

24. For a discussion of Freud in relation to *Haskalah*, see Marianne Krull, *Freud and His Father*, trans. Arnold Pomerans (New York: Norton, 1986), and also Yosef Hayim Yerushalmi, *Freud's Moses: Judaism Terminable and Interminable* (New Haven, Conn.: Yale University Press, 1991), 62–63.

25. Freud, *Mass Psychology*, 98.

26. Ibid., 11.

27. Ibid., 98.

28. Ibid., 220.

29. Ibid., 144.

30. Ibid., 27.

31. Freud, *Civilization and Its Discontents* (1930), trans. David McLintock (London: Penguin Modern Classics, 2002), 12.

32. Freud, *Mass Psychology*, 136.

33. Ibid., 152.

34. Ibid., 120.

35. Ibid., 123.

36. Ibid., 122.

37. Ibid., 125.

38. Ibid., 135.

39. Ibid., 160.

40. Ibid., 133.

41. Bertolt Brecht, *The Life of Galileo* (1955), trans. Desmond I. Vesey (London: Eyre Methuen, 1963), 54, 42.

42. Freud, *Mass Psychology*, 161.

43. Ibid., 150.

44. Ernest Jones, *The Last Phase: 1919–1939*, vol. 3 of *Sigmund Freud: Life and Work* (London: Hogarth, 1957), 375.

45. Freud, *Mass Psychology*, 158.

46. Ibid., 153.

47. Ibid., 162.

48. Letter of 9 October 1918 from Freud to Oskar Pfister, *Psychoanalysis and Faith: The Letters of Sigmund Freud and Oskar Pfister* (London: Hogarth, 1963), 63.

49. Freud, "Address to the Society of B'nai Brith," Standard Edition 20:273–74 (translation modified); Reik's translation is cited by David Bakan, who discusses the implications of Freud's use of "*heimlich,*" in *Sigmund Freud and the Jewish Mystical Tradition* (1958; London: Free Association Books, 1990), 305–19.

50. Freud, *Mass Psychology*, 106.

51. Ibid., 162.

52. Ibid., 210, my emphasis.

53. Ibid., 217.

54. Ibid., 288, 294.

55. Ibid., 210.

56. Freud, letter to Chaim Koffler, cited by Yerushalmi, *Freud's Moses*, 13, from *Freudiana: From the Collections of the Jewish National and University Library* (Jerusalem, 1973); letter to Arnold Zweig, from *The Letters of Sigmund Freud and Arnold Zweig* (New York: Harcourt Brace, 1970), cited in Yerushalmi, *Freud's Moses*, 15; letter to Ferenczi, cited in Jones, *Sigmund Freud*, 3:88.

57. *Freudiana*, cited by Yerushalmi, *Freud's Moses*, 13.

58. Ibid.

59. Ibid., 3.

60. Freud, *Mass Psychology*, 220.

61. Ibid.

62. Ibid., 221, 178, 221.

63. Lydia Flem, *Freud the Man: An Intellectual Biography* (New York: Other Press, 2003), 159.

64. Freud, *Mass Psychology*, 202.

65. Ibid., 266.

66. Viktor Shklovsky, "Art as Technique" (1917), *Russian Formalist Criticism*, ed. Lee T. Lemon and Marion J. Rees (Lincoln: University of Nebraska Press, 1965), 23, original emphasis; Viktor Shklovsky, *Mayakovsky and His Circle* (London: Pluto, 1972), 17, my emphasis.

67. Freud, *Mass Psychology*, 193.

68. Editor's note, *Moses and Monotheism* (1938), Standard Edition 23:4.

69. Freud, *Mass Psychology*, 210.

70. For a very strong discussion of *Moses* in relation to the idea of dispossession and dissociation, see Philippe Lacoue-Labarthe and Jean-Luc Nancy, "The Unconscious Is De-Structured Like a Language" and "From Where Is Psychoanalysis Possible?" *Stanford Literary Review* 6 (1991) and 8 (1992).

71. Freud, *Mass Psychology*, 210.

72. Yerushalmi, *Freud's Moses*, 84.

73. Freud, "The Disillusionment of the War," *Thoughts for the Time on War and Death* (1915), Standard Edition 14:285.

74. Freud, *Mass Psychology*, 167.

75. Edward Said, *Freud and the Non-European*, response by Jacqueline Rose, introduced by Christopher Bollas (London: Verso/London Freud Museum, 2003); Jan Assman, *Moses the Egyptian: The Memory of Egypt in Western Monotheism* (Cambridge, Mass.: Harvard University Press, 1997).

76. Freud, *Mass Psychology*, 180, 181, 228.

77. Ibid., 182.

78. Ibid., 183.

79. Ibid., 247, 192.

80. Assman, *Moses the Egyptian*, 3.

81. Ibid., 5.

82. Ibid, 21.

83. Freud to Arnold Zweig, 30 September 1934, *The Letters of Sigmund Freud and Arnold Zweig*, 91.

84. Freud, *Mass Psychology*, 213.

85. Martin Buber, *Mamre: Essays in Religion* (Melbourne: Melbourne University Press, 1974), cited in Bakan, *Sigmund Freud and the Jewish Mystical Tradition*, 117.

86. Freud to Jung, 16 April 1909, *The Freud/Jung Letters*, ed. William MacGuire, trans. R Mannheim (London: Hogarth, 1974), 220.

87. See Bakan, *Sigmund Freud and the Jewish Mystical Tradition*.

88. Freud, "The Moses of Michelangelo" (1914), Standard Edition 13:213.

89. Robert, *From Oedipus to Moses*, 95; the thesis is central to Robert's study.

90. Freud, *Mass Psychology*, 293.

91. Bluma Goldstein, *Reinscribing Moses: Heine, Kafka, Freud and Schoenberg in a European Wilderness* (Cambridge, Mass.: Harvard University Press, 1992), cited in Assman, *Moses the Egyptian*, 167.

92. Freud, *Mass Psychology*, 208.

93. Ibid.

94. Ibid., 304.

95. Karl Abraham, "Amenhotep IV: A Psychoanalytic Contribution Towards the Understanding of His Personality and of the Monotheistic Cult of Aton" (1912), *Clinical Essays and Papers on Psychoanalysis* (London: Hogarth, 1955).

96. Freud, *Mass Psychology*, 207.

97. Ibid., 208.

98. "Dear Prime Minister Sharon," *Ha'aretz*, 19 March 2004.

99. Freud, *Mass Psychology*, 208.

100. Ibid., 255.

101. Ibid., 256.

102. Freud to Zweig, 8 May 1932, *The Letters of Sigmund Freud and Arnold Zweig*, 40.

103. Nicolas Abraham, "Notes on the Phantom: A Complement to Freud's Meta-psychology," *The Shell and the Kernel*, vol. 1, ed. and trans. with an introduction by Nicholas T. Rand (Chicago: University of Chicago Press, 1994).

104. Freud, *Mass Psychology*, 253.

105. Freud, *Totem and Taboo: Some Points of Agreement between the Mental Lives of Savages and Neurotics* (1913), Standard Edition 13:xv.

106. Freud, *Mass Psychology*, 275.

107. Ibid., 277.

108. Wulf Sachs to Sigmund Freud, 1 August 1938, Archive of the Freud Museum.

109. Freud, *The Letters of Sigmund Freud*, cited in Robert, *From Oedipus to Moses*, 35.

110. Freud, *Mass Psychology*, 279.

111. Ibid., 223.

112. Ibid., 277.

113. Ibid., 269.

114. Ibid., 270.

115. Ibid., 118.

116. Ibid., 274.

117. Ibid., 179.

118. Hannah Arendt to Gershom Scholem, letter of 24 July 1963, in Hannah Arendt, *The Jew as Pariah: Jewish Identity and Politics in the Modern Age* (New York: Grove Press, 1978), 247.

119. Letter to Meitlis from Jacob Meitlis, "The Last Days of Sigmund Freud," *Jewish Frontier* 18 (September 1951), cited in Bakan, *Sigmund Freud and the Jewish Mystical Tradition*, 49.

120. Freud, *Mass Psychology*, 277.

121. Ibid., 258.

122. Ibid., 303.

382   NOTES

Introduction to Part II

1. Jacqueline Rose, *The Question of Zion* (Princeton, N.J.: Princeton University Press, 2005), xxii.

2. Gershom Scholem, *Sabbatai Sevi, The Mystical Messiah, 1626–1676*, trans. R. J. Zwi Werblowsky (Princeton, N.J.: Princeton University Press, 1975), 8.

3. Rose, *The Question of Zion*, 8.

Chapter 5: States of Fantasy

First published as the introduction to Jacqueline Rose, *States of Fantasy*, 1994 Clarendon Lectures (Oxford: Oxford University Press, 1996).

1. Sigmund Freud, *Extracts from the Fliess Papers (1892–9)*, Standard Edition 1:250.

2. Freud, *Extracts from the Fliess Papers*, Standard Edition 1:253. Note that these quotations are all taken from letters written in 1897, only months before the famous letter of 21 September 1897, when Freud confesses to Fliess that he no longer believes in his own earlier theory of the origins of hysteria in infantile seduction.

3. Ammiel Alcalay, "Understanding Revolution," *For Palestine*, ed. Jan Murphy (London: Writers and Readers, 1993), 80.

4. *Jerusalem Post*, 30 Zionist Congress Supplement, November 1982; cited by Michael Jansen in *Dissonance in Zion* (London: Zed, 1987), 53.

5. Amos Oz, "The Israeli-Palestinian Conflict: Tragedy, Comedy and Cognitive Block, A Storyteller's Point of View," *Israel, Palestine and Peace* (London: Vintage, 1994), 112.

6. George Eliot, *Daniel Deronda* (1876; Harmondsworth, U.K.: Penguin, 1967), 190.

7. Freud, *Extracts from the Fliess Papers*, Standard Edition 1:247–48.

8. I take this concept from the work of the Hungarian émigré analysts Nicolas Abraham and Maria Torok; see esp. Abraham, "Notes on the Phantom: A Complement to Freud's Metapsychology," in Abraham and Torok, *The Shell and the Kernel*, ed. and trans. with an introduction by Nicholas T. Rand (Chicago: University of Chicago Press, 1994); originally published as "Notules sur le fantôme," *Etudes freudiennes* 9–10 (1975), and in *L'écorce et le noyau* (Paris: Aubier-Montaigne, 1978).

9. Freud, *Extracts from the Fliess Papers*, Standard Edition 1:249, 253.

10. Josef Breuer and Sigmund Freud, *Studies on Hysteria* (1893–95), Standard Edition 2:165.

11. Cited in Jansen, *Dissonance in Zion*, 42.

12. "State," *Oxford English Dictionary*, 2d edn. (Oxford: Oxford University Press, 1991), 551, my emphasis.

13. Maria Torok, "Fantasy: An Attempt to Define Its Structure and Operation" (1959), in Abraham and Torok, *The Shell and the Kernel*, 35.

14. Freud, *Moses and Monotheism*, 1934–8 (1939), Standard Edition 23:76.

15. Olive Schreiner, *Woman and Labour* (1911; London: Virago, 1978), 139; Sheila Rowbotham, Lynne Segal, and Hilary Wainwright, *Beyond the Fragments: Feminism and the Making of Socialism* (London: Merlin, 1979).

16. Machiavelli, *The Prince*, extract included in *States and Societies*, ed. David Held et al. (Oxford: Blackwell, 1983), 67, my emphasis.

17. Max Weber, "Politics as a Vocation," *From Max Weber: Essays in Sociology*, ed. H. H. Gerth and C. Wright Mills (London: Routledge, 1991), 79.

18. Ibid., 78.

19. Max Weber, *Economy and Society*, ed. Guenther Roth and Claus Wittrich (New York, 1968), 1:9–10, 14.

20. Quentin Skinner, *The Foundations of Modern Political Thought* (Cambridge: Cambridge University Press, 1978), 2:358.

21. Karl Marx, "On the Jewish Question" (1843), *Writings of the Young Marx on Philosophy and Society*, ed. and trans. Loyd D. Easton and Kurt H. Guddat (New York: Doubleday, 1967), 240.

22. Cited in Elie Kedourie, *Nationalism* (1960; Oxford: Blackwell, 1993), 30.

23. Weber, *Economy and Society*, 56.

24. Max Weber, "The Sociology of Charismatic Authority," *From Max Weber*, 245.

25. Antonio Gramsci, "The Conception of Law," *Selections from the Prison Notebooks* (1929–35), ed. and trans. Quintin Hoare and Geoffrey Nowell-Smith (London: Lawrence and Wishart, 1971), 246–47.

26. Friedrich Engels, "The Origins of the Family, Private Property and the State" (1884), *Marx and Engels: Selected Works* (London: Lawrence and Wishart, 1968), 577.

27. Emil Habiby, *The Secret Life of Saeed, the Ill-Fated Pessoptimist: A Palestinian Who Became a Citizen of Israel*, trans. from the Arabic by Salma Khadra Jayyusi and Trevor le Gassick (New York: Vantage Press, 1982), 70.

28. Gramsci, *Selections from the Prison Notebooks*, 324; cited by Edward Said, *The Question of Palestine* (New York: Times Books, 1979; Vintage, 1992), 73; also cited in Said, *Orientalism* (New York: Pantheon, 1978), 25.

29. Freud, *The Psychopathology of Everyday Life* (1901), Standard Edition 6:211n.

30. Letter to L. Jaffe of the Keren Ha-Yesod, financial arm of the World Zionist organisation, 1935; 1930 letter to Dr Chaim Koffler in response to an appeal by the Jewish Agency to prominent European Jews for criticism of British policy on access to the Wailing Wall in Jerusalem and on Jewish immigration to Palestine, cited by Yosef Hayim Yerushalmi, *Freud's Moses: Judaism Terminable and Interminable* (New Haven, Conn.: Yale University Press, 1991), 13, as Yerushalmi points out, many committed Zionists, including Martin Buber and Gershom Scholem, shared Freud's 1930 view.

31. Muriel Spark, *The Mandelbaum Gate* (London: Macmillan, 1965; Harmondsworth, U.K.: Penguin, 1967).

32. Anton Shammas, *Arabesques*, trans. from the Hebrew by Vivian Eden (New York: Harper and Row, 1988), 23, 235, 243.

33. Virginia Woolf, *Three Guineas* (1938), ed. with introduction by Morag Shiach (Oxford: Oxford University Press, 1992), 273, 313.

34. "An Interview with Israel Shahak," *Journal of Palestine Studies* (spring 1975): 5: "For Ben-Gurion, the state of Israel was an instrument for doing a presumed benefit for the Jews. But for Rabin's generation, Jews are instruments for the security of the state of Israel. It is very much worse." Shahak has been one of the most consistent and outspoken internal critics of Israel and chairman of the Israeli League for Civil and Human Rights.

35. Martin Woollacott, "After the Slaughter Israel Must Search Its Soul," *Guardian*, 16 March 1994.

Chapter 6: Just, Lasting, Comprehensive

First published as chapter 4 in Jacqueline Rose, *States of Fantasy*, 1994 Clarendon Lectures (Oxford: Oxford University Press, 1996).

1. Claudia Koonz, ed., *Becoming Visible: Women in European History* (Boston: Houghton Mifflin, 1977), and Sue Lipschitz, *Tearing the Veil* (London: Routledge, 1977).

2. Stanley Fish, "Why Literary Criticism Is Like Virtue," *London Review of Books*, 10 June 1993.

3. Iris Murdoch, *The Sovereignty of the Good* (London: Chatto and Windus, 1970; Routledge, 1991), 90, my emphasis.

4. Jacques Derrida, "Force of Law: The 'Mystical Foundation of Authority,'" *Deconstruction and the Possibility of Justice*, ed. Drucilla Cornell, Michel Rosenfeld, and David Gray Carlson (London: Routledge, 1992), 16.

5. Ibid.

6. Jonathan Freedland, "A Firebrand in the Laundry," interview with Amos Oz, *Independent*, 4 September 1993.

7. Amos Oz, *Black Box*, translated from the Hebrew by Nicholas de Lange in collaboration with the author (London: Chatto and Windus, 1988), 110–11.

8. Cited by Fouad Moughrabi, "Arab Images in Israel," in "Views from Abroad," *Journal of Palestine Studies* (spring 1977): 167. It might be worth giving this quote in full: "We have become specialists in Arab mentality. For twenty-seven years, every Jew, here in Hulda and in other places, has been a great expert on Arab mentality. . . . Force is the only language the Arabs understand. That's what they are like. Listen to me, I know them all the way back from Silberstein's orange grove in Nes Ziona in the 1920s." Elsewhere Oz makes it clear that there is no symmetry between Israeli and Palestinian grievance: "They say that the Arabs (Egypt excepted) have a 'Saladin complex' and the Israelis have a 'Masada complex.' . . . I reject this comparison. There is no symmetry between a destruction complex and an insecurity complex. . . . Moreover, the Israeli insecurity complex is, to a large extent, a product of the 'Saladin

complex' of part of the Arab world" ("From Jerusalem to Cairo: Escaping the Shadow of the Past" (1982), in Amos Oz, *Israel, Palestine and Peace*, translated from the Hebrew by Nicholas de Lange [London: Vintage, 1996], 41).

9. Jacqueline Rose, "Black Hamlet," *States of Fantasy*, 1994 Clarendon Lectures (Oxford: Oxford University Press, 1996), 38–55.

10. Yehuda Lukacs, ed., *Documents on the Israeli-Palestinian Conflict 1967–1983* (Cambridge: Cambridge University Press, 1984), 1, 10.

11. Nicholas Abraham and Maria Torok, "Mourning or Melancholia: Introjection versus Incorporation," *The Shell and the Kernel: Renewals of Psychoanalysis*, ed., trans., and with an introduction by Nicholas T. Rand (Chicago: University of Chicago Press, 1994); first published as "Deuil ou melancolie, introjecter-incorporer," *Nouvelle revue de psychanalyse 6* (1972).

12. Roberto Mangabeira Unger, *The Critical Legal Studies Movement* (Cambridge, Mass.: Harvard University Press, 1983), 65.

13. Ibid.

14. Ibid., 24.

15. Judith N. Shklar, *The Faces of Injustice* (New Haven, Conn.: Yale University Press, 1992), 87.

16. "Sayings of the Week," *Independent*, 7 May 1994.

17. Lukacs, *Documents on the Israeli-Palestinian Conflict*, 1.

18. Raja Shehadeh, *The Third Way* (London: Quartet Books, 1982), 129.

19. Lukacs, *Documents on the Israeli-Palestinian Conflict*, 9.

20. *The Palestinian-Israeli Peace Agreement, A Documentary Record* (Washington, D.C.: Institute for Palestine Studies, 1993, 1994), 117.

21. David Hirst and Charles Glass, "An Interview with Israel Shahak," *Journal of Palestinian Studies* (spring 1975): 15.

22. *The Palestinian-Israeli Peace Agreement, A Documentary Record* (Washington, D.C.: Institute for Palestine Studies, 1993, 1994), 118.

23. Edward Said, "The Morning After," *London Review of Books*, 21 October 1993; "Who Is Worse?," *London Review of Books*, 20 October 1994; see also Robert Fisk, "Remaining Issues," *London Review of Books*, 23 February 1995, and Anton Shammas, "Palestinians Must Now Master the Art of Forgetting," *New York Times Magazine*, 26 December 1993.

24. Shammas, "Palestinians Must Now Master the Art of Forgetting."

25. Jay Murphy, "Interview: Noam Chomsky," *For Palestine*, ed. Jay Murphy (New York: Writers and Readers Publishing, 1993), 229; "I Know That They Are Tapping My Phone: Interview with Hanan Ashrawi," *Yediot Ahoronot*, 17 December 1993.

26. Israel Shahak, "The Oslo Accords: Interpreting Israel's Intentions," *Middle East International*, 22 October 1993. The Oslo agreement can be interestingly compared with the 1979 Camp David agreement with which Palestinian leaders almost uniformly refused to cooperate. This comment, made at the time by the émigré Palestinian scholar Fayez Sayegh, makes the similarities all too clear: "A fraction of

the Palestinian people . . . is promised a fraction of its rights (not including the national right to self-determination and statehood) in a fraction of its homeland (less than one-fifth of the area as a whole); and this promise is to be fulfilled several years from now, through a step-by-step process in which Israel is to exercise a decisive veto power over any agreement." Cited by Howard M. Sachar, *A History of Israel: From the Aftermath of the Yom Kippur War* (Oxford: Oxford University Press, 1987), 8.

27. Amos Oz, *The Slopes of Lebanon*, translated from the Hebrew by Maurie Goldberg-Bartura (London: Chatto and Windus, 1990), 6.

28. "The Nine-Point Peace Plan, Israel's Foreign Minister Abba Eban, 8 October, 1968," in Lukacs, *Documents on the Israeli-Palestinian Conflict*, 81.

29. Ibid., 86.

30. "The Jarring Questionnaire and Replies, January 1971," in Lukacs, *Documents on the Israeli-Palestinian Conflict*, 7.

31. Yeshayahu Leibowitz, "Right, Law and Reality," *Judaism, Human Values and the Jewish State*, ed. Eliezer Goldman (Cambridge, Mass.: Harvard University Press, 1995), 230–31.

32. "The term 'right,' at least in its secular sense, stands for something which is recognised by others, not for something which someone feels very strongly about" ("The Israeli-Palestinian Conflict," *Israel, Palestine and Peace*, 102).

33. "Fundamental Policy Guidelines of the Government of Israel as Approved by the Knesset, 5 Aug. 1981," in Lukacs, *Documents on the Israeli-Palestinian Conflict*, 107.

34. Benedict Anderson, *Imagined Communities: Reflections on the Origin and Spread of Nationalism* (London: Verso, 1983).

35. Unger, *The Critical Legal Studies Movement*, 100.

36. Plato, *The Republic*, trans. G. M. A. Grube, revised by C. D. C. Reeve (Indianapolis: Hackett, 1992), 6.

37. John Rawls, "The Law of Peoples," *Critical Inquiry* 20.1 (autumn 1993).

38. Ibid., 45.

39. Ibid., 48.

40. Ibid., 50.

41. Plato, *The Republic*, 170.

42. John Rawls, *A Theory of Justice* (Oxford: Oxford University Press, 1972), 143; Linda Colley, *Britons: Forging the Nation 1707–1837* (New Haven, Conn.: Yale University Press, 1994), 35.

43. Jean Genet, "Four Hours in Shatila," in Murphy, *For Palestine*, 29; extract from *Un captif amoureux* (Paris: Gallimard, 1986).

44. Shklar, *The Faces of Injustice*, 29.

45. Ibid., 37.

46. Ibid., 101.

47. Ibid.

48. Ibid., 49.

49. Richard Dowden, "Obituary," *Independent*, 7 January 1995.

50. Stephen Greenblatt, *Marvelous Possessions: The Wonder of the New World* (Oxford: Oxford University Press, 1988), 37–38.

51. Sigmund Freud, *Civilisation and Its Discontents* (1930 [1929]), Standard Edition 21:104; *Das Unbehagen in der Kultur*, Gesammelte Werke (Frankfurt: Fischer Verlag, 1948), xiv, 464.

52. Freud, *Civilisation and Its Discontents*, Standard Edition 21:95; *Das Unbehagen in der Kultur*, 455.

53. Freud, *Moses and Monotheism*, Standard Edition 23:82, original emphasis.

54. Freud, *Civilisation and Its Discontents*, Standard Edition 21:143.

55. Ibid., 109.

56. Ibid., 102; *Das Unbehagen in der Kultur*, 461.

57. Freud, *Civilisation and Its Discontents*, Standard Edition 21:109–10; *Das Unbehagen in der Kultur*, 468–69.

58. Freud, *Civilisation and Its Discontents*, Standard Edition 21:143.

59. Judith Shklar, *Ordinary Vices* (Cambridge, Mass: Belknap Press of Harvard University Press, 1984), 41.

60. Annette Baier, "Theory and Reflective Practices," *Postures of the Mind: Essays on Mind and Morals* (London: Methuen, 1985), 223.

61. Oz, *Black Box*, 176.

62. Ammiel Alcalay, *After Jews and Arabs: Remaking Levantine Culture* (Minneapolis: University of Minnesota Press, 1992), 272–74.

63. Amos Oz, *In the Land of Israel*, translated from the Hebrew by Maurie Goldberg-Bartura (New York: Harcourt Brace Jovanovich, 1983), 140.

64. Alcalay, *After Jews and Arabs*, 118.

65. Amos Oz, *Touch the Water, Touch the Wind* (London: Chatto and Windus, 1973), 137.

66. Grace Halsell, *Prophecy and Politics: The Secret Alliance between Israel and the Christian New Right* (Chicago: Lawrence Hill, 1986), 37.

67. Max Weber, "Politics as a Vocation," *From Max Weber: Essays in Sociology*, trans. H. H. Gerth and C. Wright Mills (London: Routledge, 1973), 122.

68. Hannah Arendt, *The Origins of Totalitarianism* (New York: Harcourt Brace Jovanovich, 1957, 1979), 462.

69. Alasdair MacIntyre, *Whose Justice? Which Rationality?* (London: Duckworth, 1988), 347.

70. Freud, *Civilisation and Its Discontents*, Standard Edition 21:142.

71. For one account of these connections and parts of this history, see Paul Gilroy, *The Black Atlantic: Modernity and Double Consciousness* (London: Verso, 1993), chap. 6.

72. Nelson Mandela, "We Must End the Old Social Order and Bring in a New

One," *Intensify the Struggle to Abolish Apartheid: Nelson Mandela Speeches 1990* (New York: Pathfinder, 1990), 59.

73. Cited in Milton Shain, *The Roots of Anti-Semitism in South Africa* (Charlottesville: University Press of Virginia, 1994), 138.

74. Alcalay, *After Jews and Arabs*, 284.

Chapter 7: Apathy and Accountability

Extract from a paper first delivered at a conference on public intellectual life—"The Republic of Letters: On the Public Role of Writers and Intellectuals"—held in Oxford in 2000, whose papers were published as *The Public Intellectual*, ed. Helen Small (Oxford: Blackwell, 2002). Subsequently republished in *On Not Being Able to Sleep: Psychoanalysis and the Modern World* (London: Chatto and Windus, 2003).

1. *Truth and Reconciliation Commission of South Africa Report*, 5 vols. (London: Macmillan, 1998, 1999), 4:313. Hereafter cited in the text.

2. Eric Hobsbawm with Antonio Polio, *The New Century*, trans. Allan Cameron (London: Little Brown, 2000), 86.

3. Antjie Krog, *Country of My Skull* (Johannesburg: Random House, 1998), 73.

4. Philip Gourevitch, *We Wish to Inform You that Tomorrow We Will Be Killed with Our Families: Stories from Rwanda* (London: Picador, 1999), 7.

5. Njabulo Ndebele, "Memory, Metaphor and the Triumph of Narrative," *Negotiating the Past: The Making of Memory in South Africa*, ed. Sarah Nuttall and Carli Coetzee (Cape Town: Oxford University Press, 1998), 26.

6. Krog, *Country of My Skull*, 36. I discuss Krog and the question of representation and language in relation to the Truth Commission more fully in "Aux marges du littéraire: Justice, verité, reconciliation," *Où é en est la théorie litteraire?*, ed. Julia Kristeva and Evelyne Grossman, Actes du Colloque organisé à l'Université Paris, 7 May 1999, *Textuel* 37 (2000).

7. Hobsbawm, *The New Century*, 115.

8. Desmond Tutu, *No Future without Forgiveness* (London: Rider, 1999), 2.

9. Gerry Hugo, "Confession of a Torturer," *Wounded Nations, Broken Lives: Truth Commissions and War Tribunals, Index on Censorship* 5 (1996): 66.

10. Kader Asmal, Louise Asmal, and Ronald Suresh Roberts, "When the Assassin Cries Foul: Modern Just War Doctrines," *Looking Back, Reaching Forward: Reflections on the Truth and Reconciliation Commission of South Africa*, ed. Charles Villa-Vicencio and Wilhelm Verwoerd (Cape Town: University of Cape Town Press; London: Zed Books, 2000), 93; see also their *Reconciliation through Truth: A Reckoning of Apartheid's Criminal Governance* (Cape Town: David Philip, 1997). Compare Neville Alexander: "The fundamental flaw in the conceptualisation of the TRC as a mechanism for 'dealing with the past' lies in the fact that the question of moral debt (Habermas) is judged by both trying to 'share' it between victim and perpetrator

and by individualising it, i.e., removing it from systematic embedment" ("The Politics of Reconciliation," unpublished mimeo of chapter of book forthcoming from University of Natal Press). My thanks to Benita Parry for making this available to me.

11. Asmal, Asmal, and Roberts, "When the Assassin Cries Foul," 92.

12. For fuller discussion, see Neville Alexander and Deborah Neel, *The Making of Apartheid 1948–1961: Conflict and Compromise* (Oxford: Clarendon, 1991).

13. Tutu, *No Future without Forgiveness*, 25.

14. Ibid., 28.

15. See Arthur Chaskalson, "Human Dignity as a Foundational Value for our Constitutional Order," Third Bram Fischer lecture. My thanks to Stephen Clingman for making this text available to me.

16. Wole Soyinka, *The Burden of Memory, The Muse of Forgiveness* (New York: Oxford University Press, 1999), 25–26.

17. Ibid., 9. See Janet Cherry, "Historical Truth: Something to Fight For," in Villa-Vicencio and Verwoerd, *Looking Back, Reaching Forward*. For me the best critique of the commission in relation to the category of truth is contained in Gillian Slovo's extraordinary novel, *Red Dust* (London: Virago, 2000). See also Richard Wilson's critique of the TRC in terms of the distinction between retribution and revenge, in *The Politics of Truth and Reconciliation in South Africa: Legitimising the Post-Apartheid State* (Cambridge: Cambridge University Press, 2001). I do not, however, agree with those critiques of the commission which see it as "an officially instituted memory-loss" (Benita Parry, "Reconciliation and Remembrance," *Pretexts* 5.1–2 [1995]) or which suggest, as Alexander does at points in his chapter on the commission, that the truth offered by the commission was simply unexamined truth, or rather that this was a problem of which the commissioners were unaware. See, for example, this statement by Professor Simpson, a psychiatrist specialising in post-traumatic stress disorder, cited in the final volume chapter on Reconciliation (Oxford: "Truth is one essential component of the needed social antiseptic which could cleanse the social fabric of the systematised habit of disregard for human rights, but it needs to be an *examined truth, it needs to be considered, thought about, debated and digested and metabolised by individuals and society*" [5:356, my emphasis]); and the statement from Bishop David Beetge at the follow-up hearing workshop in Reiger Park: "We retell our painful stories so that we shall remember" (5:350).

Chapter 8: The Body of Evil

First published in *New Formations, Intellectual Work* 53 (summer 2004).

1. For a discussion of the symmetry between Bush's and Bin Laden's rhetoric, see Bruce Lincoln, "Symmetric Dualisms: Bush and Bin Laden on October 7," *Holy Terrors: Thinking about Religion after September 11* (Chicago: University of Chicago Press, 2003).

2. All quotes from Martin Kettle, *Guardian*, 12 September 2002.

3. *Truth and Reconciliation Commission of South Africa Report*, 5 vols. (London: Macmillan, 2003), 5:272.

4. Ibid.; Gillian Slovo, "Evil Has a Human Face," *Guardian*, 31 October 1998.

5. Susan Neiman, *Evil in Modern Thought: An Alternative History of Philosophy* (Princeton, N.J.: Princeton University Press, 2002, new edn. 2004), xv. For a philosophical survey of evil, see also Peter Dews, *The Idea of Evil* (Oxford: Wiley-Blackwell, 2007).

6. *Truth and Reconciliation Commission of South Africa Report*, 1:13.

7. Coetzee's essays in the voice of Elizabeth Costello were subsequently published as *Elizabeth Costello: Eight Lessons* (London: Secker and Warburg, 2003). The text of the original lecture has been slightly modified in the published version in which this quotation no longer appears.

8. *Truth and Reconciliation Commission of South Africa Report*, 5:271–72.

9. Gillian Slovo, *Every Secret Thing: My Family, My Country* (London: Little, Brown, 1997), 267.

10. Ibid., 268.

11. Ibid., 266.

12. J. M. Coetzee, *The Lives of Animals* (Princeton, N.J.: Princeton University Press, 1999), 16.

13. Coetzee, *Elizabeth Costello*, 164.

14. Ibid., 178.

15. Ibid., 179.

16. Ibid., 165.

17. Ibid.

18. Ibid.

19. Ibid., 158, 168.

20. Ibid., 168–69, original emphasis.

21. Ibid., 179.

22. Ibid., 178.

23. Hannah Arendt, *Eichmann in Jerusalem: A Report on the Banality of Evil* (New York: Viking, 1963; rev. ed. Harmondsworth, U.K.: Penguin, 1977), 150.

24. Ibid., 471, original emphasis.

25. Ibid., 291.

26. Coetzee, *Elizabeth Costello*, 177.

27. Ibid., 176.

28. *Truth and Reconciliation Commission of South Africa Report*, 1:130.

29. Jacqueline Rose, "Deadly Embrace," *The Last Resistance* (London: Verso, 2007), 125–37.

30. *Truth and Reconciliation Commission of South Africa Report*, 5:228.

31. Ibid., 5:282.

32. Ibid., 1:42.

33. Ibid., 5:292.

34. Ibid., 5:274.

35. Ibid., 5:286, 289, 292.

36. Arendt to Scholem, letter of 24 July 1963, in Arendt, *The Jew as Pariah: Jewish Identity and Politics in the Modern Age* (New York: Grove Press, 1978), 251, my emphasis.

37. Neiman, *Evil in Modern Thought*, 303.

38. Arendt, *Eichmann in Jerusalem*, 27.

39. Ibid., 149.

40. Fyodor Dostoyevsky, *The Brothers Karamazov* (London: Quartet, 1990), 255.

41. In *Holy Terrors*, Bruce Lincoln states that the first page of the document has never been made available.

42. Kanan Makiya and Hassan Mneimneh, "Manual for a 'Raid,'" *Striking Terror: America's New War*, ed. Robert B. Silvers and Barbara Epstein (New York: New York Review of Books, 2002), 303.

43. Ibid., 304.

44. Ibid., 306. All citations from the version provided in *Striking Terror*, which can be compared with the translation published as an appendix in Lincoln, *Holy Terrors* and in the *Observer*. In *Holy Terrors*, these lines appear as "Remember that this is a battle for the sake of God" (96).

45. Makiya and Mneimneh, "Manual for a 'Raid,'" 321–24.

46. Ibid., 321.

47. Lincoln, *Holy Terrors*, 94.

48. Makiya and Mneimneh, "Manual for a 'Raid,'" 312.

49. Ibid., 315.

50. Ibid., 317.

51. Ibid. For a discussion of the tension between the Islam of Mecca and Medina, see Kenneth Cragg, "The Finality of the Qur'an and the Contemporary Politics of Nations," *Islam and the West Post-9/11*, ed. Ron Greaves, Theodore Zeldin, Yvonne Haddad, and Jane Idelman (Aldershot, U.K.: Ashgate, 2004), and interview with Al-Afif Al-Akhdar, Ehud Ein-Gil, "The Roots of Jihad," *Ha'aretz*, 17 March 2006.

52. These lines appear in both the *Observer* version of the document and in Lincoln but not in the version published in Makiya and Mneimneh.

53. Lincoln, *Holy Terrors*, 12.

54. Neiman, *Evil in Modern Thought*, 285.

55. Lincoln, *Holy Terrors*, 16.

56. "Atta's Document" and commentaries, *Observer*, 30 September 2001.

57. Ibid.

58. For a discussion of the proximity between Islamic, Christian, and Jewish fundamentalism, see Karen Armstrong, *The Battle for God* (London: HarperCollins,

2001), and John Shepherd, "Self-critical Children of Abraham? Roots of Violence and Extremism in Judaism, Christianity and Islam," in Greaves et al., *Islam and the West Post-9/11*.

59. Sigmund Freud, *Moses and Monotheism* (1938), Standard Edition 23:114.

60. Freud, *Civilisation and Its Discontents* (1930), Standard Edition 21:136.

61. Christopher Bollas, "The Structure of Evil," *Cracking Up: The Work of Unconscious Experience* (New York: Hill and Wang, 1995), 189, 193.

62. Coetzee, *Elizabeth Costello*, 178.

63. Ibid., 159, 163, 178.

64. Ibid., 158.

65. J. M. Coetzee, *Disgrace* (London: Secker and Warburg, 2000), 44.

66. Ibid., 61.

67. Ibid., 67.

68. Ibid., 9.

69. Ibid., 141, 160.

70. Ibid., 74.

71. Ibid., 220.

72. Jean Amery, *On Aging: Revolt and Resignation* (1968), trans. John D. Barlow (Bloomington: Indiana University Press, 1994), 116, 117.

73. Ibid., 118, 127.

Chapter 9: Zionism as Psychoanalysis

Excerpt from " 'Imponderables in Thin Air': Zionism as Psychoanalysis (Critique)," chap. 2, *The Question of Zion*, the Christian Gauss seminars (Princeton, N.J.: Princeton University Press; Melbourne: Melbourne University Press, 2005).

1. Amnon Raz-Krakotzkin, "Binationalism and Jewish Identity: Hannah Arendt and the Question of Palestine," *Hannah Arendt in Jerusalem*, ed. Stephen E. Aschheim (Berkeley: University of California Press, 2001), 169.

2. Martin Buber, "Zionism and 'Zionism' " (1948), *A Land of Two Peoples: Martin Buber on Jews and Arabs*, ed. Paul Mendes-Flohr (New York: Oxford University Press, 1983), 220.

3. Ibid., 221.

4. Ibid.

5. Arendt, "Zionism Reconsidered," in *The Jew as Pariah: Jewish Identity and Politics in the Modern Age*, ed. Ron H. Feldman (New York: Grove Press, 1978), 146.

6. Martin Buber, "The Spirit of Israel and the World of Today" (1939), *On Judaism*, ed. Nahum N. Glatzer (New York: Schocken, 1967), 185.

7. Buber, "Zionism and 'Zionism,' " 221.

8. Ibid.

9. Ibid., 223.

10. Ibid., 221.

11. Said, "Zionism from the Standpoint of Its Victims," in *The Question of Palestine* (New York: Times Books, 1979), 89, original emphasis.

12. "What Needs to Be Done," announcement of opening Conference of the Sikkuy "Or Commission Watch" Project, *Ha'aretz*, 18 June 2004.

13. Buber, "Should the Ichud Accept the Decree of History?" (1949), in Mendes-Flohr, *A Land of Two Peoples*, 250.

14. David Grossman, "Death as a Way of Life" (May 2001), *Death as a Way of Life*, translated from the Hebrew by Haim Watzman (London: Bloomsbury, 2003), 115.

15. Buber, "Politics and Morality" (1945), in Mendes-Flohr, *A Land of Two Peoples*, 172.

16. Sigmund Freud, "The Dissection of the Psychical Personality," Lecture 31, *New Introductory Lectures* (1933), Standard Edition 22:80.

17. Jacques Lacan, "The Freudian Thing" (1955), *Ecrits: A Selection*, trans. Alan Sheridan (London: Tavistock, 1977), 128–29.

18. Buber, "The Spirit of Israel and the World of Today," 180, my emphasis.

19. Hans Kohn, "Nationalism" (1921–22), *The Jew: Essays from Buber's Journal der Jude*, ed. Arthur A. Cohen, trans. Joachim Neugroschel (Tuscaloosa: University of Alabama Press, 1980), 27, my emphasis.

20. For a discussion of the emergence of messianism in German-Jewish thought after the First World War, see Anson Rabinbach, *In the Shadow of Catastrophe: German Intellectuals between Apocalypse and Enlightenment* (Berkeley: University of California Press, 1977). Rabinbach shows how the radical messianism of Walter Benjamin and Ernest Bloch, apocalyptic and esoteric, with its "certitude of redemption" and "bleak pessimism" after the First World War, progressively detached itself from political and hence any nationalist aspirations (62). See esp. chap. 1 "Between Apocalypse and Enlightenment: Benjamin, Bloch and Modern German-Jewish Messianism."

21. Arnold Zweig, *The Face of East European Jewry*, ed. and trans. Noah Isenberg (Berkeley: University of California Press, 2004), 11.

22. Buber, "The Meaning of Zionism" (1946), in Mendes-Flohr, *A Land of Two Peoples*, 183.

23. Ibid.

24. Buber, "Zionism and 'Zionism,'" 222.

25. Ibid.

26. Ibid., 221.

27. Theodor Herzl to Baron Maurice de Hirsch, 3 June 1895, *Complete Diaries*, 1:27, cited in Amos Elon, *Herzl* (New York: Holt, Rinehart, and Winston, 1975), 137.

28. Chaim Weizmann, *Trial and Error: The Autobiography of Chaim Weizmann* (London: Hamish Hamilton, 1949), 418; "On World Citizenship and Nationalism" (Prague, 27 March 1912), in *Letters and Papers*, vol. 1, ser. B, ed. Barnet Litvinoff (Jerusalem: Israel Universities Press; New Brunswick, N.J.: Transaction Books,

1983), 89, 91; "The Jewish People and Palestine" (statement before Palestinian Royal Commission, Jerusalem, 25 November 1936) (Jerusalem: Office of Zionist Organization, 1936), 12; "States Are Not Given" (address at UPA Campaign Banquet, London, 28 January 1948), in *Letters and Papers*, vol. 1, ser. B., 687. (My emphasis throughout.)

29. Hans Kohn, "Zionism Is Not Judaism" (1929), in Mendes-Flohr, *A Land of Two Peoples*, 98.

30. Ibid.

31. Ibid., 99.

32. Buber, "Our Reply" (response to an attack by the clandestine military group, the Irgun, in their underground publication, *Herut* [Freedom] on Buber's organization, the Ichud, 1945), in Mendes-Flohr, *A Land of Two Peoples*; "Should the Ichud Accept the Decree of History?," 178, 248.

33. Kohn, "Zionism Is Not Judaism," 99.

34. Ibid.

35. Kohn, "Zionism," *Living in a World Revolution: My Encounters with History* (New York: Trident, 1964), 48; my thanks to Elliott Ratzman for giving me this volume.

36. Kohn, "Nationalism," 30, 96.

37. Ibid., 20, editor's note.

38. Ibid., 26.

39. Hermione Lee, *Virginia Woolf* (London: Chatto, 1996), 510.

40. Kohn, "Nationalism," 26.

41. Ibid., 28.

42. Ibid.

43. Ibid., 26.

44. Ibid., 25; Freud, *The Future of an Illusion* (1927), Standard Edition 21:18.

45. Judah Leon Magnes, "Like All the Nations?" (1930), in Mendes-Flohr, *A Land of Two Peoples*, 447.

46. Freud, *The Future of an Illusion*, Standard Edition 21:34; Kohn, "Nationalism," 27.

47. Edward Said, *Freud and the Non-European* (London: Verso/Freud Museum, 2003).

48. Kohn, "Nationalism," 27.

49. Leon Pinsker, "Autoemancipation" (1882), in Arthur Hertzberg, *The Zionist Idea: A Historical Analysis and Reader* (Philadelphia and Jerusalem: The Jewish Publication Society, 1997), 184, 194.

50. Buber, "Should the Ichud Accept the Decree of History?," 250, my emphasis.

51. Arendt, "Zionism Reconsidered," 156.

52. Ibid., 172.

53. Ibid., 156.

54. Ibid., 132–33.

55. Ibid., 133.

56. Ibid., 162.

57. *Dangerous Liaison: Israel and the USA*, channel 4, TV documentary, dir. Nick Read, written and presented by Jacqueline Rose, 24 August 2002, unpublished transcript of interview with Ramadan Safi, 5. See also Noam Chomsky, *Fateful Triangle: The United States, Israel and the Palestinians* (1993; rev. ed., London: Pluto, 1999).

58. J. L. Talmon, *Israel among the Nations* (London: Weidenfeld and Nicholson, 1970), 102–3.

59. Arendt, "Zionism Reconsidered," 141.

60. Tom Nairn, "Out of the Cage," *London Review of Books*, 24 June 2004, 14.

61. Kohn, "Nationalism," 30.

62. Arendt, "To Save the Jewish Homeland: There Is Still Time" (May 1948), *The Jew as Pariah*, 187.

63. Ronit Chacham, *Breaking Ranks: Refusing to Serve in the West Bank and Gaza Strip* (New York: Other Press, 2003), 60.

64. Chris McGreal, "Israel on Road to Ruin," *Guardian*, 15 November 2003.

65. Gideon Levy, "I Punched an Arab in the Face," *Ha'aretz*, 21 November 2003, 7.

66. Ze'ev Schiff, "Crazy after All These Years," *Ha'aretz*, 26 March 2003.

67. Cited in Colin Urquhart, "Hamas Barrage Follows Israeli Raid," *Guardian*, 22 October 2003.

68. Ari Shavit, "On the Eve of Destruction" (interview with Avraham Burg), *Ha'aretz*, 14 November 2003, 4.

69. Kohn, "Nationalism," 20.

70. Jonathan Spyer, "Israel's Demographic Timebomb," *Guardian*, 14 January 2004.

71. Ilan Pappe, "Encountering Nationalism: The Urge for Cohabitation," *A History of Modern Palestine: One Land, Two Peoples* (Cambridge: Cambridge University Press, 2004), 116. See also Susan Lee Hattis, *The Bi-National Idea in Palestine during Mandatory Times* (Tel Aviv: Shikmona Press, 1970).

72. Samuels to Smuts, 30 March 1948, cited in Hattis, *The Bi-National Idea*, 316.

73. Peter Hirschberg, "One-State Awakening," *Ha'aretz*, 12 December 2003, 14.

74. Cited in N. de M. Bentwich, *Ahad Ha'am and His Philosophy* (Jerusalem: Keren Hayesod [Palestine Foundation Fund] and the Keren Kayemeth Le-Israel, 1927), 22.

75. Cited in ibid., my emphasis.

76. Kohn, "Zionism Is Not Judaism," 99.

77. Ahad Ha'am to Weizmann, quoted in Yosef Gorny, *Israel and the Arabs 1882–1948: A Study of Ideology* (Oxford: Clarendon, 1987), 63.

78. Ahad Ha'am, "The Truth from Palestine" (1891), cited in Steven J. Zipperstein, *Elusive Prophet: Ahad Ha'am and the Origins of Zionism, Jewish Thinkers*, gen. ed. Arthur Hertzberg (London: Peter Halban, 1993), 57.

79. Bentwich, *Ahad Ha'am and His Philosophy*, 5; Zipperstein, *Elusive Prophet*, xxiii, Hertzberg, *The Zionist Idea*, 250.

80. Cited in Zipperstein, *Elusive Prophet*, 196.

81. Ahad Ha'am, "The Truth from Palestine," cited in ibid., 61.

82. Ahad Ha'am to Moshe Smilansky, 18 November 1913, cited in Kohn, "Zionism," 54.

83. Ahad Ha'am, "The Wrong Way" (1889), *Nationalism and the Jewish Ethic: Basic Writings of Ahad Ha'am*, ed. and introd. Hans Kohn (New York: Schocken, 1962), 35.

84. Ahad Ha'am, "Positive and Negative," *Selected Essays*, trans. Leon Simon (Philadelphia: Jewish Publication Society of America, 1912), 52.

85. Gershom Scholem to Walter Benjamin, 1 August 1931, *Walter Benjamin: The Story of a Friendship*, trans. Harry Zohn (New York: Schocken, The Jewish Publication Society of America, 1981), 173.

86. Ahad Ha'am, "Moses" (1904), *Essays, Letters, Memoirs*, trans. and ed. Leon Simon, East West Library (Oxford: Oxford University Press, 1946), 327.

87. For a discussion of Franz Rosenzweig's critique of this issue, and the question of idolatry in relation to political fulfillment, see Leora Batnitzky, *Idolatry and Representation: The Philosophy of Franz Rosenzweig Reconsidered* (Princeton, N.J.: Princeton University Press, 2000).

88. Ahad Ha'am, "Moses," 323.

89. Ibid., 324.

90. Magnes, "Like All the Nations?," 447; Arendt, "Zionism Reconsidered," 171, 166.

91. Herzl to Moritz Güdemann, 16 June 1895, *Complete Diaries*, 1:112.

92. Herzl, *The Jewish State: An Attempt at a Modern Solution of the Jewish Question*, trans. Sylvie D'Avigdor (1896; London: Central Office of the Zionist Organisation, 1934), 20.

93. Herzl, conversation with de Hirsch, 2 June 1895, *Complete Diaries*, 1:21.

94. Ahad Ha'am, "The Wrong Way," 40.

95. Ahad Ha'am, "A Spiritual Centre" (1907), *Essays, Letters, Memoirs*, 205.

96. Ahad Ha'am, "Two Masters," *Selected Essays*, 100.

97. Ahad Ha'am, "A Spiritual Centre," 206.

98. Ahad Ha'am, "Past and Future" (1891), *Selected Essays*, 87.

99. Ibid., 81.

100. Frédéric Paulhan, *L'activité mentale et les éléments de l'esprit* (Paris: Felix Alcan, 1889), pt. 3, *L'esprit*, bk. 1, *Synthèse concrète*, chap. 2, "Synthèses générale: La formation de la personnalité—Darwin," 484.

101. Ibid., introduction, 7.

102. Ibid., pt. 3, bk. 1, chap. 1, "Synthèses partielles: L'amour, la langue," 282–83.

103. Ibid., pt. 3, bk. 1, chap. 2, 504.

104. Paulhan, *Les mensonges du caractère* (Paris: Felix Alcan, 1905), 107.

105. Ibid., 109.

106. Ahad Ha'am, "Two Masters," 91.

107. Ibid.

108. Ibid., 92.

109. Ibid.

110. Ibid., 102.

111. Ibid.

112. Ibid., 94.

113. Siegfried Lehmann, "Zionism and Irrationality," in *Shorashim* (Roots) (1943), cited in Georges Bensoussan, *Une histoire intellectuelle et politique du sionisme, 1860– 1960* (Paris: Fayard, 2002), 777.

114. Ahad Ha'am, "Two Masters," 99.

115. Robert Louis Stevenson, *The Strange Case of Dr Jekyll and Mr Hyde* (1881; Oxford: Oxford University Press, 1987), 61.

116. Lacan, "Intervention on Transference" (1951), *Feminine Sexuality: Jacques Lacan and the école freudienne*, ed. Juliet Mitchell and Jacqueline Rose, trans. Jacqueline Rose (London: Macmillan, 1982), 72.

117. Haim Chisin, 10 February 1882, *A Palestine Diary: Memoirs of a Bilau Pioneer 1881–1887* (New York, 1976), cited in Josef Frankel, *Prophecy and Politics: Socialism, Nationalism and the Russian Jews 1862–1917* (Cambridge: Cambridge University Press, 1981), 92.

118. *Dangerous Liaison*, typescript of interview with Aaron and Tamara Deutsch, 6.

119. Yosef Hayim Yerushalmi, *Zakhor: Jewish History and Jewish Memory* (1982; Seattle: University of Washington Press, 1996), 8.

120. David Hartman, *Israelis and the Jewish Tradition*—the critique of messianism forms the starting point of Hartman's attempt to retrieve another Jewish spirit for modern-day Israel.

121. *Dangerous Liaison*, interview with Aaron and Tamara Deutsch, 12.

122. Nadav Shragai, "This Land Is Our Land," *Ha'aretz*, 25 June 2004, 10.

123. Compare the moment in the 1950s, recalled by the psychoanalyst Christopher Bollas at the opening of his book *The Shadow of the Object* (New York: Columbia University Press, 1987), when Paula Heimann, a member of the British Psycho-Analytic Society, posed a simple question about the patient in analysis: "Who is speaking?" "Up until this moment it had always been assumed that the speaker was the patient," Bollas comments. "But Heimann knew that at any given moment in a session a patient could be speaking with the voice of the mother, or the mood of the father, or some fragmented voice of a child self either lived or withheld from life" (1). My thanks to Martin Golding for pointing out this similarity.

124. Ahad Ha'am, "Imitation and Assimilation" (1893), *Selected Essays*, 107–8.

125. Ibid., 113–14.

126. Ahad Ha'am, "A Spiritual Centre," 203.

127. Ahad Ha'am, "Imitation and Assimilation," 112.

128. Ibid.

129. Ahad Ha'am, "Moses," 315.

130. Kohn, "Nationalism," 27.

131. Weizmann, "A Vision of the Future," New York, January 16, 1960, in *Letters and Papers*, vol. 2, ser. B, ed. Barnet Litvinoff (Jerusalem: Israel Universities Press; New Brunswick, N.J.: Transaction Books, 1983), 389.

132. Ahad Ha'am, "Ancestor Worship," *Selected Essays*, 208.

133. Ibid., 209.

134. Ibid.

135. Freud, *The Interpretation of Dreams*, 68; translation taken here from the Oxford University Press edition (1999), trans. Joyce Crick, 58.

136. Ahad Ha'am, "Ancestor Worship," 209.

137. Ibid.

138. Levy, "I Punched an Arab in the Face," *Ha'aretz*, 21 November 2003, 6.

139. McGreal, "Israel on Road to Ruin"; Amir Oren, "The Fire Next Time," *Ha'aretz*, 26 March 2004.

140. In addition to Ronit Chacham, *Breaking Ranks*, see also *Refusenik! Israel's Soldiers of Conscience*, ed. Peretz Kidron (New York: Zed, 2004).

141. Aviv Lavie, "Hebron Diaries," *Ha'aretz*, 18 June 2004, 10; see also, for extracts from the catalog, Yitzhak Laor, "In Hebron," *London Review of Books*, 22 July 2004.

142. Moshe Nissim, "I Made Them a Stadium in the Middle of the Camp," *Yediot Aharanot*, 31 May 2002.

143. Chacham, *Breaking Ranks*, 60.

144. Gordon, "Some Observations" (1911), in Hertzberg, *The Zionist Idea*, 377.

145. Buber, "Politics and Morality," 171.

146. Ibid.

147. Ibid., 175, editor's note.

148. Arendt, "The Jewish State: Fifty Years After," in *The Jew as Pariah*, 175.

149. Ibid.

150. *Dangerous Liaison*, typescript of interview with Naomi Chazan, 28.

151. Buber, "And If Not Now, When?" (1932), in Mendes-Flohr, *A Land of Two Peoples*, 104.

152. Marc H. Ellis, *Israel and Palestine Out of the Ashes: The Search for Jewish Identity in the Twenty-First Century* (London: Pluto, 2002), 35, 138.

Chapter 10: Sexuality in the Field of Vision

1. Sigmund Freud, "Leonardo da Vinci and a Memory of His Childhood" (1910), Standard Edition 11:70n.; Pelican Freud 14:159n. This essay was written for the catalogue of the exhibition *Difference: On Representation and Sexuality*, held at the New Museum of Contemporary Art, New York, December–February 1984–85 and at the Institute of Contemporary Arts, London, September–October 1985, 31–33. The exhibition, curated by Kate Linker, included works by Ray Barrie, Victor Burgin,

Hans Haacke, Mary Kelly, Silvia Kolbowski, Barbara Kruger, Sherry Levine, Yve Lomax, Jeff Wall, and Marie Yates. There was also a film and video exhibition in conjunction with the art exhibition in New York, curated by Jane Weinstock. Only part of the drawing discussed here is now attributed to Leonardo (see "Leonardo da Vinci and a Memory of His Childhood," Pelican Freud 14:161n).

2. Freud, "The Dissection of the Psychical Personality" (1933 [1932]), Standard Edition 22:79, Pelican Freud 2:112 (passage retranslated by Samuel Weber in *The Legend of Freud*, 1).

3. Peter Wollen makes a similar point on the relationship between perceptual and sexual contradiction in Manet's *Olympia*, in "Manet: Modernism and Avant-Garde," *Screen* 21. 2 (summer 1980): 21.

4. Freud, "Some Psychical Consequences of the Anatomical Distinction between the Sexes" (1925), Standard Edition 252, Pelican Freud 335–36.

5. Freud, *From the History of an Infantile Neurosis* (1918 [1914]), Standard Edition 17:29–47, Pelican Freud 9, 80–81.

6. For discussion of these issues in relation to film, see Laura Mulvey's crucial article, "Visual Pleasure and Narrative Cinema," and also Jane Weinstock's article in *Difference: On Representation and Sexuality* (New York: New Museum, 1984; London: Institute of Contemporary Arts, 1985).

7. Roland Barthes, "Change the Object Itself," *Image, Music, Text* (London: Fontana, 1977).

8. Barthes, *S/Z* (Paris: Seuil, 1970); trans. Richard Miller, *S/Z* (New York: Hill and Wang, 1974).

9. Leo Steinberg defined postmodernism as the transition from nature to culture; this is reinterpreted by Craig Owens, "The Allegorical Impulse: Towards a Theory of Postmodernism," *October* 12–13 (spring–summer 1980): esp. 79–80, and also Douglas Crimp, "On the Museum's Ruins," *October* 13 (summer 1980). Craig Owens has recently used Freud's account of the creative impulse in a critical appraisal of the Expressionist revival, "Honor, Power and the Love of Women," *Art in America* 71 (January 1983).

10. For a discussion of some of these issues in relation to feminist art, see Mary Kelly, "Re-viewing Modernist Criticism," *Screen* 22.3 (autumn 1981).

11. Freud, "Leonardo da Vinci and a Memory of His Childhood," Standard Edition 11:95, Pelican Freud 14:186–87.

12. The status of the woman as fantasy in relation to the desire of the man was a central concern of Lacan's later writing; see *Encore*, especially "God and the Puissance of the Woman" and "A Love Letter," *Feminine Sexuality: Jacques Lacan and the école freudienne*, ed. Juliet Mitchell and Jacqueline Rose, trans. Jacqueline Rose (London: Macmillan; New York: Norton, 1983), and the commentary, "Feminine Sexuality: Jacques Lacan and the *école freudienne*," in the same collection [and extracted in this reader].

13. Norman Bryson describes post-Albertian perspective in terms of such a restriction, in *Vision and Painting: The Logic of the Gaze* (London: Macmillan, 1983).

14. See Lacan on death in Holbein's "The Ambassadors," *The Four Fundamental Concepts of Psychoanalysis*, ed. Jacques-Alain Miller, trans. Alan Sheridan (London: Hogarth, 1977), 85–90.

15. Freud, "Leonardo da Vinci and a Memory of His Childhood," Standard Edition 11:111, Pelican Freud 14:203. An exhibition entitled "The Revolutionary Power of Women's Laughter," including works by Barbara Kruger and Mary Kelly, was held at Protetch McNeil, New York, January 1983.

Chapter 11: The "Mona Lisa" of Literature

1. T. S. Eliot, "Hamlet and His Problems" (1919), *Selected Prose of T. S. Eliot*, ed. Frank Kermode (London: Faber and Faber, 1975). This essay was first presented as a talk at the Pembroke Center for Teaching and Research on Women, Brown University, 1984; printed in *Critical Quarterly* (autumn 1986); a different version appeared as "Sexuality in the Reading of Shakespeare: *Hamlet* and *Measure for Measure*," *Alternative Shakespeares*, ed. John Drakakis (London: Routledge, 1985).

2. Eliot, "Hamlet and His Problems," 47.

3. Ernest Jones, *Hamlet and Oedipus* (1949; New York: Doubleday, 1954), 88.

4. Sigmund Freud, *The Interpretation of Dreams*, Standard Edition 4:264; Pelican Freud 4:366.

5. Eliot, "Hamlet and His Problems," 45.

6. Ibid., 48.

7. Ibid.

8. Ibid.

9. Ibid, 48–49.

10. Ibid., 49.

11. Ibid.

12. William Shakespeare, *Hamlet*, 1.5.47 and 1.5.80. All references to the Arden Shakespeare unless otherwise specified.

13. Freud, "The Dissolution of the Oedipus Complex" (1924) and "Some Psychical Consequences of the Anatomical Distinction between the Sexes" (1925), Standard Edition 19, Pelican Freud 7.

14. Angelo Conti, cited in Freud, "Leonardo da Vinci and a Memory of His Childhood" (1910), Standard Edition 11:109, Pelican Freud 14:201.

15. Muther and Walter Pater, cited in ibid., Standard Edition 11:108 and 110, Pelican Freud 14:200 and 202.

16. Ibid., Standard Edition 11:108, Pelican Freud 14:200.

17. John Florio, trans., *The Essays of Michael, Lord of Montaigne* (1603; London: Henry Morley, 1885), 219–310.

18. Ibid., 378–82.

19. Shakespeare, *Hamlet*, 3.2.225.

20. See, in particular, Roland Barthes, "La mythologic aujourd'hui," *Esprit* (1971) (trans. Stephen Heath, "Change the Object Itself," *Image, Music, Text* [London: Fontana, 1977]) and *S/Z* (Paris: Seuil, 1970) (trans. Richard Miller, *S/Z* [London: Hill and Wang, 1974]); Julia Kristeva, *La révolution du langage poétique* (Paris: Seuil, 1974) (excerpts from part 1 of this book have been translated in *The Kristeva Reader*, ed. Toril Moi [Oxford: Columbia University Press, 1986]).

21. Eliot, "The Use of Poetry and the Use of Criticism" (1933), *Selected Prose of T. S. Eliot*, 92, 89.

22. Eliot, "Tradition and the Individual Talent" (1919), *Selected Prose of T. S. Eliot*, 38.

23. Jacques Lacan, "Desire and the Interpretation of Desire in *Hamlet*," *Literature and Psychoanalysis: The Question of Reading: Otherwise*, ed. Shoshana Felman (Baltimore: Johns Hopkins University Press, 1982).

24. Tourneur, cited in Eliot, "Tradition and the Individual Talent," 42.

25. Lacan, "Seminar of 21 January, 1975," *Feminine Sexuality: Jacques Lacan and the école freudienne*, ed. Juliet Mitchell and Jacqueline Rose, trans. Jacqueline Rose (London: Macmillan; New York: Norton, 1982), 168.

26. Jones, *Hamlet and Oedipus*, 49.

27. Freud, "The Dissection of the Psychical Personality," *New Introductory Lectures* (1932), Standard Edition 22:80, Pelican Freud 2:112.

28. Lacan, "The Agency of the Letter in the Unconscious," *Ecrits: A Selection*, trans. A. Sheridan (London: Tavistock, 1977), 171 (translation modified).

29. See, for example, Laurence Lerner, ed., *Shakespeare's Tragedies: An Anthology of Modern Criticism* (Harmondsworth, U.K.: Penguin, 1963).

30. Freud, *The Interpretation of Dreams*, Standard Edition 4:264–66, Pelican Freud 4:364–68.

31. Ibid., 4:264; 4:366.

32. Freud, "Mourning and Melancholia" (1915), Standard Edition 14:246–47, Pelican Freud 11:255.

33. Freud, "Psychopathic Characters on the Stage" (1905 or 1906), Standard Edition 7.

34. Lessing, cited in ibid., Standard Edition 7:30n.

35. Jones, *Hamlet and Oedipus*, 70.

36. Eliot, "Hamlet and His Problems," 43.

37. Freud, *The Origins of Psychoanalysis*, letters to Wilhelm Fliers, Drafts and Notes, 1887–1902, ed. Marie Bonaparte, Anna Freud, and Ernst Kris (London: Imago, 1954), 224; Jones, *Hamlet and Oedipus*, 59.

38. Freud, "Female Sexuality" (1931), Standard Edition 21, Pelican Freud 7.

39. Jones, *Hamlet and Oedipus*, chap. 5, 105–14.

40. Shakespeare, *Hamlet*, 3.2.384–87.

41. Ibid., 3.4.20–21.

42. Jones, *Hamlet and Oedipus*, 88, 106. The concept of femininity in relation to Hamlet's character appears again in Marilyn French, *Shakespeare's Division of Experience* (London, Jonathan Cape, 1982), 149; and in David Leverenz, "The Woman in *Hamlet*: An Interpersonal View," *Representing Shakespeare, New Psychoanalytic Essays*, ed. Murray M. Schwarz and Coppélia Kahn (Baltimore: Johns Hopkins University Press, 1980).

43. Shakespeare, *Hamlet*, 5.1.281. The image of the female dove was objected to by Knight as a typographical error in the Variorum edition of the play (ed. H. H. Furness, 15th edn. [Philadelphia, 1877], part 1, 410n.).

44. Jones, *Hamlet and Oedipus*, 25–26.

45. In *Hamlet et HAMLET* (Paris: Balland, 1982), André Green continues the work he began in *Un oeil en trop* (Paris: Editions de Minuit, 1969) (trans. Alan Sheridan, *Tragic Effect: Oedipus Complex and Tragedy* [New York: Cambridge University Press, 1979]) on the psychoanalytic concept of representation in relation to dramatic form, and argues that, while the explicit themes of *Hamlet* (incest, parricide, madness) have the clearest links with the concerns of psychoanalysis, the play's central preoccupation with theatrical space and performance also falls within the psychoanalytic domain through the concept of psychic representation and fantasy. Green examines the way that theatricality, or show, and femininity are constantly assimilated throughout the play (1.2.76ff, 2.2.581ff, 3.1.50ff). In the remarks which follow, I concentrate on the concept of femininity which he sets against this negative assimilation in his final section on Shakespeare's creative art (25–62).

46. Green, *Hamlet et HAMLET*, 256.

47. D. W. Winnicott, "Split-off Male and Female Elements Found Clinically in Men and Women" (1966), *Psychoanalytic Forum* 4, ed. J. Linden (New York: International Universities Press, 1972).

48. See especially Luce Irigaray, *Speculum of the Other Woman*, and Michele Montrelay, "Inquiry into Femininity."

49. Winnicott first presented this paper to the British Psycho-Analytic Society in 1966 under the title "Split-off Male and Female Elements Found Clinically in Men and Women: Theoretical Inferences" (see n. 47 above). It was then included in *Playing and Reality* (London: Tavistock Publications, 1971). The discussion of sexual difference in the paper as a whole is far more complex and interesting than the final descent (ascent) into mythology which is addressed here, although it is this concept of femininity, with its associated emphasis on mothering, which has recently been imported directly into psychoanalytic readings of Shakespeare (see especially Leverenz and the whole anthology in which the article appears).

50. Green, *Hamlet et HAMLET*, 61.

51. Lacan, "Desire and the Interpretation of Desire in *Hamlet*," 14.

52. Green, *Le discours vivant, le concept psychanalytique de l'affect* (Paris: PUF, 1973).

53. Green, *Hamlet et HAMLET*, 256.

54. Eliot, "Tradition and the Individual Talent," 39.

Chapter 12: Virginia Woolf and the Death of Modernism

This essay was first published in autumn 1998, in the New York–based literary journal, *Raritan*, whose policy is to publish without annotation so as to avoid the weight of the academy on the writing. It was subsequently reprinted in *On Not Being Able to Sleep: Psychoanalysis and the Modern World* (London: Vintage, 2004), 72–88.

Chapter 13: "Daddy"

Excerpt from "Daddy," chap. 6 of *The Haunting of Sylvia Plath* (London: Virago, 1991), 205–38.

1. Leon Wieseltier, "In a Universe of Ghosts," *New York Review of Books*, 25 November 1976, 20.

2. Joyce Carol Oates, "The Death Throes of Romanticism," *Southern Review* 9.3: 39; Seamus Heaney, "The Indefatigable Hoof-taps," *Times Literary Supplement*, 5–11 February 1988, 144; Irving Howe, "The Plath Celebration: A Partial Dissent," in Edward Butscher, *Sylvia Plath: The Woman and the Work* (New York: Dodd, Mead, 1985), 233; Marjorie Perloff, "The Two Ariels," *American Poetry Review* (1984): 14–15. For a discussion of similar objections to Marianne Moore's poem "In Distrust of Merits" and more generally to women's war poetry, see Sue Schweik, "Writing War Poetry Like a Woman," *Critical Inquiry* 13.3 (spring 1987): 532–56, part of her forthcoming study, *A Word No Man Can Say for Us: American Women Poets and the Second World War*.

3. "The sense of history, both personal and social, found in a poem like 'For the Union Dead' is conspicuously absent from the *Ariel* poems. This is not mere coincidence: for the oracular poet, past and future are meaningless abstractions. . . . For Sylvia Plath, there is only the given moment, only now." Marjorie Perloff, "*Angst* and Animism in the Poetry of Sylvia Plath," *Journal of Modern Literature* 1 (1970): 121. For a much more positive assessment of Plath's relationship to history, see Stan Smith, *Inviolable Voice: History and Twentieth-Century Poetry* (Dublin: Gill and Macmillan, 1982), chap. 9, "Waist-Deep in History: Sylvia Plath," 200–225.

4. Perloff, "The Two Ariels," 15.

5. The criticism was first directed at Ferdinand de Saussure's *Course in General Linguistics* (1915) (London: Fontana, 1974), for what has been seen as an emphasis on the synchronic, at the expense of the diachronic, dimension of language, and on the arbitrary nature of the linguistic sign which, it was argued, made it impossible to theorise the relationship between language and reference. It has become a commonplace to reproach post-Saussurian literary theory with ahistoricism. For discus-

sion of some of these debates, see Derek Attridge, Geoff Bennington, and Robert Young, eds., *Post-Structuralism and the Question of History* (Cambridge: Cambridge University Press, 1987), especially Geoff Bennington and Robert Young, "Introduction: Posing the Question," 1–11. More specifically, I am referring here to the controversy which has followed the discovery of Paul de Man's wartime writings for the Belgian collaborationist newspaper *Le Soir*. See Werner Hamacher, Neil Hertz, and Thomas Keenan, eds., *Responses* (Lincoln: University of Nebraska Press, 1989).

6. "The Blood Jet Is Poetry," review of *Ariel*, *Time*, 10 June 1966, 118. This review is copiously illustrated with photographs from Aurelia Plath's personal collection. A letter from her to Ted Hughes suggests that she felt she had been tricked by the reviewer and that this, plus the cover of the issue of *The Atlantic* which published "Johnny Panic and the Bible of Dreams" ("Sylvia Plath on Going Mad"), had contributed to her reluctance to see *The Bell Jar* published in the United States. Letter from Aurelia Plath to Ted Hughes, 11 April 1970, correspondence, Plath Manuscript Collections, Lilly Library, Indiana University.

7. Jean-François Lyotard, *The Differend: Phrases in Dispute* (Manchester, U.K.: Manchester University Press, 1988), 27. Lyotard is discussing the issue of Holocaust denial or the Faurisson debate (see 3ff). See also Gill Seidal, *The Holocaust Denial: Antisemitism, Racism and the New Right* (Brighton, U.K.: Beyond the Pale Collective, 1986).

8. The concept comes from Sigmund Freud, *The Ego and the Id*, Standard Edition 19:31–32, Pelican Freud 11:370–71, and *Group Psychology and the Analysis of the Ego* (1921), Standard Edition 18:105–6, Pelican Freud 12:134–35. It has been most fully theorised recently by Julia Kristeva in *Tales of Love* (New York: Columbia University Press, 1987), 24–29.

9. For Kristeva this father founds the possibility of identification for the subject and is critically linked to—enables the subject to symbolise—orality, and hence the abjection.

10. Peter Orr, ed., "Sylvia Plath," *The Poet Speaks* (London: Routledge and Kegan Paul, 1966), 169.

11. Claude Lanzmann in discussion of the film *Shoah*, Channel 4 Television, 27 October 1987; see also Lanzmann, *Shoah: An Oral History of the Holocaust: The Complete Text of the Film* (New York: Pantheon, 1985); Lyotard, "Judiciousness in Dispute, or Kant after Marx," *The Aims of Representation: Subject, Text, History*, ed. Murray Krieger (New York: Columbia University Press, 1987), 64.

12. Sylvia Plath, *Journals*, Neilson Library, Smith College, July 1950, July 1953, September 1950, 60 (*The Journals of Sylvia Plath*, eds. Frances McCullough and Ted Hughes [New York: Random House, 1982], 20).

13. F. W. Eickhoff, "Identification and Its Vicissitudes in the Context of the Nazi Phenomenon," *International Journal of Psycho-Analysis* 67 (1986), 38.

14. Plath, 4 July 1958, 7 July 1958, 11 October 1959, *The Journals of Sylvia Plath*, 244, 246, 319; 13 October 1959, *Letter Home: Correspondence 1950–1963*, ed. Aurelia Scho-

ber Plath (London: Faber and Faber, 1975), 356; 13 October 1959, 19 October 1959, *J*, 319, 321; *Journals*, Neilson Library, Smith College, 12 December 1958–15 November 1959, 7 November 1959, 94 (*J*, 327).

15. Plath, *The Bell Jar* (London: Heinemann, 1963; Faber and Faber, 1966), 35.

16. "On one side I am a first generation American, on one side I'm a second generation American, and so my concern with concentration camps and so on is uniquely intense" (Orr, "Sylvia Plath," 169).

17. Letter from Thomas J. Clohesy to Aurelia Plath, 4 September 1966, Neilson Library, Smith College, Section 5, Biography.

18. Jean Stafford, *A Boston Adventure* (1946; London: Hogarth, 1986).

19. Ibid., 335.

20. Ibid.

21. Ibid., 482.

22. David Rosenfeld, "Identification and Its Vicissitudes in Relation to the Nazi Phenomenon," *International Journal of Psycho-Analysis* 67 (1986): 62.

23. Lyotard, "Judiciousness in Dispute," 59. In a reply to Lyotard, Stephen Greenblatt takes issue with him on this specific question (Greenblatt, "Capitalist Culture and the Circulatory System," in Krieger, *The Aims of Representation*, 260–61).

24. Freud, *The Ego and the Id*, Standard Edition 19:34, Pelican Freud 11:374.

25. Plath, "Among the Bumblebees" (early 1950s), *Johnny Panic and the Bible of Dreams: Short Stories, Prose, and Diary Excerpts* (London: Faber and Faber, 1977, rev. ed., 1979), 263.

26. Jacques Lacan, "Seminar of 21 January 1975," *Feminine Sexuality: Jacques Lacan and the école freudienne*, ed. Juliet Mitchell and Jacqueline Rose, trans. Jacqueline Rose (London: Macmillan; New York: Norton, 1982), 167.

27. Freud, "Psycho-Analytic Notes on an Autobiographical Account of a Case of Paranoia (Schreber)," (1911) Standard Edition 12, Pelican Freud 9; see also Samuel Weber, introduction to Daniel Paul Schreber, *Memoirs of My Nervous Illness*, ed. Ida Macalpine and Richard Hunter (1955; Cambridge, Mass.: Harvard University Press, 1988), vii–liv.

28. Otto E. Plath, *Bumblebees and Their Ways* (New York: Macmillan, 1934).

29. Otto E. Plath, "Insect Societies," *A Handbook of Social Psychology*, ed. Carl Murchison (Worcester, Mass.: Clark University Press; London: Oxford University Press, 1935), 83, 136–37. The first quote comes from the epigraph to the chapter and is part of a quotation from Thomas Belt, *The Naturalist in Nicaragua* (1874); its account of the perfect regiment belongs to a more generally utopian image of community which ends with a quotation from Thomas More.

30. Plath, "Among the Bumblebees," 262.

31. Virginia Woolf, *Three Guineas* (1938; Harmondsworth, U.K.: Penguin, 1977), 162.

32. Elizabeth Wilson, "Coming Out for a Brand New Age," *Guardian*, 14 March 1989. The same line has also been taken as a slogan to explain German women's

involvement in Nazism; see Murray Sayle, "Adolf and the Women," *Independent Magazine*, 9 November 1988: " 'Every woman adores a Fascist,' wrote Sylvia Plath. Is this why so many German women voted for Hitler, despite the male emphasis of the Nazi regime?" (caption under title).

33. For a study of this difficult question, see Claudia Koonz, *Mothers in the Fatherland: Women, the Family and Nazi Politics* (London: Jonathan Cape, 1987).

34. Thanks to Natasha Korda for pointing this out to me.

35. Sherry Ortner, "Is Female to Male as Nature Is to Culture?," *Woman, Culture and Society*, ed Michelle Zimbalist Rosaldo and Louise Lamphere (Stanford, Calif.: Stanford University Press, 1974), 67–87. For a critique of this article, see Carol P. MacCormack, "Nature, Culture and Gender: A Critique," *Nature, Culture and Gender*, ed. Carol P. MacCormack and Marilyn Strathern (Cambridge: Cambridge University Press, 1980), 1–24.

36. Alexander and Margarete Mitscherlich, *The Inability to Mourn* (London: Grove Press, 1975), chap. 1, "The Inability to Mourn: With which Is Associated a German Way of Loving," 3–68.

37. Saul Friedlander, *Reflections of Nazism* (New York: Harper and Row, 1984).

38. Edward Glover and Morris Ginsberg, "A Symposium on the Psychology of Peace and War," *British Journal of Medical Psychology* 14 (1934): 274–93.

39. Ibid., 277.

40. Excerpt from a letter to Richard Sassoon, *Journals*, Neilson Library, Smith College, 15 January 1956, 1, 97.

41. Marguerite Duras, *La douleur* (London: Fontana, 1987), introductory statement to "Albert of the Capitals" and "Ter of the Militias," 115.

42. Plath, *Journals*, Neilson Library, Smith College, 12 December 1958–15 November 1959, 28 December 1958, 28.

Chapter 14: Peter Pan and Freud

Chapter 1 of Jacqueline Rose, *The Case of Peter Pan, or, The Impossibility of Children's Fiction* (London: Macmillan, 1984), 12–42.

1. Sigmund Freud, "Screen Memories," Standard Edition 3:306.

2. Bruno Bettelheim, *The Uses of Enchantment: The Meaning and Importance of Fairy Tales* (London: Thames and Hudson, 1976).

3. Ibid., 118.

4. Gareth Matthews, *Philosophy and the Young Child* (London: Harvard University Press, 1980), 48–55.

5. Freud, preface (1920) to *Three Essays on the Theory of Sexuality* (1905), Standard Edition 7:133.

6. Freud, *Three Essays on the Theory of Sexuality*, Standard Edition 7:195–97.

7. "The first time he is founded in a *Lye*, it should rather be wondered at as a

monstrous Thing in him, than reproved as an ordinary Fault" (John Locke, *Some Thoughts Concerning Education* [London: Churchill, 1693], 153–54).

8. Locke, *An Essay Concerning Human Understanding*, 4th edn. (London: A. J. Churchill and S Manship, 1970), 280–89.

9. Freud (1914), *From the History of an Infantile Neurosis*, Standard Edition 17.

10. Freud (1899), "Screen Memories," Standard Edition 3.

11. Compare for example Elizabeth Cook, *The Ordinary and the Fabulous: An Introduction to Myths, Legends and Fairy Tales for Teachers and Story-Tellers* (Cambridge: Cambridge University Press, 1969).

12. Carl J. Jung, *The Archetype and the Collective Unconscious*, Collected Works, 9, part 1 (London: Routledge and Kegan Paul, 1959).

13. Freud (1900), *The Interpretation of Dreams*, Standard Edition 4–5:96–100.

14. There is no room here to discuss in detail Bettelheim's work on the fairy tale, but it should be noted that, while he interprets Little Red Riding Hood, for example, predominantly in terms of the girl's mastery of oedipal conflict, he does stress throughout the book the partial nature of his reading and the multifarious and contradictory meanings which fairy tales carry in themselves, and which they may represent for different children at different moments of their psychic life. In fact, I see a tension between Bettelheim's stress on this complexity and his fundamental aesthetic—his belief in the artistic coherence of the fairy tale, the facility of the child's identification with its characters and meaning, and the assumption of its final and necessary resolution of psychic and sexual conflict.

15. Matthews, *Philosophy and the Young Child*, 82.

16. Bettelheim, *The Uses of Enchantment*, 179.

17. For more explicitly psychoanalytic discussions *of Peter Pan*, see John Skinner, "James M. Barrie or The Boy Who Wouldn't Grow Up," *American Imago* 14 (1957): 111–41; Martin Grotjahn, "The Defenses against Creative Anxiety in the Life and Work of James Barrie" (a commentary on John Skinner's article), *American Imago* 14 (1957): 143–48; and G. H. Pollock, "On Siblings, Childhood Sibling Loss and Creativity," *Annual of Psychoanalysis* 6 (1978): 443–81.

18. See, however, Frederick Meisel, "The Myth of Peter Pan," *Psychoanalytic Study of the Child* 32 (1977): 545–63—one of the few articles I have found which attempts a reading of *The Little White Bird* and *Peter Pan*, not through Barrie's personal history, but in terms of the unconscious scenario of narcissistic anxiety and defence which the stories might symbolise for the child.

19. E. Benveniste. "La nature des pronoms" (1956) in *Problèmes de linguistique générale* (Paris: Gallimard, 1966), 251–7; "De la subjectivité dans le langage" (1958), in *Problèmes*, pp. 258–66; "Subjectivity in Language," in *Problems*, pp. 43–48.

20. *Times Literary Supplement*, 14 November 1902, 339.

21. J. M. Barrie, *The Little White Bird* (London: Hodder and Stoughton, 1902), 11.

22. Ibid., 10.

23. Ibid., 290–91.

24. Ibid., 22.

25. Ibid., 133, 135.

26. "At lunch, the children asked about 'the beginning of the world.' Dan (six years one month) insists, whatever may be suggested as 'the beginning,' there must always have been something before that" (Matthews, *Philosophy and the Young Child*, 22).

27. Naomi Lewis, "Peter Pan's Progeny," *Observer*, 27 May 1979.

28. Barrie, *Peter Pan in Kensington Gardens* (London: Hodder and Stoughton, 1906).

29. Barrie, *The Little White Bird*, 189–90.

30. Ibid., 226.

31. H. Gersheim, ed., *Lewis Carroll, Victorian Photographer* (London: Max Parrish, 1949); see, for example, Greville MacDonald, plate 31, and Cyril Bickersteth, plate 55.

32. Peter Llewellyn Davies, *The Boy Castaways of Black Lake Island* (London: published by J. M. Barrie, in the Gloucester Road, 1901) (Beinecke B276, 1901). References to Beinecke and date refer to the J. M. Barrie collection at the Walter Beinecke Jnr Collection at the Beinecke Rare Book and Manuscript Library, Yale University, which contains the main collection of *Peter Pan* manuscripts.

33. Graham Ovenden, *Victorian Children* (London: Academy Editions, 1972); M. Linklater, " 'Victorian' Photos Faked," *Sunday Times*, 19 November 1978.

34. Davies, *The Boy Castaways of Black Lake Island*, vii–ix (Beinecke B276, 1901, preface).

35. Andrew Birkin, *J. M. Barrie and the Lost Boys* (Constable: London, 1979).

36. D. Mackail, *The Story of J. M. B.* (London: Peter Davies, 1941), 366; Roger L. Green, *Fifty Years of Peter Pan* (London: Peter Davies, 1954), 85; Birkin, *J. M. Barrie and the Lost Boys*, 116.

37. Beinecke, 1904–5B.

38. Ibid., i.

39. Ibid., my emphasis.

40. For a fuller discussion of this question of stage space in relation to classical and Shakespearian tragedy, see Andre Green, *Un Oeil en trap, le complexe d'Oedipe dans la tragédie* (Paris: Minuit, 1969), 11–29; trans. Alan Sheridan, *The Tragic Effect; Oedipus Complex and Tragedy* (Cambridge: Cambridge University Press, 1979).

41. Freud (1939), *Moses and Monotheism*, Standard Edition 23:43.

42. Roger L. Green, *Fifty Years of Peter Pan*, 31.

43. Alan Garner, *Elidor* (London: Collins, 1963) and *The Owl Service* (London: Collins, 1967); Maurice Sendak, *Where the Wild Things Are* (London: Bodley Head, 1967). The adventure in Sendak's book can be read as a dream. On the first night of *Peter Pan* in 1904, one critic objected that the adventure in *Peter Pan* could not, but his concern was for the adult rather than the child: "Having regard to the mother's

feelings, it is customary in such cases to invoke the aid of the dream. We cannot imagine why Mr. Barrie has not done so" ("Mr. Barrie's *Peter Pan*-tomime," *Enthoven*, dated 27 December 1904).

44. Beinecke, 1904–5B, act 1, scene 5.

45. Beinecke, 1904–5B, act 1, scene 13.

46. A. Noyes, "Peter and Wendy," *Bookman* 43.243 (December 1911): 132.

47. Roger L. Green, *Fifty Years of Peter Pan*, 65.

48. Ibid., 72.

49. Both John Skinner ("James M. Barrie or The Boy Who Wouldn't Grow Up,") and Martin Grotjahn ("The Defenses against Creative Anxiety in the Life and Work of James Barrie") comment on the failure of the oedipal resolution in *Peter Pan* (Grotjahn criticizes Skinner for not making this explicit enough), but make this the basis of an aesthetic (and moral) condemnation of Barrie himself.

50. Beinecke, 1904–5B, act 2, scene 3, 26.

51. Beinecke, 1904, typescript, act 3, scene 6.

52. Beinecke, 1904, act 3, scene 2.

53. Beinecke, 1904, typescript, act 3, scene 6.

54. Beinecke, 1908B–D and Barrie, "An Afterthought," typescript of an epilogue to the play *Peter Pan* (1908), Duke of York's Theatre, in *When Wendy Grows Up* (Edinburgh: Nelson, 1957). On the reinstatement of the *Afterthought* and other aspects of the play mentioned here (e.g., the episode with Tiger-Lily) see note on the 1982 Royal Shakespeare Company production at the Barbican, Jacqueline Rose, *The Case of Peter Pan* (London: Macmillan, 1984), 113–14.

55. Beinecke, 1908C, words in parenthesis are an autograph addition in Barrie's hand facing page 21.

56. Cynthia Asquith, ed., *The Treasure Ship* (London: Partridge, 1926 [a]).

57. Roger L. Green, *Fifty Years of Peter Pan*, 119.

58. Barrie, 1926(a), pp. 92–93.

59. Freud (1900), *The Interpretation of Dreams*, Standard Edition 4–5:277–78, Pelican Freud 4:381–82.

60. Edward Lear, *A Book of Nonsense* (London: McLean, 1846).

61. See, for example, Paul Schilder, "Psychoanalytic Remarks on *Alice in Wonderland* and Lewis Carroll" (*Journal of Nervous and Mental Diseases* 87.2 [February 1938]: 159–68), which describes nonsense as the effect of incomplete object relations and analyses the *Alice* books in terms of anal regression (a long note to this effect was cut out from this article when it was reprinted in R. Phillips, *Aspects of Alice* [London: Gollancz, 1972]); Martin Grotjahn, "About the Symbolisation of Alice's *Adventures in Wonderland*" (*American Imago* 4 [1947]: 32–41), replying to Schilder, rejects the moral judgment which declares the *Alice* books unsuitable for children but also defines them in terms of psychic and artistic regression; John Skinner, "Lewis Carroll's *Adventure's in Wonderland*" (*American Imago* 4 [1947]: 3–31) does take account

of the child's pleasure in illogicality, but again concentrates mainly on Carroll's biography; an exception is Alwyn Baum, "Carroll's *Alices*: The Semiotics of Paradox" (*American Imago* 34.1 [spring 1977]: 86–108), which discusses the *Alice* books in terms of the operations which they carry out on language. There is an interesting intellectual parallel between the psychoanalytic readings of the works of Carroll and Barrie, both analysed psychobiographically in terms of artistic and psychic regression, both receiving attention more recently in terms of the internal structure of the fantasies which their books represent and how these fantasies are symbolised for the child (Baum, "Carroll's *Alices*"; and F. L. Meisel, "The Myth of Peter Pan," *Psychoanalytic Study of the Child* 32 [1977]: 545–63). Baum has this to say on the limits of psychobiography in dealing with children's fiction: "If we accuse Carroll of aberrance in his fantasies, we would similarly have to charge human society, as collective author of the world's traditional literature, with neurosis" (Baum, "Carroll's *Alices*," 87).

Chapter 15: Excerpts from Albertine

From Jacqueline Rose, *Albertine: A Novel* (London: Chatto and Windus, 2002).

Chapter 16: "Infinite Justice"

From a series of contributor responses to September 11, published in the *London Review of Books* 23.19 (4 October 2001): 20–25.

Chapter 17: We Are All Afraid, But of What, Exactly?

First published in the *Guardian*, 20 March 2003.

Chapter 18: Why Zionism Today Is the Real Enemy of the Jews

Speech delivered at the "Intelligence Squared" debate, Royal Geographic Society, London, 4 February 2005.

Chapter 19: Israel's 2008 Incursion into Gaza

First published in the *London Review of Books*, 15 January 2009.

Chapter 20: Why Howard Jacobson Is Wrong

First published, online, in the "Comment Is Free" section of the *Guardian*, 24 February 2009.

Chapter 21: Holocaust Premises

A revised version of a paper delivered, in dialogue with Judith Butler, at the opening session of "Fear of the Other and the Israeli-Palestinian Conflict," a conference organized by the Faculty for Israeli-Palestinian Peace (FFIPP), London, 25 September 2005.

Chapter 22: An Interview with Jacqueline Rose

A condensed version of two hour-long conversations between Jacqueline Rose and the editors, conducted by telephone in April 2009.

1. Jacqueline Rose, "Afterword," *Carnival, Hysteria and Writing: The Collected Essays and Autobiography of Allon White* (Oxford: Oxford University Press), 178–86.

2. Rose, "Hannah Arendt's Legacy," ed. Ben Naparstek, *Canberra Times*, 14 October 2006.

Jacqueline Rose

A Select Bibiliography, 1974–2011

1974   Trans. "Freud in Paris," by J. B. Pontalis. *International Journal of Psychoanalysis* 55: 455–58.

1975   "Writing as Auto-Visualisation: Notes on a Scenario and Film of *Peter Pan.*" *Screen* 16.3 (autumn): 29–53.

      "Comment on *The Freudian Slip* by Sebastiano Timpanaro." *New Left Review* 94 (November–December): 74–79.

1976   "Paranoia and the Film System." *Screen* 17.4 (winter 1976–77): 85–104.

1977   Translator. "Suture: Elements of the Logic of the Signifier," by Jacques-Alain Miller. *Screen* 18.4 (winter 1977–78): 24–34.

1978   "Dora: Fragment of an Analysis." *m/f* 2: 5–21.

1980   "Woman as Symptom." *Cinema in the Eighties: Proceedings of the Meeting,* 23–25. Venice: Edizione "La Biennale di Venezia."

1981   With Elizabeth Cowie et al. "Representation versus Communication." *No Turning Back: Papers from the Women's Movement 1975–1980,* ed. by The Feminist Anthology Collective, 238–45. London: Women's Press.

      "Jacques Lacan: An Intellectual Portrait." *Times Higher Educational Supplement,* 2 October.

1982   "The Imaginary." *The Talking Cure: Essays in Psychoanalysis and Language,* ed. Colin MacCabe, 132–61. London: Macmillan.

      "The Cinematic Apparatus: Problems in Current Theory." *The Cinematic Apparatus,* ed. Teresa de Lauretis and Stephen Heath, 172–86. London: Macmillan.

      Editor, with Juliet Mitchell. *Feminine Sexuality: Jacques Lacan and the école freudienne,* trans. Jacqueline Rose. London: Macmillan.

"Introduction—II." *Feminine Sexuality: Jacques Lacan and the école treudienne*, ed. Jacqueline Rose and Juliet Mitchell, trans. Jacqueline Rose, 27–57. London: Macmillan.

1983   "Femininity and Its Discontents." *Feminist Review* 14 (summer): 5–21.

"Feminine Sexuality: Interview with Juliet Mitchell and Jacqueline Rose." *m/f* 8 (summer): 3–16.

"Complete Diversity or Disarray?" Symposium on English Studies. *Times Higher Educational Supplement*, 11 February.

1984   *The Case of Peter Pan, or, The Impossibility of Children's Fiction*. London: Macmillan. Revised edition, Philadelphia, Pa.: University of Pennsylvania Press, 1993.

1985   "Sexuality in the Field of Vision." *Difference: On Representation and Sexuality*, 31–33. New York: New Museum.

"Sexuality in the Reading of Shakespeare: *Hamlet* and *Measure for Measure*." *Alternative Shakespeares*, ed. John Drakakis, 95–118. London: Methuen.

1986   "*Hamlet*: The 'Mona Lisa' of Literature." *Critical Quarterly* 28.1–2 (March): 35–49.

Sexuality in the Field of Vision. London: Verso.

"Jeffrey Masson and Alice James." *Oxford Literary Review* 8.1–2: 185–92.

1987   "The State of the Subject II: The Institution of Feminism." *Critical Quarterly* 29.4 (December): 9–15.

" 'The Man Who Mistook His Wife for a Hat' or 'A Wife Is Like an Umbrella': Fantasies of the Modern and Postmodern." *Identity: The Real Me*, ed. Lisa Appignanesi, 237–50. London: Institute of Contemporary Art Publications.

1988   "Margaret Thatcher and Ruth Ellis." *New Formations* 6 (autumn): 3–29.

"Sexuality and Vision." *Vision and Visuality (Discussions in Contemporary Culture)*, ed. Hal Foster, 115–27. Dia Art Foundation. Seattle: Bay Press.

1989   "Shakespeare and the Death Drive: On *Measure for Measure*." *L'Eros in Shakespeare*, ed. Keir Elam and Alessandro Serpieri, 29–46. Parma: Pratiche Editrice.

"Julia Kristeva: Take Two." *Coming to Terms: Feminism, Theory, Politics*, ed. Elizabeth Weed, 17–33. New York: Routledge, Chapman and Hall.

"Where Does the Misery Come From? Psychoanalysis, Feminism and the

Event." *Feminism and Psychoanalysis*, ed. Richard Feldstein and Judith Roof, 25–39. Ithaca, N.Y.: Cornell University Press.

"Psychoanalysis and History: A Comment." *History Workshop* 28 (autumn): 148–54.

1990   "On the Concept of the Female Spectator." *Camera Obscura* nos. 20–21: 274–79.

"Interview with Hanna Segal." *Woman: A Cultural Review* 2 (autumn): 198–214.

Review of *Sylvia Plath: The Critical Heritage*, by Linda W. Wagner; *Sexton: Selected Criticism*, by Diana Hume George; and *The Unbeliever: The Poetry of Elizabeth Bishop*, by Robert Dale Parker. *Journal of American Studies* 24.3: 446–48.

Review of *Am I That Name? Feminism and the Category of Women in History*, by Denise Riley. *History Workshop* 29 (winter): 159–62.

1991   *The Haunting of Sylvia Plath*. London: Virago. Reissued by Harvard University Press, 1992.

"Why War?" *Winnicott Studies* 6: 66–83.

"Strange Dissociation of Ideas." Review of *Lacan and Co.*, by Elizabeth Roudinesco. *Times Higher Educational Supplement*, 4 January.

"Faking It Up with the Truth." Review of *Anne Sexton: A Biography*, by Diane Wood Middlebrook. *Times Literary Supplement*, 1 November.

1993   "Afterword." *Carnival, Hysteria and Writing: The Collected Essays and Autobiography of Allon White*, 178–86. Oxford: Oxford University Press.

Why War? Psychoanalysis, Politics and the Return to Melanie Klein. The Bucknell Lectures in Literary Theory. Oxford: Blackwell.

1994   "On the 'Universality' of Madness: Bessie Head's *A Question of Power*." *Critical Inquiry* 20.3 (spring): 401–18.

1995   " 'Undone, Defiled, Defaced': Christina Rossetti." Review of *Christina Rossetti: A Literary Biography*, by Jan Marsh. *London Review of Books*, 19 October.

"Freud and the Crisis of Our Culture." *Critical Quarterly* 37.1 (spring): 3–19.

1996   "Dorothy Richardson and the Jew." *Between "Race" and Culture: Representations of "the Jew" in English and American Literature*, ed. Bryan Cheyette, 114–29. Stanford, Calif.: Stanford University Press.

States of Fantasy. The 1994 Clarendon Lectures. Oxford: Oxford University Press.

"Of Knowledge and Mothers: On the Work of Christopher Bollas." *Gender and Psychoanalysis* 1.4: 411–28.

Editor and introducer, with Saul Dubow. *Black Hamlet* (1937), by Wulf Sachs. Parallax Series. Baltimore: Johns Hopkins University Press.

1998   "Conversation with Edward Said." *Critical Quarterly* 40.1 (spring): 72–89.

"Sylvia Plath: Tribute." *Journal of the Poetry Society of America* 51 (spring): 4–5.

"Virginia Woolf and the Death of Modernism." *Raritan* 18.2 (fall): 1–18.

1999   "Freud in the Tropics." *History Workshop Journal* 47 (summer): 49–67.

"The Cult of Celebrity." *London Review of Books*, 20 August.

" 'Go, Girl!': Adrienne Rich and Natalie Angier." Review of *Midnight Salvage: Poems 1995–1998*, by Adrienne Rich; and *Woman: An Intimate Geography*, by Natalie Angier. *London Review of Books*, 30 September.

2000   "Bizarre Objects: Hallucination and Modernism: Mary Butts and Elizabeth Bowen." *Critical Quarterly* 42.1 (spring): 75–85.

"Aux Marges du Litteraire: Justice, Vérité, Reconciliation." *Ou en est la Theorie Littéraire?*, ed. Julia Kristeva and Evelyne Grossman. *Textuel* 37: 99–108.

Introducer and translator. *Jacques Lacan and the Question of Psychoanalytic Training*, by Moustapha Safouan. London: Macmillan.

2001   *Albertine*. London: Chatto and Windus.

2002   "This Is Not a Biography: Sylvia Plath." *London Review of Books*, 22 August.

2003   "Apathy and Accountability: The Challenge of South Africa's Truth and Reconciliation Commission to the Intellectual in the Modern World." *The Public Intellectual*, ed. Helen Small, 159–79. Oxford: Blackwell.

"Response to Edward Said." *Freud and the Non-European*, by Edward Said, 65–79. London: Verso.

On Not Being Able to Sleep: Psychoanalysis and the Modern World. London: Chatto and Windus; Princeton, N.J.: Princeton University Press.

"The Body of Evil." Proceedings of the Conference of the Nexus Institute, Brabant, University Tilburg, *The Quest for Life–Part 2: "Evil,"* Nexus, 96–105.

2004   "Failed State." Review of *Death as a Way of Life: Dispatches from Jerusalem* and *Someone to Run With*, by David Grossman. *London Review of Books*, 18 March.

"Freud and the Rise of Zionism." Essex University Freud Memorial Lecture. *London Review of Books*, 8 July.

"Introduction." *Mass Psychology and Other Writings*, by Sigmund Freud. New Penguin Freud Series. London: Penguin.

Preface to Simone de Beauvoir, *All Men Are Mortals*. London: Virago.

"Deadly Embrace." Review of *My Life Is a Weapon: A Modern History of Suicide Bombing*, by Christoph Reuter; and *Army of Roses: Inside the World of Palestinian Women Suicide Bombers*, by Barbara Victor. *London Review of Books*, 4 November.

2005   "Zionism as Psychoanalysis." *Bulletin of Psychoanalysis* (February): 27–42.

"Entryism." Review of *Specimen Days*, by Michael Cunningham. *London Review of Books*, 22 September.

"Introduction." *Born Jewish: A Childhood in Occupied Europe*, by Marcel Liebman. London: Verso.

"Edward Said: Continuing the Conversation." Tribute to Edward Said. *Critical Inquiry* 31.2 (winter): 512–18.

The Question of Zion. The Christian Gauss Seminars. Princeton, N.J.: Princeton University Press; Melbourne: Melbourne Univeristy Press.

2006   "Displacement in Zion." *Displacement, Asylum, Migration*, ed. Kate Tunstall, 264–91. Oxford: Oxford University Press.

"On Being Nadine Gordimer." Review of *Get a Life*, by Nadine Gordimer. *London Review of Books*, 20 April.

"The Zionist Imagination" (on the writings of Ze'ev Jabotinsky). *The Nation*, 26 June.

2007   *The Last Resistance*. London: Verso; Calcutta: Seagull Press.

"Words without Borders" (on Israeli poetry marking the fortieth anniversary of the Six-Day War). *Guardian Review*, 2 June.

2008   "Chroniclers of Pain" (on Israeli writers marking the sixtieth anniversary of the founding of the State of Israel). *Guardian Review*, 10 May.

"The Political Edge of Fiction." *Waiting for the Barbarians: A Tribute to Edward W. Said*, ed. Muge Sokmen, Basak Ertur, and Rasha Salti, 15–33. London: Verso.

"On the Myth of Self-Hatred." *A Time to Speak Out: Independent Jewish Voices on Israel, Zionism and Jewish Identity*, ed. Jacqueline Rose, Brian Klug, Anne Karpf, and Barbara Rosenbaum, 84–96. London: Verso.

"Editors' Introduction." *A Time to Speak Out: Independent Jewish Voices on Israel, Zionism and Jewish Identity*, ed. Jacqueline Rose, Brian Klug, Anne Karpf, and Barbara Rosenbaum, vii–xi. London: Verso.

"The Iron Rule." Review of *Homecoming*, by Bernard Schlink. *London Review of Books*, 31 July.

2010   *Conversations with Jacqueline Rose*. Calcutta: Seagull Press.

2011   *The Jacqueline Rose Reader*. Edited by Justin Clemens and Ben Naparstek. Durham, N.C.: Duke University Press.

Proust among the Nations. Chicago: University of Chicago Press.

Index

White, Allon, 341, 347
Wilson, Elizabeth, 37
Winnicot, D. W., 48, 238–39
Woolf, Leonard, 243–47, 249, 256
Woolf, Virginia, 1, 2, 26, 135, 193–94,
   215–17, 242–56, 268, 347–48

Yeats, W. B., 118

Zionism, 2, 13, 17–19, 101, 108, 118, 121–
   22, 126–28, 134, 140, 151, 188–211,
   322–25, 329, 331, 337–40, 346, 355–59

JACQUELINE ROSE is a professor of English at Queen Mary, University of London, and is a regular contributor to the *London Review of Books*. Her most recent publications include *The Last Resistance* (2007), *The Question of Zion* (2005), and *On Not Being Able to Sleep: Psychoanalysis and the Modern World* (2003).

JUSTIN CLEMENS teaches in the School of Culture and Communication at the University of Melbourne. He is the author of several books, including *The Romanticism of Contemporary Theory* (2003), as well as the co-editor of numerous anthologies, including *Jacques Lacan and the Other Side of Psychoanalysis* (2006), also published by Duke University Press.

BEN NAPARSTEK graduated with degrees in English and Law from the University of Melbourne before taking up a graduate fellowship with the Humanities Center at the Johns Hopkins University. He returned to Melbourne in 2009 to become the editor of the national Australian magazine *The Monthly*. His collection of literary journalism, *In Conversation*, has been published in three languages.

GRATEFUL ACKNOWLEDGMENT IS MADE TO THE FOLLOWING
FOR PERMISSION TO REPRINT PREVIOUSLY PUBLISHED
MATERIAL BY JACQUELINE ROSE:

Blackwell: *Why War: Psychoanalysis, Politics and the Return to Melanie Klein* (1993), 137–71.

Chatto and Windus: *Albertine* (2002), 18–29, 85–91.

Chatto and Windus / Princeton University Press: *On Not Being Able to Sleep: Psychoanalysis and the Modern World* (2004), 72–88, 216–37.

The Guardian: "We Are All Afraid, but of What, Exactly?" (20 March 2003).

The London Review of Books: "Infinite Justice" (4 October 2001); "Reflections on Israel's 2008 Incursion into Gaza" (15 January 2009).

Oxford University Press: *States of Fantasy* (1996), 1–15, 78–97.

Palgrave Macmillan: *The Case of Peter Pan, or, The Impossibility of Children's Fiction* (1984), 12–41.

Palgrave Macmillan / W. W. Norton: *Feminine Sexuality: Jacques Lacan and the école freudienne*, by Jacques Lacan, edited by Juliet Mitchell and Jacqueline Rose (1982), 30–44.

Princeton University Press: *The Question of Zion* (2005), 68–107.

Verso: *Sexuality in the Field of Vision* (1986), 81, 83–103, 123–40, and 225–33; *The Last Resistance* (2007), 62–88, 139–55, and 214–22.

Virago: *The Haunting of Sylvia Plath* (1991), 205–38.

Library of Congress Cataloging-in-Publication Data
Rose, Jacqueline.
The Jacqueline Rose reader / Jacqueline Rose ;
edited by Ben Naparstek and Justin Clemens.
p. cm.
Includes bibliographical references and index.
ISBN 978-0-8223-4963-1 (cloth : alk. paper)
ISBN 978-0-8223-4978-5 (pbk. : alk. paper)
1. Psychoanalysis. 2. Psychoanalysis and culture.
3. Psychoanalysis and feminism. I. Naparstek, Ben, 1986–
II. Clemens, Justin. III. Title.
BF173.R64 2011   150.19'5—dc22   2010035887